WALTER BENJAMIN

AND **THE CORPUS** OF

AUTOBIOGRAPHY

For Erin,
With all good wishes,

[signature]

WALTER BENJAMIN

AND THE CORPUS OF

AUTOBIOGRAPHY

GERHARD RICHTER

 WAYNE STATE UNIVERSITY PRESS DETROIT

KRITIK: GERMAN LITERARY THEORY AND CULTURAL STUDIES
Liliane Weissberg, Editor
A complete listing of the books in this series
can be found at the back of this volume.

Library of Congress Cataloging-in-Publication Data
Richter, Gerhard, 1967–
    Walter Benjamin and the corpus of autobiography / Gerhard
Richter.
        p.   cm.—(Kritik)
    Includes bibliographical references and index.
    ISBN 0-8143-2880-6 (alk. paper)
    1. Benjamin, Walter, 1892–1940—Political and social views.
2. Authors, German—20th century—Biography.   3. Autobiography.   I. Title.   II. Kritik (Detroit, Mich.)
PT2603.E455 Z855 2000
838'.91209—dc21   99-048541

DESIGNED BY   S. R. TENENBAUM

FOR STEPHANIE

Language has a body and the body has a language.
Walter Benjamin, "Review of Mendelssohn"

It is the gift of the good writer to grant to thinking, through his style, the spectacle that an intelligently trained body offers.
Walter Benjamin, "Der gute Schriftsteller"

What does a word touch, if not a body? But there you have it: How can one get hold of the body? I am already speechless.
Jean-Luc Nancy, "Corpus"

CONTENTS

Note on Citation and Translation   9

Preface   11

INTRODUCTION:
BENJAMIN'S CORPOREALITY AND THE POLITICS
OF SELF-PORTRAITURE   19

1

BENJAMIN'S FACE: DEFACING FASCISM   93

2

BENJAMIN'S BODY: THE ALTERITY OF THE
CORPUS IN THE *MOSCOW DIARY*   125

3

BENJAMIN'S EAR: NOISE, MNEMONICS, AND
THE *BERLIN CHRONICLE*   163

4

BENJAMIN'S EYE/I: VISION AND THE
SCENE OF WRITING IN THE
BERLIN CHILDHOOD AROUND 1900   199

EPILOGUE:
TOWARD A POLITICS OF THE UNUSABLE   231

Notes   247

Works Cited   281

Index   299

NOTE ON CITATION AND TRANSLATION

In quoting Benjamin's writings, the first citation refers to an English translation, the second to the original German. Where only one citation is given, no commonly available published English translation exists and the citation refers to the German text only, in my own translation. While I use standard English translations of German and French texts wherever available, I have modified these when necessary in order to increase their faithfulness to the original. Unless otherwise indicated, quotations from Benjamin's German works are indicated by volume and page number only. They refer to the following edition:

Walter Benjamin, *Gesammelte Schriften*. Ed. Rolf Tiedemann and Hermann Schweppenhäuser. 14 books in 7 vols. Frankfurt am Main: Suhrkamp, 1972–89.

QUOTATIONS FROM OTHER BENJAMINIAN TEXTS AND FROM
ENGLISH TRANSLATIONS USE THE FOLLOWING ABBREVIATIONS:

B   *Briefe*
BA *Theodor Adorno/Walter Benjamin: Briefwechel, 1928–1940*
BK *Briefe an Siegfried Kracauer*
BW *Walter Benjamin/Gershom Scholem: Briefwechsel, 1933–1940*
C   *The Correspondence of Walter Benjamin, 1910–1940*
CB *Charles Baudelaire: A Lyric Poet in the Era of High Capitalism*
CBS *The Correspondence of Walter Benjamin and Gershom Scholem: 1932–1940*
CP "Central Park"

D   "Doctrine of the Similar"
I   *Illuminations*
MD *Moscow Diary*
N   "N [Theoretics of Knowledge; Theory of Progress]"
O   *Origin of German Tragic Drama*
OWS *One-Way Street and Other Writings*
P   "Program for a Proletarian Children's Theater"
R   *Reflections*
T   "Theories of German Fascism"
W *Selected Writings.* Volume 1: *1913–1926*

In cases where a quotation continues onto the following page, I have used the abbreviation (f.) to indicate this. Where the quotation or passage in question continues for more than one additional page, the abbreviation (ff.) is used.

PREFACE

In a seminar on Walter Benjamin I recently taught, there
came a point toward the end of our discussions when the possibility of political intervention in a Benjaminian sense was at stake.
Having read most major texts from his so-called early metaphysical
or theological phase, through his preoccupation with the German
and French literary traditions, to the engaged materialism and the
critique of technology and mass culture that characterize his late
phase, we had reached a discomforting conclusion. Despite certain
Marxist gestures here and various appeals to the political there, there
was very little in Benjamin's celebrated corpus that would provide
a clear itinerary to follow. This seemed especially disconcerting in
light of his sustained empirical struggle against German fascism,
which ended his life prematurely when he, persecuted by the Nazis,
committed suicide in September 1940. As Benjamin once explained
his enigmatic politics to his lifelong friend Gershom Scholem, "my
stance would be to behave always radically and never consistently
when it came to the most important things" (C 300; B 425). I thus

11

suggested to the group that the absence of a stable political program was not necessarily something negative or mournful. I proposed that it signals the very possibility of something radically new to come, something that exceeds existing political agendas, something that has no name yet and whose potential cannot be delimited as a mere formula, by us, now, in advance. The Benjaminian "magic spark," I reminded them, what he calls the "leap between the word and the motivating deed" (C 80; B 127), will not occur within the confines of a set political agenda, much less in a conventional theological or mystical space. What is essential to Benjamin's oppositional spirit, however, is the "perhaps" of the redemptively charged possibility itself, what in an autobiographical text he once termed "the traces of what is to come" (7:407). This hope may or may not be for us. It may be almost too much to hope. The politics to come is, for Benjamin, fundamentally predicated on a radical openness toward, and even hope for, the other. It is this other or otherness that, precisely because it remains infinitely out of reach, can still be considered something that may yet come to pass. For what is to come, hopelessness is as much a condition of possibility as hope itself. "Only for the sake of the hopeless ones," Benjamin tells us, "have we been given hope," echoing Kafka's axiom that there is an infinite amount of hope, but not for us (W 356; 1:201). Puzzled by Benjamin's enigmatic sense of the political, one student raised her hand and asked, "But what do we do in the meantime?" Struck by the beauty and urgency of this question, I realized that what I had been trying to accomplish in my own thinking about the enigma we call Benjamin actually was nothing but a sustained meditation on this very question. This book, in a sense, returns again and again to the difficulty of the question: What do we do in the meantime?

In this study I hope to show that any understanding of Benjamin's sense of the political, and the history to which it belongs, cannot be found in unified concepts and fully deducible theses that might simply be verified or refuted. That is, instead of reading Benjamin's sentences literally, we must follow the shifting movements of language itself. Because for Benjamin the political can only become legible in and as something else, it is most itself when it is read through a series of deferrals and mediations, in short, figuratively. To assume the ethical responsibility of weaning ourselves off what Benjamin once called "the strongest narcotic of the century," that is, the kind of mimetic realism of a concept of "history that showed things 'as they really were'" (N 51; 5:578), we must learn to read history and politics as they appear in the guise of what they are not. As we learn in his theses "On the Concept of History," this reading may well require us "to brush history against the grain" (I 257; 1:697) in order for the true historicity of a text or political object to emerge.

While Benjamin famously predicates his struggle against fascism on the development of a series of new concepts that would be "useless" for the purposes of fascist politics, he defers the specification of these concepts. This deferral has consternated his readers, because they sense that there is more at stake than a simple substitution which would counter Nazism with Marxism, or the fascist aestheticization of politics with the politicization of art. In these pages, I wish to suggest that Benjamin's silence about the multiple historical and political relays in his call for unusable concepts is not a political foreclosure, but an affirmation or possibility: it sets for his readers the necessary and Sisyphean task of thinking in his wake by learning how to read the politics of concepts that have never been written. The implications of Benjamin's confrontation with fascism and his engagement with more general questions of politics and ethics demand that we take seriously Benjamin's insistence on thinking through the complicated relationship between a text and its culture, between the idiomatic artifact and its historical formation, in a way that shows itself responsible for the figurative or linguistic dimension of both. Through this insistence on the rhetorical nature of history and politics, Benjamin invites us "to open the book of what has come to pass," so "that we can read the real like a text [*daß man das Wirkliche wie einen Text lesen kann*]" (N 52; 5:580). The reading that Benjamin calls upon us to perform always occurs in and as a moment of crisis, a dangerous instant in which nothing may remain what it seems: "The image that is read, that is, the image of the Now of recognizability, bears to the highest degree the stamp of that critical, dangerous moment that lies at the ground of all reading" (N 50f.; 5:578).

These issues can be addressed most poignantly in the often overlooked corpus of Benjamin's autobiographical writings. Written at important stages in the development of his career, his autobiographical documents interact in complex ways with his larger theoretical oeuvre. Benjamin's reflections on history, politics, the self, the body, reading, and writing can hardly be understood in separation from his innovative art of self-portraiture. Indeed, we could cast the essential rapport between his autobiographical works and his philosophical ones in the terms Benjamin offers us in his 1924 essay on "Goethe's Elective Affinities." He writes: "Let us suppose that one makes the acquaintance of a person who is handsome and attractive but impenetrable, because he carries a secret with him. It would be reprehensible to want to pry. Still, it would surely be permissible to inquire whether the person has any siblings and whether their nature could not explain somewhat the enigmatic character of the stranger. In just this way critique seeks to discover siblings of the work of art. And all genuine works have their siblings in the realm of philosophy" (W 333; 1:172). The relation that Benjamin describes here also signals the elective affinities between his confessional and his philosophical corpus; placed in a constellation, they illuminate each other in ever new ways. And because his autobiographies stage the radicalization of his theoretical corpus in the figures of a writing self, they contain, as Benjamin himself unambiguously tells us, "the most precise portrait that I shall ever be able to give of myself" (C 424; B 589).

The hypothesis of my reflections, to my knowledge the first book-length study of his three major autobiographical texts taken together, is that Benjamin does not *explain* what his innovative political concepts are but rather *stages* their transgressive movement in his language. Specifically, Benjamin's complex rhetorical mobilizations of the corporeal subject in his autobiographical writings, composed between 1926 and 1938—the *Moscow Diary*, the *Berlin Chronicle*, and the *Berlin Childhood around 1900*—can be read as pointing toward his new concepts. In these texts, the body of Benjamin's confessional self is always in retreat, unemployable by ideologemes that rely on a single and stable meaning, and on presence, closure, and self-identity. For Benjamin, "language has a body and the body has a language" (3:138), and both remain suspended in the corporeal subject that is perpetually caught between construction and dispersal in the act of self-portraiture. In his autobiographical writings, Benjamin's corporeal figures, the face, the ear, and the eye, become visible as sites of the political struggles that illuminate the intricate relationship among politics, history, and rhetoric in his writing, even—and especially—when they do not seem to refer explicitly to political and historical concerns on the surface. They perform "useless" concepts with every

14

undoing of the self, staging a negation of fascism with every trope—or turn away from—an essential, fully legible self.

To realize that "the core of Benjamin's philosophy," as his friend Theodor W. Adorno reminds us, is traversed by "the paradox of the impossible possibility" is to grasp that Benjamin "overcame the dream without betraying it and making himself an accomplice in that on which the philosophers have always agreed: that it shall not be" ("Portrait of Walter Benjamin" 241). The paradox of the impossible possibility: it signals Benjamin's theoretical and political interests, and it touches all of his sentences. That "everything he ever wrote originates in that paradox," means, as Adorno suggests, that it "was nothing other than the explication and elucidation of this paradox . . . that drove Benjamin to immerse himself without reserve in the world of multiplicity" (241). Benjamin's autobiographical writings, I wish to suggest, can be read as a meditation on the impossible possibility and on the political concerns that lodge this impossible possibility in the variegated linguistic movements of his signature.

If, through the theories of the body inscribed in them, Benjamin's acts of self-portraiture work to re-treat the figurative dimension of the political, then it becomes possible to begin to address the question, "What do we do in the meantime?" Indeed, it is in the bodily tropes that the ethical and political import of his thinking can be made vivid. Our task, then, is to trace the hidden material figures that traverse Benjamin's writings and to activate their performative potential. These tropes will help us to take seriously the urgency with which Benjamin in "On the Program of the Coming Philosophy" evokes the power of what is transitory and elusive, "the dignity of an experience that is ephemeral" (W 100; 2:158). This is also the dignity of Benjamin's corpus.

Earlier versions of chapters 1 and 2 appeared in *Monatshefte* (fall 1998) and *Modern Language Studies* (fall 1995), respectively. A few sentences and paragraphs of the introduction and the epilogue enjoyed an earlier incarnation as part of a review essay in *Philosophy and Literature* (April 1996). I am grateful to the various editors and publishers for permission to include this material here. For their assistance in securing illustrations as well as the necessary permissions, I wish to thank Julian Cox and Jacklyn Burns of The J. Paul

Getty Museum in Los Angeles; Uta Hoffmann at the August Sander Archiv in Cologne, Germany; and the staff at Medical Photography at the University of Wisconsin. Faculty Summer Research Grants from the Graduate School of the University of Wisconsin supported the writing and research of this project. Earlier, a generous Whiting Foundation Fellowship in the Humanities allowed me to dedicate myself exclusively to this project for a year. Audiences at the University of Wisconsin, Rutgers University, the conference "Construction Site: A Colloquium on Walter Benjamin" at Princeton University, the Northeast Modern Language Association in Boston, the International Association for Philosophy and Literature in Irvine, California, and the Inaugural Walter Benjamin World Congress, organized in Amsterdam by the newly founded International Walter Benjamin Association, listened patiently to my arguments about Benjamin and offered valuable comments.

All friendship is a work-in-progress, and it allows work to progress. During the writing of this book, I have had the good fortune to benefit from the generosity, support, and kindness of friends and colleagues. It gives me pleasure to record, however inadequately, my gratitude to them here. I am especially grateful to Stanley Corngold and Michael Jennings, under whose guidance an earlier version of this study was first carried out at Princeton. Their enormous intellectual and personal generosity and friendship, both during my years at Princeton and since, far exceed the boundaries of these pages. I am indebted to their kindness, their integrity, and the rigor of their scholarly example. I am also grateful to my friend and teacher Eduardo Cadava, who painstakingly concerned himself with this project, offering invaluable insights and wonderful comments. He has been a tireless source of friendship, inspiration, and encouragement. I also wish to record my indebtedness to those other friends and colleagues from whose wisdom and encouragement I have benefitted in the course of this project—in Princeton, Madison, and beyond. For readings, comments, or discussions, I thank especially Klaus Berghahn, Fritz Breithaupt, Donald Brown, Jost Hermand, Walter Hinderer, Thomas Levin, Marc Silberman, Uwe Steiner, Victor Udwin, and David Weberman. As my research assistant, Eric Jarosinski helped reliably with library tasks. Benjamin's nephew, Prof. Michael Benjamin, shared with me delightful stories about "Uncle Walter" and how Benjamin would devise philosophical "word puzzles" especially for his brother's son. I wish to thank Liliane Weissberg for her unflagging interest in and support of this project. In addition, she and James Rolleston each provided valuable comments and suggestions on my text. At the press, Arthur Evans, its director, was a delight to work with; Kristin Harpster and Mary Gillis took scrupulous care in preparing the manuscript for print.

Benjamin once wrote that "one need only take love seriously to recognize in it . . . a 'profane illumination.'" My deepest gratitude belongs to Stephanie Richter, to whom this book is dedicated. Without the marvels and pleasures that the illuminations of her love, support, and companionship have given me, this book could not have been. I offer it to her as a small gift.

INTRODUCTION

BENJAMIN'S CORPOREALITY AND
THE POLITICS OF SELF-PORTRAITURE

Jetzt muß man Benjamin erst mal neu lesen, glaube ich.
                                    Heiner Müller (1991)

The work of Walter Benjamin stages a perpetual confrontation with the politics of German fascism. Fascism belongs to the image-space of the famous Benjaminian alarm clock that rings for sixty seconds in every minute. Like the ringing of the alarm clock, the face of fascism haunts Benjamin's writings: from his early work on the *Passagen-Werk* in the late 1920s, through his well-known meditations on art, technology, and reproducibility of the mid-1930s, to his final text, the quasi-testamentary theses on the concept of history of 1940. One year earlier, in September 1939—on the eve of the Vichy regime—Benjamin, along with thousands of other Parisian exiles of German and Austrian descent, was forced by the French authorities to report to one of the local collecting stations. He was subsequently transported to the gruesome French internment camp at Vernuche near Nerves. Within a few days of his arrival at the camp, which made few concessions to its prisoners' human dignity, Benjamin began to hold an outdoor seminar "for advanced students," charging a tuition fee of three cigarettes or, alternatively, one button. Along with a small group of interested inmates, he convened regular meetings on straw-covered ground beneath a suspended blanket in order to launch an academic camp journal. Drinking contraband schnapps from a thimble, Benjamin, to the amazement of the other prisoners, conducted these editorial meetings with a ceremonious rigor that stood in marked contrast to the camp's macabre living conditions.[1] This exercise of intellectual rigor was Benjamin's only hope in the face of constant alarm. It was as though his ghostly seminar, an atavism from less barbaric times, could somehow rescue him from "the swastika aimed at me."[2]

Benjamin leaves many questions behind for us. In what way does his resistance to what the poet Paul Celan once termed "the thousand darknesses of death-bringing speech" call upon us to face fascism as the specter of what is never finished, what always threatens to return? How can we begin to articulate the attempts of the empirical and textual Benjaminian "self" to pull the emergency break on the onrushing train of catastrophe? And what are the implications of this confrontation with fascism for our understanding of Benjamin's engagement with more general questions of politics and ethics?

Benjamin rejects fascism's conceptual arsenal of "outmoded concepts" such as "creativity and genius, eternal value and mystery" because they lend themselves "to a processing of data in the fascist sense" (I 218; 1:473). Instead, he predicates the urgency and effectiveness of his "fight against fascism" (I 257; 1:697) upon the development of a series of concepts that would "differ from the more familiar terms in that they are completely useless for the purposes of fascism [für die Zwecke des Faschismus vollkommen unbrauchbar sind]" (I 218; 1:473). But even though he suggests that, in general, they might be developed in a new theory of art, Benjamin famously defers the specification of such concepts as delimited notions or representative examples. This deferral has provided the impetus for much speculation. Clearly, the radically disruptive concepts that are at stake here cannot be reduced to those that inform the critical apparatus of an orthodox historical materialism, even while in their oppositional spirit they exhibit an essential elective affinity to it. Benjamin himself comments on the rather enigmatic thinking performed

20

in his "Work of Art in the Age of Its Technical Reproducibility" when he writes to his Frankfurt School colleague Max Horkheimer on 16 October 1935 that the essay's "reflections attempt to give the questions raised by art theory a truly contemporary form: and indeed from the inside [*und zwar von innen her*], avoiding any *unmediated* reference to politics [*unter Vermeidung aller* unvermittelten *Beziehung auf Politik*]. These notes almost nowhere refer to historical material and are not extensive. They are merely fundamental in nature [*haben grundsätzlichen Charakter*]" (C 509; B 690f.).[3] Benjamin here links the actuality of his reflections on aesthetics and the political both to a formal critique—that is, to a full reading that seeks to do justice to its object's singularity and self-differentiation—and to the avoidance of a crudely historicist thinking of politics. Instead, in order to think through the historical and political specificity of his concerns, the rigor of his stance must never allow a reading to stray into false immediacy or revel in the treacherous security of mimesis. Benjamin's emphatic negation of what is "unmediated" [*unvermittelt*] suggests that his confrontation with the political is meant to reach its fullest potential when the political is not illuminated directly. Because for Benjamin the political can only exhibit itself in and as something other, it is most itself when it is read through a series of deferrals and mediations, that is, figuratively. This movement also illuminates the relays between his thinking of the political and his abiding interest in reevaluating the theory of allegory, whose traditionally lower standing in relation to the notion of the allegedly more transparent and immediate symbol he works to question. The task is to learn to read political concepts according to the disruptive force of allegorical figuration itself.

But for Benjamin's readers it has been far from clear what such a learning to read might entail. Indeed, it seems that a wrestling with these unspecified unusable concepts has become something of a hidden leitmotif for critics attempting to come to terms with Benjamin's enigmatic sense of the political. As one reader complains, "Benjamin self-consciously opted for a hermetic and forbidding mode of discourse, further compounding the difficulties of reception by steadfastly refusing in most cases to supply outright the meta-theoretical bases of his conceptual train" (Wolin xi). "What are these concepts," a more recent critic asks, "to what degree did Benjamin accomplish his own task, and to what extent have his demands been given their due? These are questions that have posed themselves to his readers from the beginning" (Bolle 207). And another recent reader of Benjamin's essay bluntly expresses our predicament by asking, "Why does Benjamin not explain what he means by a 'series of completely unusable concepts'?"[4] I wish to suggest that Benjamin does not need to *explain* what these concepts are because he *stages* their transgressive movement in his language. Instead of paraphrase or example, he relies on the narrative gesture of allegorical enactment. As he states in the *Passagen-Werk*, "I have nothing to say. Only to show" (N 47; 5:574). The hypothesis of this book is that Benjamin's complex rhetorical mobilizations of the modern subject, as it emerges in its corporeal form throughout his autobiographical writings, can be read as pointing toward these new concepts. The body of Benjamin's autobiographical subject is useless. It is always in retreat, unemployable by ideologies and programs that rely on presence, stability, closure, and self-identity. In its withdrawal from stable meaning, the corporeal subject belongs to those Benjaminian words that approach us in the image of what does not yet have a name and always remains still to come. These concepts are like a "flag under which sails a cargo that cannot be declared because its name is still lacking" (R 183f.; 2:301).

To begin to address such issues, this initial chapter will devote itself to a network of more general and conceptual Benjaminian concerns. It will clear the way for a detailed reading of Benjamin's acts of self-portraiture in the political terms that I suggest by first reconstructing his novel thinking of the relationship between texts and their political and historical contexts within the realm of the figurative; by discussing Benjamin's fundamental reflections on autobiographical writing and the historical archaeologies of his confessional self; by tracing his theoretical preoccupations with the problem of the body, both as idiomatic meditations and as responses to more general contemporary debates; by situating Benjamin's imbrication of language, the body, and the political in his ethical demand that questions of history and culture be addressed rhetorically; by linking his innovative reading of the tropes of fascism to this demand; and, finally, by meditating on issues and challenges that arise in the reading of Benjamin more generally.

Texts and Con-texts

By calling for radically innovative political concepts that have yet to be thought, Benjamin imagines a language that both binds him to his historical and philosophical context and divorces him from it. Indeed, his entire corpus of texts is traversed by this uneasy simultaneity, posing special challenges both to readers of his writings and students of intellectual history. It is in part this problematic simultaneity too that has prevented Benjamin's readers from articulating more fully his complex intellectual debts to the rich network of competing intellectual traditions on which he draws at different moments in his career, including, among others, "neo-Platonism, neo-Kantianism, early Romanticism, Goethe's aesthetics, Surrealism, [and] Marxism."[5] Already in 1928, his friend Siegfried Kracauer marvels at how Benjamin's "manner of presentation [*Darstellungsform*]" is "the antithesis of the philosophical system, which wants to secure its grasp of the world by means of universal concepts" ("On the Writings of Walter Benjamin" 259). Benjamin's ally and best reader, Theodor W. Adorno, echoes Kracauer's observation in 1965 when he writes that in "contrast to all other philosophers . . . his thinking, as paradoxical as it may sound, was not one that took place in the realm of concepts. . . . He unlocked what could not be unlocked as though with a magic key" ("Erinnerungen" 83). More recently, even such subtle critics as Rodolphe Gasché concede that "it is ultimately impossible to tie Benjamin to any of the philosophical currents that characterized his time" (84). And when one wishes to systematize Benjamin's politics and philosophical stance into a conceptually unified, traditional apparatus of concepts, his language begins to slip away before one's eyes. In his seminal study of the early Benjamin, Bernd Witte thus reminds us that Benjamin privileges the radical moment of uncontainable critique itself rather than the veil of security and stability promised by a "system." Witte therefore cautions us that Benjamin performs a "thinking which attempts to utter in critique the truth that denies itself to any philosophical system" (*Kritiker* 5).

What, in Benjamin, denies itself to any theoretical systematization is precisely the intricate and self-reflexive movement of his language. Benjamin's friend Hannah Arendt senses this difficulty when she suggests that what "was so difficult to understand in Benjamin is that he, without being a poet, *thought poetically* [*dichterisch dachte*], and that for him metaphor had to be the greatest and most enigmatic gift of language, because its 'carrying over' made it possible to make the invisible sensuous" (*Essays* 22). Even though one might take issue with Arendt's slightly ontologizing gesture which distinguishes between those who "are" poets in their essence and those who, even though they *act like* poets, "are" not—as though it were some allegedly unchangeable essence and not the performative act itself that could define one—she does point to the vital importance of addressing the figurative dimension of Benjamin's thought. I wish to suggest that what any engagement with Benjamin's critical confrontation of politics, much less fascism itself, demands, then, is the urgent Benjaminian promise to think through the complicated relationship between language and culture, between the idiomatic artifact and its historical formation, in a manner that takes seriously his insistence on the rhetorical or figurative character of both.

Any understanding of Benjamin's "politics" is predicated upon an examination of the relationship he wishes to forge between the language of his texts and that of his culture. His encounter with the political seeks to avoid forcing a hasty assimilation of a text or object into a crudely mimetic model. It would question the ways in which linguistic events are reduced to illustrative or evidential material. For him, the historicity of a text (which is not simply its own history or its historical context) and its ethico-political resonances are always elsewhere. This Benjaminian "elsewhere" turns around three main axes.

The first axis emerges out of the assumption that the tension between a text and its culture, between language and politics, is reenacted in the tensions that exist in the internal linguistic breaks of any historically mimetic model. This moment becomes clearer in Benjamin's understanding of historical traces and their contingent relationship to a particular context. The thinking of an object or text occurs at a particular point in time and explodes that particularity. Kracauer speaks of this Benjaminian procedure as the consequence of a "thinking that stands in a strange [*fremd*] relation to its time."[6] It is precisely in this strange or alien (*fremd*) relationship to its context and its time, this simultaneous immersion and distancing, that a Benjaminian thinking registers, and then theorizes, the representational phenomenon upon which it fastens. Even though the traces of an object to be examined in this way are inscribed historically, they do not necessarily belong to a particular time. This is to say that just because a text bears historical traces does not mean that it stands in a *necessarily* determined or transparent relationship to the time in which it was produced. As Benjamin puts it in an early study, "The time of history is infinite in every direction and unfulfilled at every moment. This means that no single empirical event is thinkable that would stand in a necessary relationship to the particular historical situation in which it was produced" (W 55; 2:134). To read Benjamin's relation to language and the political therefore means to attempt to account for the perpetual tension between the textual event, on the one hand, and history and politics, on the other. Indeed, his encounter with and struggle against fascism are lodged in this tension.

For a historian of culture and politics to confront this tension requires a sensitivity to the inevitably textual nature of historical insight. In the *Passagen-Werk*, Benjamin takes up the problem of reading historically from his early text when he extends it to the textual activity of the historian himself. He explains that the "events surrounding the historian and in which he takes part will underlie his presentation [*Darstellung*] like a text written in invisible ink. The history that he lays before the reader will, as it were, shape the quotations in the text, and the quotations alone are put forward in a fashion readable to anyone. To write history therefore means to *quote* history. But the concept of quotation implies that any given historical object must be ripped out of its context" (N 67; 5:595). In Benjamin's rhetorical understanding of the historical, there can be no writing of history that is not a form of citation. This means that the language of historical writing is traversed by many other competing languages. The writing of history depends on a textual gesture of quotation, of letting something else speak. But in this moment of *Darstellung*, in which history is confronted with the problems of its own modes of presentation,[7] the historical is already becoming something else. Just as the relation between a phenomenon and its historical context is not fully transparent, the act of writing that attempts to come to terms with this relation confronts the moment in which the historical is torn out of its trajectory. The historicity of an object is thus to be found not simply in its historical chronology but rather—through the textual practice of citation—in the movements of its very shift into something else.

The second axis belongs to the realm of Benjamin's view that the historical significance of a text or a work cannot be thought in separation from the figure of a disjunction. For him, the task of reading historically involves tracing the ways in which the historically inflected dimension of a text enters into a complex elective affinity with the time in which the act of reading occurs—its actuality. "In this way, the work," Benjamin writes in his 1931 essay "Literary History and Literary Scholarship," "transforms itself within itself into a microcosm or rather: a microaeon. After all, the task is not to present works of literature in the context of their time but, rather, to give over to presentation, within the time that produced them, the time that comes to know them—that is our time. Thus literature becomes an organon of history; and to make it so—rather than to make literature the material field of the historical, is the task of literary history" (3:290). To read historically does not mean simply to place works in their own chronological configuration and to find in them, in a mimetic temptation, the material content necessary for the confirmation of what we already believed to be true of their historical moment; nor does it mean superimposing on texts of the past, in a violently retroactive projection, the concerns and issues of the later age in which they are read. Rather, to read historically in this way means to read in and through the historicity of a text the obscure constellations that traverse our own time. The condition of possibility for this demand is the disruption of history: both past and present are torn from their immediate contexts or, as in Benjamin's theses on history, blasted out of their putative teleology. In this double rupture, the historicity of a text may become legible only once it is radically removed from its historical embeddedness in the past; and the present in turn can only be approached when it is viewed through the prism of a historical time that is not its own. Thus, both past and present must first disown what is properly theirs in order to become themselves. Only after this act, the renunciation of their self-identity, can they become what they are—and even then only in and as an other. For Benjamin, the space of this multiple disjunction is the historicity of the act of reading.

The third axis concerns the relentless self-reflexivity of Benjamin's texts. While Benjamin's texts are always historically inscribed, they also unfold in a singularity that often seems to resist assimilation into a larger systemic structure, be it a unified concept of his "theory" or "approach" or a larger cultural paradigm posited as a transparent historical category. This is so in part because the particular beauty—

and challenge—of Benjamin's texts lies in the presence of narrative gestures that provide their reader with the tools with which to make sense of them. We could say that, like the *Trauerspiel* study and its famous "epistemo-critical prologue," all of Benjamin's texts contain their own implicit epistemo-critical prologue.[8] Any understanding of Benjamin's texts and the experience of singularity they afford is thus predicated upon our ability and willingness to read them the way they teach us to read them. For they are instances par excellence of those texts that "solicit an understanding," in Paul de Man's formulation, that "poses the problem of its intelligibility in its own terms" (*Blindness and Insight* 107). Another way to put this is to say that by directing the reader through a laborious reading process toward a particular mode of reading—a mode of reading that as such did not exist before or could not be performed in that particular, necessary way prior to this new rhetorical event—they produce, or, in Jacques Derrida's language, "invent" their own reader ("This Strange Institution" 74). In his own subtle acts of reading, Benjamin allowed himself to be invented as a reader in this sense. To become something like an ideal reader of Goethe's *Elective Affinities*, for example, Benjamin attempted to construct a theoretical stance that would allow him, as he writes in his curriculum vitae, "to illuminate the work fully from within itself" (6:218). And the singularity of the act of reading a Benjaminian text extends, by the same token, to the singularity of a certain *type* of reading performance, albeit in a way that simultaneously addresses—still from the perspective of the singular textual event and in a parallel yet different movement— more general, generic, and necessarily plural concerns of a textual understanding of history and the political.

If Benjamin therefore engages the political struggles of his time through an encounter with language itself, it is because he wishes to illuminate the intricate relationship among politics, history, and rhetoric. As he writes in an early letter to Martin Buber, the questions concerning the relays between language and politics, just as much as those between theory and activism, need to be recast. There, taking "the concept of 'politics' in its broadest sense," Benjamin states:

> The opinion is widespread, and prevails almost everywhere as self-evident, that writing can influence the moral world and human behavior, in that it places the motives behind our actions at our

disposal. In this sense, therefore, language is only a means of more or less suggestively *laying the groundwork* for the motives that determine a person's actions in his heart of hearts. What is characteristic about this view is that it completely fails to consider a relationship between language and action in which the former would not be the instrument of the latter. . . . Every salutary effect, indeed every effect not inherently devastating, that any writing may have resides in its (the word's, language's) secret. In however many forms language may prove to be effective, it will not be so through the transmission of content, but rather through the purest disclosure of its dignity and essence. . . . My concept of matter-of-fact and, at the same time, highly political style and writing is this: to move toward what was denied to the word; only where this sphere of speechlessness reveals itself in unutterably pure power can the magic spark leap between the word and the motivating deed, where the unity of these two equally real entities resides. Only the intense aiming of words into the core of innermost silence is truly effective. (C 79f.; B 126f.)

What Benjamin suggests in this passage traverses his entire corpus, from the so-called metaphysical or mystical writings of his youth to the materialistically inflected texts of his mature phase: namely, that there is an essential rapport between language and politics. For Benjamin, language is not a mere instrument for the mobilization of this or that ideological position. Rather, it stages within itself the very principles or ground of political action. To the extent that Benjamin wishes to privilege a model of political intervention that collapses the false binarism of word and deed, he envisions an approach to the urgent issues of his historical context that is not dependent upon communication, that is, transmitting something *through* language, but that takes place *in* language itself. This "being-in-language," which names the space in which word and deed touch one another, is for Benjamin the condition of possibility for any political inter-vention. What is at stake for Benjamin is, in a very real sense, not a politics *of* language but a politics *in* language.

   Benjamin's celebrated early meditation, "On Language as Such and the Language of Man," written in the same year as his letter to Buber, bears out this reading. This text is important not only because it is a significant predecessor to his later language-theoretical essays on the task of the translator and on the mimetic faculty but also because it illuminates the view of language with which Benjamin associates his innovative thinking of politics. Here, he stresses the self-referential qualities of language. "That is to say," Benjamin writes, "the German language, for example, is by no means the expression of everything that we could—theoretically—express *through* it, but is the direct expression of that which communicates *itself* in it. This 'itself' is a mental entity" (W 63; 2:141). For Benjamin's linguistic theory, the task is "to survive suspended precisely over this abyss" (W 63; 2:141). Because the "answer to the question 'What does language communicate?' is . . . 'All language communicates itself'" (W 63; 2:142), language confronts us with an aporetic double movement. It communicates, and it signals that it cannot communicate. "For language," Benjamin continues, "is in every case not only communication of the communicable but also, at the same time, a symbol of the noncommunicable" (W 74; 2:156).

Benjamin elaborates on this line of thought in his 1935 review essay for the Frankfurt School's *Zeitschrift für Sozialforschung*, "Problems of the Sociology of Language." Citing Kurt Goldstein's suggestion that the purely instrumental and communicative aspect of language corresponds to the language used by a patient suffering from aphasia, he claims that language unfolds on the far side of any transparent transmission of meaning. Using the words of Goldstein, Benjamin writes that one

> could not find a better example for showing how wrong it is to view language as an instrument. What we have seen [i.e., aphasia] is the creation of language in cases where it only functions as an instrument. . . . But this instrumental function presupposes that language, at its core, presents something fundamentally different, the same way that it presented something different to the patient before he fell ill. . . . As soon as a human being uses language in order to forge a living relation to himself or to his peers, language is no longer an instrument, no longer a means, but rather a manifestation, a revelation of our innermost being and the psychical band that binds us to ourselves and our peers. (3:480)

To understand language simply in terms of its use value for communication is akin to aphasia because it disregards the otherness that, traversing the speaking voice and the receiving ear, prevents language from simply transmitting this or that content. Indeed, Benjamin suggests that what structures our *polis* cannot be thought in separation from the difficulties of the language that ceaselessly makes and unmakes it. If to confront politics means to confront language, and if to confront language means to experience both its referential, communicative aspects as well as its self-reflexivity, its retreat from transparent communication, then any reading of the political in a Benjaminian sense must attempt to do justice to this double movement of language.

Benjamin casts the political stakes of this double movement into sharp relief in his 1923 "The Task of Translator." There, he suggests that the aesthetic and political dimension of a work of art unfolds on the far side of transparent, teleological communication of this or that content. "In the cognition of a work of art," Benjamin writes, "consideration of the receiver never proves fruitful. . . . No poem is intended for the reader, no picture for the beholder, no symphony for the audience" (W 253; 4:9). This means that to understand a text or artwork is to appreciate the specific ways in which it resists full comprehension: "For what does a literary work 'say'? What does it communicate? It 'tells' very little to those who understand it. Its essential quality is not communication or the imparting of information," so that the crux of a text or artwork is "the unfathomable, the mysterious, the 'poetic'" (W 253; 4:9). Rather than straightforward expression, Benjamin here privileges what he calls *das Ausdruckslose*, the "expressionless." Artworks and texts are tools for the transmission of content only in conventional, *bürgerlich* conceptions of language. Seven years earlier, in 1916, Benjamin had explained his specifically political motivation for challenging the referential, purely communicative view of language: "This view is the bourgeois conception of language, the invalidity and emptiness of which will become increasingly clear. . . . It holds that the means of communication is the word, its object factual, and its addressee a human being." Benjamin's own notion of language, "in contrast, knows no means, no object, and no addressee of communication" (W 65; 2:144). Opposed to bourgeois notions of language as the transmission of closed meanings, Benjamin hopes to think the politics of language in terms of its truth content—pure language (*die reine Sprache*)— that wrestles with its own inability to transmit a stable content and that recognizes its status as a vital supplement to any performance of signification, even that of "the original" itself.[9] Benjamin believes that translators such as Luther, Voß, Schleiermacher, Hölderlin, and George approached their texts in these terms. Hoping to activate a critical legacy that wrestles with the poetic excess encoded in *das Ausdruckslose*, Benjamin's conception of language strives to make vivid how the self-reflexive obscurity of the aesthetic may help us to address political and ethical concerns. Indeed, if his later materialism is unthinkable in separation from these intensely linguistic concerns, it is because, as he writes to Max Rychner in 1931, "there is a bridge to the way dialectical materialism looks at things from the perspective of my particular stance on the philosophy of language, however strained and problematic that bridge may be. But there is no bridge to the complacency of bourgeois scholarship" (C 372; B 523).

For Benjamin, then, it is always a matter of registering the extent to which the figural or representational dimensions of a text, be it philosophical or political, are structurally related in that they may be at odds with what they seem to name on the surface—whether with regard to literary figures such as Proust or Kafka, surrealism or fascism, or in the *Passagen-Werk* (the phantasmagoria of Paris and the nineteenth century in general, the ghostly origins and procedures of photography or the haunted nature of modern technology, painting, railway travel, and metropolitan street scenes). Just as Benjamin's "Storyteller" in the essay of 1936 is said to be the one who would have "the wick of his life be slowly but completely consumed by the gentle flame of its very narration" (I 108f.; 2:464f.), the cultural critic's political task would be to register, as Benjamin writes in the essay on Goethe's *Elective Affinities*, the "enigma of the flame itself," which is to say, with regard to the relationship between language and culture, "the truth whose living flame continues to burn over the heavy logs of what is past and the light ashes of what has been experienced" (W 298; 1:126).

The challenge that Benjamin offers us in our attempt to read his transformative understanding of politics through the linguistic is therefore to establish a mode of inquiry that does justice to the complicated relation between the language of a text and that of a culture in a more general sense. The problem may well turn out to lie not, as is often assumed nowadays, in the non-referential qualities of language but rather precisely in its *excess* of reference. For Benjamin, language cannot but refer to culture, and culture, in turn, is a matter of language. What this means, among other things, is that it will be incumbent upon Benjamin's readers to trace this excess as a structural feature of the relation between the idiomatic textual artifact and the cultural context to which it refers and by which it is referred to—a relation through which we operate as readers. But precisely because this relation, inversely, also operates through us, we are not in full control of it, and it may turn on us, betray us. We have the choice of either attempting to read this relation despite its potential instability or of not reading it at all. As Benjamin would have it, this choice is a political and ethical one. In spite of the frightening prospect of the "paradoxical transformation [*Umschlag*] of the one into the other," Benjamin writes to Scholem, this political choice must be made: "The task is therefore not to make a finite decision once and for all, but rather to decide at every moment. But to *decide*" (C 300; B 425). Benjamin's decisions, if there are any, are always already lodged in the structure and logic of the turnover. As products of perpetual *Umschlag*, they are born out of the tension of the aporia.

AUTOBIOGRAPHY

The politics of Benjamin's language can perhaps best be approached in his important but often overlooked acts of self-portraiture. The autobiographical writings are especially significant in his corpus not only because they contain theoretical and aesthetic reformulations of the modern autobiographical act as it has been conceived since Rousseau and Goethe but also because they enact on a literary level the historico-political concerns of his more overtly speculative texts. Indeed, the bulk of Benjamin's corpus can hardly be understood in isolation from his autobiographical texts. As Werner Hamacher puts it in his stunning reading of the word "Wolke" (cloud) in Benjamin's *Berlin Childhood*, "it cannot be doubted that Benjamin's memoirs represent the impetus as well as the explication, extrapolation and fulfillment of the program that his theoretical writings formulate. But the memoirs are, for this very reason, also its radicalization" (166). Between 1926 and 1938, at significant points in the trajectory of his development, Benjamin wrote three major autobiographical texts: the *Moscow Diary* (1926–27), the *Berlin Chronicle* (1932), and the *Berlin Childhood around*

1900 (1932–38). The fragmentary *Moscow Diary* was written during
Benjamin's visit to the Soviet Union in the winter of 1926–27 and
represents Benjamin's longest surviving autobiographical document.
In its narrative gesture of free indirect discourse and the rhetoric
of the quotidian, it holds a unique place among the texts of his
autobiographical corpus. As a loose series of chronologically dated
entries, it appears more paratactical[10] and tentative than the *Berlin
Chronicle*, the text Benjamin wrote in the spring of 1932 while
on vacation in Ibiza. The *Berlin Chronicle* was Benjamin's attempt
to make the strategy of literary montage—enacted in his Weimar
book of aphorisms *One-Way Street* a few years earlier—productive
for the language of autobiography. In it, he composes a series of
fragments that interweave general confessional recollections with
theoretically charged material to form a kind of montage of self-
portraiture. The *Berlin Chronicle* is located somewhere in between
the laconic, quotidian language of the *Moscow Diary* and the ornate
prose snapshots of the *Berlin Childhood,* and contains, in a number
of self-reflective passages, some of his most sustained statements on
the very possibility of autobiographical discourse. Like Benjamin's
allegorical miniatures of the *Berlin Childhood,* by far the most stylized
and polished among his autobiographies, the *Berlin Chronicle* stages
Benjamin's idiosyncratic relationship to various Berlin quarters, specific streets, and places such as Tiergarten and Peacock Island, and to
his family and relatives. The images of the subject that emerge from
these autobiographical reflections inform Benjamin's entire corpus.
His confessional texts can be read as symptoms of an ailing Weimar
culture that buries itself somewhere along the one-way street between
one historical catastrophe and another and as urgent documents
that perform an innovative historical materialism that intertwines
general and political questions with highly personal reflections. As
literary enactments of his aesthetic theories that perpetually confront
their own aporias, Benjamin's autobiographical texts are traversed by
the melancholia of absence and finitude. Together, they offer an
experience of singularity and transgression in which the history of
the self is inseparable from the history of its culture and in which
the autobiographical act becomes visible as a salient instance of the
ways in which Benjamin works to illuminate "the connection between
historiography and politics" (1:1248).

But to suggest that the politics of Benjamin's radically innovative "unusable" concepts takes place in his often neglected autobiographical corpus is to confront an enigmatic tension. On the one hand, the high esteem in which Benjamin himself held his autobiographical writings can hardly be overstated. As he writes to Scholem in July 1933, "they contain the most precise portrait that I shall ever be able to give of myself" (C 424; B 589). Benjamin also articulates his desire to map the self semiotically one year earlier when he writes, "For a long time, years really, I have toyed with the idea of structuring [gliedern] the space of my life—bios—graphically on a map. . . . I have devised a sign system, and on the ground of such a map there would be a real hustle and bustle" (R 5; 6:466f.). On the other hand, if to write an autobiography is, in classical terms, to rely upon the grammatical first-person singular pronoun, Benjamin undermines the viability of drawing up such an autobiographical map of the "I." As he writes in 1926, "Writers should get accustomed to regarding the word 'I' as their iron rations. . . . The sooner they come to rely upon it, the worse is their understanding of their craft" (3:68). He continues this thought a few years later in his *Berlin Chronicle:* "If I write a better German than most writers of my generation, I owe it in good part to my twenty-year long observation of a single little rule: never use the word 'I' except in letters. The exceptions to this prescription [*Vorschrift*] that I have permitted myself could easily be counted" (R 15; 6:475).[11] Here, even though he valorizes his autobiographical acts, Benjamin decenters the grammatical subject as the sovereign ruler of discourse, skeptically calling the singularity of writing and the subject's signature into question. A *Vorschrift* is a regulation, rule, or law, here a self-imposed principle that the subject follows. But it is something else as well: a *Vor-Schrift* is literally a "pre-scription" or "pre-writing," a "pre-text" that is always already written and in place from the outset of an act of writing, much the way that—within the general "text" of a culture or a language into which one is born and which, as the text of arche-writing, is always already in place—writing precedes speech. In the case of this Benjaminian *Vor-Schrift*, the subject's linguistic displacement ("never use the word 'I' ") becomes the condition of possibility of a certain textual production: the pre-scription of displacement. The tension to which Benjamin alludes here—that between the impetus to construct the subject through the act of writing and the narrative renunciation of such a project—is the space in which his autobiographical corpus unfolds.

Benjamin's Subject of Modernity

Benjamin's skepticism vis-à-vis the autobiographical self is linked to his more general critique of the modern subject. Indeed, his obsession with articulating a theory of the modern subject is one of the principal tropes of his entire corpus. It is no accident that in the introduction to his friend's *Schriften* Adorno alerts readers to the contested status of subjectivity in Benjamin's writings by emphasizing that just "as Benjamin's thought does not respect the boundary line between the conditional and the unconditional, neither does it, conversely, claim definitive self-completion—a claim raised wherever thought marks out its own circle, the kingdom of subjectivity, in order to reign supreme within it" ("Introduction" 5). For Benjamin, the fragmented, constantly revised subject eludes the desire for completion and closure, even as it strives toward them. The subject's textual figures trace the contours of this perpetual deferral.

In contrast to Hegel, whose definition of the subject as the one that is "capable of maintaining within itself its own contradiction" has remained the dominant understanding of the metaphysical subject,[12] Benjamin rejects the notion of a continuous and self-identical subject that could account for its own multiplications and reconfigurations in the scene of writing. As he tells us in an autobiographical fragment, the "seemingly *whole* (unified) individual does not matter" (6:71). Benjamin's deep suspicion of the notion of a transparent "self" prompts him, already in a letter to Ernst Schoen from September 1919, to question the idea that a human subject could fully emerge through its texts and contexts. Instead, Benjamin prefers to speak of a textual event "whose relation to a subject is as meaningless as the relation of any pragmatic-historical testimony (inscription) to its author" (C 149; B 220). He makes a similar point a decade later, when, in the essay "On Surrealism," which is often considered one of the transitional points between his so-called metaphysical and Marxist phases,[13] he again privileges language over the self: "It [language] is primary. Not only to meaning. Also to one's self. In the configuration of the world, the dream loosens individuality like a hollow tooth" (R 179; 2:297). For Benjamin, language tends to exceed both stable meaning and the self. This excess, though, need not be considered merely destructive or nihilistic. It also opens up the very possibility of thinking through the subject along innovative paths, traces that only come into presence when the ideology of the transparent subject is destroyed. " 'Construction' presupposes 'destruction' " is Benjamin's maxim in the *Passagen-Werk* (N 60; 5:587). And as Adorno points out, "In all his phases, Benjamin thought the demise of the subject and the salvation of humanity as one thing" ("Portrait of Walter Benjamin" 231).

If Benjamin attempts to articulate a genealogy and material historiography of a subject that vacillates between construction and disarticulation, then, as his friend Ernst Bloch once put it, Benjamin's "[c]onstantly new 'I's . . . are to be seen here and extinguish one another. Indeed . . . nobody at all really walks in the street, its things appear to be solely among themselves" ("Revue" 335). This movement, which makes the self visible at the same time that it eclipses it, is a specifically Benjaminian dialectic of perpetual turnover (*Umschlag*) rather than harmonious mediation (*Vermittlung*).[14] For Benjamin, another name for the erratic velocity of this perpetual turnover is the "dialectical standstill," that is, the experience of a break or rupture in historical temporality. This notion of time is no longer subject to the continuity of the sequential progression of time assumed by conventional historicism and the ideology of progress. The historical signature of Benjamin's subject—a subject that is at once constructed and dispersed—begins to become readable in the relation between selfhood and language, between the corporeal subject and its inscription within (and as) a text. This relation never ceases to traverse Benjamin's writings.

What is at stake for Benjamin's articulation of the self may be illustrated by a question from an early note to the *Passagen-Werk*. There, Benjamin asks, "Am I the one who is called W. B., or am I merely called W. B.? [*Bin ich der, der W. B. heißt, oder heiße ich bloß einfach W. B.?*]" (5:1038). Though the act of signification, whose status is involved in *heißen*, is not denied here, signifier and signified do not necessarily coincide. The subject lives in the fear and urgency of having to acknowledge the possible nonself-identity of "the self," thereby calling into question the referential dimension of language.[15] But, significantly, the conjunction "or" suspends our capacity to make a finite choice between rejecting and affirming the possibility of a disjunction between signifier and signified, that is, between a proper "W. B." on the one hand, and the questioning voice of the subject on the other. The syntactical *conjunction* thus places the conceptual *dis*junction into the field of doubt—so that the possibility that the signifier and signified, the subject's voice and its proper name, will coincide is, *in potentia*, both possible and impossible.

By the same token, reading the logic of the sentence against the backdrop of Heidegger's "The Principle of Identity"—which demonstrates the fundamental rupture and plurality inherent in the concept of identity—opens two possibilities of identity, or rather, of non-identity. Were one to emphasize the ontological dimension of *heißen*, Benjamin's sentence could be read as a consequence of the assumption that "I am not myself," which signals a dissolution or negation of identity. But it could also be understood as the consequence of the assumption that "I *am the one* who is not himself," that is, as an affirmation of the subject's identity. This identity, however, is linked to rupture and displacement. If Witte rightfully downplays the differences between the early and the late Benjamin by suggesting that we read his texts from the Youth Movement fully alongside those of his later materialist phases, and if he predicates this way of reading on the argument that "Benjamin is, in his writings, immediately and fully himself" (*Intellectual Biography* 22), then we should here invert this logic. For what allows us to read Benjaminian texts from various phases of his development alongside each other is precisely that they share a sense of rupture and displacement as well as a self that will not remain what it is. If Benjamin's texts define the writer's struggle as a negotiation of the construction and dispersal of selfhood, then they allow us to redefine his self as the one who is not himself.

This definition also serves well as an illustration of the problems that haunt Benjamin in his autobiographical acts. In them, Benjamin sets a task for his readers that has yet to be accomplished: to follow the traces of his autobiographical self as the one who is not himself. As one reader of Benjamin, Fredric Jameson, recently observed, Benjamin's corpus poses a challenge to us not least of all because Benjamin "seems to dissolve into multiple readings fully as much as he turns into a unique 'self' that remains to be defined" ("Benjamin's Readings" 19).

Historical Traces of the Material Self

The historical moment of Benjamin's reflections on the idea of the subject occurs at a time when time is strangely out of joint, a rupture that, for Benjamin, is simultaneously cultural and personal. As Norbert Bolz puts it, Benjamin's "transition from Fritz Heinle to Bert Brecht, that is to say, from the Berlin Youth Movement to a kind of anthropological communism is exemplary for the dynamics of thought in the Weimar Republic: Benjamin embodies its failure" ("Zwerg" 42). It is a moment in the wake of the alienating mechanisms of the industrial revolution, the age of infinite technological reproducibility, and of a growing suspicion of representability and redemption. This suspicion requires the subject to conceptualize history in a new way. As Benjamin writes in his sixteenth thesis on the concept of history, the "historical materialist cannot do without the concept of a present that is not a transition, but in which time comes to a standstill. For this concept defines precisely *that* present in which he writes his own history" (*I* 262; 1:702). The present appears to the subject that writes its own history, its autobiography, as a momentary stasis, a space in which time is suspended. For instance, the Benjaminian child who, in his Berlin autobiographies, plays on the threshold of two centuries, experiences such an historical moment of suspension when the telephone (what Benjamin calls his "twin brother") is introduced into German households. There, the impact of the initially disturbing apparatus remains undecidable and the sheer intrusion of this seductive technological apparatus threatens to blot out the possibility of its evaluation and historicization.

At the turn of the twentieth century, roughly—the threshold of the centuries upon which young Benjamin is playing in the *Berlin Childhood*—the crisis of the modern material subject becomes increasingly intertwined with new media technologies such as photography, the gramophone, and film. As Friedrich Kittler argues, it is possible to specify a rupture between the self-identical, coherent, bourgeois subject of eighteenth-century idealism and the subject of the late nineteenth century—a subject now determined, even overdetermined, by the cultural mechanisms of new technological media.[16] The very nature of writing—and, by extension, the writing of the subject—changed dramatically. "In order to optimize writing through the machine," Kittler writes, "it must no longer be dreamed as the expression of individuals or as the trace of bodies. The so-called human being is split into physiology and information technology" (*Grammophon* 29). While prior to the advent of new forms of recording and storing data traditional forms of writing had no competition, now the media-specific quality of words and information moves into the foreground. The materiality of the signifier becomes decidedly more visible. "Along with the technical differentiation," Kittler explains, "of optics, acoustics, and writing, as it exploded Gutenberg's monopoly on storage around 1880, the so-called human being became manufacturable. His essence runs over into the apparatus" (29). Here, the line of demarcation between a subjective consciousness and various technological machines (such as the typewriter, the telephone, or the camera) ceases to be clearly discernible. Benjamin registers precisely this moment in his essay on Kafka when he speaks of the "age in which the degree of alienation of human beings from each other, along the immeasurably mediated relations which became their only ones, have been intensified to the highest degree," an age in which "film and the gramophone were invented. In a film, the human being cannot recognize his walk or his own voice in the gramophone" (*I* 137; 2:436). The subject is, at the turn of the twentieth century, dispersed and then reconstituted in these new materialities of communication in a way that situates it at the material interstices of competing discursive systems and media technologies. Autobiography is the genre that is the most fully invested with the perpetual shifts of this self.[17]

For Benjamin, there can be no historicization of the modern subject that is not touched by a rethinking of the historical itself. In this rethinking of history, he distinguishes between two different modes of conceptualizing that intermediate moment in time between past and future, one of which he terms *Gegenwart*, or present, the other *Jetztzeit*, or "now-time." In his Baudelaire fragments Benjamin privileges now-time over the present and its conceptual sequelae. The present, according to Benjamin, represents merely a transitory phase that is part of a continuous trajectory, emerging out of the past and pointing toward the future. Now-time, by contrast, takes the form of a historiographic snapshot, a frozen quasi-photographic image that depicts the unique historical conditions of a particular moment in time in its relation to the past. How one thinks about the present moment, then, has important consequences for the ways in which the subject makes sense of its own history. For Benjamin, the relation of present to past is merely chronological, whereas the connection between now-time and "the former" (*das Gewesene*) is dialectical and, as such, represents an economy through which historical insight might be gained. Now-time, embedded in the larger present, contains those elements of the present that refer to historical events and that allegorize history by giving rise to dialectical images. A view of the subject established by this logic would be, by extension, not stable and self-identical but, like its image, at least dialectical.

Benjamin sets this problem into sharper relief in his theses on history. There, he distinguishes between traditional historicism and an unorthodox materialist historiography. Historicism, we learn, is ill-equipped to comprehend the present as now-time, that is, as more than what we could call an inhabitant of the transitory guest-room of the historically incidental. Historicism is only capable of conceiving of the present as a temporal condition flowing swiftly into the past. Benjamin's innovative historiography, on the other hand, conceptualizes the present strategically as a temporal stasis.[18] A fleeting image is here brought to a momentary standstill, and elusive traces of history fasten upon the cultural and representational chart of now-time. By constructing the concept of now-time in this way, the materialist historiographer is able to cite what is contemporaneous to him without immediately falling prey to the elusiveness of a temporality that historicism conceives in an all-too-facile empiricist, realist, or positivist manner.

Benjamin's strategy of the subject, then, is to disrupt the deceptively continuous flow of the "film" of its history, freezing, as it were, the frame of immediate experience in an effort to discern the potentially revolutionary struggle for the disclosure of a suppressed past. The truly radical element in Benjamin's argument may well lie in the fact that it allows for the continuous unfolding of previously suppressed historical trajectories and tensions within the framework of the static moment—rather than conceiving of that stasis as merely the absence of movement: "The gain of his method is that the work sublates [i.e., contains, preserves, and cancels—*aufgehoben*] his lifework, his lifework the epoch, and the epoch the entire movement of history" (*I* 263; 1:703). Here, Benjamin reads history through a language of perpetual disclosure, reminiscent, one could say, of the marvels sparked by the Slavic wooden dolls, each of which contains within itself yet another doll. The moment of stasis, intended to yield insight into the dialectical structure of temporality, is itself dialectical, and contains within it the antagonistic impulses of movement and motionlessness. This kind of stasis is not merely aporetic, it also opens up the possibility of reading the protocols of a subject's experience through a series of negations.

To undo, with Benjamin, the subject and its canonical privileges as a way of opening up certain other modes of insight is also to acknowledge that any attempt to consider the political question "Who?" would proceed—like all of Benjamin's questions—in accordance with a rhetorical mode of analysis. In a 1924 letter to Hofmannsthal concerning Benjamin's magisterial essay on Goethe's *Elective Affinities*, he emphasizes his belief in the importance of close linguistic analysis, his "conviction, namely, that every truth has its home, its ancestral palace, in language," so that what is needed is an analysis of the 'oldest *logoi*' and a sustained examination of the "semiotic character of language" (C 228f.; B 329). And, in "The Task of the Translator," Benjamin argues that what is essential in negotiating the movements of meaning is not to be sought within the subjectivity of those who are born in the wake of the scene of writing ("Subjektivität der Nachgeborenen") but rather "in the most proper life of language and its workings," lest we fall prey to the danger of a theoretical confusion, that is, "to confuse cause and essence of a thing or, put more rigorously, to deny one of the most powerful and fruitful historical processes due to an inability to think" (I 73; 4:13). To take these Benjaminian precepts seriously is not to suppress what may be thought of as more properly "historical" concerns but rather to suggest that a conscientious thinking of history proceeds through an analysis of the structure and temporality of presentation. For the temporality of presentation is itself an image of how time—precisely in the temporal distance between an apperception of an instance of signification and our attempt to read it—presents itself to us. History, in Benjamin's corpus, is always to be negotiated as a form of presentation, as "the object of a construction" (I 261; 1:701). This Benjaminian procedure makes it possible to accentuate the force field of differences that is at the core of history itself.

Textual Archaeologies of the Autobiographical Self

Only through the laborious work of "textual archaeology" suggested by Benjamin's figure of the autobiographical archaeologist can the historical trajectory of a subject in crisis be traced, and only in such a textual approach can the *relation* between that subject and a historical or cultural concept, such as "Weimar" or "fascism," be articulated. This procedure requires not an exercise in paraphrase or summary but a thinking of relations that constantly questions what it might mean for a trope to enter into a relation (with culture, with history) and what compels us to articulate this relation in a particular way.

If it is true that Benjamin's texts provide his readers with the conceptual tools with which to read them according to their own logic, then the autobiographical texts that are so central to his thought should be no exception. And, indeed, in his *Berlin Chronicle* Benjamin offers us a remarkable passage that teaches us both how to read his self-portraitures and how they themselves were conceived:

> Language has unmistakably signified that memory [*Gedächtnis*] is not an instrument for the exploration of the past but rather its scene [*Schauplatz*]. Memory is the medium of what has been experienced the way the earthen realm is the medium in which dead cities lie buried. He who wishes to approach his own buried past must act like a man who digs. This determines the tone [*Ton*], the stance of real memories. They must not be afraid to return again and again to the same fact of the matter [*Sachverhalt*], to strew it [*auszustreuen*] the way one strews soil, to churn [*umgewühlt*] it the way one churns the earthen realm. Because facts of the matter are only deposits, layers which deliver only to the most meticulous examination what constitutes the true assets hidden within the inner earth: the images which, torn from all former contexts, stand—like ruins or torsos in the collector's gallery—as the treasures in the sober chambers of our belated insights. And, in order to dig successfully, a plan is certainly required. Yet just as indispensable is the spade's careful, probing penetration of the dark earthen realm; and he who only keeps the inventory of his finds, but not also this dark bliss of the finding itself, cheats himself of the best part. The unsuccessful search belongs to it just as fully as the fortunate search. This is why memory must not proceed by way of narrative, much less by way of reports, but must, rather, assay its spade, epically and rhapsodically in the most rigorous sense, in ever new places and, in the old ones, to delve into ever deeper layers. (R 25f.; 6:486f.)

This infinitely rich passage contains Benjamin's autobiographical poetics. For Benjamin, the condition of possibility of the autobiographical act, memory itself, is not an instrument to be employed in order to gain access to a system of reference external to it but rather a scene, space or site, a spectacle or stage (*Schauplatz*). Memory is not a hermeneutic tool which assures the conjuring up of what is no longer the case. Rather, it is itself the scene in which what it cites takes place. Only in the scene of memory itself, Benjamin suggests, can what is called forth be narrativized and emplotted in the virtual drama performed on its stage.

But in what way can Benjamin claim that this movement of memory is "unmistakably signified" by language itself? First of all, etymologically *Gedächtnis*, or memory, is vitally intertwined with thinking (derived from the Old High German *kithehtnissi*, which means "the thinking of," "rapt attention," "remembrance"; the word is actually a noun derived from the past participle of *denken* [to think]). *Gedächtnis* is thus not an instrument for activating the process of thinking; it *is* the very scene of thinking itself. Second, the structure of memory, like that of language, is not necessarily a tool for communicating the external referential world but rather the scene or space in which experience and the memory of this experience take place. This is not to say that for Benjamin language is non-referential—after all, it signifies *that* it may not be referential. It is in this paradoxical sense, then, that both language and memory signify "unmistakably" that they are not referential instruments but rather the scene or site of experience itself.

This mnemonic scene, Benjamin's passage suggests, specifies that memory is the medium of experience in the same way that the earthly realm is the medium in which "dead cities" are buried. To dig one's way to one's past—say, in the process of autobiographical writing, the specific act performed by the text in which this specific passage is buried—is to dig ever more deliberately and, ultimately, to become a kind of archaeologist of the self. Specific mnemonic events may be encountered along the way of this archaeological activity—this, Benjamin tells us, "determines the tone [*Ton*], the stance of real memories." It is no accident that Benjamin's text would privilege *Ton*, for at least four semantic layers of this German word are operative here. First, *Ton* signals the digger's "tone," his very stance or attitude (toward his own past, his method of digging, etc.). Second, *Ton* is the hue or coloration of what the digger is likely to find in his mnemonic excavations (and the particular bent or slant with which he will report such findings to himself and others). Third, *Ton* is also a sound, here presumably the sound of the digging spade, of digging itself, that is, the phenomenologically accessible correlate of the activity which gives birth to mnemonic images in the first place. Finally, *Ton*, as "clay," names the very substance in which the archaeological material for the work of memory is situated, or rather, flexibly encrypted (though the mnemonic material is interred in clay, this clay can also be shaped and manipulated into new forms and formulations).

But, as Benjamin would have it, the memories to be found by means of such archaeological work strew, scatter, or disseminate [*ausstreuen*] their very contents. Indeed, they must never cease to disseminate their hard-won property. Only by first disseminating their contents the way one would scatter a handful of earth can they eventually be scrutinized. For Benjamin's *ausstreuen* is the exact counterpart to *auflesen* or simply *lesen*, which means both to gather and to read. (We recall his comments on the "strange double meaning of the word *Lesen*" in "Doctrine of the Similar" [D 68; 2:209], a double meaning that also plays a role in Heidegger.) The moment of being able to read the various mnemonic finds thus depends on their prior gathering, which in turn is only enabled by an initial radical dissemination. In the activity of collecting the scattered pieces to prepare a "gathering-reading," the Benjaminian archaeologist will have learned that collecting is always strategic and will always have been indebted to the rhetorical requirements of narrativization.

The contents of memory, those crusty layers and hardened sedimentations, Benjamin continues, need to be *umgewühlt* (ploughed through, churned, rototilled) in order to yield mnemonic images. But, in the moment of churning that Benjamin invokes, the particular sedimentation of memory, the very topography that needs to be articulated, is also destroyed. For what the churning leaves behind forms new and unexpected sedimentations that, when churned again by the archaeologist of the self, will yield rather different images of the past. Each time the layers of memory are thus accessed to articulate, through disconnected images, archaeological fragments broken out of context, a certain past of a specifiable somebody, their particular rhetorical constellation is also disrupted and shuffled. As Benjamin suggests, the *same* text of history can never be read more than once, as it will always become something else in subsequent

44

readings. There can never be a self that possesses a stable past that can be fully emplotted at will.

Benjamin's passage subtly stages, at the level of syntax, the conceptual argument it makes. At precisely the moment in the narrative when the archaeologist's spade penetrates the earth in order to churn it, Benjamin's syntax registers a kind of penetration or insertion ("what constitutes the true assets hidden within the inner earth: the images"). Benjamin's colon orthographically marks the penetration of the earth by the spade. While prior to that point in the paragraph, the syntax was smooth and uninterrupted, it is now punctuated by the intruding colon. (The very sentence containing the colon introduces a certain syntactical "piling up" of inserted sentence parts, as if to stage grammatically the layers and sedimentations of the earthly realm and thus to prepare the scene for the coming incision.) The "puncturing" of the spade figures simultaneously as a scission in the realm of memory. The syntax of this sentence enacts the poetological principle Benjamin evokes in *One-Way Street:* "A period that, constructed metrically, afterward has its rhythm upset at a single point yields the finest prose sentence imaginable" (W 457; 4:105). Finally, this is the poetological pendant to what Benjamin, in the section on the theory of knowledge in the *Passagen-Werk,* refers to as "the caesura in the movement of thought" (N 67; 5:595).

When specifying the mnemonic images that are found in the earth, Benjamin refers to "the images which, torn from all former contexts, stand—like ruins or torsos in the collector's gallery—as the treasures in the sober chambers of our belated insights [*die Bilder, die aus allen früheren Zusammenhängen losgebrochen als Kostbarkeiten in den nüchternen Gemächern unserer späten Einsicht—wie Trümmer oder Torsi in der Galerie des Sammlers—stehen*]." Set off by diacritical markers, the ruins and torsos disturb the syntactical flow of the sentence in order to make their presence felt. As torn fragments, these empty historical shells continue to linger in an age that has outlived them and that now can hardly make sense of them. Their conceptual status is specified syntactically: they are placed—between diacritics— in the most disruptive and ghostly place of German syntax, that is, immediately prior to the deferred climax of the sentence, the verb (*stehen*). This is how they strangely defer the already deferred climax of the relative clause even further. These empty Benjaminian ruins of memory, then, inhabit the space of a certain deferral of sense.

But the impetus that leads the collector of mnemonic images to place his archaeological finds in a gallery or museum also gives us pause. The broken fragments and stranded torsos appear precious and interesting even though they are divorced from the flow of contemporary life—and are, in a certain sense, unreadable. It is, in Benjamin's passage, precisely because its earlier signification is no longer fully readable that cultural material is put in museums in the first place. Thus, when the autobiographer or archaeologist of the self becomes the curator of his own gallery of the self, that moment is not simply one of remembering, enhancing, or preserving. It is also one of resignation.

The movement of the spade by which the Benjaminian archaeologist of the self accesses mnemonic layers and sedimentations is both planned or teleological ("a plan") and tentative or provisional ("careful, probing"). What he encounters can only inadequately be categorized as an "inventory of findings." We understand, by extension, that the historicist inventory par excellence, the chronicle, will not yield the best mnemonic results ("cheats himself of the best part"). Thus, the methodology presented in this autobiographical text, the *Berlin Chronicle*, problematizes the fact that it has announced itself in its title as a chronicle. It implicitly calls into question its own generic mode.

The chronicle, as a genre, relies on a systematic ordering of historical events and experience deemed significant. Its narrative gesture is that of linearity, continuity, and progression. The alternative to the chronicle is the archaeologist's "dark bliss" registered at the site of a find. From the perspective of the subsequent narrativization of the finds, searching in vain is just as significant as finding, and Benjamin valorizes the gap between seeking and finding. Archaeologically driven memory, therefore, must not proceed by way of linear narration, much less by hypotactical reportage. For Benjamin, it must be rigorously epical and rhapsodic: it must prompt one to start to dig in ever new and unexpected sites and simultaneously to penetrate the layers of one's existing historical construction sites ever more deeply. The space of autobiographical unfolding is thus both horizontal and vertical, extensive and intensive. Benjamin's text allegorizes the methodological need for broad historical awareness and the closest possible reading of individual moments of representation.

Along these same lines, to say, as Benjamin does, that memory is to proceed rhapsodically means to reject its pretension of linearity and closure. To think and write rhapsodically means, among other things, to operate in a disconnected style, to valorize the torn fragments of consciousness and narration without obliterating broad historical (or "epic") trajectories. One can think of the rhapsodical in connection with the privileged status Benjamin accords to constellation and montage: here, the rhapsodic is the name of montage in the realm of autobiography.

If we can think of the mode of autobiography in Benjamin as that of "archaeological montage," then certain moments of a subject's historical trajectory of experience briefly come to the fore without being forced into the fiction created by the continuous narrative of a putatively stable subject's life. It is well-known that Benjamin's ideal utopian text always remained that of a strategic montage of quotations, a textual constellation that would illuminate its internal relations not by way of added commentary or paraphrase but by virtue of its playful yet calculated juxtaposition of citational fragments. Indeed, for a while, Benjamin conceived of the entire *Passagen-Werk* in this manner.[19] The archaeologist's rhapsodic treatment of loose fragments found in the excavated past, which are then put into relation with one another without the added conceptual linearity of a chronicling narrative, names Benjamin's thinking of montage in the realm of autobiography.

This archaeological procedure can finally be thought as an allegory of writing and reading. An archaeologist's *Scharren*, or digging, is etymologically related, through the practice of scratching and engraving, to writing itself—in all the allegorical ways of Kafka's writing and digging animal in "The Burrow."[20] It is no accident either that Benjamin prefers to name this archaeological process of writing down *Niederschrift* as opposed to, say, the more common *Aufschreiben*. *Niederschrift* seals both the pen's downward movement onto the page—a writing *down*—and the spade's incisive downward movement into the depth or netherworld of mnemonic layers, giving full emphatic valence to the parallelism of pen-spade and writing-digging. That *Niederschrift* also echoes *Niederkunft*—or giving birth—emphasizes the creative moment that gives the text over to presence. In this sense, Benjamin's passage stages as much a theory of memory as it outlines a mode of autobiographical writing and—if we allow ourselves to be constructed or "invented" by Benjamin's text—of reading. We must become, "epically and rhapsodically," textual archaeologists of the Benjaminian subject and the politics of its culture.

If Benjamin wishes to situate his archaeological discussion of the self primarily in the art of self-portraiture, it is because he knows that, while the problem of the subject is inherent to a certain degree in all moments of representation, it is most acute in autobiographical discourse. The subject of an autobiography is traditionally located in the difficult attempt to project a unified, autonomous self in its pellucid historical and social context. The key figure of what Benjamin once termed his apprenticeship in German literature, Goethe, already recognized in his own confessional writing the difficulty of this autobiographical demand, what he calls "something nearly impossible to achieve," that is, "that the individual know himself and his century—himself, as a constant entity in the midst of all the circumstances" (*Poetry and Truth* 17). This is a theoretically arduous task because autobiographical texts are more and less than the attempt to render a written account of a life story. In their self-reflexivity, these texts problematize the interrelation of the self (*autos*), life (*bios*), and the act of writing (*graphe*). Autobiographical language projects the image of a self that strives to come to grips with itself by manipulating the inscription of this or that chronology. The constructability, "the subjectivity-effect," is only guaranteed—"underwritten"—by the writer's proper name and signature. The reader is asked to enter this "autobiographical pact,"[21] to submit to a fiction which is then legalized, countersigned by the signature of an other, a reader. This temporary legalization permits the examination of a subjective consciousness that turns itself into an object, thematizing—in the question of just what constitutes the self and differentiates it from an other (if the citation of the subject always involves such an ironic objectification)—its own conditions of possibility.

The Problem of Genre

Yet despite the promise of such an autobiographical pact, it remains extremely difficult to treat autobiography as a genre, and Benjamin, in the *Berlin Chronicle*, registers the instability of his own text as autobiography: "Memories, even when they go into great breadth, do not always represent an autobiography [*stellen nicht immer eine*

Autobiographie dar]. And this is certainly not one, not even for the Berlin years which, after all, are my only concern here" (R 28; 6:488). If Benjamin problematizes the moment of presentation in which memories are to figure as texts, it is because for him presentation always threatens to run awry. Benjamin's statement also suggests that his *Berlin Chronicle* is a document that wrestles with its own status as text. The *Berlin Chronicle* announces itself, then, as a text of distinctly philosophical concerns and proportions. It intertwines questions of the "bios" with questions of presentation.[22] Benjamin continues his thought in the *Berlin Chronicle* when he writes: "For autobiography is concerned with time, with sequence and what constitutes the continuous flow of life. Here, however, I am talking of a space, of moments and discontinuities. For even though months and years appear here, it is in the figure they have in the moment of remembrance [*Eingedenken*]. This strange figure—one may call it fleeting or eternal: in no case is the material from which it is made that of life. . . . The air of the city that is conjured here allots them [the people] only a brief, shadowy existence" (R 28; 6:488f.). While the status traditionally accorded to the autobiographical performance names a chronological, hierarchical unfolding of the narrative of a life—on the order of what Adorno would call hypotaxis—Benjamin's text unfolds not in a linear fashion as the word "Chronicle" would suggest but as the protocol of a paratactically arranged montage of experiences and textual miniatures. His self-portraits reside, Benjamin tells us, not so much in time but in a space [*Raum*], a topography or constellation which the writing subject endows with certain significations. While the space of these constellations can never be outside of temporality, time is here a trope that names not a linear unfolding of a vital trajectory (of the *bios, des Lebens*) but rather a "strange figure," that is, as a rhetorical form through which time is constructed in the moment of remembrance (*Eingedenken*). This strange figure of time is thus not the product of some natural life, the mimetic product of lived experience, but rather what emerges as the figural image of temporality in the scene of writing an autobiography. Benjamin's strange figure of time thus encodes both temporality (it is written, thought, or remembered in time) *and* its suspension (it is, we are told, radically divorced from the natural material of life). This is why, in the moment of the autobiographical act, the strange figure of time is both ephemeral and eternal. The scene of autobiography opens up precisely in the distance between what Benjamin terms the ephemeral and the eternal, between the struggle to capture the presence of meaning and the prospect of its absence. This scene is populated, to use Nietzsche's famous image, by a moveable army of metaphors, by dialectical images and haunting figures that conspire to call into question the certainty of reading and making sense even while enabling these activities in the first place.

The "strangeness" of autobiography Benjamin addresses here has not escaped students of this mode of writing. Symptomatically, the noted historian of autobiography James Olney laments, "if autobiography is the least complicated of writing performances, it is also the most elusive of literary documents. One never knows where or how to take hold of autobiography" (3). And according to de Man, it is problematic to treat autobiographical texts as a distinct genre. This is so because they retreat from referentiality and because they are determined by the specificity of their linguistic medium, by "the illusion of reference" ("Autobiography" 69). Instead, de Man suggests that the concept of *prosopopeia,* a rhetorical term signifying the impersonation or mask of an absent or dead speaker or voice, may be employed in the examination of autobiographical writing. To speak of autobiographically constructed selves is therefore to speak of their prosopopeially assumed textual identities, their construction of a specific mask or voice that is designed to give the impression of presence. An analysis of such an autobiographical construction would hence scrutinize tropes less in an effort to assemble an essential presence, an "authentic" identity, but rather to examine the montage and subsequent employment of one possible mask among many competing ones, what Benjamin in the *Berlin Childhood* calls his "arsenal of masks" (7:418).[23] These masks are designed to produce rhetorically the most plausible "subjectivity effect," that is, the mechanisms by which, in the Nietzschean sense, the subject becomes what it is through representing itself to itself.

There are certain crucial relays between de Man's figure of prosopopeia and Benjamin's reading of the scene of autobiography. Both prefer to think autobiography not as the mimetic reflection of an empirical subject's life ("in no case is the material from which it is made that of life"), but as the staging of a mask (de Man) or figure (Benjamin) of an absent or deceased voice. De Man stages autobiography as the "giving and taking away of faces," while Benjamin speaks of the brief, shadowy appearance, the *kurzes, schattenhaftes Dasein* of the faces and voices featured in his autobiographies. Like de Man's ghostly voices from beyond the grave, the selves of Benjamin's autobiography appear as ghosts, specters, and detached names, they "appear ghost-like in their windows only in order to disappear again, they sniff along thresholds like a *genius loci,* and even if they fill entire quarters of the city with their names, it is only in the way a dead man's fills the headstone on his grave" (R 28; 6:488f.). Readers of his autobiographical writing encounter a Benjaminian prosopopeia in "places and moments when it [the city] bears witness to the dead, shows itself full of the dead" (R 28; 6:489). The mask or voice that Benjamin's autobiographies assume is as much connected to life and presence as to death and absence. Thus, the life emplotted in the *Berlin Chronicle* "approaches the realm of the dead, where it protrudes into the realm of the living, in the same preciously attached manner . . . as it approaches life itself" (R 28; 6:489).[24]

This thanatographical moment of Benjamin's self-portraiture traverses not only his written corpus but also his empirical one, his entire intellectual being. In Adorno's terms, neither corpus corresponds to the idea of a self-present subject: "Just as Benjamin's thinking forms the antithesis to the existentialist concept of the person, empirically he seems, despite extreme individuation, hardly the person but rather the scene of the movement of the subject matter that pushed through him toward language" ("Letter Writer" xvii). This de-subjectified scene of the movement of thought takes place as though from beyond the grave. According to Adorno, it "was as if he [Benjamin] had paid a horrible price for the metaphysical power of what he saw and what he attempted to express in infallible words; as if he spoke as a dead man in return for his ability to recognize, with sobriety and calm, things which the living are not normally capable of recognizing" ("Erinnerungen" 82). Benjamin's autobiographical texts act as a kind of metonymy for this general thanatographical scene. They name the subject's finitude. It is as if Benjamin's voice were always already a prosopopeia, coming from beyond the grave—even before death.

THE CORPUS

In order to understand the complicated ways in which Benjamin's fleeting autobiographical subject participates in the development of innovative political concepts, it is necessary to appreciate the extent to which Benjamin is obsessed with the subject's body or corpus. For him, there can be no history of the self that is not simultaneously a history of the body. If he suggests that "language has a body and the body has a language" (3:138), then any attempt to understand the mechanisms by which we strive to assure ourselves of ourselves in language is a matter of reading the text of the body. To say that the body has a language is to say that it operates according to a certain grammar, a network of symbolic structures that can be made meaningful and that may be learned by an attentive reader. But the language of the body is also subject to the threats that other forms of language face, such as the breakdown of communication and the retreat from transparent meaning. Conversely, to think of language as possessing a body is to allow for the possibility that it can behave in a corporeal way: it can become tactile, it may digest, regulate, and sense pain, it can grow tired, be infected and injected, register pleasure, even procreate. And like the mortal body, language would face its own finitude.

In his remarkable essay on Karl Kraus (1931), Benjamin injects the written body with a series of linguistic morphemes. Evoking what he calls Kraus's singular *Sprachdenken,* or "linguistic thinking," Benjamin writes: "If style is the power to move freely in the length and breadth of linguistic thinking without falling into banality, it is attained chiefly by the cardiac strength [*Herzkraft*] of great thoughts, which drives the blood of language through the capillaries of syntax into the remotest limbs [*das Sprachblut durchs Geäder der Syntax in die abgelegensten Glieder treibt*]." Pointing to Kraus's "suffering, that he exposes with all its wounds, all its nakedness," Benjamin argues that Kraus's rhetorical thinking demands a reader "for whom even in a subordinate clause, in a particle, indeed in a comma, mute torn scraps and nerve-fibers quiver" and for whom even "from the obscurest and driest fact still hangs a piece of mutilated flesh" (R 251; 2:346). To read the written corpus is thus to read the history of its wounds and the syntax of its torments. Benjamin could not have given us a more poignant image of his own writing.

From this perspective we can also begin to understand why in the context of autobiographical writing, a writing that returns incessantly to the question of the self, the body emerges as especially significant for Benjamin. As he writes already in an early fragment, the question of the self is not primarily a matter of freedom or individuality but can be thought as a problem of its material basis: "The question of the spontaneity of the *I* belongs in a very different, a (biological?) context" (6:55). Benjamin sets for the readers of his autobiographical corpus the task of realizing the implications of this view.

In order to approach Benjamin's acts of self-portraiture through the body, it is helpful to consider what one of his most incisive readers, Derrida, has to say about the autobiographical corpus of one of Benjamin's intertextual relays, Nietzsche. According to Derrida,

> Neither "immanent" readings of philosophical systems (whether such readings be structural or not) nor external, empirical-genetic readings have ever in themselves questioned the *dynamis* of that borderline between the "work" and the "life," the system and the subject of the system. This borderline—I call it *dynamis* because of its force, its power, as well as its virtual and mobile potency—is neither active nor passive, neither outside nor inside. It is most especially not a thin line, an invisible or *indivisible* trait lying between the enclosure of philosophemes, on the one hand, and the life of an author already identifiable behind the name, on the other. This divisible borderline traverses two "bodies," the corpus and the body, in accordance with laws that we are only beginning to catch sight of. (*Otobiographies* 5f.)

What is at stake in responding to autobiographical discourse is, among so many other things, to question the ways in which what separates the empirical self from its mobilizations, even constructions, in language can itself be thought in terms of another separation. This other separation—that between what presents itself as systemic (or, one might add, as cultural and political) and what, in the scene of writing, appears to be idiomatic and organic—simultaneously redoubles and displaces the first separation. The second separation redoubles the first because it, too, hovers on the mobile and variable border between two spheres, and the second inversion displaces the first because it shifts attention away from an ontologizing specification of the borderline to the ways in which this line can be conceptualized as an interaction of bodies and texts. To the extent that these shifting movements can be thought as being governed by certain "laws," as Derrida suggests, Benjamin's negotiations of the embodied self within his autobiographical corpus are fruitful territory. They self-consciously stage their own traversal by the ghostly and ever-shifting borderline that would separate the idiomatic from the systemic, the personal from the political, and the private from the cultural—all precisely in terms of the body. Benjamin's autobiographical corpus enacts itself to the same extent that it threatens to vanish from sight.

Benjamin's Trajectory of the Body

To grasp what this might mean in Benjaminian terms, it is instructive to situate the emphasis on the body in the development of Benjamin's thinking, where it remains, in different modulations, a permanent concern. Benjamin became interested in the problem of the body as early as 1918, as a variety of often neglected notes and fragments suggest. Many of the notes and drafts concerning the body were made available by Benjamin's editors in 1985 in the penultimate volume of his *Gesammelte Schriften*, which collects fragments and a series of autobiographical documents. These fragments of varying length address issues of the body in such contexts as the philosophy of language, anthropology, aesthetics, and history.[25]

What all of Benjamin's texts about the body share is an insistence on the materiality of the corpus as a linguistic structure, whether the body is conceived in psychological, politico-historical, or theoretical terms. In a short fragment from 1918, for instance, Benjamin departs from the precepts of conventional psychology by emphasizing the ways in which the self is structured by the semiotic nature of its body. Here, what is at stake for Benjamin is the "relationship of human form to language," which may be traversed by something "unintelligible [*unverständlich*]" (6:66). In his comments on this fragment, Rainer Nägele has noted that Benjamin's shift from the psyche to a physiognomy of inscription is "not a naive physiologism. As the body of a being that speaks, the human body is permeated by language, and the perceptual world is structured by language." This shift "is the basis of all of Benjamin's later work. It also defines his distance from romanticism and from any philosophy based on self-consciousness and self-reflection" (*Echoes of Translation* 7). From early on in his career, Benjamin registers the ways in which the corpus is aporetically traversed by language, that is, how it is both constructed and disarticulated by it.

While the corpus and its relationship to language already was a central issue for the early Benjamin, from the mid-1920s onward his theoretical concerns become increasingly preoccupied with it.[26] Benjamin's major publications of 1928, *One-Way Street* (which he had begun in 1923), and his study of the baroque German *Trauerspiel*, *Origin of the German Mourning Play* (completed in 1924), register an increasing emphasis on the body, culminating in his first major autobiographical document, the *Moscow Diary*. Both earlier texts are preoccupied with the body and the ways in which it functions as a theoretical and cultural marker: *One-Way Street* culminates in the construction of a new concept of the body, and the *Trauerspiel* book thematizes the baroque allegorization of the suffering, dismembered body as an emblematic instance of the modern subject in pain. In these texts, Benjamin regards the body both as a material inscription of the self and as a collective and aggregate corpus. It is thus hardly an accident that Kracauer in 1928 refers to the *Trauerspiel* study as a text that "contains the presentation and interpretation of the modes of being which embodied themselves [*sich verkörpert*] in the reality of the Baroque mourning play" ("Benjamin" 259). "Embodied": Kracauer's playfully precise language registers how Benjamin's text traces the conditions of baroque culture in a state of embodiment. The *Trauerspiel* book not only features the multitude of dismembered, bloody, and sexualized bodies that occupy the baroque stage but also shows how certain philosophical and cultural discourses of the period are "embodied" allegorically on that stage. Significantly, the "modes of being" in the reality of the mourning play embodied *themselves* or turned *themselves* into body (*sich verkörpert*). Seen through the prism of this emphatically reflexive form, it is as though the truth of subjective and cultural representation made itself felt by traveling through the body, that is, as a somatic existence that is not always understood by our conscious critical capacities.

If the final segment of *One-Way Street* evokes a new sense of *physis*, it is intertwined with the 1929 essay "On Surrealism" which develops two innovative concepts that Benjamin calls *Leibraum*, or "body-space," and *Bildraum*, or "image-space." Through these terms, Benjamin wishes to reconsider the difficult relationship between the body and history. In *One-Way Street*, Benjamin emphasizes the body's suffering of technologically mediated traumas as they erupted in World War I. As Benjamin tells us, in "technology, a new *physis* organizes itself for humanity in which the latter's contact with the cosmos forms itself in new and different ways" (W 487; 4:147). He continues, "In the nights of destruction of the last war, the limb structure of humanity was shaken by a feeling similar to the bliss of the epileptic. And the revolts that followed it were the first attempt of mankind to bring the new body under its control [lit.: to bring it under its power/violence, *in ihre Gewalt zu bringen*]" (W 487; 6:148). But does it follow for Benjamin that in a technologically mediated historical crisis, the individual and collective body exposes itself to finite meaning, to closure? Is the corpus historically legible as a determinate limit?

To be sure, Benjamin's historically inflected body is here messianically or revolutionarily charged.[27] Technology itself becomes an organ of the collective body which would abandon the imperative—driven by a reductive form of instrumental reason—to dominate and exploit nature. Instead, Benjamin seeks to disrupt this thinking with the new imperative to master the *relation* between man and nature. This could be called, positively, an apocatastatic moment ("apocatastasis," a term significant to Benjamin, refers to the redemptive recovery of everybody and everything) of the historical body.[28] But at the same time we must question the ways in which a historical body can be represented in the first place. At first, there are innumerable historical events of the body in which it becomes invested with meaning (say, for instance, its birth, illnesses, or technological inventions such as hearing aids). Though these instances signal the continued existence of a body, as a random group of isolated events they are not yet historical. That is to say, they do not participate in a thinking of time, and they are not yet readable as instances of a historical self across time. Although these isolated instances lay claim to certain properties of the traditional, autonomous subject, such as self-identity, determinacy, and self-presence—in each individual instance, being as such seems to be affirmed—they cannot be read historically. For historical readability to emerge in Benjaminian terms, the isolated events must first be put into a set or constellation in which not only their formal or configurational relatedness emerges, but also their *temporal* connectedness. It is only through such a constellation that evidence of historical subjectivity and its body can be established. But to establish such a constellation—to establish "history"—is also to expose the individual instances of the subject to time. And to think the subject in time is to consider time itself, which is a matter of finitude. Thus something peculiar happens in the moment in which this historically constituted subjectivity emerges: though it becomes visible as the temporal manifestation of self-presence, it is also exposed to the radical absence, non-linearity, and nonself-identity that are embedded in its very temporality. The delimitation of the historical subject's being is thus also the opening up of its abyss or death: the historical alterity of the subject and its *physis*.

This is precisely why, in Benjamin's formulation, historical forces and movements have difficulty, *den Leib in ihre Gewalt zu bringen*, meaning both "to control the new body" or "to dominate the new body violently [*Gewalt*]." For to control this new historical body is also, because of its representational vicissitudes, to do violence to it. Any historical appropriation of the body, based on violence, will thus fall prey to a vertiginous "frenzy of destruction" (W 487; 4:148) and decay.[29] For the historical body to survive this violence of appropriation and destruction, it must continually reinvent itself. It must never cease to come into presence, and it must not stop becoming something else. That is why it must, in order to remain alive, a *Lebendiges*, partake of the eternal dionysian "ecstasy of pro-creation [*Zeugung*]" (W 487; 4:148). In the form of *Zeugung* it both reproduces itself (*Zeugung* as procreation) and bears witness to itself (*Zeugung* as *bezeugen*). Benjamin's historical body—a corpus that links the personal body and the body politic—is thus always already something else, something that escapes hermeneutic delimitation. As history, it is no longer among the living.

This aporetic moment—the simultaneity of the body's redemption and decline—unfolds in the space of the image. As we learn in "On Surrealism" the body even *becomes* image in Benjamin's image-space (R 192; 2:309). The movement of this image-space is the destruction, "in accordance with dialectical justice," of the "inner human being, the psyche, the individual, or whatever else we might accuse them of, so that no limb remains untorn" (R 192; 2:309). According to Benjamin, this destruction accounts for the identity of "image-space" and "body-space"—"precisely after such a dialectical destruction this space will be an image-space, or, more concretely: a body-space" (R 192; 2:309). The destruction of every limb within the image-space is here the advent of the body-space. Benjamin continues: "A residue remains. The collective, too, is corporeal. And the *physis*, which organizes itself for the collective in technology, can, in its entire political and factual reality, only be created in this image-space in which a profane illumination makes us feel at home. Only once body-space and image-space have interpenetrated so deeply that all revolutionary tensions become bodily innervations, and all bodily innervations of the collective become revolutionary eruptions, only then has reality exceeded itself by as much as the *Communist Manifesto* demands" (R 192; 2:310). For Benjamin, to be at home in the space in which body and image interpenetrate is thus to experience the profane illumination that exposes the movement of the historically inflected body of the subject between affirmation and negation.[30] Benjamin's *physis*, then, emerges as the image of a body, and the body of an image, in a way that bears witness not only to the simultaneity of a historically recognizable physical subjectivity (and, by extension, the revolutionary potential this recognition may engender), but also to the moment of uncontainable excess, or even destruction, that mars this prospect.

This double movement of the body could be linked, following Adorno, to Benjamin's "anthropological materialism." In a letter from 6 September 1936, Adorno registers his friend's obsession with the body, an emphasis that is indebted to, among others, Bergson, Nietzsche, Proust, and Kafka, and that cuts across his entire corpus. There, naming the Benjaminian corpus a kind of anthropological materialism, Adorno remarks on the extent to which for Benjamin the experience of the body gives us access to our experience of what can be known: "It is as though for you the human body were the measure of all concretion" (BA 193). Adorno makes a similar point when he contrasts his friend's rejection of inwardness with his emphasis on external materiality, the surface of signification: "Inwardness for him is not merely the seat of torpor and dull complacency; it is also the phantasm which distorts the potential image of the human being— he always contrasts it to the bodily exterior [*das leibhaft Auswendige*]" ("Portrait of Walter Benjamin" 236). Following Adorno's lead, we can begin to suggest that Benjamin's theory of subjectivity and its culture belongs to a rather literalized anthropological materialism that, in its textual forms, depends on an insistence on the material substratum of cognition. The human body emerges for Benjamin as a figure for the extent to which subjective and cultural knowledge can be concretized.

While Adorno's comment registers the perpetual presence of the body in Benjamin's thinking, its significance had been impressed upon Benjamin by Henri Bergson's *Matter and Memory,* with which he was familiar through Wilhelm Windelband's 1908 German translation and which later came to play a key role in his own writings (most notably perhaps in his reflections on memory in "On Some Motifs in Baudelaire").[31] It was one of Bergson's concerns to argue for a renewed philosophical emphasis on the material substrate of cognition, to emphasize the embodiedness of mind and the view of the human subject's body as a condition of possibility for knowledge.[32] While Benjamin was especially receptive to Bergson's proposed links among memory, perception, and the body, he was, in the context of his German sources, sensitized to the notion of tactility and the tactile critique of the artwork by Alois Riegl's seminal *Late Romantic Art Industry* (*Die spätromantische Kunstindustrie*) (1901), which develops a theory of perception and representation in terms of the sense of touch, and Wilhelm Worringer's *Abstraction and Empathy* (*Abstraktion und Einfühlung*), where Benjamin found an elaboration of theories of the tactile into a critically potent moment of "abstraction," which Benjamin felt had been missing in Bergson.[33] His 1932 review essay "Rigorous Study of Art," which, *inter alia,* discusses Riegl, should be understood in this context (3:363ff.). This interest in the relation between the corporeal and the presentational leads Benjamin, in his 1935 "Problems of the Sociology of Language," to speak of a "language physiognomy [*Sprachphysiognomik*]" (3:478). For Benjamin, the relays between bodies and texts finally become so significant that he states in a 1936 fragment that the "insight that the first material upon which the mimetic faculty attempts to operate is the human body should be put to use . . . more forcefully than it has" (6:127). Here, he suggests an innovative textual and historical research program centered on the corpus. If the theoretical importance of the body arises in the intertwining of the corporal and the mimetic, Benjamin links the body to the scene of writing and reading in such a way that it becomes a site in which both the possibility and the limit of meaning are negotiated.

The body is not only a privileged site because it encodes certain material conditions of experience but also because it records and stores memories. As a mnemonic device, the body presents itself to us as the constellation of vital inscriptions that archive—for and on us—certain images of the past. Benjamin discerns this mnemonic function of the body archive specifically in his work on Proust, who, next to Baudelaire, Breton, and Aragon, figured prominently in his engagement with the French literary tradition. Here, Benjamin, reading Proust alongside Freud and Bergson, writes of those structures and systems that in A la recherche du temps perdu (*Remembrance of Things Past*) intertwine images and bodies: "Proust speaks of these 'other systems' frequently. Limbs are his favorite representation of them, and he does not tire of speaking of the memory images deposited in them, that is, how they, dependent on no prompting from consciousness, suddenly break into the latter when a thigh, an arm, or a shoulder blade suddenly takes the position in bed that they had once assumed. The *mémoire involontaire des membres* is one of Proust's favorite subjects" (*CB* 115; 1:613). Benjamin's reading of Proust's text as a kind of memory of the limbs suggests that the process of constructing a genealogy of the self proceeds through the body as a site where images and memory meet. It also serves as a springboard for Benjamin's own theorizations of the body. It sets the stage for his meditations on how mnemonic images, in the form of body parts, "break into" the surface of writing, how the body and language interact in the moment of remembering. One could say that just as Benjamin's *Berlin Childhood around 1900* is conceptually and formally indebted to Proust's A la recherche, Proust's emphasis on thighs, arms, and shoulder blades is reconfigured in Benjamin's confessional writing as an emphasis on ears, eyes, faces, and bodies.

But while the body is a privileged site from which to pose questions about what we can know, it can never serve as the moment of closure that casts an ultimate stable meaning upon the critical reading activities out of which the body's image emerged. While any attempt to understand the mechanisms by which we strive to assure ourselves of our identity in language is a matter of reading the text of the body, it does not provide a stable hermeneutic key to interpreting the bodily signs that constitute it. This corporeal scene can be called "semeiotic" in the full etymological sense of reading and interpreting clinical symptoms. The body becomes affected by the same problems of interpretation that vex all texts.

If Benjamin's friends and contemporaries, including, among others, Adorno, Kracauer, Bloch, Horkheimer, Scholem, and Ernst Schoen—all of whom, like Benjamin, attempted to articulate a critical reading of modernity—sensed Benjamin's particular fascination with multiple codings of the body, they were also aware of the difficulties that Benjamin located in the corpus. For while the body is inscribed as the material text of our experience, the subject that attempts to read itself as and through the body can never be simply itself. Bloch writes in a 1928 review of Benjamin's *One-Way Street* that although the "question of the 'I' or 'We' " arises again and again in his friend's constantly revised constructions of the self, this " 'I' in the street is admittedly only the strolling body" ("Revue" 336). As Bloch senses, Benjamin conceives of the subject's body in a way that simultaneously affirms its importance and traces its demise.

Bloch's intuition about the retreat of his friend's image of the body is born out by Benjamin's fragment "Perception and Body." There, he argues that, on the one hand, our body is a primary site of cognition that places us in a privileged linguistic sphere through which we "are ultimately placed into the world of perception, into one of the highest realms of language, by our corporeality, our own body" (6:67). But, on the other hand, our body signals the advent of a strange blindness, our inability to distinguish among the signs our corpus gives us to read, and we become "blind, for the most part incapable" (6:67). Benjamin elaborates on the body's inaccessibility when he suggests that it is "highly significant that our own body is in so many ways inaccessible to us. We can see neither our face nor our back, nor our entire head, the primary part of our body; we cannot pick ourselves up with our own hands or embrace ourselves etc. We rise up into the world of perception with our feet, but not our head. Thus the necessity for our body to transform itself in the moment of pure perception; thus the sublime physical torture of what is eccentric" (6:67). This body does not sign in the name of the self. Embodying a tenacious alterity, the body remains an inaccessible other to the self, disrupting the self-identity of the tactile subject and its consciousness. Thus it is not the head and, by extension, brain and mind, that link the corporeal subject to its object world, but rather its feet. In their mundaneness they are the physical other to the head as locus of consciousness and cognition. This constellation cannot give rise to the conscious cognition of a bodily self and world through a physically mediated experience. The text of such a bodily self and its world are indecipherable. The body will hence not remain "fixed" or stable in the process of the act of reading. It is constantly metamorphosing into another form, another text. For Benjamin, the moment of bodily cognition, then, is always also a moment of blindness. This is our sublime torture.

This moment of blindness that Benjamin so eloquently lodges in the body deepens Jean-Luc Nancy's intuition that, within the realm of writing, the body is the site where sense and meaning expose themselves to us precisely when the conditions and limits of intelligibility become an issue of materiality. Nancy reminds us that "the body never ceases to contradict itself" ("Corpus" 192), so that a "body is what cannot be read in a writing" (198). As Nancy suggests, this "is indeed what writing is: the body of a sense that will never tell the signification of bodies, nor ever reduce the body to a sign" (197). Following this schema, one could even view literature and, with it, the literature that, like Benjamin's, comes under the sign of self-portraiture, as the site on which our engagement with the vicissitudinous body is most properly at home. For, Nancy continues, "Literature as much as, if not more than, philosophy exposes this problematic. . . . [I]f there has never been any body in philosophy—other than the signifier and the signified—in literature, on the contrary, there is nothing but bodies" (193). The literary writing that approaches us in and as Benjamin's autobiographical corpus permits us to analyze in some detail the specificity of this uneasy encounter of language and the body. Benjamin's corpus would even suggest that this encounter is what reading the figures of a text is all about.

This reading of the bodily text must be allegorical and anchored in the corpus and, indeed, the corpse. Benjamin suggests this figurative function of the corporeal scene in his *Trauerspiel* book, when he brings the body into relation with the sphere of the allegorical. While such figures as ruins and broken fragments embody the allegorical, the dismembered body is a prime object of allegorical intensity. On the stage of the baroque play, we learn, in a passage that echoes many similar ones,

> the human body could be no exception to the commandment which ordered the shattering of the organic so that the true meaning, as it was written and ordained, might be picked up [or read: *aufgelesen*] from its fragments. Where, indeed, could this law be more triumphantly presented than in the human being which abandons its conventional, conscious physis in order to scatter it to the manifold

regions of meaning? . . . And if it is in death that the spirit [*Geist*] becomes free, in the manner of ghosts [*auf Geisterweise*], it is not until then that the body too comes properly into its own. For this much is understood: the allegorization of the physis can only have its way, energetically, on the corpse. And the characters of the *Trauerspiel* die, because it is only thus, as corpses, that they can enter into the homeland of allegory. It is not for the sake of immortality that they meet their end, but for the sake of the corpse. (O 216ff.; 1:391f.)

As Benjamin elaborates this thought:

Seen from the point of view of death, the product of the corpse is life. It is not only in the loss of limbs, not only in the changes of the aging body, but in all the processes of elimination and purification that everything corpse-like falls away from the body piece by piece. And it is no accident that precisely nails and hair, which are cut away as dead matter from the living body, continue to grow [or regrow: *nachwachsen*] on the corpse. There is in the physis, in the memory itself, a memento mori. (O 218; 1:392)

There can be no truth of the body that emerges in a moment other than the one of its demise. Like a text, whose meaning can never be fully arrested, the body shatters when the allegorical gaze falls upon it. The body is dismembered, falls into pieces, just as a text cannot sustain the appearance of organic wholeness. The physical and textual fragments of meaning return to haunt the allegorical reader. For Benjamin, it is the physical and textual corpse, rather than the unified living substance of the organic, that underwrites the moment of remembrance. To the extent that it signifies anything at all, the allegorical corpus, both in the textual and physical sense, signifies the fragility and finitude with which our reading of it must come to terms. Like the allegorical writing that becomes visible only when it is inscribed in "history as petrified primordial landscape" (O 166; 1:343), the corpus becomes legible only as the "mortification of the flesh" (O 222; 1:396). Benjamin's tortured corpus thus seals within itself—always already and in excess of itself—the contours of its own demise. It is most fully itself when it is read allegorically, that is, with an eye to its tears of dissolution and an ear to the echoes of its whispered melancholia.

Corporeal Contexts: Klages, Kafka, Nietzsche

Certainly, Benjamin's reading of the body in textual terms injects a virulent dose of singularity and difference into the corpus of his historical frame. The difference between his dialectical conception of the body as allegorical corpse and contemporary theories that posited a unified or transparent body can perhaps best be illustrated by juxtaposing Benjamin with his vitalist contemporary Ludwig Klages. Klages, the psychologist, cultural philosopher, and graphologist who, together with such writers as Max Kommerell and Friedrich Gundolf, belonged to the George circle Benjamin so despised, was tireless in expounding new theories of the body throughout his prolific writings. Although Benjamin was well aware of Klages's latent anti-Semitism, his right-leaning *Lebensphilosophie*, and his problematic notions of cosmology and characterology, he certainly took his work very seriously, reading it conscientiously and even finding in it occasional moments of inspiration for his own work.[34] In Klages's major treatises, such as "On Dream Consciousness" (1914), "Spirit and Soul" (1917), *Of Cosmogonic Eros* (1922), and *Movement of Expression and Power of Shaping* (1923), he attempted to articulate a theoretically grounded approach to cultural renewal and bodily regeneration. Like Benjamin, Klages emphasized what he termed the subject's *Körperlichkeit*, or corporeality, as the condition of possibility for speaking about a self's "here and now," its very "space" ("Traumbewußtsein" 203). Klages and Benjamin would also converge on the notion that the representational qualities of corporeality mediate the subject's experiences of its senses, its space, and its culture. As Klages writes, the "power of representation of corporeality in motion is not subordinated to all other traces of appearance but rather is superior to them in such a way that the symbolism of colors, sounds, smells, tastes, and temperatures show themselves to their best advantage only in accordance with this power and only *when they are mediated* by it (*Ausdrucksbewegung* 233). But Benjamin departs from Klages when the latter, in his *Principles of Characterology*, inscribes the body in an "immediately certain identity of the 'I'" (*Prinzipien der Charakterologie* 168). Even though Klages concedes that "today we are someone else than we were yesterday or years ago," and even though "the body is subject to change," he posits a fundamental and deep-seated "consciousness of the unity of our being" (168). To the extent that the body is "the carrier of the 'I,'" it too participates in a discourse of stable identity and continuous selfhood. From the perspective of Benjamin's obsession with the dialectics of the corporeal subject, one that is constantly made and unmade, and with the politics that he hopes to articulate through that aleatory and fickle subject, few ideas would seem more suspect and in need of revision than Klages's. It is not least of all because of this urgency that, as Benjamin writes to Scholem in 1926, a "confrontation with . . . Klages is unavoidable" (C 288; B 409). Although Benjamin never carried out his plans for a comprehensive written critique of Klages, it became ever more obvious over the next few years that, as Adorno writes in a 1935 missive to Benjamin, "Klages appears as a danger" for any attempt at critical demystification (C 497; B 675).

While the subject's encounter with an aporetic corporeal moment that both constructs and disperses it is one of the many aspects that separates Benjamin from Klages, the aporias of the body to which Benjamin perpetually returns are enacted in the writings of another contemporary, Kafka, without whom Benjamin's writings would be unthinkable. It is in his essay on Kafka that Benjamin observes that "the most forgotten strangeness or alien land [*Fremde*] is our body— our own body" (I 132; 2:431). Here, Kafka's troubled corporeality becomes a modern cipher for what Benjamin had identified a few years earlier as a special kind of baroque melancholia, associated both with the theater stage and with the art of Dürer, in which the "deadening of the emotions, and the ebbing away of the waves of life which are the source of these emotions in the body, can increase the distance between the self and the surrounding world to the point of alienation from one's own body" (O 140; 1:319). Benjamin makes a similar point in his 1931 radio talk on Kafka when he argues that "[t]oday's human being dwells in his body the way that [Kafka's] K. dwells in the village at the foot of the castle: [as] a stranger, an outcast, who knows nothing about the laws that connect his body with higher, broader orders" (2:680). Commenting on Kafka's corpus, Benjamin stages the body as a site of self-differentiation that cannot be known by the being that dwells in it. Indeed, if Benjamin's corpus names the alterity, the unreadable otherness within the self that is edged deeply into the flesh of the subject of modernity, then nowhere does his departure from Klages become more visible than in his engagement with Kafka's corpus.

We can begin to measure the urgency of Benjamin's corporeal obsessions when we place them into syntactical relation with Kafka's view that the treacherous act of writing and the experience of the vulnerable body enter an interdependent relationship. In so many of Kafka's texts, whether in "The Burrow" or "In the Penal Colony," the body is a necessary but unreliable element without which the unstable act of writing itself would be impossible.[35] In 1912, having just completed "The Judgment," Kafka enters into his diary: "*Only in this way* can writing be done, only with such coherence, with such complete opening out of the body and the soul" (*Diaries* 276). And in the following year he adds: "This is necessary because the story came out of me like a real birth, covered with filth and slime, and only I have the hand that can reach the body itself and the strength of desire to do so" (*Diaries* 178). For Kafka, this corporeal materiality, this transformation of the body into a piece of writing, is the condition of possibility for all signification. Benjamin, as a close reader of Kafka, deepens just this uneasy relay between writing and the encounter with the textualized body. In a letter to Scholem about Kafka, Benjamin registers the ways in which the subject depends on the legibility (and thus textual nature) of its body, so that on the scene of the corpus "writing . . . is not writing, but life" (CBS 135; BW 167). As Benjamin elaborates on Kafka's corporeal inscriptions:

> In the *Penal Colony* those in power use an ancient machine which engraves ornate letters onto the backs of the guilty ones, increasing the number of the needle-pricks and the ornaments until the back of the guilty one becomes clairvoyant, capable of deciphering the writing from whose letters it must learn the name of its unknown guilt. It is the back, then, whose burden this is [*dem es aufliegt*]. And the back is always heavily burdened in Kafka. For instance in an early diary entry: "In order to be as heavy as possible, which I deem advantageous for falling asleep, I had crossed my arms and put my hands on my shoulders, so that I was lying there like a soldier loaded with a heavy pack." (I 133f.; 2:432)

In this passage, Benjamin registers the ways in which writing and the body enter a problematic relationship.[36] Again, it is not the traditional locus of thought and consciousness—the head and its eyes—that emerges as the site of cognition, but rather the back, the site prominent in the moment when the subject has turned its back on the event or text to be hermeneutically deciphered. Through the inscription, on its back, of a text that it cannot understand, the subject faces the impossible task of distinguishing between letter and ornament, syntax and pain, meaning and the disappearance of meaning. Aporetically, the body becomes a hermeneutic machine whose workings are continually sabotaged by the object of its inquiry. Confronting the moveable army of tropes and metaphors that is its proper domain, the subject's body figures as an isolated, immobilized soldier.

While Benjamin's understanding of the body takes issue with Klages and shares its concerns with Kafka, it also stands in implicit dialogue with Nietzsche, whom Benjamin studied carefully. As Scholem tells us, Benjamin, as early as 1919, positioned his considerations of the nineteenth century and modernity more generally vis-à-vis the writings of Nietzsche (*Friendship* 60).[37] Indeed, Benjamin's encounter with the Nietzschean corpus well exceeds the early years of his infatuation with the Youth Movement and with its leader, Gustav Wyneken. Whether in his reflections on Baudelaire or on "Experience and Poverty," whether in the *Trauerspiel* study or in his theses on history, Benjamin never fails to register the presence of Nietzsche's ghost. Not only does Benjamin share Nietzsche's rejection of the single, monolithic subject, he also shares his understanding of the "subject as multiplicity," a multiplicity that can best be addressed in the sphere of the body. If Nietzsche suggests that the "belief in the body is more fundamental than [the] belief in the soul" and that the "body and physiognomy [are] the starting point" (*Will* 271), it is because it is the notion of the coherent body that has traditionally supported the idea of the coherent subject. In the body, it was idealistically assumed, the multiplicities and internal breaks of the self could be contained in the moment of the here and now. Likewise, if for Benjamin the history of the self cannot be written other than as a history of the body, he takes up Nietzsche's idea that a "[p]sychological history of the concept 'subject'" would involve a tracing of the ways in which the "body, the thing, the 'whole' construed by the eye" had left the self behind (*Will* 294). And when Benjamin suggests an innovative approach to the self that is anchored in a rearticulation of its corporeal nature, a nature, however, that can never be fully understood, he implicitly deepens the point made by Nietzsche that the "phenomenon of the body is the richer, clearer, more tangible phenomenon: to be discussed first, methodologically, without coming to any decision about its ultimate significance" (*Will* 270). Benjamin would not only share this view of the body with Nietzsche, he would also agree that this bodily point of departure raises political questions and that one might well speak, as Nietzsche once did, of the "body as a political structure" (*Will* 348).

In 1883, Nietzsche published the first section of his central work, *Thus Spoke Zarathustra*, which contained a key meditation on the body. There, in an effort to stage the ways in which the subject needs to exceed and undo itself to assume its new position in a world without transcendental signifieds, Nietzsche has Zarathustra predicate his new vitalism upon a critical affirmation of the body. Taking issue with the "despisers of the body," Nietzsche suggests the vital relationship between the body and language. To take leave of the body, Nietzsche claims, would mean to fall silent (*Zarathustra* 146). To activate the potential of the body means to realize, according to Nietzsche, that there "is more reason in your body than in your best wisdom" (146f.). Since for Nietzsche the self is not a stable given but rather a creative performance, a rhetorically mediated construct, the self's corpus, too, is to be understood as a vital component in this perpetual construction. Despising the body can thus be read as a sign of despair when a self is faced with the prospect of its own demise. As Nietzsche would have it, the "self wants to go under, and that is why you have become despisers of the body! For you are no longer able to create beyond yourselves" (147). But while Nietzsche's Zarathustra links the demise of the stable self to the demand that it strive toward its own excess, the "more" in which its body could go beyond itself, Benjamin takes a more guarded approach to such a philosophy of life. What Nietzsche conceives of as the body's excess is transformed in Benjamin's thought into the experience of shock. This is to say that, while the body of Nietzsche's feeble self is inscribed in a history that gestures toward the immanent advent of the *Übermensch*, the corpus of Benjamin's self relates to what is historical through the technologically and aesthetically mediated moment of shock—and not through the Nietzschean "more." Here, Benjamin both follows and departs from Nietzsche's corpus. Or, rather, in the Nietzschean sense, he follows it precisely by departing from it.

If, therefore, Benjamin thinks the "body" as one of the names of "the function of the historical present within the human being"

(W 395; 6:80), then the history to which this body ultimately belongs is one precipitated by shock. In *One-Way Street*, Benjamin, still traumatized by the first fully technologized World War and the fundamental religico-philosophical consequences of this war elaborated by the Jewish theologian Franz Rosenzweig, suggests that the human body in modernity is experienceable and citable for and as history only in painful grimaces and erratic convulsions. As a body in pain, it both belongs and does not belong to history.[38] That is to say, the body belongs to history most fully when it is not embodied by it, when it is exiled from it. Our body, then, names our simultaneous inscription in, and exile from, history.

This strange Benjaminian simultaneity embodies what separates the significance of the body's historicity from the telos of traditional historicism. In this view Benjamin also exhibits certain links to Michel Foucault. The historicity of the body is formulated in the critical desire, as Foucault puts it, "to expose a body totally imprinted by history and the process of history's destruction of the body" ("Genealogy" 148). If, as Foucault suggests, what is needed is not a "history of mentalities" but a "history of bodies" and the discourses invested in them (*Sexuality* 152), then for Benjamin these bodies belong to the specific historical images that flicker up briefly only to disappear again. "The true image of the past," Benjamin states, "*flits* by. The past can be captured only as an image that briefly flashes up in the moment of its recognizibility never to be seen again" (I 255; 1:695). Embodying the contours of its own finitude, the image of Benjamin's body, flitting by, traverses history as a ghost. My pages trace its perpetual returns.

THE ARGUMENT

By suggesting that Benjamin stages his confrontation with politics in general, and with fascism in particular, in the body of his confessional rhetoric, I have wanted to take seriously his notion that any thinking of history and culture proceeds through questions of presentation. I am guided by Benjamin's claim that "theory must not refer to reality but rather must be a matter of language" (2:601f.). This is not to say that texts and theories have no reality for Benjamin. On the contrary, there can be no text and no theory that is not traversed by the many ghosts of other texts and theories that came before. Likewise, texts and theories have a specific time and a particular historical reality. But Benjamin urges us to rethink their relationship to that historical reality in ways that we have yet to learn. Indeed, a responsible thinking of the relationship between texts and their historical particularity can only occur when we no longer assume this relationship to be transparent and separate from language. Therefore, Benjamin calls upon us to think through the consequences of the fact that texts and theories always stand in a mediated relationship to history and politics, and that this mediation is textual. If Benjamin wishes to establish a rhetorical approach to historical and cultural analysis, in which what we call the political becomes touched by language, then it is our task to address ourselves to those points in our readings of cultural texts where the complicated relationship between our objects of study and their rhetorical nature becomes visible. But to follow the textual nature of our objects of study also means to be open to the possibility that they might lead us astray, that language may turn away from what it is meant to present. To uncover the reality of the real may thus require us to follow language on its unpredictable paths away from what had presented itself to us as something incontrovertibly real and natural. Sometimes, therefore, we may have to betray what is immediate in our objects of study, the "real" and the "factual," precisely in order to enhance our fidelity to it. As Benjamin would have it, to follow the laws of the real we must break them. Benjamin insists on this point when he writes, "Only he who has made his dialectical peace with the world in the moment of deciding can comprehend what is concrete. But to him who wishes to make that decision 'on the basis of the facts,' these facts will refuse to offer themselves [*dem werden diese Fakten ihre Hand nicht bieten*]" (R 97f.; 4:317).

In these pages I try to take seriously this Benjaminian admonition. Following Benjamin's premise that language, the body, and the self are inextricably intertwined, I wish to suggest that the new political concepts he calls for in his struggle against fascism can best be read in the rhetoric of the corpus in his autobiographical writings. Although the corpus belongs to a wider network of innovative Benjaminian concepts—which still remain to be fully analyzed as such—my interest in this particular Benjaminian concept is not entirely arbitrary. After all, Benjamin himself makes the link between

70

a new conceptualization of the body and the thinkability of certain political interventions. As he writes in a note two years after the Nazis' seizure of power: "There would result, in these connections, a polarity of the centers of the mimetic faculty within the human being. It shifts from the ear to the lips, taking a detour through the entire body. This process would include the overcoming of myth" (2:958). For Benjamin, the passage from vision to the mouth, that is, from the passive gaze of cognition to a voiced maturity (the German *Mündigkeit* that since Kant has become inseparable from any form of enlightenment) could serve as an interruption of myth, even its perpetual transgression. This transgressive unmaking of myth signals, for Benjamin in 1935, no doubt primarily the undoing of the chief myth machine, Nazi ideology itself. Benjamin here thinks the dislodging of the ideologemes—which Nancy and Philippe Lacoue-Labarthe have aptly called the "Nazi Myth" and which the historian George Mosse names the "fascist myth" ("Theory of Fascism" 184)— in terms of the corpus.[39] For Benjamin, this body, tortured and vexed, is invested with a political significance whose logic we have yet to comprehend.

To approach this ethical and political investment of the body, we may register that in a 1928 review of Anja and Georg Mendelssohn's *Der Mensch in der Handschrift* (*The Human Being in Its Handwriting*), Benjamin praises not only the authors' insightful departure from the vitalist determinism of Klages but also outlines what such an ethico-political reading of the body may involve. "Everything that is moral," Benjamin tells us, "is without physiognomy, something expressionless that, invisible or blinding, jumps out of the concrete situation. It can be guaranteed but never ever prophesied" (3:137). He continues to claim that the antagonism between Klages and the Mendelssohns, crystallized in a reading of graphology that emphasizes the movements of presentation rather than those of alleged expression, is situated precisely in the body. This antagonism in turn is one between "body and language" (3:138). According to Benjamin, "Language has a body and the body has a language. Nevertheless—the world is grounded in what, within the body, is not language (the moral) and in what within language is not body (the expressionless). . . . Klages proceeds from language, that is, expression, and, from the body, that is, the image" (3:138). Here, Benjamin links language and the body in a surprising manner. He suggests that our experience of the world cannot take place outside of (a) what within the body has a language but refuses to be represented; and (b) what remains without a body and without expression within a corporeal language. Benjamin links the first moment to something ethical. Note that he does not say that language *is* ethical. Rather, language becomes the site of something ethical in the moment when it appears as an other, as a marker of difference within the logic of the corporeal system which is governed by linguistic rules. Language, then, becomes a site of the ethical when it does not remain itself. Its political potential is most properly in play when the linguistic moment breaks out of the syntax of the body. Language encounters the ethical when it transgresses its own laws.

The grounding force, then, is a double displacement that simultaneously connects and forever separates language and the body. This grounding is predicated upon what remains an elusive, aporetic other within each of the poles of the binarism of body and language. Language is touched by the ethical when it retreats from the body it structures, and the body retreats from language in the movement of what refuses to express anything. If Benjamin in both cases has language retreat from the category of expression, then the ethical is precisely the undoing of a readable physiognomy. It is what departs from the body as a legible text. On the far side of expression and legibility, the body's retreat signals its politics: its uselessness for an ideology of stable bodies and stable hermeneutic meanings.

This political function of the constellation of language and the body as something expressionless that retreats from meaning and that cannot be mobilized is tied, Benjamin says, to its own invisibility or hyper-visibility (that is, its blinding moments). Yet this ethics of the expressionless body cannot simply be turned into a fixed program or system to follow in this or that political struggle. Even while the linguistic body in retreat does not belong to the repertoire of concepts that may be usable by ideologies such as fascism, it is not simply another tool for a transparent politics of intervention. Rather, its ethical and political potential lies precisely in its refusal to be used by any kind of program. It cannot be contained, for it is always "jumping out" of its own context, its own situation, as Benjamin writes. It emerges when it can no longer be accounted for by the logic of the structure that produced it. What *is* predictable ("can be guaranteed") about it is that its departure from itself *will* take place, that it will open itself up to self-differentiation in order to become unpredictable. But this erratic departure cannot be appropriated a priori to follow any program toward this or that end ("never ever prophesied"). The ethical and political potential with which Benjamin's idea of the linguistic body is invested flashes up, in the act of reading, as an image only to disappear again.[40] Its dark traces outline the contours of a future that is always still to come, a future whose futurity is that it cannot be programmed as a fixed meaning.

Language, Politics, and the Corpus: A Note on Method

This study not only hopes to address a lacuna in Benjamin scholarship, which has not yet analyzed Benjamin's three major autobiographical texts in a single, book-length discussion; my analysis of Benjamin's autobiographical corpus is also meant to contribute to a growing discussion that attempts to rearticulate our understanding of Benjamin in terms of the materiality of the body. The ground for such a reexamination has been laid, as we have seen, by the intuitions of such early Benjaminian readers as Adorno, Bloch, and Kracauer. It is now pursued by critics such as Winfried Menninghaus, Rainer Nägele, Sigrid Weigel, Norbert Bolz, and Michael Taussig, all of whom have, on rather diverse terms, proposed to take the corporeal seriously as a category in Benjamin's oeuvre.[41] What my study hopes to add to this discussion is a better understanding of how Benjamin's figures of the body—particularly in his autobiographical texts, which are usually not considered in Benjamin's discussion of the body—are not merely rhetorical motifs but gesture toward an engagement with the political that unfolds according to unexpected figurative terms which have yet to be fully grasped. I also wish to show how specific figures of particular body parts, such as the ear, the eye, and the face, cannot be thought apart from Benjamin's more general confrontations of history and culture. Likewise, I hope to suggest that the Benjaminian corpus names the site in which traditional distinctions between a self's private history and the public history in which it is embedded breaks down. His often overlooked autobiographical writings form the corporeal link between his archaeology of modernity, performed in the *Passagen-Werk*, and the archaeology of the self. Finally, I wish to suggest that Benjamin's rearticulation of the body, and the new physiology that comes in its wake, can be read as what Derrida once called a "paleonomy," a strategy that relies on the "maintenance of an old name in order to launch a new concept" (*Positions* 71).

The reading of Benjamin's subject and its body that I propose here suggests that the corpus can hardly be reduced to the fugal convenience of a leitmotif in his writings. As a paleonomy, it exceeds the merely thematic, illuminating more general movements of Benjaminian language and thought. This is to say that even though Benjamin, as one of Weimar Germany's premier intellectuals, was certainly aware of the many contemporary discourses surrounding the politics of the body, he engages this politics only indirectly, that is, in the movement of his rhetoric. To be sure, the German cultural obsessions involving the body in the 1920s and 1930s, such as *Lebensreform*, vitalism, *Körperkultur*, the cult of nudism, mythically transfigured versions of vegetarianism, clothing reforms, and the like, as well as National Socialism's total coordination of the iron body of subject and collective, were all symptoms of growing alienation in a rapidly modernizing world, a technocracy that had paid little respect to the human body, especially after the very real annihilations of the body in World War I.[42] Indeed, these movements can be understood in the context of the technologically mediated undoings of the body that Benjamin describes in "The Storyteller": "A generation that had gone to school on a horse-drawn street car now stood under the open sky in a countryside in which nothing remained unchanged but the clouds, and beneath these clouds, in a force field of destructive torrents and explosions, was the tiny, fragile human body" (*I* 84; 2: 439). Often, these movements drew on questionable notions of *Lebensphilosophie* and ideologies of cultural reformism and internal renewal. Whereas for Ernst Jünger's transfigurations of war as a "storm of steel" as well as for "Weimar's right-wing nationalists, the violence of the battlefields, the efficiency and power of tanks and ships, and the explosions of grenades were the external expression of inner impulses toward 'life'" (Herf 34), for Benjamin they signaled "a bloodbath" in which "the frame of mankind was shaken by a feeling that resembled the bliss of the epileptic" (*W* 487; 4:147f.). Benjamin became increasingly aware of the reactionary qualities of these ideologemes drawing on *Lebensphilosophie* after his early infatuation with the Youth Movement had waned and he became utterly disillusioned by it. Klaus Theweleit's monumental work has elucidated for us the phantasmagorical logic of pre-fascist and fascist fantasies of the body.[43] For Benjamin, these mobilizations of the modern corpus, for all their frenzy, denoted a peculiar kind of poverty of experience. As he writes in his essay "Experience and Poverty" of 1933, in the world of a technically mediated modernity human beings have been struck "with an utterly new miserableness. And the reverse side of this miserableness is the frightening inventiveness which descended among—or better: upon—people with the revival of astrology and yoga wisdoms, Christian science and palmistry, vegetarianism and gnosis, scholasticism and mysticism. For it is not a true revival that is taking place here, but a galvanization" (2:214f.). These questionable preoccupations with the experienceability of the corporeal self lead Benjamin to speak of a "new barbarism" (2:215).

Yet what his own theory of the body performs is not primarily a *direct* intervention in these discourses of the body of his time— be they progressive, reactionary, or fascist—even while his body is inscribed in them. Rather, I want to suggest that what makes Benjamin's politics of the body political is its engagement with issues of presentation. Because for Benjamin, there can be no body that does not have a language, and no language that does not have a body, the politics he locates in that body must also be a matter of language. Benjamin's body, then, is political precisely to the extent that it performs the double movement of construction and dispersal, of exhibiting itself and retreating. The figures of Benjamin's body behave in ways that fascism, which relies on stability, presence, and closure, cannot accommodate. In this way, we could say that the body, in Benjaminian terms, can be read as a "thought-image" or even a "dialectical image"—a sign or figure of thought that gives rise to an analysis of larger cultural and theoretical questions. Because for Benjamin the political can only be addressed indirectly or allegorically, his project is ethically and politically charged, even— or precisely—when it is not cloaked in the familiar language of the political. For Benjamin's thinking of politics is a thinking of double aberration: it is an aberration from conventional political models and it takes aberration as its course. As Benjamin tells us, "What for others are aberrations, for me are the data that determine my course" (N 43; 5:570).

We can begin to make vivid this Benjaminian requirement of aberration, and its reading of politics in other terms, by turning to one of his actual thought-images. Commenting on a child's game, popular in the Biedermeier era, whose object is quickly and decisively to put a random string of seemingly unrelated words, such as *pretzel, quill, break, sorrow,* and *nonsense,* into meaningful relation with each other, Benjamin writes:

> Especially in children, this game yields the most beautiful finds. For them, words are still like caves whose secret connecting channels they know. But let us suppose the inversion of this game and look at any sentence as if it had been constructed according to this principle. All of a sudden, the sentence would appear to us to have a strange, upsetting face. Yet part of such a view is encrypted in every act of reading. It is not only the common people who read novels in this way—looking for names or formulae that jump out at them from the text. The educated reader, too, lies in wait for tropes [*Wendungen*] and words; and meaning is only the background upon which the shadow rests that they cast like relief figures. . . . Commentary, which operates in their service, takes words out of such a text as if they had been placed into it according to the rules of that game and as if its task were to come to terms with them. . . . And it is true, the sentences that a playing child generates out of these words have more in common with divine texts than with the everyday language of adults. (4:432f.)

Here again, Benjamin gives us the tools with which to read his texts. This passage suggests, among so many other things, the generative rhetorical strategy that a Benjaminian reading against the grain may perform. Like children—who for Benjamin are always the utopian image of shrewd insight and acute political sensitivity—the subtle reader may wish to tear the false veil of homogeneity that lies cast upon a given text by placing individual signifiers into a new and unexpected relationship. As the children playing in the debris of the Benjaminian construction site isolate individual pieces of garbage to place into an innovative and potentially revolutionary constellation (W 449f.; 4:92f.), and just as quotations which in Benjamin work "like wayward robbers who leap out, armed, and relieve the idle stroller of his conviction" (W 481; 4:138), the act of allegorical reading is most powerful and sinuous when it defamiliarizes and estranges. To follow the movement of an allegorical trope we must follow its numerous shifts into other forms and other allegories. To extract figural language from its encrusted, mortified landscape is Benjamin's project: "To free metaphor from its objects means to discover its anthropological core, which in turn is identical to presenting its political significance" (6:417). To uncover this political significance within the figurative is the Benjaminian ethics of reading.

Yet this ethics needs to be explained further. To say that the figure of the body can not only come to be invested with a political significance but may actually enact the development of certain political concepts is to say that in Benjamin's language the engagement with one domain can generally be expressed, as something figurative, in terms of an other. Indeed, the condition of possibility for the truth of something to emerge is its movement into something else. Rilke puts it well: "That which would remain what it is becomes ossified" (*Sonette an Orpheus* 758). In Benjamin's own language, "Nothing is more miserable than a truth expressed as it was thought. Committed to writing in such a case, it is not even a bad photograph. And the truth refuses (like a child or a woman who does not love us), facing the lens of writing while we crouch under the black cloth, to keep still and look amiable" (W 480; 4:138). If any truth ever emerges in writing, it is the truth that says something else. "Truth," Benjamin continues, "wants to be startled abruptly. . . . Who could count the alarm signals with which the . . . true writer is equipped? And to 'write' is nothing other than to set them into motion" (W 480; 4:138). In other words, in the movement of Benjamin's rhetoric, words and concepts may at any time enter into a new relationship with what they present. The task of reading his writings, then, involves a tracing of the complex ways in which words and concepts change alliances, positions, and meanings in order to become something else. The "truth" of our reading would then be measured not in terms of how Benjamin's language remains identical to itself, linear, and referential, but rather in its constant movement toward what it is not yet. We could say that this truth can be approached precisely by following those multiple traces that define the distance between the word's or concept's previous positions, and the position that they assume in any new, specific act of reading, here and now. This web of traces and relays brings disparate words and concepts into grammatical relation. Another way to put this is to say that one must read not with an eye toward presentational unity but toward the excess of figuration, not symbolically but allegorically in the Benjaminian sense. If in the postlapsarian world of modernity we are called upon to read allegorically, as Benjamin maintains throughout his *Trauerspiel* book, then the basic predicament of reading (in) modernity can be summed up in the realization that "[a]ny person, any object, any relationship can mean absolutely anything else" (O 175; 1:350).[44] This is not to say, however, that the movement by which this "anything else" is touched cannot be traced or that its internal logic cannot be accounted for. On the contrary, the burden of following the intricate design of his tropes is placed squarely upon us. The figurative or allegorical mode of reading Benjamin calls for is thus simultaneously a predicament and an opportunity. It is a predicament because it seals off from us the idea of a transparent, fully readable world; it is an opportunity because it invites us to accept the challenge of reading modernity's enigmatic and complicated texture. Indeed, the very opportunity for our productive modes of figurative reading could only have been called into being by the absence of what is self-evident or immediately comprehended. There can be no birth of responsible reading without the death of transparency. It is here that questions of ethics, responsibility, and politics may begin to be articulated. Our hope, then, is not just to illuminate the opacity of the figurative and thus to undo it; it also *is* this opacity.

The Tropes of Fascism

To the extent that my pages also hope to revisit larger questions of Benjamin's politics and the relationship of his often enigmatic language to larger cultural and historical concerns, I stress this double movement of figurative language. Certainly, the question of how literally or figuratively to read Benjamin's theoretical encounter with the political, and especially fascism, has long vexed his critics. While the mature Benjamin clearly confronts fascism with every turn anew, the complex movements of his tropes do not easily yield to a literal reading in which conceptually unified and historically fully deducible theses could simply be verified or refuted. His confrontation with fascism is often cast either exclusively in terms of his reevaluation of the technology of art in the realm of cultural production or said to contain its theoretical actualization only after the event itself, such as the cultural revolution of the 1960s, in which his writings first gained canonical relevance.[45] Here, unlike more literal readers of

Benjamin's confrontation of fascism such as Ansgar Hillach, Russell Berman, and Howard Caygill—valuable as their perspectives may be for appreciating some of the more concrete networks in which Benjamin's reflections are embedded—I suggest that we follow the logic of his tropes and thought-images from within.[46] It is in them that we may encounter most fully the innovative and complex figures in which Benjamin presents us with "a pictorial atlas of the secret history of National Socialism" (*CBS* 100; *BW* 128).

The forms of fascism and the ideologemes of National Socialism that Benjamin confronts in my pages can be put in the following terms. According to Benjamin's "Theories of German Fascism," fascism was characterized by a rhetoric of presence; the delusions of subjective heroism; the questionable ability to show the masses their own face; the effacing of differences (such as that between civilian and military populations); the radical application of *l'art pour l'art* to politics; historical misreadings; cultist thinking in a variety of guises; a war-driven technophilia; the rhetoric of eternity; the efforts of total coordination; and myth-inspired irrationalism (*T* 120ff.; 3:238ff.). Add to these the concepts that Benjamin evokes in the Artwork essay as being so eminently usable by fascism, among them the cult of creativity, the rhetoric of originality, the genius, eternal value, and the mysterious (*I* 218; 1:473). What organizes these features around a fascist core is, for Benjamin, that fascism relies on a totalitarian rhetoric in which its beliefs and meanings are given a false essence, an immediacy that is tied to the doctrine of a single, stable meaning.[47] Benjamin confronts National Socialism by attempting to expose the blind spots that work to disrupt its monolithic presentational logic from within. This occurs "at a time when," as Adorno tells us apropos of the antifascist stance of Benjamin's book of letters, *German People* (*Deutsche Menschen*), "disregarding the *specific differences* in which spirit has its life, [National Socialism] had confiscated everything, including things that were *completely heteronomous*" ("On Benjamin's *Deutsche Menschen*" 329; emphasis added). Working to respect difference as something irreducible and the alterity of what remains wholly other, Benjamin focuses on the impossibility of revealing a single meaning within a transparent textual or political system initiated by a self-identical sovereign subject that revels in presence and closure.

This alleged singularity of meaning and its appearance as a stable concept is precisely what Hitler, in *Mein Kampf* desires, namely, a "transformation of a general, philosophical, ideal conception of the highest truth into a definitely delimited, tightly organized political community of faith and struggle, unified in spirit and will, since on its happy solution alone the possibility of the victory of an idea depends" (381). Through its cult of the *Führer*, fascism works to guarantee the stability and continuity of a single, highly aestheticized collective subject endowed with a determined meaning—the state, destiny, the *Volk*, "Germanness" itself—and the capability of revealing the essence of that subject through film, the arts, radio technology, and indeed the entire network of Nazi coordination (*Gleichschaltung*). The ideology of singularity and presence inscribed in National Socialism has no place for the uncertainties, differences, and dissimulations that the ghostly figures of Benjamin's unusable concepts enact. It is no accident that the Nazi regime's minister of propaganda, Joseph Goebbels, in "Why Are We Enemies of the Jews?," can imagine a German socialism, what he calls a "comradeship in arms," only in terms of a "forward-driving energy of a newly awakened nationalism. Without nationalism it is nothing, a phantom, a theory, a vision of air, a book. With it, it is everything, The Future, Freedom, Fatherland!" (137). Goebbel's fear of phantoms, theories, and books—in other words, everything that Benjamin's corpus is—stems from the need of German National Socialism to reveal in a total transmission what is essential, material, and self-evidently immediate. It has no place for Benjamin's phantoms, theories, and books, all of which signal the uneasy return of the repressed, the marginalized other, the breaks and fissures that threaten the dominant subject of Nazi master narratives.

The Nazism against which Benjamin writes struggles to mask its heterogeneities and constitutive multiplicities by repressing aberrations from its alleged singularity. To construct this single meaning, it intertwines the idea of transparent subjectivity with the aestheticization of its political maneuvers; the symbolic dominance over nature with the phantasmagoria of an organic community; the notions of heritage and originality with its racial claims; and its program of racial purification with calls for internal renewal. This is why Benjamin opposes Ernst Jünger's stance assumed in the anthology *War and Warriors* (*Krieg und Krieger*)—that served as the basis for Benjamin's extended review essay on theories of German fascism—which "understands every thought and every emotion as a symbol of a *unified* and *unchangeable* being which is incapable of withdrawing from its own

80

laws."[48] Indeed, the delusion of unhaunted meaning can be said to be vital in the construction of a fascist subject body politic. Benjamin hopes to challenge this delusion, especially as it relates to the notion of the state as a secure essence.[49]

In his deconstructive reversals of the corpus, Benjamin struggles against this phantasmagoria of presence. This struggle, exemplarily crystallized in his autobiographical writings and shared by his larger oeuvre, is a political or ethical one, even when its tropes do not appear political on the surface. His tropes are always already touched by the shadow of the political. Adorno registers this point when he writes that the haunted narrative images of his friend's *Berlin Childhood* are "neither idyllic nor contemplative. The shadow of Hitler's *Reich* lies cast upon them" ("Nachwort" 74). To be sure, for Benjamin, confronting the ideologemes of fascism is, again, a matter of language. As he tells us in "Theories of German Fascism," "language is the touchstone [*Prüfstein*] for each and any position taken, and not just . . . for that of the writer" (*T* 125; 3:245).

That a confrontation of fascism proceeds through language implies that its opponents must be sensitive and responsible readers. This is so not only because "Benjamin's sense of revolution," as Stanley Corngold and Michael Jennings remind us, "has more to do with an act of inspired reading than it does with seizing railroads" ("Walter Benjamin/Gershom Scholem" 363), but also because for Benjamin the very actuality of any revolution cannot be thought in separation from the figures through which it presents itself as well as the language it hopes to confront. Fascism cannot read ambiguities and double meanings. Its movement is linear and its efforts "culminate in one thing: war" (*I* 241; 1:506). But the phrases "to win a war" and "to lose a war," for instance, have a hidden significance. To win a war, Benjamin points out, can mean both to be victorious and to come to be the new owner of war. He who wins the war unhappily must keep it, too. It will remain with him, in his possession, and it will return to haunt him. On the other hand, to lose a war means both to be defeated and to get rid of war. The defeated has not won any new property (war) and comes to live without it. Such hidden double meanings, Benjamin explains, are to be read both in the most general and fundamental acts of war and in the "most subtle chess moves" imaginable (*T* 123; 3:242).[50] Certainly, fascism is deaf to such nuances of meaning. The Nazis eventually reinforced their own singularity by having Berlin's secret police strip Benjamin, a reader who read against the grain, of his German citizenship.[51]

The corpus of Benjamin's autobiographical writings, then, invites us to rethink his political strategies, both in terms of certain oppositional strategies and of a Nazism that we have yet to comprehend fully. The reevaluation is necessary because the sense that his engagement with certain trajectories of Marxism cannot fully account for the theoretical stance assumed in his political fights has been a prominent but unresolved issue among his critics. It will remain an open issue. I am in sympathy with Arendt's observation that Benjamin often had more in common with certain Heideggerian sensibilities of reading "than he did with the dialectical subtleties of his Marxist friends" ("Introduction" 46). Indeed, from the perspective of a "second generation" Frankfurt School, which simultaneously embraces Benjamin and views him with a certain guardedness, Jürgen Habermas has detailed Benjamin's many departures from orthodox historical materialist critiques of ideology.[52] And a more recent critic, Anson Rabinbach, implicitly shares Habermas's sense of ambivalence with regard to Benjamin's historical materialism, though he wishes to keep the possibility of a special Benjaminian messianic Marxism alive, suggesting that for Benjamin "fascism could not be defeated by denouncing it as false consciousness," because "as a socially powerful myth of redemption it could fill the 'hollow space' that a Marxism divested of utopia could not even imagine. Nor did . . . Benjamin join Lukács and other orthodox Marxists in a rationalist rejection of aesthetic modernism" (63f.). While Benjamin's readers have traditionally conceived of his politics either in Marxist or messianic terms, or have questioned the political validity of his so-called mysticism altogether, I implicitly hope to recast our reading of Benjamin's politics in textual terms. In contrast to Habermas, who claims that "Benjamin did not consider the special property of language to lie in its syntactical organization (in which he had no interest) or in its representational function (which he regarded as subordinate to its expressive function)" ("Consciousness-Raising" 110), I hope to show that Benjamin's politics are enacted in his language, in the space of presentation, rather than explicated as coherent concepts in the realm of transparent expression.[53]

While Benjamin's project is inscribed in the critical tradition of an oppositional sprit that includes, among others, Marxism itself, his sentences never allow themselves to stand in a mimetic relationship to such a critical tradition. If his language "exceeds, or allows us to think about that which exceeds," as Alexander García Düttmann suggests, "the limitations of a description which would be restricted to retracing the lines of a historical movement or development" (531) it is because Benjamin wishes us to rethink not this or that tradition—thus remaining within the tradition that thinks of traditions in a determined, teleological manner—but rather the very concept of tradition itself. This rethinking would entail the realization that in order to remain faithful to a tradition one must depart from it and from what makes it possible, rather than claiming to see oneself embodied or reproduced in it. In this sense, "[f]ascism, as Benjamin seems to understand it, marks the *forgetting* of tradition, while revolution, is tradition's *memory*" (Düttmann 545). To appropriate a tradition or legacy of critique is therefore inseparable from a revolutionary event which both keeps a memory alive and—precisely *as* a revolutionary act—breaks with it. For Benjamin, there can be no faithful relation to a tradition that is not informed by the radical perturbation that this double movement constitutes. On the far side of this double movement, there is only the forgetting of tradition, even when ideologemes such as fascism dissimulate this forgetting in terms of an alleged continuity with tradition. What emerges as political in a tradition is inseparable from what transgresses it at every moment that it is evoked.

That Benjamin hopes to recast the political in terms of its vexing relations to language also means that he diverges from the tradition of so-called vulgar Marxism and the sense of activist immediacy promised by the strategies of "crude thinking" that held certain attractions for him during his work with Brecht and that prompted him to compose a series of essays on the writer.[54] His fascination with Brecht's epic theater, which Benjamin believed to be on a level of technical and medial sophistication similar to that of film and radio, reignited in him the sense of admiration he had felt for the analyses of class struggle in Lukács's *History and Class Conscience*, which he had read in 1924. Yet while his important and complex friendship with Brecht sensitized him to the requirements of a dialectical optic capable of taking into account the monstrosities of bourgeois ideology as well as the political use value of shock and the theatrical gestures of critical unmasking, the theoretical base of Benjamin's self-understanding as a "strategist in the literary struggle"

(W 460; 4:108) ultimately lay elsewhere. The dialectical materialism Benjamin engaged so intensely is perpetually restructured by his innovative thinking of a non-teleological model of historiography and by his conviction that there can be no politics and no historically informed analysis of literature and culture that is not decisively affected by questions of language and presentation.

Along these same lines, critics have often attempted to approach the abiding question of the political in Benjamin either, as in John McCole's reading, through his radical reworking of a specifically German intellectual tradition of idealism and historicism or, as in Susan Buck-Morss's work, through a reconstruction of his later engagement with mass culture in terms of a proletarian revolution that remains tied to a peculiar materialist messianism.[55] Even when the perennial discussions of Benjamin's innovative political interlocking of messianism and materialism are recast and elevated to serve as the whetstone for a "politico-theological positioning" of Benjamin's project, as in the work of Irving Wohlfarth ("Zur theologisch-politischen Standortsbestimmung"), a consideration of Benjamin's language itself has tended to play only a minor role. That is to say, the specifically figurative element in Benjamin's project that eludes the promises of conceptual closure or historical certainty—an elision that works to recast the very notion of the political—has remained a blind spot for his readers. In my engagement with the innovative politics of the Benjaminian corpus I am ultimately guided by two fundamental sentences that provide the tools for reading any of his texts. The first one not only stands as the famous first line of the epistemological prologue to the *Trauerspiel* book, it also formulates an axiom that touches all of Benjamin's corpus: "It is the property of philosophical writing that it must with each turn confront the question of representation anew" (O 27; 1:207). The second sentence comes from a little known fragment on translation, written two years after the Nazi's seizure of power: "There is no world of thought that is not a world of language, and one only sees in the world what is pre-conditioned by language" (6:158).

The Chapters

The following chapters analyze the rhetorical, philosophical, and political strategies Benjamin sets to work in his delineation of a corporeal theory of the modern subject that is "useless" for the purposes of fascism. Focusing on his major autobiographical texts, I trace the innovative forms of self-portraiture and modes of self-presentation that are inextricably intertwined with Benjamin's analyses of the physiognomy of Weimar culture and the politics of fascism. In my analysis, I evoke a network of references from Benjamin's entire corpus in order to demonstrate that the problem of the corporeal self remains a permanent concern from Benjamin's earliest to his latest writings. The signature of Benjamin's subject traverses the relation between subjectivity and language, between the body and its inscription within a text. It is precisely in this double movement that the subject's vicissitudinous body becomes visible as one of the innovative political concepts Benjamin calls for but never explicitly delineates in his struggle against fascism. Because the logic of fascism relies on stability, presence, and closure, it cannot appropriate the corporeal subject Benjamin develops. His corporeal self is perpetually in retreat, even in the moment in which it is posited. As such, it is quite literally *unbrauchbar*, or useless, for ideological mobilizations.

Benjamin's staging of the corporeal subject is performed in different ways in his three major autobiographical texts, each one mobilizing a specific anatomical trope. The chapters that follow are consequently organized around a particular aspect of the body. The first chapter focuses on the theoretical problem of the face throughout Benjamin's corpus; the second chapter focuses on the body in its entirety in the *Moscow Diary*; the third chapter focuses on the ear in the *Berlin Chronicle*; and the fourth chapter focuses on the eye in the *Berlin Childhood around 1900*. This strategy makes it possible to follow Benjamin's complex staging of subjectivity in relation to a series of corporeal figures that give form to his genealogy of the self.

The first chapter, "Benjamin's Face: Defacing Fascism," sets the conceptual and political stage for an analysis of the corporeal subject in Benjamin's autobiographical texts. Here, I show that within the context of his problematization of the body, Benjamin's figure of the face, which traverses his entire corpus, enacts the transgressive movement called for by his new thinking of politically useless concepts. Indeed, among the many body parts that Benjamin enlists in his project, the face is one of the most significant figures, constituting a Benjaminian constellation of the other bodily features central to his thinking, such as the ear and the eye. As I show in a series of detailed readings, the figure of the face, which places Benjamin into an illuminating constellation with such contemporaries as Kracauer, Bloch, Simmel, Brecht, and Rilke, becomes visible as a site of self-differentiation upon which key Benjaminian notions of politics, culture, and reading converge.

The second chapter, "Benjamin's Body: The Alterity of the Corpus in the *Moscow Diary*," focuses on the role of the body in the *Moscow Diary*. As an irreducible alterity, the body is semiotized as a potentially readable text but finally remains unknowable. This predicament is enacted by the perpetual deferral of Benjamin's access to the eroticized body of his love, the Latvian actress and stage director Asja Lacis, who introduced him to Brecht and Marxist theory. Benjamin's ambivalent relation to Lacis's eroticized body enables us to analyze the oscillation between proximity and distance, passion and deferral, attraction and repulsion, that also structures his conception of relation in general. I argue that Benjamin's relation to Lacis's body can best be read in terms of an eroticization of reading that connects sex with the activity of interpretation. Redirecting his desire for Lacis onto reading, Benjamin sets the stage for a thinking of the deferral of desire and meaning that arises in relation to corporeal inaccessibility—whether in the form of the body of a loved one or the body of language itself. It is this inaccessibility that prevents the subject from finding itself—either in itself or in an other.

The relation between the body and the reading process is extended in the third and fourth chapters by focusing on the two organs that make reading possible: the ear and the eye. In the third chapter, "Benjamin's Ear: Noise, Mnemonics, and the *Berlin Chronicle*," I trace his relation to noise—from street traffic to telephones and beyond—in order to describe Benjamin's interest in the technological and material conditions that enable the corporeal subject to emerge even as they signal its demise. The noise penetrates Benjamin's ear and, in so doing, helps to make him who he is: the one whose selfhood is interrupted by the acoustic. Here, noise both functions as a mnemonic trigger and as a disruption of consciousness, a movement that parallels the simultaneous articulation and dissolution of the corporeal self.

In the fourth chapter, "Benjamin's Eye/I: Vision and the Scene of Writing in the *Berlin Childhood around 1900*," his recourse to the language of seeing elucidates the role of vision in the formation of the self. Benjamin's text is obsessed with the vicissitudes of the eye/I whose gaze is tied to a constellation of flashlike moments of insight and dialectical images that also betray the subject. While the narrating subject strives to construct itself through the language of vision, it is constantly exposed to the threats posed by moments of reversal, such as the competition of sight and sound, the treacherous photograph, and the unstable ocular gift. Because the status of the writing subject is a shifting one, Benjamin's continuous revision of the *Berlin Childhood* can be read as a textual enactment of the endlessly shifting and ceaselessly changing status of the Benjaminian self.

In the epilogue, I return to the figure of the aleatory bodily subject that haunts Benjamin's corpus. The ethico-political consequences of Benjamin's dialectical conception of the corporeal subject are predicated on our understanding of Benjamin's politics in terms of unusable concepts of which the body of the confessional self is a prime example. If the relations that Benjamin forges among texts, bodies, and cultures exceed any form of dialectics, they not only tell us how our corporeal selves are made and unmade in writing but also that a Benjaminian reading of fascism, and politics in general, depends on an engagement with language itself.

If the following chapters tend less to tell an unfolding story or progressive narrative about the body and its relation to reading, language, and politics than to place this relation into a *constellation*, it is because I wish to take seriously what Benjamin teaches us about his own procedures. Benjamin's aesthetic and political lessons cannot be thought in separation from his anti-teleological stance and his favoring of rupture. Indeed, as Jennings aptly reminds us, Benjamin's theoretical stance relies on "his own attack on narrative and its cognate concepts of totality, organicism, and progress" so that "the reader will emerge not only with 'hard knowledge' but with a sense for the cognitive processes that produced such knowledge" (*Dialectical Images* 10). Therefore, rather than construct a false sense of closure or continuity in Benjamin's autobiographical texts, my specific argument regarding the political explosiveness of the *unusable* in Benjamin's writing is enacted in the very organization of the book. I stay away from a conventional story line because this would bring the project itself too dangerously close to eclipsing what it theorizes as Benjamin's own privileged moment. Thus, there is no false veil of a completed story or of argumentative finality. On another level, I also have decided not to construct a more predictable story line within and among the individual chapters in order to be able to remain faithful to Benjamin's own preferred mode of thought, what he calls the constellation. The concept of the constellation, in which heterogeneous elements are juxtaposed in order to make visible otherwise hidden links and patterns, is central to his project on a variety of levels—historical, theoretical, political, and aesthetic. As we learn in the *Passagen-Werk*, "the Then [*das Gewesene*] and the Now [*das Jetzt*] come into a constellation like a flash of lightning" (N 49; 5:576). I have tried to do justice to the requirements of the constellation's persistent flash of lightning in that the shape of my book performs this Benjaminian figure of thought even as it thematizes it.

While my study limits itself to an analysis of the face, the body in its entirety, and the aural and visual senses, one could extend the discussion to include other senses and body parts as well. Among the other corporeal figures that permeate Benjamin's writings are, for instance, his frequent evocations of noses and smells (especially in his writings on Baudelaire and Proust),[56] not to mention his obsession with actual and figurative hands as, for instance, in the Artwork essay. His interest in the problem of the gesture, which Benjamin shares with Brecht, also belongs in this context. Indeed, Adorno noted as early as 1950 that in Benjamin's work, "thought approaches the body of the subject matter as though it wanted to transform itself into touching, smelling, and tasting" ("Portrait of Walter Benjamin" 240), and much work remains to be done in this area.

My limitation also imposes itself in part from what I perceive to be the major tropes and themes in Benjamin's autobiographical texts which specifically mobilize the ear and the eye—both as organs that enable reading and as the constellation that constitutes a face—in addition to the body as a whole. Indeed, as Benjamin's contemporary, Heidegger, tells us, the visual and the aural are privileged modes of thinking through the distance at which our corporeal experience holds us from ourselves since "[s]eeing and hearing are tele-senses [*Fernsinne*] not because they are far-reaching but because it is in them that *Dasein* as deseverant mainly dwells" (*Being and Time* 141). This moment of visual and aural distancing is the proper moment of the self. Indirectly, my choice is also informed by the historical privileging of the eye and, to a lesser extent, the ear, over other senses in literary-philosophical discourses since the eighteenth century.[57] According to Hegel's aesthetics, the "sense of touch, taste, and smell" are excluded from "the capacity to apprehend works of art," whereas vision and hearing, which he calls the "theoretical senses," can encounter the aesthetic structure.[58] Benjamin's Artwork essay emphasizes the significance of considering such historical dimensions in analyzing the ways in which the senses give us access to who we are. As Benjamin tells us, during "long historical periods, the human collective's mode of sense perception changes along with its entire mode of being-in-the-world. The ways in which human sense perception organizes itself—the medium in which it takes place—is determined not only naturally but also historically" (*I* 222; 1:478). These historical and theoretical concerns, too, inform my choice of senses here.

A final note about my procedure is in order. The question of whether Benjamin "intended" in his autobiographical corpus to stage the body in the terms that I wish to suggest here is as insignificant as it is uninteresting. His confessional writings belong to the same realm as Hölderlin's hymnic poetry of which Benjamin writes in his essay on Goethe's *Elective Affinities* that "one could not characterize this rhythm [of the hymn as objection] any more aptly than by asserting that something beyond the poet interrupts the language of poetry" (W 341; 1:182). There is always something peculiar that informs, traverses, even ruptures writing that cannot be reduced to authorial control. Thus, what matters is that these texts *are* traversed by an obsession with particular body parts, and that their language stages encounters with the body that are shared by the entire Benjaminian corpus. This is not to say that my readings veer toward the arbitrary. On the contrary, they attempt to do justice to Benjamin's texts by following their rhetorical movements closely and by illuminating the ways in which the latter share relays with larger cultural and political concerns. My readings are thus meant to respect Benjamin's texts by acknowledging that their many "truths" can only emerge when the category of intention is displaced. "Truth," Benjamin teaches us, "is the death of intention" (O 36; 1:216) fully as much as the "work is the death mask of its conception" (W 459; 4:107).[59] Instead, he tells us, it "is illuminating to think that the observation that a work issues forth from the subjective disposition of its author means nothing" (O 52; 1:233). If the category of intention survives in Benjamin beyond the stage of fallacy, it is in the form of what he once called the "intention toward language [*Intention auf die Sprache*]" (*I* 76; 4:16). It is this linguistic striving that I wish to trace.

To trace the movement of language in excess of intention means, for Benjamin, to dwell in the materiality of thoughts. To dwell there, in turn, is to linger in those topographies that have remained unknown to the thinking and writing self. As we learn in a fragment from 1928: "Everything is thought. It is a matter of making stops at these many little thoughts. To spend the night in a thought. Once I have spent the night in it, I know something about it that its architect did not suspect" (6:200). To dwell in the thoughts of Benjamin, then, would require one to inhabit their nooks and crannies, to sleepwalk in their hidden chambers, to roam the unsuspected underground terrains of which the master of the house was not fully aware. And if thoughts and their linguistic figures can dwell not only in houses but also in organic matter, such as trees and rootlike surfaces—sharing perhaps the logic of what Gilles Deleuze and Félix Guattari have called the rhizome—then here too the reader encounters not the stability of authorial intention but a multitude of interwoven figures. In an autobiographical note from 1931, Benjamin writes:

> While I was watching the foliage and followed its movement, the thought occurred to me, how many images [and] metaphors of language nestle in a single tree alone. These branches, and with them the tree-top, sway consideringly [*wiegen sich erwägend*] and bow rejectingly; the branches show themselves, depending on the wind, as something inclining towards or as something supercilious; the mass of leaves resists the impositions of the wind, trembles before them or makes concessions to them [or moves toward them: *entgegenkommen*]; the trunk has its solid ground, on which it stands, and one leaf casts its shadow upon the next. (6:441)

We may inhabit the lush thicket of images and metaphors Benjamin evokes only if we make ourselves at home in the treacherous paths and root lines in which his texts are inscribed. Only in the thicket (*Dickicht*) of the dense (*dicht*) undergrowth that is Benjamin's writing (*Dichtung*) may one encounter the complex interlacing of linguistic figures that traverse his texts.

Finally, by focusing on the subject's corpus in my attempt to think through what Benjamin's innovative political concepts might entail, I wish to argue that the body is one of the concepts that teaches us more generally how to read Benjamin's concepts politically. That is to say, I hope to show that what is required of us in confronting the rather enigmatic corpus of texts that we call "Benjamin" is a rigorous sensitivity not simply to what his language says, but to what his language does in performing the very arguments it makes. To find the truly political element in Benjamin's thought we must follow the movements of his tropes, and the figure of the body guides us in our efforts to grasp any of Benjamin's figures. Thus, if we are to learn to read historically, culturally, and politically in a responsible way, we are obliged to come to terms with what is at stake in Benjamin's admonition that "every language is inhabited by its own incommensurable, singular infinity" (W 64; 2:143).

1

BENJAMIN'S FACE: DEFACING FASCISM

> If I were asked to recall his outward appearance, I would
> have to say that Benjamin had something of a magician. . . .
> One could well have imagined him with a very tall hat
> and some kind of magic wand. . . . His face was actually
> rather evenly shaped. Yet at the same time he had—and
> again, it is difficult to find the right words—something of
> an animal that stores supplies in its cheeks. The moment
> of the antiquarian and the collector, which played such a
> prominent role his thinking, was also pronounced in his
> physiognomic appearance.
>
> Theodor W. Adorno, "Erinnerungen"

> Not to look at oneself, that is something.
>
> Ernst Bloch, *The Principle of Hope*

In suggesting that we link Benjamin's engagement with
tropes of the body to larger questions of history and politics, I have
argued that Benjamin stages, rather than explains, his development
of innovative concepts that would be unusable for the purposes of
fascism. If his complex constructions of the body and its undoings
can indeed be read as belonging to those concepts that are always
already in retreat—and thus unemployable by political ideologies
that rely on the singularity, presence, and self-identity of concepts—
then the ethical and political significance of these concepts remains
to be thought in the context of Benjamin's culture. Before turning
to his autobiographical texts themselves, we may therefore begin
to set the stage for the political importance of the illegible corpus
that Benjamin's confessional writings stage by first turning to one
significant corporeal figure: the face.

The entire corpus of texts that we call "Benjamin" is traversed by rhetorical figures and dialectical images of the body and its members, as well as the visual, aural, and other senses. But among the various body parts that Benjamin enlists in his engagement with the corpus in retreat, the face is one of the most significant figures, and it in turn forms, as it were, a Benjaminian *constellation* of the other bodily features that are so central to his autobiographies, namely, the eye and the ear. The problem of the face is a trope not only in Benjamin's essays on photography and on Baudelaire but also in his writing on Proust, surrealism, the Artwork essay, in thought-images such as "Hashish in Marseille," and throughout the *Passagen-Werk*. While the trope of the face assumes different shades of meaning depending on its specific context and modulation within the trajectory of Benjamin's oeuvre, its affiliation with self-differentiation, with what remains at odds with itself, is remarkably consistent. The face reminds us that the corpus for Benjamin is not only the condition of possibility for reading the self and its culture historically but also signals an unreadable alterity, a monstrous dis-figuration. The face of the corpus belongs to the "ghostly crowd of words" of which he speaks in his Baudelaire material (*CB* 120; 1:618). The face ultimately works as a metonymy for Benjamin's political undoing of the body in its entirety. Like Proust's limbs which, as we have seen, break into the scene of writing, Benjamin's face works to disrupt the economy of its own presentation. And like the Benjaminian corpus itself, the face exceeds the status of the thematic in his writing, illuminating more general movements of Benjamin's political reading of the body and of unusable concepts in general.

The general sense that Benjamin is obsessed with the physiognomy of objects, thoughts, and human beings has not escaped his attentive readers. After all, in the *Passagen-Werk* Benjamin speaks of collectors—and, by extension, of himself, the greatest collector of all—as "physiognomists of the object world" (5:274). There, his physiognomist's gaze fastens upon a variety of cultural semiotics, from railroad travel and iron construction to the color of words and the gestures of style. It is thus hardly an accident that in 1972 Hermann Schweppenhäuser devoted a seminal general essay to the complex logic by which Benjamin's movements of thought are touched by physiognomic considerations ("Physiognomie eines Physiognomikers"). And in his 1982 introduction to the first publication of the

Passagen-Werk, Rolf Tiedemann alerts us to the ways in which the "prolegonomena to a materialist physiognomics that can be gleaned from the *Passagen-Werk* counts among Benjamin's most prodigious conceptions" ("Dialectics at a Standstill" 281). Since then, critics have begun to investigate the historical indebtedness of Benjamin's new physiognomy to the tradition of physiognomic interpretive strategies, including the general influence of the eighteenth-century Swiss theologian Lavater and the physiognomic interests of Lichtenberg, whose work Benjamin hoped to honor by compiling an extensive critical bibliography.[1] But not until recently have the specifically theoretical contours of Benjamin's rethinking of the figure of the face begun to emerge. As part of his examination of the role of art, aura, and the media in Benjamin's writings, Samuel Weber has pointed to the significance of the face for Benjamin's reading of fascism in a crucial but often neglected footnote to the Artwork essay ("Mass Mediauras" 102ff).[2] Following Weber's lead, I wish to elaborate on the Benjaminian figure of the face by considering it within the framework of his reading of the body as such; by tracing it through the corpus of his oeuvre; by linking it to his more general tropes about fascism and the masses; by putting it to work in connection with specific National Socialist and oppositional cultural productions; and by placing it into conceptual relation with discourses on the face by other thinkers, especially contemporaries such as Kracauer, Brecht, Georg Simmel, Bloch, and Rainer Maria Rilke. Benjamin's obsession with the figure of the face signifies one of his theoretical attempts to interrupt or dislodge the logic of National Socialism. His thinking of the face claims for his own political project what he, in a letter to Horkheimer, admired most about Adorno's study of Wagner, that is, how "*one tendency of this work was of particular interest to me: to lodge what is physiognomic immediately, almost without any psychological mediation, in the societal space*" (*C* 549; *B* 741). Ultimately, Benjamin's multiple transgressions of the ideology of the fascist face belong to the theoretical constellation that he terms his "position in the fight against fascism" in his theses on the concept of history (*I* 257; 1:697). As Benjamin would have it in a little-known fragment on criticism, "The stronger the critic, the more he can work the whole opponent through, down to the physiognomic details" (6:163).

The Face of Fascism

While Benjamin's figure of the paleonomic face is inscribed in a whole network of theoretical concerns, it plays the most crucial role in his reading of the politics of German fascism. According to Benjamin, the technologized aesthetics of the Hitler regime was aimed at constructing an image in which the mobilized masses could see themselves reflected, that is, in which they were given a face. In Hitler's aestheticization of politics, the propagandistic effectiveness of the mass rallies is tied to its ability to depict the image of the masses, indeed, it must, as Hitler insists throughout *Mein Kampf*, exhibit a capacity for mass effect and influence. This Nazi mass effect is enacted on the stage of the face. As Benjamin explains apropos of the propagandistic newsreel of the Nazi regime:

> In the big parades and monster rallies, in mass sports events, and in war, all of which nowadays are captured by the recording apparatus, the mass looks itself in the face [*sieht die Masse sich selbst ins Gesicht*]. This process, whose significance need not be stressed, is intimately connected with the development of the techniques of reproduction and photography. Mass movements usually present themselves more clearly to a camera than to the naked eye. A bird's-eye view best captures gatherings of hundreds of thousands. And even though such a view may be as accessible to the human eye as it is to the camera, the image received by the eye cannot be enlarged the way a negative is enlarged. This means that mass movements, including war, constitute a form of human behavior which particularly favors the apparatus. (*I* 251; I:506)

And in a preparatory note to the Artwork essay Benjamin elaborates this thought: "The life of the masses has always been decisive for the face of history. But that the masses consciously, as if they were the muscles of its face, exhibit its facial expressions—that is an entirely new phenomenon. This phenomenon comes to the fore in multiple ways, and especially drastically in art" (1:1041). Benjamin suggests that the fascist production of a face, in which the masses can see themselves mimetically reflected as if in a hyperreal simulation, is mediated by certain technological structures. The masses are made to assume that they are the face of history. The technical mediation of the fascist face creates for the masses the illusionary simulacrum of seeing themselves reflected and identified everywhere, and the public productions and aesthetic disseminations of Nazi ideology become the very locus of a *Volk*'s essence or identity.[3] Once this structure is in place, the members of the masses can be manipulated much more easily by the reigning hegemony because they succumb to the temptations of what promises them the possibility of identity and stability, indeed, the narcissistic enjoyment of mimesis and identification reproducible and extensible at will. It is thus no accident that Goebbels in a 1935 speech defines the propagandistic task of the National Socialist regime in terms of the face. He speaks of "great technical projects . . . which are to give the spirit of the times its vivid face [*dem Geist der Zeit das plastische Gesicht geben sollen*]." For Goebbels, to bestow a face onto the spirit of the masses is an act which "returns national sovereignty to a *Volk* shackled by a ghastly treaty" (*Reden* 224).

If Benjamin reads this mimetic moment of giving and receiving a face as a fascist delusion, as the ideology of self-identity and reproducible community, then his own understanding of the face ultimately signals a break with mimetic revelation and transparent identification. The critical stance vis-à-vis fascism that Benjamin assumes here can hardly be reduced to the simple proposal of a "model that would convene a collective recipient (the 'masses') endowed with an active and critical character," as one of his critics claims.[4] On the contrary, Benjamin rejects the very ideology of "convening" any kind of stable "collective" in the interest of some common set of principles and programs that are assumed implicitly to structure a communal subject.[5] This ideology, even if it is harbored by well-meaning leftist interests, runs the risk of metamorphosing into a tacit perpetuation of the intoxication with a self-identical Germanic community. Rather, Benjamin works to suspend the Nazi narrative of the face by introducing into its addictively narcissistic economy a moment of withdrawal from this intoxication. His work signals a series of powerful withdrawal symptoms from such addictive drugs as the concepts of mass community, the aestheticized political spectacle, and the desire to see oneself reflected in the production mechanisms of one's culture. At stake is a weaning oneself from the drug of the self, "the most horrible drug of all—ourselves" (R 190; 2:308).

Writing in the face of fascism, Benjamin's close friend Kracauer, to whose writings Benjamin is indebted, develops a similar point when he speaks of this fascist production of the face in propagandistic material as the construction of a recognizable mass ornament. In an as yet unpublished outline concerning fascist propaganda, commissioned in 1936 by the Frankfurt School's Institute for Social Research, Kracauer attempts to think through what is at stake in the Nazi production of a mass face: "The mass is forced everywhere to look at itself [*sich überall selbst zu erblicken*] (mass rallies, mass parades etc.). The mass is thus always present to itself and often in the aesthetically seductive form of an ornament or of an effective image."[6] The force and violence of fascist propaganda is thus predicated upon the aesthetic productions with which it compels the masses to discern their own face everywhere they look. There is no outside to the image of the face here. In this treacherous simulacrum of their own face, the masses, according to Benjamin and Kracauer, are hard-pressed to resist the temptation to succumb to fascism's delirious promises. The failure of the masses to resist this temptation renders them complicit subjects of the propaganda machinery.

Fascism's deliberate construction of this face of mass identification is also of concern to Brecht, Benjamin's friend-in-exile, whom he considered his best critic. In a 1939 review of Heinrich Mann's essays, Brecht emphasizes that one of the most illuminating pieces of Mann's collection deals with an analysis of a Hitler speech. Quoting Mann, Brecht reproduces an imaginary conversation Hitler has with himself:

> My *Volk* and my genius, they each reflect and multiply the other, an endless gallery of mirrors sparkling emptily. Because of all the immense lighting, both are empty, my genius, my *Volk*. . . . The mirror image and its observer are one. No image without the one who is mirrored. Where would the *Volk* be if it were not lucky enough that I mirror myself in it and that it is allowed to mirror itself in me. We are inseparable; no scrap of paper shall force itself between us to prevent us from looking at each other. And nothing else may step before my mirror and conceal my image from me: especially no theories, and least of all the dead. ("Notizen" 475)

In the theoretical orbit of Kracauer and Benjamin, Brecht, speaking through Mann, depicts a fascist scenario of seduction and persuasion that is fueled by the mimetic drives of mirroring, identification, and narcissistic reproduction. In this economy of gazes and faces, the mirror image of the masses is shown to merge with that of the personified Nazi ideology to such an extent that the seductions and promises of mediated desire become hard to resist. Indeed, the face is here made to insure the ultimate returns on a *Volk*'s libidinal investments. It tolerates no interruption of this economy—neither by theory nor by death itself, two of Benjamin's preferred tropes.

The intricate imbrication of fascist propaganda and the image of the face signals, then, a seductive mass appeal. If, by extension, "fascist art is an art of propaganda," as Benjamin argues in "Parisian Letter I," this is because it is "executed for the masses. Fascist propaganda must, furthermore, penetrate the entire life of a society. Fascist art is thus executed not only for the masses but also by the masses" (3:488). This mass execution of fascist art relies on the Nazi myth that "the masses confront themselves in this art [*die Masse habe es in dieser Kunst mit sich selbst zu tun*]," that they allegedly "communicate with themselves," even though in reality this is "not the case" (3:488.) Simultaneously, the propagandistic movement of presentation, in which the masses are constantly confronted with the mirage of their own face, encrypts the stability of a static status quo. "In fascist art," Benjamin elaborates, "the immortalization of the existing conditions is achieved by paralyzing the executing or receiving people who could change these conditions. Fascism teaches us that only through the stance forced upon the masses by this spell do they acquire their expression" (3:489). This false promise of expression (*Ausdruck*) is the proper face of fascism, and Benjamin constantly warns us against the threat of giving in to the unwarranted hope that this moment of expression could signal the essence of a community and its interests. For Benjamin, as opposed to the fascists, the community is touched by an irreducible difference that prevents its members from achieving unity. Nothing underwrites this community, as there can be, as he writes in the "Announcement of the Journal Angelus Novus," "no unity, let alone a community." What the word community ought to signal is a "mutual alienness [*wechselseitige Fremdheit*]," in order to reflect on "how unspeakable any community these days [*wie unaussprechlich in diesen Tagen jede Gemeinsamkeit*]" must be (W 296; 2:246). This mutual strangeness, and not the phantasmagoria of the coordinated masses, is precisely the promise of any community to come.

If fascism's wish was to bestow a face onto the masses, this desire was perhaps nowhere more evident than in its filmic production.

Prominent Nazi film directors such as Veit Harlan, Leni Riefenstahl, Wolfgang Liebeneiner, and Wolfgang Staudte, Hans Schweikart, Helmut Käutner, Paul Verhoeven, and Hans Steinhoff worked to realize this fascist dream of the face.[7] As filmmaker Hans-Jürgen Syberberg cynically suggests, one might speculate that Hitler and Goebbels staged the elaborate Nuremberg rallies mainly for the benefit of Riefenstahl's camera and produced World War II as a gigantic big-budget film to be shown in Hitler's bunker (*Die freudlose Gesellschaft* 74f.).[8] Whether in Steinhoff's *Hitlerjunge Quex* (1933) or Riefenstahl's highly aestheticized "documentaries," such as *The Triumph of the Will* (1934) or her films about the 1936 Olympic games: the masses are made to look at themselves, to turn themselves into the mythologizing delusion of a gigantic national film.

In her photographic volume documenting the making of *The Triumph of the Will*, Riefenstahl repeatedly evokes the importance of capturing beautiful, determined German faces that could reflect back to the *Volk* the simulacrum of its own visage. As Riefenstahl glosses her mission: "The *Führer* has arrived. Cheers everywhere. The people can hardly restrain themselves. Our camera people fight for the images. A laughing face over there. The *Führer* here, his men there— everything, everything must be captured" (*Reichsparteitag-Film* 19).[9] She further praises her German subjects' "vigorous faces" (21), emphasizing how "most important to us are the glorious heads of the youths. Using our telephoto lenses, we pick out the most beautiful ones" (23). In Riefenstahl's highly aestheticized images of jubilant young German faces celebrating the arrival of Hitler (figure 1) and of German workers violently determined to serve their country and *Führer* (figure 2), the *Volk* is given the illusionary perfection of a beautiful and politically eroticized Aryan countenance. It thus comes as no surprise that the inside cover of Riefenstahl's book proudly carries the official Nazi seal of approval ("The N. S. D. A. P. does not object to the publication of this text"; 2) and that her acknowledgments prominently feature Hitler's minister of propaganda, "Dr. Goebbels, who supported work on this film in every way" (7). The stakes are so high here because the aestheticized face carries as much political cargo as any Nazi image. Indeed, our ability to read the syntax of this fascist face measures nothing less than our ability to read any kind of fascist cultural production.[10]

Fig. 1. Jubilant young German faces greeting Hitler in Nuremberg. From Leni Riefenstahl, *Hinter den Kulissen des Reichsparteitag-Films* (Munich: Zentralverlag der NSDAP, 1935), 38. Reproduced by Medical Photography, University of Wisconsin, Madison.

Fig. 2. "Soldiers of Work" gazing at Hitler in Nuremberg. From Leni Riefenstahl, *Hinter den Kulissen des Reichsparteitag-Films* (Munich: Zentralverlag der NSDAP, 1935), 62. Reproduced by Medical Photography, University of Wisconsin, Madison.

Yet film was not the only medium in which the cultural fantasy of the face of the German *Volk* was politically mobilized. The stakes were just as high in still photography, where there were attempts to enlist the ideology of the stable German face for nationalistic purposes. For instance, in 1932 the photographer Erna Lendvai-Dircksen published *Das Deutsche Volksgesicht* ("The German *Volk*'s Face"), a substantial volume of 140 photographic images of "exemplary" German faces.[11] The parallels between her volume and those projections of the face that Benjamin attempts to intermit could hardly be more striking.

Introduced by an ambitious preface and accompanied by a running commentary and quotations from German literary history, the faces in Lendvai-Dircksen's volume are meant to represent what is German about German faces, the essence of the *Volk*—from the charming young farmer's daughter in Pomerania to the stern violin-maker in Mittenwald, from the pipe-smoking old woman in the Eifel area, through the determined lumberjack from the Harz region, to the grim miller in Mecklenburg wearing a traditional costume. While her images lack the overtly militaristic rigor of official Nazi photography and remain more ambiguously restrained, they nevertheless strive to idealize and transfigure the German face into an expression of essence and communal presence. Proceeding from the assumption that the "human face is the strongest focal point of everything that ever was and will be on this earth" (3), the photographer stresses that her photographs depict the true face of a natural German community. "*Volk*," she tells us, "is a unified natural community, anchored with all its roots in the soil of a landscape. It is an essential singularity [*Einmaliges an Wesenheit*] . . . simply organic" (6). "Just like everything about a *Volk* has, or better is physiognomy," she continues her ontologizing gesture, "its external forms of life are the expression of a soul, which could be called a landscape soul [*Landschaftsseele*] or the spirit of a tribe" (10). It is through the essential German faces captured in these photographs that "the culture of a Volk finds its expression" (11). Focusing mainly on German countenances found in the country and thereby seeking to avoid the internationalized and putatively more degenerate faces of city dwellers, Lendvai-Dircksen seeks to render portraits that illustrate the stability and ultimate determinacy of German culture. Thus, for example, she accompanies the face of a man from the North-Frisian island of Sylt with the caption: "There are faces in which one sees: 'After all, that's how it is.' One feels resignation. About others, one feels: 'It could be approximately like this.' Yet one is not convinced. But there are also faces of which one knows exactly: 'It cannot be otherwise!' And these faces possess the enormous stability [*Festigkeit*] of the belonging-together of all parts. This is the case here" (26). It is precisely the stability of the superior German face that differentiates it from the faces of other cultures and races, and it allegedly guarantees the expression of a *Volk*'s communal essence. The photographs and texts of Lendvai-Dircksen's remarkable volume attempt to permit the German *Volk* to enjoy this state of affairs by prompting it to look itself in the face on every page—an aestheticizing spectacle whose workings are seductive even when there seems to be little aestheticism at play in the faces themselves and whose dissemination augurs a politically exploitable racial and cultural narcissism par excellence.

Defacing Fascism

The Nazis' strategy of inventing and disseminating the images and narratives that present the German masses with their own face can be thought as an attempt to construct the people's cultural autobiography, a complex temporal and rhetorical structure that purports to reveal the identity or essence of its empirical referent. As de Man reminds us, there can be no autobiographical discourse that is not concerned "with the giving and taking away of faces, with face and deface, figure, figuration and disfiguration." This movement of bestowing a face or voice on an absent or dead speaker in order to simulate his momentary narrative presence is named by the trope of prosopopeia. "The figure of prosopopeia," de Man writes, is "the fiction of an apostrophe to an absent, deceased, or voiceless entity, which posits the possibility of the latter's reply and confers upon it the power of speech." Through this tropological maneuver, the absent subject "assumes mouth, eye, and finally face, a chain that is manifest in the etymology of the trope's name, *prosopon poien*, to confer a mask or face (*prosopon*)" ("Autobiography" 76).

Yet how to face this face? How to account for its seductive play and its promises of insight, stability, and closure while facing it with a critical guardedness? How to respond to the face which calls upon us and our sense of responsibility? After all, it would be a mistake to confuse the momentary, illusionary simulacrum of the face with its empirical referent, the fiction of autobiographical presence with a referential other who must remain forever absent from the scene of (re)presentation. To face the prosopopeia, then, is to allow for the experience of an aporetic structure, that is to say, the simultaneity of recognizing in this structure's simulacrum of the face the contours of a discourse calling upon us for authentication or verification— our counter-signature—and of resisting the temptation to succumb to its ultimately unsustainable phantasmagoria of immediacy and presence. That this double movement is the proper gesture of the image of the face propels de Man to argue that as "soon as we understand the rhetorical function of prosopopeia as positing voice or face by means of language, we also understand that what we are deprived of is not life but the shape and sense of a world accessible only in the privative way of understanding" (80f.). This means, ultimately, that, in the structure of the prosopopeia, death itself "is a displaced name for a linguistic predicament, and the restoration of mortality by autobiography (the prosopopeia of the voice and the name) deprives and disfigures to the precise extent that it restores. Autobiography veils a defacement of the mind of which it itself is the cause" (81). A full reading of the posited face would thus have to take account of the complexity of this simultaneous presentation and disfiguration, the giving and taking away of the face, the image of a face that hovers on the border between life and death.

Yet the Nazi logic of constantly confronting the German masses with their own face cannot account for this uncomfortable simultaneity, a simultaneity that signifies a deep disturbance to the fascist ideology of presence, immanence, and the revelation of stable meanings. That this double movement of the prosopopeia cannot be accounted for by the logic of the fascist system means that the fascist operation remains blind to the perpetual non-closure and deferral of its own narrative and imagistic productions, the constant turnover of the face that it produces. The monolithic Nazi myth can thus only insist—blindly, violently—on the giving of a face while remaining deaf to the perpetual threat of the face's retreat.

Benjamin, on the other hand, wishes to stage precisely this simultaneous bestowing and taking away of the face. This double movement is visible, for instance, in his demand that all historiographical insight proceed through the face—"to write history means to give dates their physiognomy," as we learn in the *Passagen-Werk* (N 67;

5:595)—and the concurrent acknowledgment of the face's excess that prevents it from being reducible to a positive fact of knowledge. Benjamin works to identify a blind spot in the fascist system of the face—not so much as a redemptive intervention extrinsically applied as a polemical tool but rather in an effort to lay bare the internal contradictions and masked aporias that are always already at work in what occurs in the name and face of Nazism. For instance, Benjamin contrasts the fascist formation of the face for the masses with the moment in Baudelaire's poetry in which the mass is never personified as a face or stable subject. There, the omnipresent metropolitan mass infiltrates every last orifice of intellectual and everyday cultural life, becoming the underlying pattern of modern consciousness. However, according to Benjamin, Baudelaire is careful to speak only of an "amorphous mass of passers-by," so that this "mass, whose existence Baudelaire never forgets, did not pose as a model for any of his works. But it imprinted on his work as a hidden figure" (*CB* 120; 1:618). The internalized presence of the mass as a hidden figure corresponds to its disappearance as a readable phenomenon with a legible countenance: "The masses are so much an internal part of Baudelaire that, with him, one looks in vain for a depiction of them" (*CB* 122; 1:621). Benjamin makes a similar point in the *Passagen-Werk* when he speaks of the image of the mass as it emerges in E. T. A. Hoffmann and Gogol. In both of these writers, Benjamin claims, the "understanding of the mass is instructive" because the image of the mass they present is never that of an organic whole with a stable countenance but rather a blurry and exhausting vortex, so dizzying and unstable, as Benjamin quotes Gogol, "that everything is swimming in front of one's eyes" (5:564). The mass can never be presented as an image and, unlike the image of Hitler in Mann's scenario, its gaze never returned.[12]

Another scene of Benjamin's staging of the face unfolds in his essay "On the Image of Proust," in which he traces the relays between physiognomies and tropes in Proust, what he calls "physiognomies or ways of speaking [*Physiognomien oder Redeweisen*]" (*I* 204; 2:313). There, he presents us with an aging face that in the moment of its presentation already outlines the contours of its own eventual demise, encrypted in its wrinkles: "The wrinkles and creases on our faces are the entries of the great passions, vices, insights that called on us; but we, the masters, were not home" (*I* 211f.; 2:321). The face, traversed by flaws and wrinkles, registers—like a text—an entire network of desires, insights, and missed opportunities, opportunities to respond to the call of the now. The double coding of the face as simultaneously revealing and denying, of marking the traces both of opportunities and their missed realization, corresponds to the erratic movement by which the prosopopeia gives and takes away, figures and disfigures.

The movement through which the image of the face both posits itself and retreats from its claims to signification is also one of the names of Benjamin's understanding of allegory. In his *Trauerspiel* book he distinguishes the symbolic from the allegorical through the figure of the face:

> Whereas in the symbol the transfigured face of nature fleetingly reveals itself through the idealization of destruction, in allegory the observer is confronted with the *facies hippocratica* of history as a petrified, primordial landscape. Everything about history that, from the very beginning, has been untimely, sorrowful, unsuccessful, is expressed in a face—or rather in a death's head. And although such a thing lacks all "symbolic" freedom of expression, all classical harmony of form, all that is human—nevertheless, what expresses itself significantly as an enigmatic question [*Rätselfrage*] in this figure most sunk into nature is not only human existence as such, but also the biographical historicity of the individual. (O 166; 1:343)

In his unraveling of allegory, Benjamin privileges the moment in which the historicity of what allegory stages is presented as the face of a petrification. As opposed to the idealizing logic of the symbol, which valorizes presence and revelation, the face of allegory confronts the marginal, the repressed other to its own unfolding. This is why the face of allegory is always also a death's head. The allegorical face of the death's head is for Benjamin not merely the undesirable mortal other to the security promised by symbolic understanding in its classical form. Rather, it is precisely through the moment in which what constitutes the face of the death's head poses an enigmatic question (*Rätselfrage*) that the most urgent issues of human being-in-the-world and its historicity may be addressed in the first place. The allegorical face of the death's head dissimulates the symbolic gesture of bestowing a face upon what is presented in order to uncover its internal breaks.

Benjamin, then, will always have insisted on deconstructing the simulacrum of the face as a moment of identification and self-identity. For him, the face comes together as a constellation but simultaneously threatens to break apart, serving as a privileged stage for the dialectical movement of the asserted and disarticulated subject itself. Far from the territory of expression or revelation, this "sense-less," unreadable face is the visage of silence whose contours Benjamin recognizes in the first photographically reproduced human beings whose "face had a silence about it" (OWS 244; 2:372). Like Baudelaire's "eccentric play of grimaces" (CB 117; 1:616), the dialectical aura of this silence of the face belongs, in its retreat from expression and straightforward readability, to the realm of Benjamin's resistance to the revelations of fascism.

That Benjamin resists the notion of a face that is in some *essential* way linked to the figure of what is human means that he wishes to think the face as also belonging to what can no longer be delimited by the discourses of the human and its referentiality. In a 1927 review, he delineates the transgressive moment which moves away from the human and toward the enigmatic face of the inhuman. There, he evokes precisely what transforms itself "not into the vaguely human." Instead, we learn, "it is a matter of creating a new, more enigmatic face: a political enigma [*politisches Rätsel*], if you wish, a sphinx's face. . . . This face rises up into the book [*Dieses Gesicht ragt in das Buch herein*]" (3:62). In Greek mythology, the sphinx names the figure of a winged monster that possesses the face of a woman attached to the body of a lion. It destroys those who cannot solve its riddles. Reading the face, we are confronted with the text of a riddle, or the riddle of a text, whose meaning we cannot access. It is the face of an alterity that is simultaneously readable and unreadable or, more precisely, is unreadable because, paradoxically, it is readable.[13] This is so because, on the one hand, one must read the face of the sphinx or a text (and Benjamin emphasizes the link between the enigmatic character of the sphinx's face and a text—"This face rises up into the book"). The sphinx's face or text demands to be read. It cannot not be read, as there is no other way to engage it but to *read* it carefully. In this sense it is readable. But this reading of the text of the sphinx can never arrive at a stable meaning or at hermeneutic closure— the enigmatic text to be read cannot be arrested, its laws cannot be broken for good. It thus remains unreadable. That a readability represents precisely the cause for an unreadability is the political alterity encoded in Benjamin's figure of the sphinx's face. If the face is here staged as a riddled text whose meanings and codifications cannot be arrested for good and if the reader of the facial text is called upon to decipher it, its textual riddles remain nevertheless unsolved. Benjamin enacts such a scene when in his unpublished fragment "La Traduction—Le Pour et le Contre" from the mid-1930s he speaks of a French translation of Nietzsche as possessing an enigmatic, disfigured textual face: "But when I looked them [Nietzsche's passages] in the face, I had the uncomfortable feeling that they recognized me as little as I recognized them" (6:158). Again, the face of a seemingly familiar text remains strange. The transgressive moment encoded in Benjamin's figure of the sphinx's face unfolds when hermeneutic desire is deferred because it cannot be fulfilled by a stable meaning. Like Benjamin's image of the face of a death's head in allegory and its evocation as an enigmatic question, a *Rätselfrage*, the sphinx's face always threatens to retreat from its own presentation as a fully legible text. Rather than revealing itself to the desire for revelation, it remains a hardly controllable other, a fleeting figure that is unusable—refuses to be used—by a program and thus remains a political enigma—*ein politisches Rätsel.*

This hermeneutic retreat of the face simultaneously points to the (frustrated) expectation that, in the moment of the prosopopeia, the face might in fact speak, that it is linked to language and the promise of communication. Benjamin makes this relay between language and the face explicit in the *Passagen-Werk* when he theorizes the world of hashish:

> When we say that a face resembles another, this means that certain features of the second face appear to us in the first, without the first ceasing to be what it was. The possibilities of appearing in this way are not subject to any criteria and are thus unlimited. The category of resemblance, which for our waking consciousness possesses only limited significance, assumes in the world of hashish an unlimited one. After all, everything in it is a face; everything possesses a degree of corporeal presence which allows one to search it like a face for traces of appearance. Under these circumstances, even a sentence assumes a face (not to mention individual words), and this face resembles the one of its opposite sentence. Every truth therefore evidently points to its opposite, and this fact of the matter explains doubt. Truth comes alive; it lives only in this rhythm in which sentence and counter-

sentence [*Satz und Gegensatz*] displace themselves in order to think themselves. (5:526)

This remarkably rich passage contains something like Benjamin's poetics of the face. Benjamin suggests, among so many other things, that we interact with the face as a corporeal presence in which we recognize the semiotic contours of language. But even though every sentence and every word has a face, this face (and with it, its meaning) may at any given time turn into its opposite, its other. The truth of this face is revealed precisely when it does not remain what it is. It assumes its proper self most fully in the moment in which it is shifting toward something else, another face, another identity. This moment of the shift *is* the proper self of the face. The language of truth, as it is staged upon the scene of its face, is always already traversed by its other, indeed, it comes alive when truth and its opposite (or sentence and counter-sentence, *Satz und Gegensatz*) leave their respective positions in the binary opposition in order to deconstruct the valorizations assigned to them by their hierarchical relation. For Benjamin, then, the face is another name (or prosopopeia) for the aporetic structure of the language of the body and the experience of finitude inscribed within it.

Genealogies of the Disfigured Face

Benjamin's obsession with the politics of the face ranges from his engagement with classical authors to his contemporary context, and it even continues to resonate posthumously. It is no accident, for instance, that in the *Passagen-Werk* he evokes the face in the work of Ovid: "Where is the passage in Ovid that says that the human face was created to send out the reflection of the stars?" (5:336).[14] Here, the human face becomes a stage for the drama enacted by a constellation of stars, for Benjamin always ciphers of uncertainty. But turning the historical gaze the other way, the contours of Benjamin's face become visible in our own discourses as well. For instance, Benjamin's emphasis on the fundamental undecidability of the face links him to the work of Emmanuel Levinas, the French-Jewish philosopher and great thinker of the face. While Benjamin emphasizes the political implications of the face's indecipherability, Levinas develops the ethical implications of the incomprehensible face as part of a more theological analysis of the encounter with the absolutely Other. In Levinas's work, the face becomes a prototype of our response to the Other as such, an Other whom we cannot understand, but whose language nevertheless binds this Other inextricably to ours. Here, the "face is present in its refusal to be contained. In this sense it cannot be comprehended, that is, encompassed" (194).[15] Levinas and Benjamin share the responsibility of answering to the ethical demand of a face that presents itself only on the far side of stable knowledge. Along similar lines, in its refutation of hermeneutic closure and its opening up to the moment of reversal, Benjamin's image of the face is also linked to that of Roland Barthes who speaks of a filmic face as something "which could be neither reached nor renounced," but which is instead "constituted by an infinite complexity of morphological functions" ("The Face of Garbo" 57). For both Benjamin and Barthes, the face exhibits a morphological complexity that can never be fully arrested.

In Benjamin's own historical orbit, it is precisely through this morphological complexity that his intricate deconstructive reversal of the face exhibits decisive links to the work of his teacher Simmel, specifically the latter's 1901 essay "The Aesthetic Significance of the Face." As a student in Berlin, Benjamin regularly attended the lectures and seminars of the great social philosopher, among whose other students were Lukács, Cassirer, L. Marcuse, Kracauer, and Bloch. According to Simmel, the aesthetic specificity of the face lies in the fact that, like no other body part, a minute change in one of its features drastically alters its appearance and interpretation. The entire texture and signification of a face is suddenly changed by "a twitching of the lips, a wrinkling of the nose, the way of looking, a knitting of the forehead" (140). To be sure, other body parts and even the body itself are also subject to change and transformation, but these changes do not result in the same immediate reconfiguration of their readability as occurs in the case of the face: "At first the trained eye can distinguish bodies much like faces. However, they do not *interpret* this difference the way a face does" (142). In the face, "the determination of each figure stands in solidarity with the determination of the others, that is, the whole. The cause of this is the incredible and monstrous [*ungeheure*] mobility of the face" (144). For Simmel, the face is what it is because of its erratic mobility, its shifts and sudden transformations of expression and meaning. Unlike the fascist mobilization of the face, which relies on the stability and monolithic meaning of certain phases of the face in order then to bestow it upon the masses for purposes of nationalistic exploitation, Simmel's image of the face unfolds as a complex and ever-shifting semiotic force field in which the meaning one assigns to a given face can suddenly be challenged and undermined by competing meanings and significations. Following Simmel, Benjamin, unlike the fascists (whom we could now call "face-ists"), ultimately emphasizes the face's potential retreat from meaning, its unreliability as a stable hermeneutic concept, its hovering, as Simmel would have it, between disclosure and disguise, *Enthüllung* and *Verhüllung* (145). The intricate Benjaminian relays that generally link problems of representation to political concerns also link this aporetic structure of the face to its political dimensions.

Benjamin's political reading of the face as what remains self-differentiated is also shared by Bloch, his philosopher friend and fellow Simmel student. We could even say that the general theoretical overlap between Bloch and Benjamin of which Adorno speaks[16] unfolds in part within the figure of the face. For instance, Bloch's 1930 *Spuren* (*Traces*), which in tone and style resembles Benjamin's *One-Way Street*, contains a section entitled "No Face" ("Kein Gesicht"). There, Bloch presents us with the story of a young girl's suffering, emphasizing, however, the inability of her suffering to assume a face. While the girl's ruptured identity emerges as that of one who suffers, this rupture cannot be captured in the image of a face, so that her "face did not emerge [*Gesicht kam nicht hervor*]" (*Spuren* 40). The essence or identity of the subject can thus not be given a face. Similarly, in Bloch's *The Spirit of Utopia*, the section "The Face of Will" considers attempts at human emancipation from the alienating mechanisms of the state in terms of the face, that is, "as a *will to our face* and finally as the *face of our will*" (*Geist der Utopie* 345). While the search for, and positing of, a face is for Bloch an ineluctable component of acts of resistance, he emphasizes the simultaneous necessity to remain vigilant vis-à-vis the promises and figures of this self-presentation: "Not one of our forms must any longer be allowed to become anonymous; the human being must no longer permit himself to be swallowed up by the means and wrong reifications of himself" (345). What is required is the complex double movement that searches and posits a face while constantly resisting the delusion that this face presents self-construction, liberation, and autonomy, lest we fall prey to the reification and erasure of any possible resistance. Bloch also alludes to such a double movement when he quotes the Kabbalah's maxim, "know that there is a double gaze for all worlds" (345). Finally, in a 1920 essay "On the Ethical and Spiritual Leader or the Double Nature of the Human Face," Bloch speaks of the "respect, a highest affect," which "is never directed at a single human being but always at the human face buried within him, the way that the 'I' wishes to encounter it in every creature and in all evidence of production" ("Menschengesicht" 210). As Bloch teaches us, while what we wish to encounter is the face as the text of a subject's essence or identity, this face remains hidden, no matter how strenuously we strive to access it as a stable text.

In addition to Bloch, Benjamin's paleonomic sensitivity to the figure of the face shares certain connections with that of Rilke, whom he read as a pupil and with whom he attended a seminar offered by the Americanist Walter Lehmann at the University of Munich in 1915. Five years earlier, Rilke had published his novel *The Notebooks of Malte Laurids Brigge* which stages the narrator's predicament in the language of the face. In a remarkable passage, Rilke's narrator tells us:

> Have I said it already? I am learning to see. Yes, I am beginning. It still goes slowly. But I intend to make the most of my time. For one thing, it has never occurred to me before how many different faces there are. There are masses of people, but there are even more faces, for each person has several. There are some who wear the same face for years: naturally it wears out; it gets dirty; it breaks at the folds; it stretches, like gloves one has worn on a journey. These are thrifty, simple folk; they do not change their face; they never even have it cleaned. It is good enough, they claim, and who can prove the contrary? Now the question of course arises, since they have several faces, what do they do with the others? They keep them [*heben sie auf*]. Their children are to wear them. But sometimes, too, it happens that their dogs go out with them on. And why not? A face is a face.
>
> There are others who put on their faces in uncannily rapid succession, one after the other, and wear them out. At first they think they have enough to last them forever; but they have scarcely reached forty when behold, they have already come to the last of them. This naturally has its tragedy. They are not accustomed to being frugal

with faces. Their last is worn through in eight days, has holes in it, and in many places is as thin as paper; and then gradually the lining— the no-face [*Nicht-Gesicht*]—comes through, and they walk about with that.

But the woman, the woman: she had completely sunk into herself, her head in her hands . . . The woman took fright and tore herself too quickly out of herself, too violently, so that her face remained in her two hands. I could see it lying in them, its hollow form. It cost me an indescribable effort to remain with these hands and not to look at what had torn itself out of them. I shuddered to see a face from the inside, but I was still more afraid of the naked, flayed head without a face. (6f.)

In Rilke's playful transgression of the semiotics of the face, there can be no self whose identity is tied to its face. This is so because no single face can be representative of the multiple faces that present and disarticulate the subject at any given moment. Indeed, there is a plethora of possible faces competing for validation as the signature of the self, a network of different possible identities and self-images Benjamin calls in his *Berlin Childhood around 1900* the self's "arsenal of masks" (7:418). This is also why no *single* face can stand in for the multiple faces of the masses ("masses of people, but . . . even more faces.") The text of the face is volatile and wears thin— through repeated use or readings perhaps—only to yield its other, what Rilke calls "the non-face" (*das Nicht-Gesicht*). Like Benjamin's face that breaks with mimesis to resemble its own opposite, Rilke's non-face signals the advent of what cannot be contained by the positing of a face as a figure of identification and hermeneutic closure. The double movement of thinking and undoing a face of which Bloch and Benjamin speak is displaced in Rilke's rhetoric onto the anxiety that comes with seeing the inside of a face—the unthinkable inside of something that is the very definition of the outside—and the frightening prospect of thus disturbing the logic of the face altogether. After all, to disturb the logic of the face as what is (the) outside means to face what no longer has a face—"a head without a face," as Rilke says—the disfiguration of the face. For Rilke, then, the disfiguration of the face is tied to its inversion and transgression as a concept. What Benjamin's allegorical reading of the face shares with that of his friends and contemporaries Rilke, Bloch, Kracauer, and Simmel is the refusal to view the face as a self-identical set of mobilizable essences. There is no unproblematic expression here, no stable program to reflect in the presentation of the face. Herein lies part of the genealogy of Benjamin's theoretical break with the stable face.

The Politics of the Portrait

This theoretical break simultaneously interacts in subtle ways with more transparently political concerns.[17] For in the realm of concrete cultural production, too, Benjamin detected artistic attempts to engage the human countenance along unexpected trajectories. The work of such seminal photographers as Eugène Atget, David Octavius Hill, Gisèle Freund, and Germaine Krull, who took several portraits of Benjamin and whose photographs Benjamin hoped would eventually illustrate the *Passagen-Werk*, held special interest for him. In Weimar Germany, the avant-garde photomontages of Sasha Stone, a fellow member of the "G-Group" and designer of the brilliant dust jacket for *One-Way Street*, and the photographs of August Sander were especially significant for him. In the photography of Stone and Sander, Benjamin sensed certain overlaps with his own theoretical concerns, and he was receptive to the ways in which they probed the epistemological complexity and political irreducibility of the problematic human subject. Indeed, they provided a counterweight to an affirmatively stale, right-leaning photographic rhetoric. While Stone's photomontages pointed toward a decisive rearticulation of the language of photography as such, Sander offered a high modernist engagement with the figure of the German face itself. His 1929 book of faces, *Antlitz der Zeit: Sechzig Aufnahmen deutscher Menschen des 20. Jahrhunderts (Face of the Times: Sixty Photographs of German People of the 20th Century)*, contained not only penetrating images of the bourgeoisie and the leaders of society but also bleak portraits of the unemployed, communists, cleaning women, students, bohemians, and other marginal groups. Sander's complex confrontation of the German face and its social and political inscriptions is considered by historians of photography to have been the "first properly discursive photo-book in the history of the medium" (Jeffrey 135). Both Alfred Döblin, whose essay "Of Faces, Images, and Their Truth" introduced Sander's volume with a meditation on the flattening and death of the face, and Benjamin, who refers to Sander's book in his essay on photography, emphasize the incommensurate, resistant qualities of Sander's socially critical work. As Benjamin writes of Sander's facial photographs in "A Short History of Photography," "immediately the human face appeared on the photographic plate with new and immeasurable significance. But it was no longer a portrait" (OWS 251; 2:380). In the work of Sander, the photographic portrait enacts its own retreat.

Sander's image entitled "Revolutionäre, Berlin, 1929," for instance, depicts in strict formal composition three men sitting side by side on brick steps in front of a white door (figure 3). The man in the middle is the socialist politician and writer Erich Mühsam. It is impossible to determine if the three are sitting in front of or behind the house, if they are the proud masters of their space or marginal characters pushed out of their house and its symbolic laws—outlaws, as it were. They are dressed in dark, serious attire that has seen better days. Their faces appear somber and strangely withdrawn from the photographic event. Only Mühsam faces the camera directly, while the comrade to his right stares into an invisible space to the left. The trajectory of the latter's gaze crosses that of the comrade sitting on the other side, who, cross-eyed and meager, wears a slightly crazed expression. He seems to enact what Benjamin praises as the *scheele Blick*, an odd looking awry, in the work of Kafka. Despite their impenetrable individual countenances, the three revolutionaries are linked by a subtle trace of solidarity, embodied by the arm and hand placed on the shoulder of Mühsam and the left leg of the man on the left, whose left-pointing foot parallels the hand on the shoulder, providing, as it were, a bodily "framing" of the entire scene. Traversed by a nameless melancholia and a politically oppositional spirit, these faces would be useless in the archives of the propagandistic images of glorified German faces.

Along these same lines, Sander's photograph entitled "Cleaning Woman (Putzfrau)," 1927, a portrait of an aging cleaning lady, retreats in its proletarian sadness from the official ideology of the German worker's face (figure 4). The woman's plaintive face is inscribed with wrinkles of age and hardship. The image sets into motion an allusive interplay between the wrinkles on her face and those on her stained smock. Far from basking triumphantly in the glow of a polished uniform, she is dressed in a worn blouse which, under her smock, is held together not by a button but, in makeshift fashion,

Fig. 3. August Sander, "Revolutionäre, Berlin, 1929." © Die Photographische Sammlung/SK Stiftung Kultur-August Sander Archiv, Cologne; ARS Artists Rights Society, New York; VG BildKunst, Bonn.

Fig. 4. August Sander, "Cleaning Woman (Putzfrau)," 1927. Gelatin silver print, 23.0 cm x 15.9 cm. The J. Paul Getty Museum, Los Angeles.

merely a safety pin. The quiet dignity of her posture is disturbed by the broom stick that she clutches in her soiled worker's hands, a figurative slash diagonally across her worn torso. Like the faces of the revolutionaries, she seems to be looking awry, even as she faces the camera head-on.

Echoing certain early Russian films, which moved away from the concept of physiognomic expression, Sander's photographed subjects can be read in terms of what Benjamin calls a "nameless appearance that they carry in their faces [*namenlosen Erscheinung, die sie im Antlitz haben*]" (OWS 251; 2:379), not with a view toward the organic presentation of a stable subject but with a view toward putting "people before the camera who had no use [*keine Verwendung*] for their photographs" (OWS 251; 2:380). For Benjamin, Sander's photographs tend to remain in a space that cannot be fully measured and that is haunted by an otherness, a specter that is on the far side of the stability promised by a conventional portrait. They are referential and politically inscribed only to the extent that they remain useless: *keine Verwendung*. It is not surprising that the Nazi Ministry of Culture eventually outlawed Sander's book, seizing its plates and confiscating its remaining copies. The way had to be cleared for the "official" German faces produced by photographers such as Riefenstahl and Lendvai-Dircksen.

If Benjamin's engagement with the photographic face stresses its unusable qualities, it exhibits an essential rapport with another key text of Kracauer's. Writing under the shadow of the swastika, Kracauer's 1933 "Comment on Portrait Photography" criticizes precisely those portraits that are taken and displayed in the name of particular ideological agendas and that project a photographic face not according to its own internal laws and contradictions, but with an eye toward appropriating it for ideological purposes. The danger of such portrait photography "consists in the way in which this photography does not present the physiognomy to be portrayed but is used as a means to an end that lies outside of the object. What photographic possibilities does a head contain?" ("Anmerkungen über Portrait-Photographie" 196). Disturbing the economy of the face's political mobilization, Kracauer instead privileges the moment when the photographed face retreats from transparent meaning in order to fold back upon itself, to follow the singular paths and wrinkles of its own composition, its formal specificity. In Kracauer's aesthetics of the portrait, the images of the face do not aim at "egotistical special aims but have the function of providing commentary on the text of the face [*den Text des Gesichts zu kommentieren*]" (197). Here, what is at stake is the very act of reading and commenting. The task of the commentator is the close reading of the face itself, not the administration of its putative meaning. And like the reading of a written text, the reading of the text of the face can never be quite complete. This is why, Benjamin tells us as if echoing Kracauer, "Reading [is] the highest traditional physiognomy" (6:170). To the extent that this reading of the facial text remains open to its own deferral, the connections between Kracauer and Benjamin are crucial. Just as for Benjamin the image of the face holds a promise that can only be fulfilled if it does not remain fully accessible to hermeneutic penetration and to the assignment of this or that meaning, Kracauer illuminates the unique event-structure of the face that flashes up in the delimited realm of its singular appearance, that is to say, in the moment when the facial text requires the sensitivity of a reading that is open to the possibility of its own impossibility. Echoing Benjamin's admonitions against the fascist aestheticization of politics, Kracauer warns against the "inevitable stylizations" (198) of the photographed face, calling upon us as facial readers to engage these stylizations as dangerous delusions. If Kracauer and Benjamin thus locate the value of a facial image precisely in its uselessness, this uselessness is one of the names of the melancholic promises the photographed face may still hold in store.

Unusable Faces

For Kracauer's and Benjamin's "useless" face, the stakes are so high because, ultimately, the fascist desire to present the masses with political spectacles and cultural productions in which they may see their face reflected as if in a mirror is one of the strategic movements of the elaborate Nazi myth that claims alternately to contain or reveal the expression, essence, and community of the people. If, as Nancy and Lacoue-Labarthe suggest in "The Nazi Myth," Hitlerism can be thought as a strategic exploitation of the modern masses' receptivity to myth, then this exploitation is achieved precisely by virtue of the fascist promise of a stable realization of the mass image—in short, the identificatory myth. The Nazi myth, which claims to be capable of expressing the identity of a closed communal subject, is ultimately inscribed in a certain trajectory within the Western tradition that conceives of the subject as a total, coherent, self-identical entity, stable across time and revealable at will as a secure essence.[18] Nancy and Lacoue-Labarthe therefore remind us not to assume an all-too-comfortable complacency vis-à-vis the face of fascism today, an indifference that would mistake it for an aberration of history. Instead, our task is to specify fascism as a pattern that calls for "a general deconstruction of the history in which our own provenance lies" (312), a strategy, however, that can never be normative or prescribed. Because the Nazi myth is in essential ways related to a larger network of master narratives that structure our culture, the full unraveling of the Nazi myth and its prosopopeia is always still to come.[19] In order to be effective, it must never (be thought to) be fully present. Any single analysis of the Nazis' political and cultural semiotics is thus thinkable only as one subversive gesture within a wide network of interlocking discourses, lest the return or perpetuation of Nazi ideology and its ghosts be misread as a closing-off, a final transcendence.

The history of the master narratives from which the Nazi myth emerged—including certain historicist images of history itself—must thus be recognized for what it is: a construction that masks a force field of differences and heterogeneous movements as historico-cultural homogeneity. For Benjamin, therefore, "history is the object of a construction" whose site is "not the homogenous or empty time." It is our task "to explode the continuum of history" (*I* 261; 1:701). His image of history, like that envisioned by Nancy and Lacoue-Labarthe, warns against seeing the face of fascism as an accidental intrusion into the otherwise pastoral scene of historical progress. Benjamin rejects a model of containment and progress in an effort "to brush history against the grain" (*I* 257; 1:697).[20] In 1940, he thus argues that the

> tradition of the oppressed teaches us that the "state of emergency" in which we live is not the exception but the rule. We must attain to a conception of history that is in keeping with this insight. Then we shall see that it is our task to bring about a real state of emergency, and this will improve our position in the fight against fascism. . . . The current amazement that the things we are experiencing are "still" possible in the twentieth century is not philosophical. This

amazement is not the beginning of knowledge—unless it is the knowledge that the idea of history from which it stems is untenable. (*I* 257; 1:697).

For Benjamin, any reading of fascism would have to attempt simultaneously to analyze its seductions, promises, and assumptions and to deconstruct the entire myth of politics and history out of which it emerged, its wide network of discourses, in short, its episteme. Only here does the project outlined in Benjamin's preparatory notes to the theses on history crystallize, that is, to respond to the "necessity of a theory of history through which fascism can be viewed" (1:1244).

The deconstructed face is one of the figures of indeterminacy that emerge in the moment when the constructed linearity of history is exploded in favor of charged interruptions or shocks and of what is still to come. Here, the face belongs to those Benjaminian illuminations that rearticulate their own relation to the historical. "[O]nly if," Benjamin writes in his essay on the translator, "all that of which there is history [*wovon es Geschichte gibt*], and which is not merely its scene, is granted life, then justice is done to its concept" (*I* 71; 4:11). Our task, then, is to read a figure not merely as the scene of history, conceived as a socio-historical totality redoubled in the figure itself, but rather to theorize the ways in which *there is history of* this figure (*wovon es Geschichte gibt*). A reading of this *wovon* would propel us to read the ways in which a figure stages a new sense of its historicity within its own tropological maneuvers. This historicity does not belong to the continuum of organic or natural history: the figure instead formulates its historicity on its own terms. The face, for Benjamin, is such a figure. It cannot easily be inscribed into the singularity of a particular historical narrative, because it confronts within itself the historicity that emanates from the constant movement of its own retreat.

Benjamin's engagement with fascism depends on his engagement with the figurative because, as we recall, "There is no world of thought that is not a world of language, and one only sees in the world what is pre-conditioned by language" (6:158). If, therefore, one of the sites of Benjamin's opposition to the Nazi myth and its seductions is located in his analysis of fascism's aetheticization of politics, and if by way of a countermove he calls for the radical politicization of art, then this inversion is indeed performed by his transgressive reading of the language of the face, an aporetic structure that exceeds any form of a

harmonious dialectic. Likewise, if Benjamin's Artwork essay emphasizes the importance of thinking a realm of concepts that cannot be
appropriated by fascism, we can now suggest that the deconstructed
face—as a metonymy for the unmade corpus as such—can itself be
thought as such a concept. If fascism operates by giving a face to
the masses, by giving them over to expression—"giving these masses
certainly not their right but instead their expression. . . . Fascism
seeks to give them an expression" (*I* 241; 1:506)—then Benjamin
refuses to take fascist semiotics at face value. Instead, he defaces
them. Just as he evokes in his "Hashish in Marseilles" the moment
which "turned me into a physiognomist" who sinks his teeth into the
faces surrounding him ("I sank my teeth into the faces surrounding
me") in order suddenly to find there countenances full of folds and
wrinkles, even "distorted visages," he works to disfigure the fascist
face (*R* 139ff.; 4:411ff.). The moment of transgressing the monolithic
face of fascism and its delusional promises of expression ultimately is
one of responsibility and resistance. In Benjamin's textual web, there
are, as in his essay on Proust, only "isolated, only enigmatically present
images of the face [*isolierte, nur rätselhaft präsente Gesichtsbilder*]"
(2:323), a constellation in which, as in the essay on surrealism, "the
true surrealist face of existence breaks through" (*I* 205; 2:314). Here,
Benjamin's face aligns itself more with the grotesquely montaged
visage that one encounters on the cover of John Heartfield's and
Kurt Tucholsky's subversive photo book *Deutschland, Deutschland
über alles* (1929) than with the facial images of mobilization. Indeed,
Benjamin's enigmatic other to fascism names what he once called
his desire to imagine the face of another, a secret Germany beyond
fascism—"*das Antlitz eines 'geheimen Deutschland'*" (4:945). It is in
this simultaneously aporetic and oppositional sense that Benjamin's
face remains a political enigma, a sphinx's face.

The ethics and politics of Benjamin's paleonomic face thus invite
us to decide not to decide. We are faced with the decision to defer
a decision in the name of what is yet to come, with an eye toward
what is other to immanence, presence, and the pull of the empirical.
The angel of history, and the promise of destruction and redemption
whose fate is inextricably tied to its appearance, reveals itself only
when its face is in retreat. As in Paul Klee's painting, the countenance
of Benjamin's angel appears disfigured, its eyes staring madly, its
mouth gaping open as it faces the hieroglyphs of what has come

to pass. A poem by Heiner Müller memorializing Benjamin evokes this uncomfortable demand of history:

> The Angel I still hear him
> but he does not have a face anymore other than
> Yours which I don't know
>
> (Der Engel ich höre ihn noch
> aber er hat kein Gesicht mehr als
> Deines das ich nicht kenne) (29)

There can be no reading of Benjamin that will not have been touched by the melancholia of this *nicht*.

2

BENJAMIN'S BODY: THE ALTERITY OF THE
CORPUS IN THE *MOSCOW DIARY*

> The only direction that eros or love takes is toward the
> common death of the lovers. Love unravels like the thread
> in a labyrinth whose center is the "chamber of death."
>> Walter Benjamin, "Über die Ehe"

> If the union of two lovers comes about through love, it
> involves the idea of death, murder or suicide. This aura of
> death is what denotes passion.
>> Georges Bataille, *Erotism: Death and Sensuality*

To trace the movements of the signature that will have
been Benjamin's "self" means to encounter at least three different
selves as they inhabit, and are traversed by, an other. For Benjamin,
the eros of love transforms the self into something else: it becomes
like the other. As he writes in an autobiographical note from 1931,
"whenever a great love came over me, I changed so fundamentally
that I was very astonished to have to say to myself: the man who
said such unanticipated things and who displayed such unexpected
behavior was I. This is so because true love makes me similar to
the beloved woman." Benjamin continues: "My most forceful and
violent transformation into the similar was . . . my union with Asja
(Lacis). . . . To write the story of my life would mean to present
the construction and undoing of these three men as well as the
compromise among them—one could say: the triumvirate that my
life now is" (6:427). To think through his relation to the other,

125

Benjamin here hints at what he once called *Leibähnlichkeiten*, or corporeal similarities that establish unexpected links between the subject and its physical surroundings (6:193). There is no other document that traces the contours of the Benjaminian self as it is inflected by the beloved other more vividly than the often overlooked *Moscow Diary*. This text stages, on the site of the unavailable body of Asja Lacis, the enigmatic process of "becoming similar," a process that for Benjamin is always also a form of disfiguration, of *enstellte Ähnlichkeit*.[1] This chapter traces that eroticized body in retreat.

While the last chapter set the stage for the ways in which Benjamin's image of the face unhinges the fascist desire for stable concepts, this chapter further elaborates Benjamin's staging of the corpus as a vicissitudinous and ultimately "unusable" concept. The ethico-political significance of the body as a concept is again tied to the ways in which it remains elusive, an alterity to any system of stable meanings. To demonstrate this, the thesis I want to put forward is that in the *Moscow Diary* one finds not only a general preoccupation with the subject's body but also that Benjamin's language itself becomes affected by this corporeal sensitivity. Like Proust, whose "sentences are the entire muscular activity of the intelligible body" (*I* 214; 2:324), Benjamin composes sentences that cannot be understood separate from his preoccupation with the links between bodies and texts. But while the body metamorphoses into a text, it always threatens to remain illegible. This scenario is enacted, I argue, on Lacis's eroticized body, access to which is continually deferred. It remains an alterity. This deferral can best be traced along a series of intertwined axes that traverse the *Moscow Diary*: illness, rejection, impotence, interference, and the transformation of the other. The body thus remains the elusive excess of hermeneutic consummation. What could be called Benjamin's erotics of reading, his attempts to inhabit Lacis's body by linking sex and the act of interpretation, invites a meditation on the ways in which desire and meaning are set into motion precisely by the inaccessibility of the corpus. The body names the space in which what Derrida once called the *Moscow Diary*'s "so very successful failure," its "abortion destined to survive," can be made vivid ("Back from Moscow" 232). In the *Moscow Diary*, the deferral of the body prevents the self from coming into its own, either in itself or in an other.

In order to begin to trace this deferral, we might note how, in spite of its seemingly quotidian character, the *Moscow Diary* has tended to make its readers feel ill at ease. Although hailed by Scholem as a unique autobiographical document, even as Benjamin's most personal and revealing text, the journal notes compiled under that title have haunted their readers. Already the very first reader, Benjamin himself, was aware of his text's opacity and incommensurability, hoping to give "at least a halfway communicable summary of my stay" but conceding, in a letter to Kracauer, that it "can in no way be more than a small image of Moscow," "disparate notes" at best (BK 37f.). And Scholem, in his foreword to the text's first publication in 1980, ambivalently refers to it as "bitter and depressing" (Preface 7). Susan Buck-Morss complains that the "reader of Benjamin's Moscow diary feels impatience" (32). The document's editor, Gary Smith, registers how it strangely "resist[s] our impulse to taxonomize" and that it "exceeds the conventions of genre," being readable only "as if through a palimpsest" (Afterword 137). Even the otherwise matter-of-fact prose of Benjamin's biographer, Bernd Witte, is interrupted by a moment of uneasiness when he characterizes Benjamin's desire to understand Moscow, the city, and, in particular, his love, Lacis, as an instance of "tenacious, almost desperate courtship" whose failure was "inevitable" (*Intellectual Biography* 101). Finally, a recent critic points to "Benjamin's slippery routes and awkward insights" in the *Moscow Diary*, comparing the text to "the unedited footage of a documentary film in the style of Dziga Vertov or the Constructivists" (Boym 125, 118). Given that Benjamin constructed the *Moscow Diary* as a text dependent upon an especially patient and rigorously discerning reader, a text in which "for the better part the reader will be left to his own devices" (*BK* 38), we are led to ask, what accounts for this litany of unease and discomfort? What is it that ails these readers? The disturbing answer may well lie in what may be called the alterity of the corpus.

A Friendship of Strange Friends

The *Moscow Diary* was written during Benjamin's visit to the capital of the Soviet Union, between 9 December 1926 and 1 February 1927. Ever since childhood, Benjamin, born into the mores and traditions of the established European bourgeoisie, had been sent on the obligatory educational journeys (*Bildungsreisen*). As an adult, too, his gaze now that of the cultural physiognomist, Benjamin was a relentless traveler. Starting in the early 1920s he spent several weeks, sometimes months, traveling through Europe every year. Along the way, he composed a significant and largely still unexamined part of his corpus: travel narratives, diaries, city portraits, aphorisms, dream protocols, autobiographical snapshots, and essays. Most of his surviving autobiographical texts were written on such trips. His stay in Moscow, however, was more specifically motivated and revolved around three main axes. First, he wanted to clarify his wish to become an active member of the Communist Party, a prospect with which he had wrestled ambivalently for over two years. Second, he wished to chart a social and cultural map of a city whose changes—since the Revolution, the end of World War I, and the emergence of the contours of a Stalinist regime—he regarded both as emblematic for the future of dialectical materialism and as an intriguing other to Weimar culture and the threat of fascism. Third, and most importantly, he was driven passionately to pursue the woman of his desire, Lacis, the Latvian actress and director whom he had met in 1924 in Capri. She embodied for him the heady conflation of eroticism and living Marxism into which she had initiated him. Upon their first meeting, Benjamin wrote to Scholem that a "Bolshevist Latvian woman from Riga, a stage actress and director, a Christian, is the most noteworthy. . . . I spoke with the Bolshevist woman until half past twelve" (C 242f.; B 346f.). Lacis became for Benjamin "one of the most extraordinary women that I have ever met" (C 255; B 351), and he dedicated his One-Way Street to her. Scholem tells us that Lacis "was, after Dora Keller and Jula Cohn [-Rath], the third woman to assume central significance in Benjamin's life. His erotic attachment to her was tied to the strong intellectual influence that she . . . exerted on him" (Preface 7).

But from the beginning, their relationship, characterized by passion and deferral, physical attraction and repulsion, obsession and denial, sexual desire and cynicism, was enigmatic. According to those who saw Benjamin and Lacis together, the strange lovers were constantly quarreling—even in 1929 and 1930, when Lacis came to Berlin and Frankfurt, and Benjamin divorced his wife Dora, from whom he had been estranged since the mid-twenties, in part due to his relation with Lacis (Scholem, Preface 8). Even Scholem capitulates before this riddle, this simultaneous excess and shortfall of desire—and meaning—that was their relation: "An inexplicable residue remains, one that is appropriate for a life like that of Walter Benjamin" (Scholem, Preface 8). It is as though their strange relationship enacted what Benjamin had once termed, in an early letter to another female friend, "a friendship of strange friends [*eine Freundschaft der fremden Freunde*]" (C 57; B 96). A friendship of strange friends: Benjamin and Lacis come together as loving friends while remaining strangely and infinitely foreign to each other—an "encounter" par excellence.[2]

The fragmentary *Moscow Diary*, the text of a friendship of strange friends, is Benjamin's longest surviving confessional document and holds a unique place among the texts of his autobiographical corpus. Its narrative gestures of free indirect discourse register, with much less aphoristic density than is typical for his other autobiographical writings, strings of frustrations and moments of consternation, from the long, harsh walks through the icy and overcrowded streets of Moscow to Benjamin's personal isolation during theater performances that he cannot understand or even during domino games. Its gloomy descriptions, encrypted in a series of chronologically organized dated entries, of mostly quotidian aspects of life in the wintry Russian capital appear more paratactical and tentative than the *Berlin Chronicle*, and much less ornate and hermetically sealed than the allegorical prose snapshots of the *Berlin Childhood around 1900*, those elegant "fairy-tale photographs," as Adorno called them, which Benjamin continued to polish until shortly before his suicide.[3] In its rhetorical gestures of the everyday and the obsessively mundane, the *Moscow Diary* reads like the Russian literature of Benjamin's Moscow, namely, as he puts it in "The Political Formation of Russian Writers" (published a month after his Moscow stay), as "nothing but baroque." This is so because of the "blatancy" of the material and its strange "predominance of materiality [*des Stofflichen*]" (2:744). The reader of the diary, too, registers a tendency, as Benjamin observes in the closely related "On the Situation of Russian Film," to wrest what is vital from life itself (*"ohne dekorativen und schauspielerischen Apparat schlechtweg dem Leben selber abzugewinnen"*; 2:749). As a self-absorbed travelogue, the *Moscow Diary* makes few concessions to the demands of its readers. Instead, it replaces the narrative momentum of a story line with obsessive meditations on, say, Russian culture, weather, politics, toys, literature, and uncommon women's fashion (for instance, those loose-fitting felt boots which, by comparison, suddenly give tight-fitting Western boots the air, as Benjamin says, of both intimacy and seediness). Such meditations tend to be interlaced with highly personal reflections on food, film, and erotic frivolity. Formally, the *Moscow Diary* unfolds paratactically by juxtaposing individual impressions and images without coordinating or subordinating one to the other. Thematically, the text ranges from incisive commentaries on Stalinist politics and discussions that Benjamin had with specific revolutionary cultural producers such as Mayakovsky, Bely, or Lelevich, to the bafflement Benjamin experiences when confronted by the journalistic practices of the daily newspaper *Vecherniaia Moskva* (to which he had granted an interview that was, however, published only in disfigured form), or even when he and Lacis, having stumbled onto a film set, accidentally become the witnesses of an ongoing film shoot in the snowy streets of Moscow. Finally, Benjamin's laconic prose and terse syntax in the *Moscow Diary* bespeak the abiding frustration of an intellectual in a foreign metropolis whose language is not his own and whose constellation of images, unlike those of Berlin and Paris, remains largely illegible. After all, to the foreign reader, the text that is the city never appears self-identical. "Nowhere does Moscow look," Benjamin notes in his Moscow travel essay, "like the city itself" (R 125; 4:343).

Moscow and/as the Corpus

Although the possibilities of the body—including its feebleness, its unreliability, and its repulsive qualities—had been an ongoing concern to Benjamin, during the year of his trip to Moscow he intensified his theoretical preoccupation with the concept of the body and with its narrative and philosophical inflections.[4] We can find what is at stake here condensed in the formulations that link writing and the body. "In the moment of introspection, there occurs, rather fleetingly," he writes in his so-called drug protocols of 1927, the year of the *Moscow Diary*, "something like a desire to stylize one's self, one's body [*sich selber, seinen Körper zu stilisieren*]" (6:559). The self and its body are to be "stylized," that is, staged in a specific aesthetic pattern they did not possess before. It is because the body becomes attuned to itself that it can be stylized. The body must be stylized also because to style it is to remain faithful to what it is—to what is proper to it. But what "style" here also encodes is the Latin *stilus*, which is "an instrument made of metal, bone, etc., having one end sharp-pointed for incising letters on a wax-tablet, and the other flat and broad for smoothing the tablet and erasing what is written" (OED). Benjamin's phrase links the body both to its inscription as a text and to the undoing or erasing of that corporeal text. That this image of the written body, moreover, is vitally intertwined with the status of the self that signs or underwrites a text, becomes clear in several meanings of the verb "to style." For "style" signifies that one has "a right to be called (so-and-so)" as well as to "sign (a letter) with one's name and title" (OED). In Benjamin's formulation, then, signing a text in which the body is staged is a precarious but crucial means by which a subject attempts to assure itself of its self-identity, of the right to be a certain somebody possessing a specific name. Therefore Benjamin's urgent question in an early note to the *Passagen-Werk*, "Am I the one who is called W. B. or am I merely called W. B.?" (5:1038), asserts the right to be called by a specific name or title in the moment of writing a "bodily" text and of then signing that text with and in one's name. But this potentially felicitous moment of becoming the signatory of a bodily text also carries within itself the threat of the undoing of this project, indeed, the eradication of the one who signs. The German *stilisieren*, according to the Grimms' dictionary, also means *erstechen*, to pierce with a stylet or execute, effectively encoding in the same signifier writing and execution. The desire to sign a bodily text corresponds in Benjamin's trope with a moment of thinking one's relation to finitude and of being haunted by death.

To stylize the body, then, which is to write, to sign, or to pierce it, means to confront the looming impossibility of this very project, a displaced name for which is "death," the execution by the stylet. Writing the body is, as it were, learning to love the ghost—precisely in the scene of writing that takes place despite the danger of its own impossibility. It is learning to love what Benjamin evokes in a 1920/21 fragment as the "skeleton of the word," that is, as the word eerily grinning back at its speaker: "Weakening of the symbolic and communicative power in the skeleton of the word. (The word is grinning)" (6:15). Under these conditions, the act of writing the body can only occur if it is not expected to result in the construction of a subject present to itself. Rather, the bodily scene of writing is linked to the self's potential displacement, its anonymity. Benjamin stresses this point in a fragment from around 1926: "The highest moral interest of the subject is: to remain anonymous to itself. 'Seigneur, donnez-moi de contempler mon coeur et mon corps sans dégout,' Baudelaire writes. This wish can only be fulfilled if the subject remains anonymous to itself. . . . The anonymity of the moral subject, then, rests on a double pre-condition. First: I have everything to expect of myself; I believe that I can do anything. Second: Though I believe that I can do anything, I can prove nothing to myself" (6:59f.). When read specifically against the backdrop of Benjamin's language of the body, this passage suggests that to write a text of the body in this way is indeed to welcome the structure of the "perhaps"—the possibility and anticipation of what is not yet the case, the love of an unknowable future. Everything is to be expected of the subject, for example, the future construction of a legible self in writing a bodily text. But the historical traces upon which the subject could base such hopeful expectations are indecipherable. This welcoming of the perhaps and of the future thus can be regarded as the condition of possibility for Benjamin's writing (about) the body. In the language that Benjamin employs in his essay on revolutionary children's theater—the text written for Lacis—this welcoming, this love, is, perhaps, "the *secret* signal of what is to come [*das* geheime *Signal des Kommenden*]" (P 32; 2:769).

Reading the *Moscow Diary*, one can hardly fail to be startled by its rhetoric of the body. Emphasizing the link that Benjamin's essay "Moscow" establishes between the material, physiological character of the Russian city and its potential legibility ("Every thought, every day, and every life here lies on a laboratory table" [R 106; 4:325]), the diary is suffused with long physiological descriptions, minute bodily observations, and astute corporeal reflections which, taken together, yield a special physiognomy of the Russian capital and its characters, something on the order of "Moscow's signature" (MD 17; 6:298). To begin with, the experience of the city sensitizes the narrator in an unexpected way to his physiological being, making his own body symptomatically conspicuous. Benjamin notices the irreducible phenomenon of bodily pain, his "stomach ache [*Leibschmerzen*]" (MD 92; 6:378) and his relentless "back pains" (MD 120; 6:408); he is "freezing horribly" (MD 80; 6:365) and is constantly subject to an abnormal fatigue, often being "very tired," able to follow conversations "only with half an ear" (MD 10; 6:293). Under these new conditions, even his normal physical functioning is strangely out of joint, so that "[m]y hair is very electric here" (*MD* 18; 6:300). The frosty conditions of the Russian winter climate force Benjamin to devise ever new ways to ensure the survival of his body. For the body, the time of warmth is the time of life. This is what Benjamin tells us in his Moscow essay when, suggesting that warmth turns time itself into ecstasy, he finally reaches a restaurant and orders a glass of vodka and a cup of tea: "Warmth turns fleeting time itself into a drink of ecstasy. It flows into the tired one like honey" (*R* 129; 4:347). The narrating self here experiences a sensitization to the complex somatic signifying system that is its body.

In a little-known introductory text from 1 May 1927, which was intended as a preface to the (eventually aborted) contemporary publication of excerpts from the *Moscow Diary*, Benjamin states in no uncertain terms that the overall framework of the text is the one constructed by the masterful reader of the body, the physiognomist: "It is in the same sense that I visited Moscow at the beginning of this year and lived there for two months. . . . The following pieces are excerpts from a diary that I kept without interruption for eight weeks. In them I have tried to capture the image of proletarian Moscow that one only knows if one has also seen it under snow and ice; I have attempted to capture *primarily the physiognomy* . . . and the new rhythm" (6:782; emphasis added). "Primarily the physiognomy": the gaze of the material anthropologist is thus in Benjamin's Moscow project that of the cultural physiognomist, the shrewd decipherer of the vital signs of both the body politic and the bodily selves that inhabit it. Likewise, in the 1927 essay "New Russian Literature," in which Benjamin draws extensively on his experiences with Russian culture during his stay in Moscow a few months earlier, he stresses the physiological dimension that interests him. His remarks concerning Russian literature apply as well to his own "Russian" text, the *Moscow Diary*: "Contemporary Russian Literature fulfills the physiological task of liberating the body of the people from the excess of materials, experiences, and constructions," a process which, invoking the image of monstrous bodily excretion, Benjamin terms "a horrible process of excretion [*ein ungeheurer Auscheidungsprozeß*]" (2:761). It is in this sense, too, that Benjamin, in his travel essay, speaks of Moscow's poor as "a corporation of the dying" (*R* 105; 4:324).

Along these same lines, Benjamin registers with utmost precision the bodily shapes and forms of people and images around him in the semiotic web of Moscow. He comments upon the cruelty of the generally "uninhibited exploitation of physical force" (*MD* 31; 6:313) in the Russian capital and describes, anticipating a passage on the wrinkled face in his essay on Proust, his acquaintance Roth's face as "creased with wrinkles." It possesses "the unpleasant look of a snoop" (*MD* 30; 6:311). He depicts an image of Christ in terms of a physiological absence, the holy icon being "bereft of genitals" (*MD* 26; 6:307). Likewise, he renders a painfully minute physiognomist's description of his friend Reich's jaw cramps, during which the latter's "gums were inflamed and an abscess had developed" (*MD* 87; 6:373). Benjamin's topographical impressions of the city, that is, the implicit identification of its difference from the Western metropolitan cities with which he is intimately familiar, are staged as bodily metaphors: "But the crosses atop the domes often resemble gigantic earrings attached to the sky." And, as Benjamin continues, taking up the image of Reich's diseased mouth, "The luxury that has lodged itself in this impoverished, suffering city like tartar in a diseased mouth: the N. Kraft chocolate store" (*MD* 22; 6:304). Even the political tradition of repression that Benjamin senses in Moscow is figured in the language of the body, culminating in the summation "how servility is still lodged in people's bones here" (*MD* 120; 6:408). This is why what interests Benjamin in Russian commercial establishments and companies are the colorful posters and warning signs depicting the dangers of various machines to physical health. As we read in the Moscow essay, "One worker is portrayed with his arm caught between the spokes of a driving wheel, another, drunk, causing an explosion with a short circuit, a third with his knee stuck between two pistons" (*R* 123; 4:341). Hence one could say that the identity of the city and its inhabitants is vitally mediated, before the physiognomist's gaze, by the body politic, in both a concrete and figurative sense. The gesture that illuminates the historical scenario of the city of Moscow in the late 1920s—on the ambivalent eve of the Revolution's transformation into full-fledged Stalinism—through the subtle reading of its physiognomy, enacts what Benjamin later theorizes in the *Passagen-Werk* as the very process of historiography, namely, that to "write history means to give dates their physiognomy" (*N* 67; 5:595).

Yet, while Benjamin describes the body as a hermeneutic machine, it is simultaneously unreliable as an understandable constellation of signs. On the level of the human body, there is Benjamin's depiction of Lelevich, the Moscow writer and critic: "His appearance is quite difficult to describe. Fairly tall, wearing a blue Russian tunic, he makes few movements. . . . The most curious thing is his long, apparently unarticulated face with its broad planes. His chin is far longer than any I have ever seen, except for the one on the invalid Grommer, and it is barely cleft. He appears to be very calm, but one senses in him the gnawing silence of the fanatic" (*MD* 14f.; 6:296). Although the writer is a towering presence, his physiognomy remains unreadable—it is, we are told, "unarticulated." The "grammar" of his face, its bodily syntax, is strangely disturbed. His broad, long, and flat face lacks contours—or editing, as it were—and it is not crisp or formed enough to be decodable. It confronts the narrator with a bodily text that he cannot understand. This unreadability of the body is allegorized as well in Lacis's narratives, in which she repeatedly speaks to Benjamin of physical mutilation: "For the second time I heard the story about the child in her care who had had his skull bashed in by another" (*MD* 21; 6:303). The disfiguration of the body names both a concrete mutilation and the dissolution of a narrative figure—the protagonist of Lacis's story—which would enable hermeneutic understanding.

To the extent that in the 1920s Benjamin became increasingly obsessed with the problem of the body, it was essential to him while writing the *Moscow Diary*, and an examination of the document from the perspective of the body should therefore help us understand Benjamin's theory of *physis*. Indeed, in a letter to Hugo von Hofmannsthal from June 1927, Benjamin emphasizes that in his writings connected with the Moscow journey he was primarily interested in the concrete, physical modes of being he had encountered in the Soviet capital, precisely "those concrete phenomena of daily life which affected me most deeply"—they are part of what in Moscow he found incommensurable ("even far more incommensurable than I had expected") (*C* 314; *B* 443f.). Along these same lines, in a letter to Martin Buber that again discusses his Moscow text, Benjamin stresses within the bodily, creaturely preoccupation of the project not only its theological dimension (in response to Hermann Cohen and the Marburg neo-Kantians) but also, implicitly, its theoretical or semiotic one: "I can assure you of one thing . . . my presentation will be devoid of all theory. I hope to succeed in thereby letting the creaturely [*das Kreatürliche*] speak." And then, citing Goethe,

Benjamin continues: "I intend to render a presentation . . . in which 'all factuality is already theory'" (*C* 313; *B* 442f.).[5] Benjamin here not only alludes to the privileging of documentary-style literature and art—advocated in Soviet Russia primarily by the editors of *Left Front* and the surrealist branches of the Soviet Constructivists, and in Germany by the movement in photography termed Neue Sachlichkeit or New Matter-of-Factness[6]—but he also encrypts the avoidance of theory that in the *Passagen-Werk* he explains by invoking his strategic preference for montage: "Method of this work: literary montage. I have nothing to say. Only to show. I will purloin nothing valuable and will appropriate no witty formulations. But the rags, the garbage: I do not want to make an inventory of them but rather to do justice to them in the only way possible—to use them" (*N* 47; 5:574).[7] This deliberate avoidance of theoretical commentary is in the letter to Buber, precisely in the narrative advent of the bodily creature, extended as an autobiographical gesture toward a flight from theory, conceived in this quasi-Kantian way also because a theoretical system no longer suffices to delimit and tame the body, the uncontrollable other which may not coincide with its theoretical image. The body for Benjamin is an alterity that is intimately familiar and infinitely strange all at once: indeed, this is so, as we recall, because "the most forgotten strangeness is our body—our own body" (*I* 132; 2:431).

But something else is at stake in Benjamin's apparent avoidance of theory. If his presence in Moscow permits the thinking of a mode of presentation that is "devoid of all theory," then "this does not mean," as Derrida reminds us, that "the purely descriptive text that results will be atheoretical." On the contrary, this "means that the theory, the theoremes, the very meaning will not be due to the intervention, the 'construction,' the projection of the author-subject; in a word, they will not be constituted, a phenomenologist would say, by Benjamin." But this also means that the "facts are theoremes in themselves; it is enough to *describe* them, which is also to say, to *relate* the referent, since it is history that is in question, so that theory is produced by the very 'object' of description, as the very meaning of the things themselves. This meaning presents itself in the presentation of self that the 'presentation' of Moscow would have to be" ("Back from Moscow" 227). Theoretical presentations of the self and its body would then be inseparable from the empirical or factual presentations of the objects that present their own theories precisely through the movement by which they seek to conceal them.

If the creaturely body relentlessly inscribes itself in Benjamin's autobiographical text, then it is no accident that Benjamin wished to reformulate parts of his travel text as a contribution to a journal edited by Buber, who had commissioned Benjamin to write a critical city portrait—an essay which was eventually published as "Moscow." Benjamin seems to have chosen the venue of publication for his Moscow essay rather well, for Buber's journal was entitled *Die Kreatur*. In that essay Benjamin again addresses the theme of the creaturely, the physical dimension that commanded his interest in the Russian capital. Here, he emphasizes, for instance, the physical experience of crowds and claustrophobia in public transportation (*R* 111; 4:330), or the Moscow sleighs that present "an incomparable experience for the sense of touch" (*R* 112; 4:331). Likewise, it is hardly an accident that "Russian Toys," an essay closely related to his Moscow journey, makes a point of registering, not without ironically allusive concern, that one of the prime materials for Russian toys is "bone" and that among favorite toy items one finds "huge groups of monsters" (*MD* 124; 4:624). The "creaturely," physiological approach Benjamin suggests here points to what is at stake in the *Moscow Diary*, namely, the alterity of the body. In his discussion of the general Benjaminian moment of the "expressionless," Menninghaus suggests that Benjamin urges a deconstruction of the representational or imagistic readability of the body; for Benjamin, "as far as self-perception is concerned, the body is, philosophically speaking, monstrous. It disfigures any possible image of itself as a figured entirety; in this sense, it is as much without images [*bilderlos*] as the ethical being of humans" ("Das Ausdruckslose" 59).

Lacis and the Corpus of the Other

In these corporeal preoccupations of the *Moscow Diary*, the eroticized body of Lacis is not only Benjamin's object of passionate desire, it also works to condense allegorically in a single body the more general preoccupation with the corpus that traverses the entire text. If Lacis represents to Benjamin both the carnal ecstasy of lived experience and the erotic pleasure of the act of writing, then we might, borrowing a concept from Roland Barthes's meditation on the erotics of writing, think of Lacis as a kind of "tmesis" (*Pleasure of the Text* 10ff.). A tmesis is simultaneously the source and figure of pleasure. Lacis is readable as a tmesis precisely because, as a *source*, she both embodies the quickening of sexual desire and becomes the elusive narrative *figure* that attempts to name that desire rhetorically.

The intense desire that Lacis arouses in Benjamin informs his entire text. From the very outset of their Moscow reunion, Benjamin does not fail to comment upon her body. For instance, he remarks apropos of her face: "We had only been underway a few minutes, driving down the broad Tverskaia with its gleam of snow and mud, when Asja waved to us from the side of the street. Reich got out and walked the short remaining distance to the hotel, we took the sleigh. Asja did not look beautiful, wild beneath her Russian fur hat, her face somewhat puffy from all the time she had spent bed-ridden" (*MD* 9; 6:292). Though the narrating voice here seems, at first sight, to focus its commentary upon the absence of anticipated beauty, it does not fail subtly to notice the "wild" and possibly passionate face under the enormous Russian fur hat. (In the *Passagen-Werk*, Benjamin elaborates on the erotic possibilities of a woman's hat.)[8] And when she touches his neck, her hand triggers his awareness of prolonged sexual frustration: "Suddenly I felt her hand on my neck. My coat collar had gotten turned up and she was folding it back into place. At this contact I realized just how long it had been since any hand had touched me with gentleness" (*MD* 57; 6:342).

Supplementing attempts at direct physical contact, Benjamin's erotic attraction to Lacis is frequently expressed through the act of reading. Indeed, the mystique and eroticism of reading mediates their economy of desire. Consider, for instance, the following scene in Lacis's room: "Then we go to Asja's. Maybe it was only then that the domino game took place. In the evening, both Reich and Asja intended to drop by my place. But only Asja came. I gave her presents: blouse, pants. We talk. I observe that she basically forgets nothing that involves us. (That afternoon she had told me she thought that I was doing well. That it was not true that I was going through a crisis.) Before she leaves, I read her the section on wrinkles from *One-Way Street*. Then I help her into her galoshes" (*MD* 15; 6:297). Here, as in numerous other scenes throughout the diary, Benjamin reads from his own texts. Citing from his own writing, he speaks and does not speak directly, constantly quoting his previous language to Lacis. He speaks indirectly, only "in his name," as though through and for an

Fig. 5. Portrait of Asja Lacis, 1918. Reprinted from *Asja Lacis, Revolutionär im Beruf*. Ed. Hildegard Brenner. Munich: Rogner and Bernhard, 1971. Reproduced by Medical Photography, University of Wisconsin, Madison.

other that is also himself. It seems that Benjamin's relation to the desired Lacis can only be sustained in this highly mediated linguistic performance.

In numerous passages in the *Moscow Diary*, reading from his own writing is Benjamin's mode of simulated intercourse with Lacis. His own writing is his potency even when he is empirically impotent. For Benjamin, touching structurally corresponds to the reading of his writing. It is his way of penetrating Lacis with language, of inhabiting her being. Identifying writing and the body through the erotics of reading, Benjamin comes to her in the body of writing.

If Benjamin attempts to dwell in Lacis's body through reading and interpretation, he echoes this scenario in a letter to Gretel Adorno from 12 October 1939, the only document he wrote during his months as a prisoner in the French internment camp. There, he records a nightly epiphany in which he experienced the act of reading texts and the sight of a beautiful woman's body as one thing.[9] Benjamin writes:

> I had such a beautiful dream while lying on my cot last night that I am unable to resist my desire to tell you about it. There are so few beautiful, not to mention pleasant, things about which I can tell you. This is one of those dreams, the likes of which I may have once every five years, that center around the motif of "reading." . . . The women with whom Dausse lived were here . . . and they were very beautiful. . . . Meanwhile, one of the women was engaged with graphology. I saw that she was holding something I had written. . . . I was somewhat worried by her graphological analysis because I feared that some of my personal characteristics might be revealed. I went closer.

As Benjamin continues:

> [S]omething intriguing happened. I noticed that one of the women who was very beautiful was lying on a bed. When she heard my explanation, she made an extremely rapid movement. She pushed aside a bit of the blanket that was covering her as she lay in bed. It took her less than a second to do this. It was not to let me see her body, but to see the pattern of her sheet. The sheet must have had imagery similar to the kind I had probably "written" years ago. . . . I was quite aware that the woman had made this gesture. But the reason I was aware of it was because of a kind of extrasensory perception. For

140

my bodily eyes where somewhere else. And I was not at all able to distinguish what was on the sheet that had been surreptitiously revealed to me. After this dream, I could not fall asleep for hours. Out of happiness. (*C* 614f.; B 828ff).

In this scenario, Benjamin once again stresses the erotic dimension of reading and writing. The displacement of desire onto the textual not only heightens sexual experience, for Benjamin's textual being it also *is* this experience. This is why he focuses his gaze on the imagery—pictures or tropes—of the "written" sheet on which the woman lies rather than directly on her body itself. But what mediates his desire is that she revels in the textual material that *he* has produced, even when in the sexual moment its meaning remains out of reach. Like in the many scenes in the *Moscow Diary* in which Benjamin reads to Lacis from his own work, he intertwines sex with the reading and interpreting of texts. Benjamin thinks a deferral of desire and meaning that is articulated through the body's inaccessibility, whether this deferral occurs with regard to the body of Lacis or to that of language itself. Benjamin's self is always the one that arises in relation to the unavailability of either. And the very letter that contains this scenario, addressed to another woman, works to reenact the logic its content evokes.

Beyond the erotics of reading, the narrating voice's desire for the erotic other is mediated in the *Moscow Diary* by a broad spectrum of experiences and scenarios. From the beginning of the text, for instance, Benjamin craves to be alone with Lacis: "Here we were alone together for the first time under the same roof for a few minutes. Asja was looking at me very affectionately" (*MD* 10; 6:292). And later: "For a few minutes Asja and I were alone. All I remember is that I said the words 'preferably forever' and that she laughed so hard at this that I realized she had understood" (*MD* 28; 6:310). Lacis's prescribed stay in a forest sanatorium is postponed for Benjamin's sake (*MD* 22; 6:304), and there are numerous scenes in which Lacis, strolling through Moscow with Benjamin, exhibits interest in items of clothing such as fur coats and folk dresses. Benjamin is fascinated with these scenarios, though he typically lacks the means to purchase the items for Lacis (*MD* 22; 6:304). Likewise, he is infatuated with the unusual snow crystals forming on her coat (*MD* 57; 6:343), and the brief flashes of physical contact with Lacis elate him: "I quickly sketched out the overall scheme I had in mind and as I explained it to her she pressed her forehead close against mine" (*MD* 82; 6:367), as if in a kind of literalized telepathy. Along these same lines, he attempts to arouse her by reading to her a lesbian scene from Proust (*MD* 93; 6:379) and feels a special attraction to her when, upon learning that his *Trauerspiel* book was rejected by the University of Frankfurt as a habilitation thesis, he exchanges comforting glances with her and feels, in this odd moment of crisis, "a sense of security" (*MD* 43; 6:326). After obscure quarrels between the two, Lacis unexpectedly embraces him, and "for this 'impertinence,' she kissed me, even hugging me in the process" (*MD* 27; 6:309). He is distracted by her, his desiring gaze crowding out all other senses: "This often happens to me: I barely hear what she is saying because I am looking at her so intently" (*MD* 21; 6:303). She playfully blows him a kiss (*MD* 112; 6:399) and even inscribes an egg with the name "Benjamin" (*MD* 46; 6:329). This scenario is reminiscent of Benjamin's observation in *One-Way Street* regarding the eroticization of lovers' names: "Two people who are in love are attached above all else to their names" (*W* 467; 4:119). Beyond this inscription of the eroticized name, a speaker of German can hardly miss the sexual connotation of this symbolic gesture, the colloquial term for testicles being *Eier* (eggs). Even tough she figuratively castrates Benjamin by presenting him with only one egg or testicle—even identifying his being with a state of impotence by engraving the very signature of his identity, his name, into the object of his allegorical castration—she subverts this impotence with a moment of renewed potency. For the egg is also part of the Easter ritual, a religious celebration of the resurrection. This scenario could be read as Lacis's provocation of Benjamin's res-erection. To celebrate the prospect of his potency she embraces him when news arrives that, ostensibly because of his wife's financial hardships back in Berlin, he will be able to prolong his stay in Moscow (*MD* 94; 6:380), a city that, as he tells her, he is capable of experiencing only through her (*MD* 94; 6:380). Consider the following symptomatic scene: "Yesterday afternoon I was in a pastry shop with Asja. They serve cups of whipped cream there. Asja had a cup with meringue, I had coffee. We sat in the middle of the room, facing each other over a small table. Asja reminded me of my intention to write something critical of psychology, and I once again realized just to what extent the possibility of tackling these subjects depends on my contact with her. At any rate, we were unable to extend our hour in the café as we had hoped" (*MD* 18; 6:299). Benjamin is thus able to engage in his intellectual projects only through this ultimate teleology of desire, even if the fulfillment of this desire is limited to watching her slowly devour cream pastries and coffee during one of their frequent visits to Moscow cafes and pastry shops. While Benjamin had registered Lacis's role as his sustenance and his intellectual "engineer" in the dedication of *One-Way Street* ("This street is named Asja Lacis Street after her who as an engineer broke it through the author" [*W* 444; 4:83]), here in the pastry shop scene their encounter is once again broken off.

Deferrals

So far, I have discussed the narrative instances in which Lacis appears as Benjamin's object of desire in a tmesis. But access to Lacis and her body is continuously deferred. In order to trace this deferral of the promise of fulfillment, we may consider the specific passage from *One-Way Street* by means of which Benjamin, reading his "section on the wrinkles" (*MD* 15; 6:297), cites himself to Lacis. The passage effectively becomes, through Benjamin's logic of intertextual citation, part of the *Moscow Diary*. It invokes the romantic, sexualized trope encoded in the wrinkles of the other's body:

> He who loves is not only attached to the "flaws" of his beloved, not only to the idiosyncrasies and weaknesses of a woman. Facial wrinkles and moles, worn-out clothes and a lopsided walk bind him much more lastingly and relentlessly than any beauty. One has long observed this. And why? If the doctrine is true that says that feeling does not nestle in the head, that we experience a window, a cloud, or a tree not in our brain but rather in the very place where we see them, then we are also beside ourselves when gazing at our beloved. But here torturously tense and ravished. Blinded, the feeling flutters like a flock of birds in a woman's radiance. And just as birds seek refuge in the leafy recesses of a tree, feelings escape into the shadowy wrinkles, the graceless gestures and inconspicuous blemishes of the beloved body, where they can hide in safety. And no passer-by would guess that here, precisely in what is defective or reprehensible, nestles the arrow-swift affection of the admirer. (*W* 449; 4:92)

In this economy of desire, wrinkles bind. Wrinkles eclipse the erratic flash of beauty and physical grace only to emerge as the true harbinger of desire. The passion aroused by viewing the other threatens to blind the gazing self. That is why the erotic passion aroused by the image of the other—staged in this trope not as internalized concept but rather as a phenomenology of experience, that is, as Benjaminian *Erlebnis* rather than *Erfahrung*—hides in the minute physical flaws and shortcomings, the blind spots of the other's body. The desiring gaze of the self does not strive to eradicate the traces of what threatens to undermine the image of its object of passion but rather tries to merge with it. For wrinkles also signal aging and an eventual departure. What Benjamin loves in the other's wrinkles is precisely the other's finitude encoded in the skin. Our relation to the wrinkles on the body of our beloved also names our relation to our own finitude, our eventual death.[10] The interruption of the economy of desire that conditions the passionate gaze of the self is hence foreclosed a priori—the possible negation of that desire's being is inverted to serve as its very condition of possibility, a corporeal *Aufhebung*, or sublation, in all senses of the word. This Benjaminian interruption is staged in the *Moscow Diary*, as we are now ready to examine, along five distinct yet interrelated trajectories: illness, rejection, impotence, interference, and the transformation of the other.

First, Lacis's illness strangely removes her from Benjamin's access. Though the particular nature of her condition is never specified— readers of Benjamin have only recently learned that the empirical Lacis was living at the Rott sanatorium near Gorky Street following a nervous breakdown in September 1926—at the beginning of the diary Asja sensitizes Benjamin to the special burden imposed by her mysterious bodily affliction. In the typically laconic style of his Moscow diary he writes that "[b]efore leaving, Asja tells the story of her illness" (*MD* 11; 6:294). Her medicinal baths disrupt the rare moments when Benjamin is allowed to visit her at the hospital because they cause fatigue: "Since morning visits are prohibited, we talk to her [Lacis] in the lobby for a minute. She is tired after the carbonic acid bath" (*MD* 16; 6:297). Thus the bath, in which Lacis's naked body is to cleanse and renew itself, actually distances it further from Benjamin. Similarly, her fatigue, coupled with the general symptomatology of her illness, prevents her from accompanying Benjamin to the theater, so that he is again forced to go by himself (*MD* 18; 6:300). By the same token, Benjamin, having enlisted her help in a translation project in an attempt to remain close to her, is told laconically that "the strain of translating was too much for her" (*MD* 25; 6:306). When Lacis's illness prevents her from keeping a date with Benjamin, he trembles: "Now I was all the more upset that Asja had not come back to my place" (*MD* 58; 6:343). The atmosphere in her sanatorium always tends to subvert Benjamin's attempts at communion with her. The description, moreover, of a psychotic patient lying in the bed next to hers assumes Beckett-like dimensions (*MD* 31; 6:313f.) and thereby intensifies Lacis's "chronic bouts of anxiety" (*MD* 45; 6:329). That the sanatorium is an obstacle to Benjamin is underlined throughout the text. He writes: "I shall not see Asja today. The situation in the sanatorium is growing critical; yesterday evening they let her leave only after protracted negotiations and this morning she did not come to fetch me as previously arranged. We were planning to buy material for her dress. I have only been here for a week and already I have to confront the ever-increasing difficulties of seeing her, not to mention of seeing her alone" (*MD* 21; 6:302f.). The sanatorium thus emerges as the site of a paradox. While its ostensible function is to heal and strengthen Lacis's body and to return it to its world in an improved and healed condition, it is also instrumental in making her body increasingly inaccessible. The following image of Lacis embodies this dilemma perhaps most fully: "Over her dress Asja wears a gray woolen sanatorium smock" (*MD* 46; 6:329). This image outlines the movement by which Lacis's illness makes her illegible and inaccessible. To the narrator's gaze, her eroticized body is utterly indeterminate under the thick layers of "illness-clothing." Here, her elegant dress—the part of her wardrobe to which she pays particular attention throughout the text—is disfigured by the gray, shapelessly coarse wool coat of the sanatorium. The coarse hospital coat functions as a veil that obscures vision and perception, a veil incapable of being removed in order to reveal what is hidden at the core.

In this sense, the perception of the body cannot yield the apperception of (or be encompassed by) something sublime. It belongs to the order of what Benjamin calls the creaturely. As he explains in his reading of Goethe's *Elective Affinities*, "the more distinctly this duality [of nakedness and veiling] expresses itself in order finally to confirm itself as the highest within the human being, the clearer it becomes that, in the veilless nakedness, the essentially beautiful has vanished and that, in the naked body of the human being, a being beyond all beauty is reached—the sublime" (W 351; 1:196). According to this view, a body draped in a coarse hospital coat is not the unveiled nudity of the sublime. All that this body can be is a merely "essential" beauty, which is to say, precisely not the unveiled, hovering sublime. Lacis's thickly disguised body remains on the creaturely, merely material circumference of the sublime. Here, the body can be read as one of the names of the sublime's uncanny other.

This moment of physical deferral or inaccessibility within the *Moscow Diary* is further staged in Lacis's frequent gestures of rejection, renunciation, and negation. It is no accident that Benjamin comments on this economy of rejection while pondering a garment on her body: "Conversation about the ochre-yellow Italian scarf she is wearing. I explain to her that she feels uneasy in my presence" (*MD* 16; 6:298). What is at stake is more than what the narrator, perhaps somewhat naively, reduces to "embarrassment," for Lacis's physical rejections of his advances appear strategically playful and consistent. A prime example of her physical rejections can be located in her subtle denial of the kiss: "I was writing my diary and had given up hope that Asja would stop by. Then she knocked. As she entered the room, I wanted to kiss her. As usual, it proved unsuccessful. . . . Another failed attempt to kiss her" (*MD* 27; 6:309). And in a parallel scene, on New Year's Eve, "I asked her . . . for one last kiss in the old year. She would not give me one. I turned back, now, on New Year's, lonely after all" (*MD* 57f.; 6:343).

The Problem of the Touch

Lacis's withholding of the kiss, the most intimate and semiotically significant of all touches, naturally presupposes the possibility of kissing, of touching the other during an encounter in the first place. But that is a problematic presupposition, for in a certain sense the possibility of touching the other's body, and of being touched by the other's body, does not exist. Or, more precisely, the possibility of touching the specific body of a certain, self-identical other is not a given. If there is a space or being "behind" a face—assuming that this space or being can be identified or named—then that "being behind," at odds with itself, is already outside of, or absent from, its face.[11] For the "being behind" exists in the alterity between, on the one hand, the multitude of thoughts, languages, and differences that is its being and, on the other hand, the eyes, ears, bones, skin, lips and so forth that conspire to yield part of its corporeal "image." To touch, then, is to "touch" part of the physical image of an other whose alterity from that image is not contained or delimited by the touch. Our touch is thus thrice removed from the being of the other: first, what we touch is merely one possible sur-face of an other who does not necessarily coincide with that sur-face and whose being cannot be contained by it; second, what we touch when we touch the other is part of the *image* that we have of the other and its body, not its "actual" body as it is when no one is looking; third, the image of the other's body being touched is not the "actual" image of that body but rather our very specific construction of the image of the other's body, a construction perhaps precariously distorted by our desire, our language, our history. There is never an unproblematic "touch" of the body—at least not of an identifiable someone.

To touch the other's body—in the case of lovers like Benjamin and Lacis, a gesture of desired physical intimacy and proximity—may thus emerge as an aporetic experience. Once an "I" touches an other during an encounter, this "I" enters a relation which may result in a loss of self-identity. The sensations, thoughts, and significations that overwhelm the "I" in the process of touching the other render it different from the "I" that first decided to initiate this touching. Likewise, the other reveals itself to the "I" as a ghostly alterity—for the "I," in the moment of the touch, senses that what is being touched is not identical with the image of the other and its body that were once encoded in the mind of the "I." The touch is thus not the signatory of the self-identity of the self and of the other—though certain effects of love, desire, and proximity may be called forth temporarily—but rather the site of a triple metamorphosis: the self metamorphoses during the touch; the other reveals itself to be a radical alterity, indeterminably different from its face or image; and, on a more structural level, the moment of the touch, intended to yield a hitherto unachieved *proximity*, actually metamorphoses into something that shows the unbridgable alterity between self and other. It produces the greatest and most irreducible *distance*.

If these metamorphoses prompted by the touch name a distance, the touch also prepares us for an eventual absence, even the other's death. If we are nevertheless drawn to the other's body, if we desire to touch it despite the looming impossibility of the touch, then we behave like the reader of a novel who, as we learn in "The Storyteller," lives and reads in the ghostly hope "to warm his frosty life on a death" (*I* 101; 2:457). The subject that, though exposed to the uncanny alterity always already encoded in the touch, desires to touch the other, lives, like Benjamin's "destructive character," among "ruins" and debris. Here, the "willingness with which he at all times observes that everything can go wrong" is tied to the ways in which he "lives not out of the feeling that life is worth living but rather that suicide is not worth the effort" (*R* 303; 4:398). The truth of the touch is—to use a figure that Benjamin employs in a note on Rilke written in late January during his Moscow stay—a kind of eulogy, a *Totenrede*, or necrology, in which one encounters "the naked truth within naked death" (4:453). Such is the haunted space that Benjamin's and Lacis's attempts at touching inhabit. Benjamin not only delineates this space in the *Moscow Diary* but also discerns it in Proust, the master writer of the impossibility of the touch. In the essay on Proust, Benjamin speaks of Proust's stance of emphasizing the impossibility of the touch as if it were his own in the *Moscow Diary*, namely that in "friendly socializing, in conversation, there is a another gesture: the touch. This gesture is not stranger to anybody than to Proust" (*I* 212; 2:321).

Along these lines, it is no accident either that throughout the *Moscow Diary* Benjamin reads to Lacis specifically from his *One-Way Street*. For it is there that he casts the specificity of the touch's difference from itself in terms of the experience of disgust (*Ekel*)[12]: "All disgust [*Ekel*] is primarily the disgust at touching. Even a becoming-master [*Bemeisterung*] exceeds this feeling only by an erratic, excessive gesture: what is disgusting will tightly embrace it, devour it, while the zone of the lightest epidermal touch remains taboo. . . . One must not deny one's bestial kinship with the creature to whose call one's disgust responds; one must become its master" (*W* 448; 4:91). The primal feeling of disgust that inhabits touching can thus not be mastered by applying to it a rational economy of containment, for such a becoming-master (*Bemeisterung*) would only be eradicated by the disgusting. A becoming-master over the moment of tactile disgust only resides, if it exists at all, in the movement that erratically exceeds ("with an erratic, excessive gesture") the process of becoming-master, by which tactile disgust is to be overcome. The becoming-master inhabits the excess of the overcoming, which is to say, the excess of itself, the excess through which it becomes itself functionally. Only now, excessively, can it keep its promise of mastering. The moment of identity or containment is therefore also the moment of excess and non-identity. Coming to terms with the touch, then, means to learn to come to terms with an erratic excess, with a movement toward the "more" that is shared structurally by all forms of the encounter, whether in experience or in language. To acknowledge this structural excess is to respond to the monstrous call from the creature with whom we stand in bestial relation ("bestial kinship").[13]

To the extent that love and the erotic are predicated upon the distant possibility of touching, they, too, are subject to the same laws of excess and disgust as touching itself. To be subjected to excess means to be exposed to the moment of transgression in which finitude and limitation are struck. In other words, to think the specificity of this striking of the limit is to think the experience of finitude and, finally, of death. This is why in an early meditation on marriage, Benjamin writes that "eros, love, has only one direction: the common death of the lovers" (6:68). In this topography of love and the erotic, there is only one possible direction—that toward death—precisely because, if this direction is changed, say, in the moment when the experience of finitude is no longer thought or ceases to be thinkable, love and the erotic vanish. It is in this sense, too, that the direction is simultaneously labyrinthine—it follows a dazzling maze of turns or tropes—and oriented toward a specific center at which finitude itself resides: it "unravels like a thread in a labyrinth whose center is the 'chamber of death'" (6:68). The reality of love, and the love of the real, thus take place in the struggle with death and the striking of finitude, so that the experience of the limit—the looming possibility of its transgression in the form of death or perhaps of the unsayable— is the experience of love itself. "The reality of the sexual," Benjamin tells us, "enters love only when even the struggle with death becomes a struggle with love" (6:68). But as a consequence of the failure to intertwine this experience of the reality of love (and the love of the real) with the striking of finitude in love and death, eros veers off on its own, fleeing finitude instead of striking it ("flees from its own death") and thus ultimately escaping only towards the nothing. "It [the escape] leads toward the nothing, toward the misery in which life is merely a non-death and death merely a non-life" (6:68) and produces a ghostliness of the living dead. The tension between, on the one hand, striking finitude in order to intertwine death and love and, on the other hand, the movement by which sexuality itself flees from death only to enter the nothingness of the un-dead—this tension is precisely the horrible, even "monstrous danger of sexuality [*die ungeheure Gefahr der Sexualität*]" (6:69). Benjamin and Lacis encounter each other in the space of that tension. Here, the abyss itself is the ground of the encounter. As Benjamin registers in the fragment "Proximity and Distance": "This abyss is the primordial fact that is experienced in any passionate, erotic intimacy" (W 400; 6:87).

The Interfered Body

This deferral of the desired other is, moreover, a concrete function of several instances of the narrator's implied impotence. The image of impotence is not limited to the *Moscow Diary*: it appears more than once in Benjamin's corpus. As he writes in "Central Park": "Male impotence—key figure of solitude: the standstill of all productive forces occurs under its sign; an abyss separates the human being from his kind" (CP 47; 1:679). There, we also learn that for "male sexuality, impotence is the fundament of the Way to Calvary [*Passionsweg*]" (CP 36; 1:663). Benjamin first alludes to this scenario of impotence when he strolls in frustration through the disorienting streets of the Russian metropolis: "In the afternoon, I wander aimlessly through the city; I cannot come to Asja [*zu Asja kann ich nicht kommen*]" (MD 22; 6:304). While he states that he cannot visit her that afternoon, we can suggest another reading of this sentence, one which points to the sexual inhibition that will later turn out to be impotence: he cannot, climactically speaking, "come" to her or to her image. This figure of impotence is repeated in a later scenario in which Benjamin is in bed with Lacis: "Asja had me remove the letters and she lay down on the bed. We kissed at length. But the thing that excited me most deeply was the touch of her hands; she herself had in fact once told me that everybody who was attached to her felt the extremely powerful forces that emanated from her hands. I placed my right palm directly against her left one and we remained in this position for a long time. . . . Then I read her the lesbian scene from Proust. Asja grasped its wild nihilism" (MD 94; 6:380f.). In this moment of intense desire

150

("excited me most deeply"), Benjamin and Lacis cannot consummate their passion. Even though the *Moscow Diary* registers Benjamin's obsessive sexual desire, the two only hold hands. Benjamin's inability to perform is subtly implied. He decides to resort, as he so often does in the text, to reading to her—a substitutive gratification through which he works to penetrate her with language, to inhabit her being as a text. Thus, even in instances where physical deferral seems least at work, when the body of the other appears within concrete, tactile reach, a consummation of the erotic passion is out of reach. The momentary presence of the desired body weighs down on virility, and the act of reading remains fruitless as an attempt at rhetorical persuasion. Here, Benjamin literalizes the figurative axiom he had cast as the shortest thought-image of *One-Way Street*, ironically entitled "For Men": "To convince is to conquer without conception [literally, unfruitful: *Überzeugen ist unfruchtbar*]" (W 446; 4:87).[14]

This moment of impotence is further complicated as the text unfolds. Shortly after the scene on Lacis's bed, physical impotence translates into intellectual impotence in the realm of writing: "But— as is the case at this very moment—with such poor writing material that nothing comes to mind" (*MD* 101; 6:386). Later, Lacis contrasts Benjamin's current lack of virility—which he is now forced to admit— to the prowess he had once exhibited, presumably in Berlin:

> I said that I hoped things would have improved by the next time we saw each other.—You mean you'll be able again to lie on top of me twenty-four hours a day?—I said this was not exactly what I had had in mind, I was only thinking of being closer to her, of talking to her. Only if I were closer to her would this other desire then return. "How lovely," she said.—This conversation left me very unsettled all the following day, and even throughout the night. But my wish to travel had in fact been more powerful than my desire for her, even though this may very well have only been due to the many obstacles [or inhibitions, *Hemmungen*] the latter had encountered. Just as it continues to encounter them now. (*MD* 108f.; 6:394)

There is an inability to come to terms with, or to mourn properly, the state of impotence: the haunting difference from those twenty-four hours once spent making love. Instead, Benjamin seems to repress the problem, claiming instead, improbably, that he is actually only interested in talking and that his desire to travel is more intense than his desire for her (though he undoes this trope by admitting that the reason for this displaced focus of desire is most likely to be found in his own *Hemmungen* or inhibitions). The final scene of Benjamin's diary will seal this experience and figure of impotence in a teary good-bye scene in which Benjamin, kissing Lacis's hand one last time, is whisked away in a sleigh through the icy streets of Moscow.

Yet Benjamin's impotence and the inability to know the body of the other can also be understood as an implicit retreat from a certain tradition that evokes a metaphysics of presence in which the voice and word of the logos, as well as the absolute founding character of the phallus, are mobilized to guarantee the truth of an allegedly stable meaning. Derridean thought criticizes this tradition as "phallogocentrism." In a 1916 text entitled "Socrates," Benjamin himself criticizes the peculiar conflation of erotic desire and epistemophilia through the logos of the phallus as "an erection of knowledge" (W 53; 2:131).[15] If in the *Moscow Diary* this erection cannot penetrate truth because this phallus, like the body of the other or meaning itself, is always in retreat, then Benjamin's text stages a certain break with phallogocentrist delusions. Here, Benjamin remains the one who continues to strive to penetrate what cannot be penetrated, the one whose tools are never sufficient to access what is desired. He can never arrive, either in texts or in bodies.

On a rather concrete level, it is also the presence of Bernhard Reich, Lacis's steady companion, who interferes with Lacis's accessibility. Reich, the Austrian dramatist, stage director, and critic living with Lacis in Moscow, generates the double movement of granting access and sealing off. On the one hand he is instrumental in guiding Benjamin through the Russian capital, arranging tours and meetings with Moscow luminaries, translating for Benjamin, and discussing with him issues of journalism and cultural aesthetics on the eve of the Stalinist regime. But simultaneously, since the two men are in love with the same woman, Reich attempts to interfere with Benjamin's ability to see her. Two examples of this omnipresent interference will suffice to suggest the narrator's intense frustration: "They had already given her [Lacis] the injections at the sanatorium. She was as a result in a somewhat agitated state and when we were alone in the corridor (both she and I had telephone calls to make), she embraced my arm in a momentary access of her former exuberance. Reich had taken up his position in the room and was making no signs of leaving. So that even though Asja had finally come to my room in the morning once again, it was totally pointless" (*MD* 74; 6:361). Similarly, "Asja was planning to drive out to see [her daughter] Daga the following morning, so I had to take into account the possibility that I might not see her again before my departure. I kissed her. When Reich returned, Asja went into the next room to listen to the radio. I did not stay very much longer" (*MD* 120; 6:407). Benjamin had hoped to take advantage here of Lacis's excited state, especially since she showed interest in entering his physical orbit, but Reich successfully aborts this prospect. Likewise, Reich's intrusion leads, in the second example, to a form of interruption that soon drives Benjamin away altogether. Reich thus emerges paradoxically as a character that enables Benjamin's stay in Moscow pragmatically, even while he sabotages his emotional investments and the fulfillment of his desire. This is how Reich, too, inscribes himself into the text of bodily deferral.

While Reich's interference partakes of Lacis's inaccessibility rather concretely, there is a more perplexing and structural mode of deferral: namely, that of the transformation of the other. There are several scenes in the *Moscow Diary* in which Lacis as the desired other metamorphoses into an unexpected image. She metamorphoses, as it were, into something that cannot be read. (We already encountered one version of this problem in our discussion of the touch.) The person that Benjamin thought he knew and loved turns suddenly and erratically strange, both unpredictable and unfamiliar. In these moments, "Asja . . . [is] almost enigmatic" (*MD* 34; 6:317). Suddenly, we are told, "there was a short argument," and later "in the evening a tremendous quarrel broke out" (*MD* 36; 6:319). At times, the other seems so pluralized in its changes as to be no longer recognizable as the image it once was: "I have no idea why it should be that of late all the life has vanished from our being together and the gazes we exchange. But my unsettled state makes it impossible to hide the fact" (*MD* 56; 6:341). All liveliness exiled, this relationship threatens to become inexplicably mortified: it is touched by death. Lacis fails, moreover, to notice the special inscription with which Benjamin had adorned the plastic bag he gives her (*MD* 59; 344f.). And when a conversation about Lukács's historical materialism threatens to turn sour, Benjamin again attempts to read to her from his text-in-progress—ironically, the *Moscow Diary* itself—all to no avail: "So I resorted to the Moscow diary and read her random passages that happened to catch my eye. But things did not turn out well . . . 'It's all nonsense,' Asja said" (*MD* 82; 6:367). Similarly, Lacis is oddly transformed into an unreliable liar, and the enraged Benjamin "finally, beside myself with anger, told her that she had lied to me" (*MD* 84; 6:369). In this way the other's perpetual transformations participate in its continual deferral. Lacis is both present and absent. She is the one who will not remain herself.

Elaborating on the problem of the touch discussed earlier, we may now add the observation that the other is not only an other to us but also, at least from our perspective, to itself. The other inhabits us as an image. The vast heterogeneity of impressions created by or projected upon the other is condensed into a single figure. But in the moment of contact with the other, the other fails to coincide with, to remain congruent with, our image of it. The other is thus always already pluralized and at odds with itself. Were we to adjust our image of the other according to our most recent impressions, it would just as soon have transformed itself yet again—during a conversation, perhaps, or by some change in physical appearance, or by an unexpected act. The very fact of having to reconfigure an other's image—another image—would already in itself, regardless of the specific turn it took, alter our relation to that other which would cease to be what we once thought it was. As Nietzsche observes, when "we have to change our opinion about someone we hold the inconvenience he has therewith caused us greatly to his discredit" (*Beyond Good and Evil* 125). This problem of the transforming other never leaves Benjamin. It stays with him in the figure of Asja Lacis.[16]

If the corpus of Lacis is the other who refuses to remain itself, this refusal is also the condition of possibility for desire. Benjamin's eros dwells in the abyss of the contradiction that is linked to this refusal. On the one hand, there is the desire to magnify the self by merging with the other (by engulfing, consuming, or appropriating it). On the other hand, there is the necessity of perpetuating desire through distance and separation.[17] As Benjamin writes in a fragment, proximity and distance are the vexing poles of erotic life. For him, the "life of eros is ignited by distance. On the other hand, there is an affinity between proximity and sexuality" (W 397; 6:83) so that "what is decisive in love is presence and separation" (W 400; 6:86). Here, erotic love exists only elliptically. It is suspended between the drive toward an affirmation of the self through the gentle eradication of the difference between self and other and the torturous yet vital radicalization of that difference as distance.[18]

That Benjamin would interlace his more general meditations on the body with a private experience of it can be understood in terms of the segment "Betting Office" in *One-Way Street*. There, Benjamin stresses the significance of undoing the exclusive "regime of private affairs" which, in its sinister philistinism housing "the most shabby instincts," strives to perpetuate the false binarism of public and private. Instead, Benjamin works radically to transform the private into the public in a politically charged way, that is, to expose "the privatization of one's love life" as ideologically questionable to such a degree that the historical and political signification of the subjective body becomes fully visible. This is Benjamin's strategic "transposition of the erotic into the public sphere" (W 485; 4:144), in which the personal and immediate body also names the public and historical body. For Benjamin, the simultaneous availability and unavailability of the other's body in the *Moscow Diary* is shared by the relationship of the body to history more generally. The language of the eroticized body in the *Moscow Diary* shares with the historical body the movement by which the desire to master or control the corpus is either impossible or violent, linked to decline. Because the body that Benjamin stages is always already something else, and because these constant shifts are historically and politically inscribed, the corpus emerges not only as an alterity that vexes the self but also as one that, like the *Leibraum*, or body-space, of *One-Way Street*, cannot easily be mobilized by this or that political force. Here, the private body also interacts with, but remains an other to, public ideologies such as Marxism and fascism.

Letting Go of the Corpus

To say that the body is constantly shifting is also to question the status of the self that encounters this body. How does the self respond to these moments of crisis? What is at stake for Benjamin in the moment when the corpus that does not remain itself is captured by his interpretation of "presence of mind" (*Geistesgegenwart*)? Presence of mind is linked to the corpus in crisis. As Benjamin defines presence of mind in a fragment from 1931, "to have presence of mind means:

to let oneself go in the moment of danger" (6:207). Presence of mind thus names not the subject's conscious attentiveness in the moment of crisis. Rather, in the rhetorical figure of *sich gehen lassen*, "to let oneself go" in the face of danger is a loosening of hypervigilance. Simultaneously, this loosening is a taking leave of oneself as a conscious, autonomous subject. This kind of *presence* of mind is thus at the same time an *absence* of mind. It is a presence insofar as the letting go is staged within a consciousness. It is an absence insofar as the result of this radical letting go is the negation or withdrawal of the subject's intentionality.[19] The truth of *Geistesgegenwart* or presence of mind thus unfolds in the space between the presence and absence of mind and intention.

In *One-Way Street* Benjamin establishes the interrelation of *Geistesgegenwart* and the body as follows: "But one does not switch the intentions unpunished or hand the unlived life over to cards, spirits, and stars, which live and use it up immediately and then return it to us disfigured; one does go unpunished for cheating the body of its power. . . . To transform the threat of the future into a fulfilled now— this is the only desirable telepathic miracle effected by a corporeal presence of mind [*leibhaftiger Geistesgegenwart*]" (W 483; 4:142). *Geistesgegenwart*, according to Benjamin, is *leibhaft*, or corporeal. Only through this corporeality of presence of mind, we are told, can the threat of the future be transformed—"telepathically"—into the lived experience of the "now." *Geistesgegenwart* as the simultaneous presence and absence of mind is enacted corporeally. As Benjamin writes in "The Way to Success in Thirteen Theses," the fact that "the secret of success dwells not in *Geist* is betrayed by language and the word '*Geistesgegenwart*.' That is, neither the 'that' nor the 'how' is decisive, but solely the '*where*' of *Geist*. It manages to be present at any given moment in a space only by merging into the tone of a voice, a smile, a falling silent, the gaze, and the gesture. For presence of *Geist* is only achieved by the body" (4:352).[20] To say that presence of mind is a presence of body is to say that the former is the opposite of what it names on the surface, and *Geist* is canceled by *Leib* (Weidmann, "Das Spiel" 532). But it also means that there can be no presence of the self's mind that does not strive to come to terms with the very movement through which its intellectual faculties are constantly shifting, namely, the motoric function of the body itself. For Benjamin, the material body is thus also a thinking body.

The body therefore enacts certain movements of thought—not in the sense that it simply carries out what has been decided by the mind but that it takes over certain shifts and realignments without which there could be no thinking. In a 1932 thought-image we learn that what must happen for such a corporeal enactment to take place is "that the will, within the space of the body, abdicates once and for all in favor of the organs—the hand, for example. . . . The hand has taken the situation over and has, by a flick of the wrist [*im Handumdrehen*], formed an agreement with it" (4:406f.), so that finally "the body and each of its limbs may act according to the hand's reason" (4:406). A gesture such as a flick of the wrist, in which the hand is no longer under the conscious control of the mind, but rather, now "severed," acts autonomously, is the enactment of the simultaneity of presence and absence of mind on the stage of the body. Benjamin here echoes the theory of the autonomous, unpredictable hand that he stages in the context of "The Lucky Hand," a thought-image concerning the gestures and movements of cunning card gamblers (4:771ff.).[21] Such declarations of independence by individual body parts presuppose the prior dismemberment of the unified corpus: already in an early fragment entitled "Death" (ca. 1920) the continuous body dramatically "passes away" and "shatters"; it "explodes," becoming "invalid" and "superfluous," so that, as in the case of the flick of the wrist, "the seemingly whole (unified) individual does not matter" (6:71). As Bettine Menke rightly suggests, Benjamin's *Handumdrehen* or *Handgriff* can be read as the figure of an encounter with the future that threatens to turn into a moment of danger or crisis— a figure that manifests a corporeal presence of mind (*Sprachfiguren* 352).[22]

We can now understand why Benjamin, in the passage from *One-Way Street*, continues thus: "In primitive times, when such behavior was part of every-day human experience, the naked body represented to man the most reliable instrument of divination. . . . Whatever was about to transform itself into a sign of horror, or an image of distress: he corporeally bound it to the second [*die Sekunde*], while turning himself into the factotum of his own body" (W 483; 4:142). A "factotum" is someone of many responsibilities and activities, a helper for all jobs, a general servant (from the Latin "fac totum"—to do everything and anything). Thus the self, by turning itself into a factotum of its body, experiences the Benjaminian presence of mind as a letting go. By becoming the servant of its own body, the subject prevents the threatening formation of time into signs of disaster and images of despair. Instead, an interruption emerges in that image of time which is about to turn into a "threat of the future." This future is not a threat because it is unknown but rather because the perception of its presence as a legible image already signals an historical belatedness on the part of the subject. Once the future has become readable, the subject is already too late. "The clock said 'too late,'" Benjamin writes in the *Berlin Childhood* (7:395). As we read in an early note to the "On the Concept of History," "there is an irrecoverable image of the past that threatens to disappear with every presence that fails to recognize that it is being addressed in it" (1:1247). "The happy message," he continues, "that the historian delivers with a flying pulse is uttered by a mouth that, perhaps already in the moment of opening itself, merely speaks into an emptiness" (1:1247). The necessary interruption of this infelicitous sequence of events is achieved by the subject through a corporeal attachment to the historical second (*die Sekunde*), the nowness of time itself, in which the subject is subsumed by its own body. The survival of the self as a dismembered body in the moment of crisis comes at the price of the effacement of the subject's intention and temporality.

What we have called the alterity of the corpus is complexly staged in the *Moscow Diary* as the hovering of the other's body between availability (or readability) and unavailability (or unreadability) in a way that casts the strange friendship between Benjamin and Lacis—to borrow Benjamin's language from the closely related Gladkov review—as an enigmatic "representation of the relationship between these two people whose unconstructable truth erases any derivation" (3:62). Not unlike the Russian politics of culture in which, as Benjamin writes in his Moscow article on contemporary Russian writers, "Russia encounters the specter of its own past" (2:746), the other and its body in Benjamin's own Moscow text remain deferred because of illness, rejection, interference from a third party, impotence, and the metamorphoses of the other during the moments of touch and encounter. The body prevents its reading from being organized into a closed hermeneutic system. In the moment of reading, it is in a certain sense already a corpse. This corpse registers its multiple and heterogeneous affinities with absence and finitude.[23] It is in this sense that the following statement, made by Horkheimer and Adorno, gains significance: "The body cannot be remade into a noble object: it remains a corpse, no matter how vigorously it is trained and kept fit" (234). Reading the body is by necessity a form of maiming or mutilation (231). As an enactment of what in his 1922 fragment "On Horror" Benjamin terms the "de-potentiation of the body in horror" (6:77), the *Moscow Diary* gives us a protocol of mourning the unreadable image of a body. "The body passes away, shatters," Benjamin tells us, "as a manometer that explodes in the moment of its highest tension and that, in the falling apart of all attachments, becomes invalid, superfluous" (6:71).

The inaccessible and enigmatic corpus, a body that will not remain itself even as an alterity, is useless for the purposes of systems that rely on presence, stability, and access to stable meanings. The dispersed body the *Moscow Diary* stages is therefore more than a private predicament. It is also an other to fascism's efforts at *Gleichschaltung*, or total coordination, of the body politic and private. In a 1933 government pamphlet concerning the principles of National Socialist education in the administrative district of the "Groß-Gau Berlin," we read that "*Gleichschaltung* . . . requires work on the head and the limbs if its essence is to be consequential. *Gleichschaltung* is familiar to us from electronic technology. We know, for instance, that through it a series of illuminating bodies [*Beleuchtungskörper*] are individually connected to the same cable [or: leadership, *Leitung*] so that they burn with the same brightness, no matter how much distance there is between them, because the same electrical current flows through all of them."[24] If Nazi *Gleichschaltung* depends on the body's total coordination, from head to toe, as a single meaning or transparent text, then the body that Benjamin attempts to think is constantly removing itself from any kind of systematicity. Instead of being employable by a stable network, it renounces its use value as a concept. It is always already shifting into something else.

This is so because the *Moscow Diary*, for all its immediacy and narrative gestures of everydayness and clarity, is traversed by a ghostly alterity of the desired other and its body. "All close human relations," Benjamin writes in *One-Way Street*, "are struck by an almost unbearable, penetrating clarity that they can hardly withstand" (W 451; 4:96). Our reading of this alterity becomes all the more haunting and unbearable the more the text rhetorically strives for immediacy and matter-of-factness. If, for Benjamin, reading to Lacis from his own writing is his way of penetrating her, of inhabiting her being, then our reading of Benjamin's reading of himself has emphasized the ways in which this erotics of reading, of coming to the other in the body of writing, is never fulfilled. This is how hermeneutic deferral corresponds to the sexual deferral of the other's body. It is as though what Benjamin gave us in the *Moscow Diary* were the visceral unfolding of what a few years earlier, in *One-Way Street*, he had only hinted at in the compactness of a one-line aphorism: "The only way of knowing a person is to love that person without hope [*Einen Menschen kennt einzig nur der, welcher ohne Hoffnung ihn liebt*]" (W 466; 4:119).

Benjamin is now ready to leave Moscow for Berlin. Both he and Lacis fear the moment of final departure. Mounting his sleigh, Benjamin notes: "We held each other tight. . . . As I was about to get in, having said good-bye to her one more time, I invited her to ride to the corner of Tverskaia with me." Then, in a final attempt at bodily communion: "She got out there, and as the sleigh was already pulling away, I once again drew her hand to my lips, right in the middle of the street. She stood there for a long time, waving. I waved back from the sleigh. At first she seemed to turn around as she walked away, then I could not see her anymore" (*MD* 121; 6:409). This last flaring up of the possibility of the impossible encounter is a structural feature of all departure. For, as Benjamin writes of departure and death in *One-Way Street*:

> Flag—
> How much more easily the leave-taker is loved! For the flame burns more purely for the one disappearing, fueled by the fleeting scrap of material waving from a ship or the window of a train. Separation penetrates the disappearing person like pigment and steeps him in gentle ardor.
> —At Half-Mast
> If someone close to us is dying, there is, in the development of the subsequent months, something about which we think we notice—as much as we would have liked to share it with him—that it could only have flourished in his absence. We greet him at last in a language that he can no longer understand. (W 450; 4:94)

For Benjamin, love and friendship, the desire for proximity and intimacy, are most present in the moment of their imminent absence.

For the self, a coming into its own is most likely to occur when what sustains it, what is closest to it, is what is farthest removed. In this simultaneity of proximity and distance, heightened at the moment of departure, the movement of friendly but ultimately incomprehensible language is shared, in necessarily different forms and registers, by all "friendships of strange friends"—and perhaps by all encounters.

That in the moment of departure or separation what once was has not yet vanished and what is imminent has yet to arrive means that the moment is strangely out of joint. It is an historical no-man's-land. In it, what was once the case—the real or imaginary relationship between the self and an other, that troubled force field of relations, desires, and differences called friendship or intimacy—continues to return. In 1930, Benjamin's friend Bloch suggests that in "the moment of separation the former Now [*das gewesene Jetzt*] remains with us in a different form, especially if it was not lived to an end, that is, haunts" (*Spuren* 72). There can be no friendship without moments of departure and separation. Because such moments are ruptures in what is never "lived to an end" without themselves being endings and are thus haunted, there can be no friendship that is not touched by a haunting.

The final sentence of the *Moscow Dairy* functions as a sort of coda to the subject's predicament: a mourning over the unavailability of the other's body that the corpus of the text enacts. It reads: "Holding the large suitcase on my knees, I rode through the twilit streets to the station in tears" (*MD* 121; 6:409). Benjamin weeps. The story or history of a friendship, the friendship of strange friends, has reached a caesura. In the moment of separation, perhaps in the sense that all history is a form of separation, the teary eye cannot cast a final glance upon the body of the other.[25] For Benjamin weeps. His gaze is blurred. Tears seize the subject, and it loses control. To see somebody cry is to see him melt away. The tear dissolves the self, along with the last hope directed toward the other. As we read in his essay on Goethe's *Elective Affinities*, "These tears, which . . . fill the eye, withdraw the visible world from him" (*W* 348; 1:191). Perhaps what is most proper to the subject's eye/I, then, is not sight and insight, but the tear—shed over the eternal play of differences that is the other, the time of the other and its body. The very truth of the subject's eyes, such as emotions, joy, sorrow, love, and prayer, is present precisely when vision and the gaze are not in normal operation, when they cannot see.[26] The crying subject is the subject fully exposed to the unavailability of the other: through the prisms of its tears it "neither sees nor does not see" (Derrida, *Blind* 127). It is exposed to the *mise-en-scène*, the ghostly *Geschehen*, of the neither readable nor unreadable body of the other. But tears also mark a limit: the limit of melancholia and, perhaps, the beginning of its end.

BENJAMIN'S EAR: NOISE, MNEMONICS, AND THE *BERLIN CHRONICLE*

I am now more of an "ear" than anything else.
Friedrich Nietzsche, Letter to Burkhardt

It is hardly an accident that Benjamin chooses to preface his essay on Karl Kraus with the writer's verse, "How noisy everything grows" (R 239; 2:334), for in Benjamin's modernity there can be no body of the self that is not disrupted by noise. In the *Passagen-Werk*, the magnum opus whose possibility of completion was terminated by his untimely death, he meditates on the relationship between noise and the materiality of the corpus. There, Benjamin speaks of a

microcosmic journey on which the dreamer travels through the realms of his own body. For he fares like the madman: the noises from within his own body, which for the healthy man unite in the surge of his health and which, if he hears them at all, bring him healthful sleep, dissociate themselves for him: blood pressure, the movements of the entrails, heartbeat, and muscular sensations each become individually noticeable to him and demand an explanation which only madness [*Wahn*] or a dream-image [*Traumbild*] hold in store. The dreaming collective, which immerses itself into the passage-ways [*Passagen*] as if into the inner realm of its own body, possesses this sharpened receptivity. We must follow it in order to interpret the 19th century as its dream-face. (5:1010)

The body of the dreamer or madman is tormented by its drive to be read and to be interpreted as a comprehensible text. But the interpretation of this corporeal text can only occur through the enigmatic sounds and noises that traverse the body. That the body can only be read in and as noise means that its interpretation also depends on particular dreams or delusions in which the question of its legibility could arise in the first place. For Benjamin, the hermeneutic moment of reading the corpus is always also a scene of madness (*Wahn*) or the advent of a dream-image (*Traumbild*).

Here, the noisy body, in the process of being read, retreats, even as this scene of reading is accompanied by a heightened awareness of the corporeal symptoms themselves. Benjamin suggests that the body of the collective—the body politic of the public sphere, of what could be called modernity—is also inscribed in this scenario. To the extent that the corporeal reading activities of the collective correspond to the subject's inability to arrest the movement and sense of its own body, Benjamin insists on the vital relays between the ways in which the subject struggles to make sense of its own materiality and the mechanisms by which its culture strives to come to terms with itself. It is precisely in order to capture this correspondence that Benjamin wishes to "attempt to move beyond Giedion's thesis. He says: 'In the nineteenth century, construction plays the role of the unconscious.' Should one not rather substitute: the role of the bodily process around which 'artistic' architectures wrap themselves like dreams around the scaffolding of the physiological process?" (5:494).

In a diary entry dated 6 March 1938, Benjamin elaborates on the role of the self's ear:

I have suffered greatly from the noises [*Geräuschen*] in my room. Last night my dream recorded this. I found myself in front of a map [*Landkarte*] and simultaneously in the landscape [*Landschaft*] which it depicted. The landscape was terrifyingly dreary and bare; it would not have been possible to tell whether its desolation was that of rocky barrenness or that of empty gray ground populated only by capital letters. These letters swiveled forth curvedly on their pad as if following mountain ranges; the words formed by them were at an approximately equal distance from one another. I knew or learned that I was in the labyrinth of my auditory canal. The map, however, was simultaneously that of hell. (6:533)

Benjamin suffers from the intrusion of the acoustic. Noise penetrates the ear which hears nothing determinable, and the sound of the *Geräusch* becomes the white noise of *Rauschen.* Because of this perpetual acoustic torment, the echoes of voices and sounds, Benjamin retreats into the ear itself. There, we learn, he strolls about in the labyrinthine inner ear channel. Although he attempts to read the ear channel as if it were a map, he cannot find his bearings there. The meaning of the figures and letters that form the soil of the ear channel elude interpretation.

Benjamin's ear thus emerges as oddly equivocal. On the one hand, it is the organ through which noise penetrates the corpus in order to disrupt the self. On the other hand, this self in turn seeks refuge in the ear. The passage thus points us to Benjamin's preoccupation with the ear and the sense of hearing as something that never releases him from this double bind. This dream scenario can also be read as a miniature of what is at stake for the corporeal self when it confronts noise: its hovering between construction and dispersal.

I started with these enigmatic passages because they allow us to begin to think the relationship between Benjamin's corporeal subject and the sense of hearing that is at stake in the *Berlin Chronicle.* This autobiographical text enacts the function of the ear in the constitution and dissolution of the self's body. Just as the ear remains a labyrinth for Benjamin, the text that intertwines his life with the urban text of Berlin is predicated upon a labyrinthine structure, a series of "many different entrances into the labyrinth" (6:491) in which the self loses itself with each turn.[1] I wish to suggest that the language of the *Berlin Chronicle* requires a reading that is attuned to the body's relation to noise, from street traffic to telephones and beyond. It stages Benjamin's sustained emphasis on the material and technological conditions that come to affect the subject's corpus. Benjamin's self, whose ear is penetrated by noise, is the one that is both enabled and disrupted. While in the *Moscow Diary* it was the body of Lacis that remained deferred and as such became visible as an "unusable" concept, in the *Berlin Chronicle* this position is occupied by the ear of the self. Because, like Benjamin's image of the face and like Lacis's corpus, the meaning of this body part remains elusive, it cannot be employed by a politics of stable concepts. I wish to show that the specific ways in which the ear, too, emerges as one of those innovative Benjaminian concepts that signal their political resonance by remaining "useless."

Chronicle and Critique

While in Ibiza in the spring of 1932, Benjamin wove a series of autobiographical notes, studies, and drafts into a textual montage. Only months before the Nazis' seizure of power, he produced an enigmatic self-portrait that breaks with the conventional narrative principles of confessional writing, such as linearity, chronology, and hypotactical ordering. The *Berlin Chronicle* attempts to make literary montage, which Benjamin had employed a few years earlier in *One-Way Street*, productive for the discourse of autobiography. As he writes from Ibiza to Gretel Adorno, "I have surprised myself by taking up again my modes of presentation from *One-Way Street* for a number of things that are connected to the most important topics of that book" (*C* 393; *B* 552). The result of this renewed montage, the *Berlin Chronicle*, is a corpus of fragments which intertwine personal recollections with theoretically charged material. As such, the *Berlin Chronicle* is located somewhere in between the laconic, quotidian language of the *Moscow Diary* and the ornate prose snapshots of the *Berlin Childhood*. It holds a unique place within the corpus of Benjamin's major texts as it contains, in a number of self-reflexive passages, some of his most sustained statements on the very possibility of self-portraiture. Like no other document, it stages in dense paratactical gestures Benjamin's idiosyncratic relationship to various quarters of Berlin, specific streets, and places such as the Tiergarten and Peacock Island. It also illuminates Benjamin's complicated relationships to his family and relatives; to particular Berlin cafés; and to his beloved deceased friend, the poet Fritz Heinle, who had committed suicide in protest against the First World War and to whom, along with Stone, Scholem, and Lacis, the *Berlin Chronicle* was originally dedicated. The *Berlin Chronicle* embodies a select compendium of individual narrative images that conspire to yield the complex topography of a corpus inhabiting a modern metropolis. This topography is mediated by the acoustic, the realm of the ear.[2]

The *Berlin Chronicle,* a text composed, in Benjamin's famously microscopic handwriting,[3] in a small, leatherbound octavo notebook of some sixty thin sheets, was first published by Scholem in 1970, thirty years after Benjamin's death. In an afterword accompanying the text's first edition, Scholem leaves no doubt about its central importance in Benjamin's corpus: "Despite their fragmentary character these notes are so valuable for an understanding of Benjamin's person and biography, but also for the complexity of his literary production, that their publication represents a substantial enrichment of our knowledge" ("Nachwort zu Benjamins *Berliner Chronik*" 174). Beyond these elements, the autobiographical text is also important as the document of a self-displacement. Benjamin's composition of the *Berlin Chronicle* may help to account for the fact that in 1932 he did not commit suicide as he had carefully planned. In Ibiza, he had already drawn up a living will that made Scholem the inheritor of his manuscripts, had designated the physician Eugen Wissig to be the executor of his will, and had composed short good-bye notes to his closest friends, including Ernst Schoen, Franz Hessel, and Jula Cohn.[4] Yet instead of terminating his life, Benjamin wrote the *Berlin Chronicle*—in a way that remains faithful to the notion, developed in the essay on "The Storyteller," that the narrating voice "could have the wick of his life be slowly but completely consumed by the gentle flame of its very narration" (*I* 108f.; 2:464f.). The traces of this threat are deeply inscribed in Benjamin's self-portrait.

Yet in spite of its importance in Benjamin's career, readers have often conceived of the *Berlin Chronicle* as merely an early version of the more aestheticized thought-images of the *Berlin Childhood around 1900,* and it has received far less critical attention than the later text. This is especially noteworthy because only some parts of the *Berlin Chronicle*—about two-fifths, according to Scholem's estimate—were eventually included, in heavily revised form, in the *Berlin Childhood.* Likewise, the *Berlin Chronicle* has often been used simply as a convenient mine for the excavation of factual information about an enigmatic life, to the detriment of its appreciation as a complex *textual* document.[5] This is the case, for instance, in McCole, who enlists the autobiography to substantiate factual points about Benjamin's youthful infatuations with German idealism and indeed his entire "intellectual identity," suggesting that "[h]ere too, the *Berlin Chronicle* offers a neat and simple account" (55). It is as though critics can hardly resist the temptations offered by the text's material content (*Sachgehalt*) while missing its truth content (*Wahrheitsgehalt*) which may unfold on the far side of any material content. That is, following the distinction between *Sachgehalt* and *Wahrheitsgehalt* that Benjamin proposes in "Goethe's Elective Affinities," such readings are concerned with mere commentary (*Kommentar*) rather than with actual critique (*Kritik*) (W 297; 1:125). While Benjamin concedes that the binarism between a text's material content and its truth content, along with the binarism between commentary and critique that attaches to it, can become affected, and even undone, by the unpredictable movement of a text's very language (W 300; 1:128), this problem becomes even more salient in biographically inflected writing. While all texts become affected by the instability of the opposition between critique and commentary, in biographically inflected writing the struggle between the two terms can only arise in a negativity, that is, in relation to their very absence from the text— "in the realm of biography, there is neither commentary nor critique" (W 325; 1:161). This is so because the language of a biographically informed text can never fully come to terms with the complexly mediated opacity it is meant to represent. It cannot deliver a complete narrative image of its subject's life, and its mimetic potential is no match for the strange infinity that it is intended to convey. "Certainly," Benjamin writes, "a particular trait and a particular relation can be illuminated, but not the totality—unless it, too, is grasped as a merely finite relation. For, in itself, it is infinite" (W 325; 1:161). The most a writing dealing with the biographical sphere of a subject can thus strive to accomplish is to give a sense of the infinite and infinitely mediated set of complex relations that constitute the fiber of the text of the subject's life. But precisely because these relations are infinite and because a full account of the forces that mediate them remains out of reach, their presentation is also impossible or doomed to failure. To put this double structure another way: the success of biographically inflected writing is always also its failure, and it succeeds most brilliantly precisely when it fails. One of the many lessons to be drawn from this is to assume a critical guardedness in relation to a stance that would conflate empirical life and its textual dissimulation. Criticizing this conflation as an organizing principle in

Gundolf's Goethe cult, Benjamin therefore argues that "human life cannot be considered on the analogy of a work of art" (W 325; 1:161).

In this chapter I will thus propose a different approach. Rather than either mining the text for biographical information or constructing a paraphrasing totality of meaning out of it—what McCole calls "a neat and simple account"—I concentrate on a seemingly trivial or accidental detail, the ear and its sphere of the acoustic. I do so because this tropological sphere seems to puncture the surface of the text, disturbing it at crucial moments in enigmatic ways. Here, I follow not only Benjamin's own concern with the theoretical importance of the marginal detail—to which we will return—but also de Man's sense that canonical readings of a text tend to gloss over its unfamiliar, hidden, and potentially subversive moments. As de Man, a perspicacious reader of Benjamin, explains, there "is no merit whatever in upsetting the canonical interpretation merely for the sake of destroying something that may have been built with considerable care." On the contrary, a "commentator should persist as long as possible in the canonical reading and should swerve away from it only when he encounters difficulties which the methodological and substantial assertions of the system are no longer able to master." To be sure, he concludes, "[w]hether or not such a point has been reached should be left open as part of an ongoing critical investigation. But it would be naive to believe that such an investigation could be avoided, even for the best of reasons" (*Aesthetic Ideology* 186). To do justice to the *Berlin Chronicle*, then, one may have to read it against the grain and focus on those moments in the text that raise questions reaching beyond what it seems to articulate on the surface. My focus on the rhetorical detail of the ear in the *Berlin Chronicle* also permits us to illuminate some hidden connections between this text and others in Benjamin's corpus that are chronologically and conceptually related.

To say that very specific moments of language play a significant role in the ways in which the *Berlin Chronicle* stages the autobiographical self is to allow for a decidedly Benjaminian concern with the linguistic dimension of knowledge to become visible. This abiding concern with the centrality of language in the production of any form of knowledge remains with Benjamin from his earliest writings to his final texts, and it effectively serves as the permanent link among his so-called early metaphysico-theological phase, his philosophical literary criticism, and his late materialist investigations of history, culture, and media technology. Thus, as early as 1918, in "On the Program of the Coming Philosophy," he situates his abiding concern with the linguistic nature of knowledge in terms similar to those with which Hamann, seen as an important theoretical leader by the later Sturm und Drang writers, criticized Kant's theory of experience. Benjamin writes: "The great transformation and correction which must be performed upon the concept of experience . . . can be attained only be relating knowledge to language, as was attempted by Hamann during Kant's lifetime" (W 107f.; 2:168).[6] If Benjamin casts himself in relation to a critical philosophy to come, and even to modernity itself, in a relation similar to the one that Hamann's linguistic critique assumed in relation to Kant's rationalist systematicity, then his confessional writings are by no means exempt from this gesture. On the contrary, they embody the enactment and even the intensification of this gesture; the *Berlin Chronicle* is a prime example of this eminently linguistic constellation.

From Autos to Otos

Unlike the *Moscow Diary* with its meditations on the alterity of the body and the *Berlin Childhood* with its optical obsessions, the language of the *Berlin Chronicle* is replete with narrative instances in which the auditory moment assumes an unsettling quality. To cite a few examples, Benjamin speaks of his whole topography as "the sober and noisy Berlin" (R 28; 6:489) whose evenings are even loud (R 48; 6:507). He can never escape the metropolitan polyphony of "cries," "voices," and "screams" (R 25; 6:484) in a city that after the various incorporations of communities and towns in 1920 had grown to a heteroglossia of over four million voices. In this space of noise, even the rust-polluted rain, an allegorical reference to the aftermath of the industrial revolution, drums down mercilessly on the Berlin street cars (R 13; 6:473). Similarly, the "bang of the doors slammed shut" (R 52; 6:511) reverberates in Benjamin, as do "the dull bang," "the screeching of the elevator," and "the falling stick of the father" (6:511).[7] Likewise, Benjamin is fully awake to the omnipresent "rattling coaches" (R 468; 6:468)[8] and he registers in carefully crafted rhetoric the "noise of the waves of conversation," the "surf of the clattering plates," and even the forceful monotony of the "carpet beating" or the resounding galloping of horses (R 43f.; 6:503). The sites of the most intense noise, the Berlin train stations, appear to the narrator as the very organs, the principle life mechanism, of the city (R 12; 6:472).[9] Even during his piano lessons, the "sound of piano études" calls forth a nightmare in the youth (R 42; 6:501).[10] And, in a gesture that criticizes the politics of military aesthetics, Benjamin suffers from the dehumanizing noise of the Prussian "blaring military bands" (R 3; 6:465).

To the extent that the rhetoric of the *Berlin Chronicle* is traversed by the notes and sounds of an intricate network of noise,[11] Benjamin's autobiography wrestles with the intrusion of the self's ear. As Benjamin tells us, "one's ear was helplessly exposed [*ausgesetzt*] to the clanking of foolish speeches" (6:474).[12] Like an eye that cannot decipher the script of a text, the ear in Benjamin's sentence is not capable of interpreting the signals that enter it. Unable to come to terms with the enigmatic order of the auditory text, the ear merely remains ex-posed (*aus-gesetzt*) to what remains out of its grasp. For the helpless ear, the law (*Ge-setz*) of having been ex-posed (*ausgesetzt*) remains suspended or fails (*setzt aus*). The abandoned ear is now at the mercy (*ausgesetzt sein*) of this perpetual suspension, release, or deferral (*Aussetzung*). Within the echo chambers of self-portraiture, Benjamin's ear sits out.

Benjamin's emphasis on the self's tormented ear resonates with his friend Brecht's observation that "our ear is doubtless in the process of a physiological transformation. Our acoustic environment has changed drastically. Just think of the noises of a modern city."[13] Benjamin's self-portrait can be read as an elaborate meditation on the corporeal transformation of the ear that Brecht invokes. Like the corporeal self's inability to orient itself by reading a map of the city in a way that "became visceral" (literally: "that turned into flesh and blood" [*in Fleisch und Blut überging*]; 6:466),[14] the ear transforms itself into something that may no longer underwrite the equilibrium of its corpus.

As the language of Benjamin's autobiography registers an obsession with the realm of the acoustic, the general link between the ear and the act of self-portraiture becomes visible. Indeed, there can be no autobiography, as Derrida reminds us in his reading of Nietzsche's *Ecce Homo,* that is not also an "otobiography," a biography of the ear. Derrida explains this shift from autos (self) to otos (ear) in terms of the other, whose receptivity and validation underwrites the text composed by the self. If, for Derrida, "it is the ear of the other that signs," this does not mean, of course, that an ear has an autonomous will or that it is physically capable of holding and manipulating a pen. Rather, the other is required to validate what the self has written. The autos of the autobiographical act depends on the counter-signature or endorsement of the other, whose ear is penetrated by the text that is the confessional self. "When, much later," Derrida explains, "the other will have perceived with a keen-enough ear what I will have addressed to him or her, then my signature will have taken place. Here one may derive the political import of this structure and of this signature in which the addressee signs with his/her ear, an organ for perceiving difference" (*Otobiography* 51). If the name and signature of the one who writes is to become visible, this is only possible when the ear of the other is attuned to the voice that emanates from the autobiographical corpus and the name that attempts to emerge in its script.

While Derrida's reading of autobiography as otobiography emphasizes the constitutive role of the other's ear, Benjamin tightens the link between the autos and the otos by shifting the terms of this dynamic back onto the body of the self. For Benjamin, the otobiographical self is not only the one who depends on the ear of the other, it equally depends on its own sense of hearing to become what it is: the one who is both constructed and undone by his ear. To be sure, Benjamin's otobiographical self can never take recourse to a stable subjectivity or rely on a secure grounding beyond or prior to an encounter with the other. Yet Benjamin's tormented otos becomes most fully the force field of tensions and contradictions that it is when it is simultaneously enabled and dispersed by the noise that penetrates it.

While Benjamin's confessional subject becomes affected by noise, it does not simply disappear into an "acoustic incognito."[15] Rather, as I hope to show here, the corporeal self that comes to be touched by noise remains *suspended* between construction and dispersal. This is an important point because Benjamin does not simply stage an undoing or negation of the corporeal self but hopes to keep the tension of its undecidability alive. For instance, as we will see, noise can both disrupt and be the trigger of mnemonic images for the Benjaminian self. In fact, I wish to suggest that what makes the corporeal self an unusable concept for fascist purposes, or any politics that relies on stable meanings and transparent essences, is precisely that it cannot be reduced to a single, determinable moment of signification, not even a negation. A negation too, as a gesture of nihilism, could be coopted by a politics of single stable meanings. It is only in the moment of the *undecidable*, when negations and affirmations perpetually trade places and when we are confronted with an object or text that we do not know how to read and arrest for good, that the ethico-political significance of what refuses to be a stable concept may emerge for us. The finality imposed by a mere negation would foreclose this political potential.

We can begin to articulate this double movement of the corporeal self through which Benjamin hopes to "structure [*gliedern*] the space of my life—*bios*—graphically" (R 5; 6:466f.) by tracing the erratic ways in which the noise that penetrates the otos of his autos serves both as a mnemonic trigger—as something that enables the self to access certain memories—and as a traumatic disruption. In one of the *Berlin Chronicle*'s richest passages, Benjamin writes:

The moment of the *déjà vu* has often been described. But I wonder whether this designation is actually fortunate, and whether the metaphor most appropriate to the process should not rather be taken from the realm of acoustics. One ought to speak of events which affect us like an echo to which the call, the sound that awakened it, seems to have at one point dissolved into the darkness of a life that has passed. To this corresponds, if we are not mistaken, the shock, accompanied by moments rising into consciousness as if already lived, which strikes us mostly in the form of a sound. It is a word, a knocking, or a rustling that is endowed with the magic power to ban us to the icy crypt of what once was, out of whose vault the present seems to sound back to us only as an echo. Yet has the counter-image of this trance ever been investigated, that is, the shock with which we hit upon a gesture or a word the way we all of a sudden discover in our house a lost glove or reticule? And just like these lead us to infer the former presence of a strange woman or strangeness [*eine Fremde*], there are words or gestures that permit us to infer that invisible strange woman or strangeness, the future which she or it forgot in our house. I was perhaps five years old. One evening—I was already in bed—my father appeared, presumably to say good night. It was probably half against his will, I thought, that he broke the news of a relative's death to me. The deceased was a cousin, a grown man who

173

did not concern me much. Yet my father gave the news with details, taking the occasion talkatively to explain, in answering my question, what a heartbeat was. I did not absorb much of this explanation. But that evening I etched into my memory my room and my bed the way one take pains to observe exactly a place in which one has the premonition that one day one will have to look in it for something forgotten. Many years later, I found out what. In this room my father had "forgotten" part of the news: that the illness was called syphilis. (R 59; 6:518f.)

In this passage, Benjamin privileges the ear in the formation of memories. These memories traverse the self not as images but rather as echoes whose origins remain forever absent but which recall the event of a past experience. It is no accident that Benjamin elsewhere quotes his teacher Simmel's observation that someone "who sees without hearing is . . . much more uneasy than someone who hears without seeing" (CB 37f.; 1:539). If the traces of memory return to the corpus as distant echoes and haunt it as acoustic ghosts, as the inchoate resounding of long lost voices, then the self becomes the site of memory and is disrupted at the same time. As Benjamin would have it, the corpus becomes a kind of ghost-hearer, and the autobiographical self, a ghost-writer. That these mnemonic sounds resonate within the crypt of the past and that they can be invested with a particular spectral structure helps to explain why Benjamin here links his meditation on the ghostly noise to his father's message of a cousin's death. The site on which Benjamin recalls the dead will itself have become invested with a ghostly memory: that of the departed father's voice. This is why Benjamin has the premonition that, one day, perhaps after his own father's death, he will have to look for something in the memory of his room—the voices of the dead parent.

If the *Berlin Chronicle* links its many figures of ghosts and phantoms to the self's auditory memory, to what "strikes us mostly in the form of a sound," then the writing corpus must also become ghostly in order to be an autobiographical subject. In a 1927 journal note Benjamin records this scene of writing when he tells us how "ghosts are hovering (vignette-like) behind my right shoulder [that is, the writing arm]. Coolness in this shoulder. . . . 'I have the feeling that, in addition to myself, there are four other people in the room'" (6:558). Benjamin's understanding of both the acoustic and ghostly dimension of memory here links him to Bergson, whom he studied carefully and who argues that "when a memory reappears in consciousness, it produces on us the effect of a ghost" (145).

That for Benjamin the corpus of the confessing otos is traversed by both memories and ghosts becomes clear in a related passage. There, Benjamin observes:

> Memories, even when they go into great breadth, do not always represent an autobiography [*stellen nicht immer eine Autobiographie dar*]. And this is certainly not one, not even for the Berlin years which, after all, are my only concern here. For autobiography is concerned with time, with sequence and what constitutes the continuous flow of life. Here, however, I am talking of a space, of moments and discontinuities. For even though months and years appear here, it is in the figure they have in the moment of remembrance [*Eingedenken*]. This strange figure—one may call it fleeting or eternal: in no case is the material from which it is made the material of life. And this is shown not so much by the role that my own life plays here, as by that of the people closest to me in Berlin—whoever and whenever they may have been. The air of the city that is conjured here allots them only a brief, shadowy existence. They flit alongside walls like beggars and appear ghost-like in their windows only in order to disappear again, they sniff along thresholds like a *genius loci*, and even if they fill entire quarters of the city with their names, it is only in the way a dead man's name fills the headstone on his grave. (R 28; 6:488f.)

Benjamin adds that the city is a topography that "bears witness to the dead, shows itself full of the dead"; indeed, it is a "realm of the dead," "seductively torturous like half-forgotten dreams" (R 28; 6:489). If what emerges in his otobiography is an elusively "strange figure" (*seltsame Gestalt*), then the corpus that attempts to write itself can be read as a phantom figure in three distinct but related ways. First, the writing corpus becomes a sort of phantom in the act of constructing a textual self. It produces a spectral version of itself which "captures" its being as presentation and thus, as it were, also prepares the self for its own death. For the autobiography will be circulated among friends and readers and will come to stand for, or replace, the actual writing subject. This is also what will be the case after the writer's empirical death, when his texts and images will be circulated and talked about as if they *were* he. Second, the cultural material upon which Benjamin's text draws is already traversed by ghosts. It is a world in which images of people and locales flicker up briefly ("appear ghost-like in their windows") in transitory "in-between" spaces only to vanish back into their shadowy, un-dead sphere, the dark "realm of the dead" from which they are "conjured" by the autobiographical corpus.[16] Benjamin's autobiographical act is, like Bergson's notion of perception, a "true hallucination" (239). Finally, the autobiographical act inscribes the subject into the "topographical tradition representing the connection of the dead to this soil" (*R* 28f.; 6:489). This tradition traces the signature of the written self "the way a dead man's [name] fills the headstone on his grave," and autobiography becomes the mourning of a thanatography.

The Ear of Technology

So far, I have argued that the ear of Benjamin's corporeal self is both disrupted by noise and accesses mnemonic images through it. We have seen, too, that these mnemonic images are not stable but haunted by the echoes and traces of specters that keep returning. If we can now read the *Berlin Chronicle* as a double otobiography, then a specific narrative image of noise penetrating the ear should illuminate this double encoding. In keeping with the text's auditory obsessions, this image is the telephone. Benjamin here anticipates what the work of such critics as Kittler, Schneider, Laurence Rickels, and Avital Ronell has shown, namely, that the modern self is no longer an a priori of the technical media with which it comes into contact but is in important ways constructed by them.[17]

The significance of the telephone first emerges in the *Berlin Chronicle*. Benjamin later takes it up again, reformulated and stylized, under the heading "The Telephone" in the *Berlin Childhood*. As Benjamin recalls:

> Here the intermediate party was perhaps a certain company of building contractors, one of whose board members, Herr Altgelt, filled the role of partner in countless telephone conversations with my father, and whose name has stayed in my memory. . . . Leaving aside mealtime conversations, it was only the telephone that intimated to us the occult world of business and traders. My father telephoned a great deal. He, whose outward manner seems to have been almost

always courteous and pliable, possessed perhaps only on the telephone the bearing and decisiveness corresponding to his sometimes great wealth. In conversations with mediating agencies the energy not infrequently grew vociferous, and the "serious side of life," which was embodied tangibly in my father's activity, found in the altercations with the telephone operator its true emblem. The telephone first came into use during my childhood. I have therefore known it nailed in some corner of the corridor, whence, shrilling from the darkness, it augmented the terrors of that Berlin apartment with the endless passage leading from the half-lit dining room to the back bedrooms. It became a truly infernal machine when my school friends phoned during the prohibited period between two and four. (R 38; 6:498)

In a reworked version of this scene written a few years after the first, Benjamin elaborates the intruding noise of the telephone as follows:

It may be a matter of the construction of the apparati or of memory— it is certain that, in their echo, the sounds of my first telephone conversations inhabit my ear differently than today's. They were nocturnal sounds. No muse announced them. The night from which they issued forth was the same one that precedes any true birth. And the voice slumbering in the apparati was a newborn one. Down to the day and hour, the telephone was my twin [*war das Telefon mein Zwillingsbruder*]. I was allowed to witness how it left the denigrations of its early years behind. For when the chandelier, the fire-screen, and the indoor palm-tree, the console, the small round table, and the bay window balustrade, all of which at the time were prominently displayed in the front rooms, had long since withered and died, the telephone, like a legendary hero once abandoned in a mountain gorge and leaving the dark corridor behind, made its royal entrance into the cleared up and lighter rooms which were now inhabited by a younger generation. The telephone became a consolation for the new generation's loneliness. It signaled to the hopeless ones, who were ready to leave this bad world behind, the light of last hope. It shared the bed of the deserted ones. Now that everyone awaited its call, the shrill voice that it possessed during exile sounded muffled.

Few of those who use the apparatus know about the devastations that its appearance once caused families. The sound with which it went off when yet another school friend wished to speak to me during two and four was an alarm signal which not only endangered my parents' after-lunch rest but also the entire age in whose heart they had entrusted themselves to this rest. Differences of opinion with the operators were the rule, not to mention the threats and thunderous words [*Donnerworte*] that my father yelled at the complaints offices. Yet his orgies [*Orgien*] were mostly directed at the crank to which he gave himself over completely [*verschrieb*] for minutes on end and in utter oblivion to the world around him [*Selbstvergessenheit*]. His hand would turn into a dervish overcome by an ecstatic trance. My heart was pounding; I was certain that in such cases the operator would be punished for her negligence with a blow.

In those times the telephone hung, disfigured and expelled, between the dirty clothes basket and the gas meter in a corner of the back corridor whence its ringing multiplied the horrors of the Berlin apartment. When, after a long journey of groping through the dark tunnel, I, barely the master of my senses, arrived to turn the riot off, ripped off the two ear pieces, which had the weight of dumb-bells, and squeezed my head between them, I was mercilessly exposed to the voice that was speaking. There was nothing to alleviate the violence or power [*Gewalt*] with which the voice penetrated me. I suffered helplessly as it destroyed my consciousness of time, my resolution, and my duty; and as the medium follows the lead of the voice that appropriated it from beyond, so I submitted to the first proposal that reached me through the telephone. (7:390f.)

Benjamin, who, as late as the 1920s, seems to have preferred the telegraph to the uncanny telephone,[18] here stages the intrusion of the telephone, the figure of electronically mediated noise, onto the stage of modernity. He portrays the telephonic noise not only as corroding the familial fiber of the Benjamin household, he also depicts it as disrupting an entire "age."[19] The telephone's emergence, Benjamin tell us, was first met with suspicion, even derision. It caused consternation and devastation among its novice users. One may hear in Benjamin's autobiographical reflections on the telephone a preoccupation with how the corpus of the self is affected by shifts in the material and technological realm.

Benjamin's sentences remind us that each medium, whether the printed book of the old Gutenberg paradigm or the modern electronic forms of storing, transmitting, and understanding codes, structures the activity of the human corpus. Far from being a neutral space for the transmission of existing ideas, the medium is always a historical and conceptual a priori. By extension, each transformation in the world of media and technology is also a restructuring of what a self can say and do, how it reads and writes. If the telephone inaugurates a new form of perception and consciousness, altering codes and information channels, Benjamin registers this transformation in the experiences of the Berlin child playing at the threshold of the centuries and a medial paradigm shift.[20]

The telephone, then, as a dialectical image of the noise that penetrates Benjamin's ear, ultimately remains suspended or deferred as a legible phenomenon. It disturbs the corpus while at the same time promising to be a trigger of memories.

To understand, first, the mnemonic qualities with which the telephone becomes invested, one may register that the first sentence of Benjamin's passage—"It may be a matter of the construction of the apparati or of memory"—links the machine to the mnemonic realm. This link is made by the surprising conjunction "or," which signals equality or interchangeability between the apparatus and memory.[21] Likewise, the distant echoes continue to resound in the realm of memory. And even though the telephone's noise may not yield "my consciousness of time," it is capable of conjuring fragments of memories in the child's mind. This is why, for instance, Benjamin so distinctly remembers his father's telephonic business partner, Herr Altgelt, as someone "whose name has stayed in my memory." We recall here that Benjamin develops the concept of autobiographical memory not in terms of a full recollection of what once was, but rather as a medium through which the past of a corporeal self may be explored. Indeed, memory, for Benjamin, is the medium of experience just as the earth is the medium in which ancient cities lie buried. This material aspect of a corpus's recollections suggests that what is at stake for the archaeological mnemonist is the meticulous recording of the space of a memory object, that is, "to designate precisely that site in which the researcher got hold of it," as we read in "Excavating and Remembering" (4:400f.).

The *Berlin Chronicle*, too, takes great pains to record the telephone's location and position in the household, placing little emphasis on an accurate or even "chronicling" explication of the child's relation to the new object. Rather, like the archaeologist, Benjamin depicts the shifting locations of the telephone with great precision. We learn, for instance, that the telephone began its life in the family's apartment in a dark corner of a corridor, even more precisely, between the dirty clothes trunk and the gas meter. This initial location suggests the family's distrust and suspicion of the new apparatus, which had not yet assumed its role as an integral member of their Berlin household. Likewise, the telephone's journey from a position of marginality to one of centrality, that is, its move from the dark recesses of the corridor into brighter chambers, receives unexpected attention. Again, instead of explaining the telephone's function in the household, the text follows its relocations, the material aspects of its topography. Only by tracing its positions materially can the telephone become part of the archeological digging site of memory. In other words, only as a material icon can it, "epically and rhapsodically in the strictest sense" (4:401), serve as a mnemonic image to be employed by the archaeologist of the self. In its relation to its own space, the telephone may become one of the objects that this archaeologist finds. As we learn in "Excavating and Remembering," "true memory [must] therefore also present an image of the one who remembers, the way a good archaeological report must not only record the layers whence its found objects stem, but primarily of all the other layers that had to be broken through first" (4:401). The telephone can be read as just such an object: its origin and meaning remain largely indeterminate, but the insights gained by a close reading of the topography in which it is inscribed render it a rich, complex tool of self-portraiture.

Yet, Benjamin's telephone, as an embodiment of the noise that penetrates the otos of writing, remains disruptive. The electronic noise the telephone emits threatens to elude interpretation. The child cannot fully make sense of its intrusiveness. It is hardly an accident that the figurative provenance of the telephone's noise is obscurity itself. Its noises, we are told, "were nocturnal sounds," even sounds of a "truly infernal machine." The telephonic noise ruptures the child's consciousness, and its ringing only intensifies the dread of the apartment's alienating interior ("shrilling from the darkness, it augmented the terrors of the Berlin apartment"). For the child, the noise is a merciless "alarm signal" whose referent remains obscure. Here, the telephone takes on the quality of a symptom that becomes visible on the sensate corpus. As Ronell has aptly argued regarding the telephone in general, "When you hang up, it does not disappear but goes into remission" (*Telephone Book*, "A User's Manual").

If Benjamin reads the telephonic noise as an invader of his Berlin apartment, he also emphasizes its disturbing impact on the technophile culture of Berlin. Thus, he tells us, "I wish to speak of this afternoon because it made so apparent what kind of regimen cities keep over imagination, and why the city, where people make the most ruthless demands on one another, where appointments and telephone calls . . . grant the individual not a single moment of contemplation, indemnifies itself in memory, and why the veil it has covertly woven out of our lives shows the images of people less than those of the sites of our encounters with others or ourselves" (R 30; 6:490f.). In this passage, telephonic interruptions corrupt the encounter with others. Casting a veil of phantasmagoria on recollection and repose, its manic noise and velocity make themselves felt.

Indeed, the telephone may act as a powerful hallucinogenic. As Benjamin states in a related autobiographical passage from his "Drug Protocols":[22] "First (moderate) laughing fit on the telephone. After the conversation, strong effect of the trance; to be noted: The telephone is not located in Benjamin's room but in the adjacent apartment; in order to get to that room, one must pass through a third. Joël wishes to remain in the room where he spoke on the telephone, but he is very uncertain" (6:571). And as Benjamin's friend, Ernst Joël, writes of the same experience: "After the telephone had been used, Fränkel could be expected in about 20–30 minutes. We left the telephone room and passed through the room with the development of the writing" (6:574). Joël continues: "When this happened, I assumed that the two would discuss the experiment in the hallway or the telephone room. This thought was immediately extended: they would talk about me, especially my personality. Then I heard steps distancing themselves and a soft clinking. Now I saw how Benjamin, holding a candelabrum with a burning candle and leading the way, accompanied Fränkel to a bathroom door and then handed the candelabrum over to him" (6:577). While the telephone in the *Berlin Chronicle* is disruptive, the telephonic experience is linked in these related texts to hallucination. The telephone is addictive, and the user is manipulated to want to remain in its immediate orbit. At the same time, the telephone is linked to paranoia ("they would talk about me, especially my personality"). As a cultural hallucinogen, the telephone can, as it were, disrupt consciousness and render the subject's desire for control over the technological apparatus an impossible dream. As in *One-Way Street*, the otos that writes its biography turns into an empty "ear that has lost the power of hearing" (W 447; 4:90).[23]

Yet the noise of the telephone not only plays a phantasmagorical role in the *Berlin Chronicle*, it also mediates another difficulty, Benjamin's experience of his father, even the paternal superego. As we have seen, Benjamin stresses that his "father telephoned a great deal," and the child becomes the witness of "countless telephone conversations." Prompted by the telephone's gesture of distancing the voice, that is, of bridging distances and making it more audible all at once, Benjamin's father appears removed and unreachable to the child. It is precisely when speaking on the telephone that the father's less desirable qualities become obvious to the child, such as his greedy authoritarianism, which under normal circumstances do not readily surface but which account for his financial success. The father's telephone conversations reinforce the effect of an overdetermined paternal presence. Here, Benjamin's father appears as a tyrant roaring unrecognizable "threats and thunderous words." He even becomes "a dervish overcome by an ecstatic trance." These telephonic episodes develop into vertiginous orgies—*Orgien* that here might be read as *Ohr-gien*, or orgies of the ear—during which Benjamin's father works himself into a frenzy that culminates in a total break with his surroundings. At this stage of the *Ohr-gie* the father, Benjamin tells us, reaches utter *Selbstvergessenheit*, the final point in his transformation. At the height of this paternal metamorphosis, young Benjamin intimates: "My heart was pounding." Here, his uneasy relation with the telephone is only heightened by the father's erratic outbreaks, figurative extensions of the disturbing electronic noise.

Benjamin's most enigmatic turn of phrase occurs when he casts the telephone as his own twin: "Down to the day and hour, the telephone was my twin brother [*war das Telefon mein Zwillingsbruder*]." This simultaneity does not simply refer to a chronological coincidence in which a birth and an invention occur at the same time. Benjamin here also casts the self in terms of an other that is inexorably linked to him. According to the Duden's etymology, the German *Zwilling*, or twin, derives from the Old High German *zwiniling*, which in turn derives from *zwinal* or "double." A *Zwilling* is thus someone who is a double, who consists of two. Because the meaning of *Zwilling* is actually *Zwei-ling*, or "two-ling," it refers to the one who is two. Benjamin's language here registers the fundamental split in the self that casts the subject in terms of an other, even when that other is no longer simply an other but represents, because it too is not simply itself, also an image of its own other, the self. The alterity of the "two-ling" is the principle of the writing subject.

Benjamin's autobiographical self is structured by this very logic. In "On the Mimetic Faculty," written in 1933 in close conjunction with his autobiographical projects, he states: "Nature creates similarities. One need only think of mimicry. The highest capacity for producing similarities, however, belongs to man. His gift of seeing resemblances is nothing other than a rudiment of the powerful compulsion in former times to become and behave like something else. Perhaps there is none of his higher functions in which his mimetic faculty does not play a decisive role" (R 333; 2:210). In the corresponding section "Mummerehlen" of the *Berlin Childhood*, Benjamin speaks of his ability to become like all the objects that surround him: through *mummen*, that is, disguising himself in their forms. But there, although he can become *like* anything else, he can never coincide with his own image. This is why "I became so clueless when I was asked to become similar to myself. . . . I am disfigured by everything that surrounds me. I dwelled like a mollusk in the nineteenth century which now lay before me like an empty shell. I hold it to my ear" (4:261). Benjamin can never become like himself because he is always like something else.[24] This being-like-something-else prevents him from being himself; becoming like himself is the only movement that presents difficulties to the economy of his perpetual transformations.

In a similar vein, Benjamin, in "Materials for a Self-Portrait" (1934), speaks of the "solution to the enigma why I do not recognize anybody but mistake people. Because I do not wish to be recognized; I want to be mistaken [*Weil ich nicht erkannt sein will; selber ver-wechselt werden will*]" (6:532). But Benjamin defers an explanation of this enigmatic passage. To unravel it, we might begin by stating that, in the same way in which relations, people, and objects in the *Trauerspiel* study "can mean absolutely anything else" (O 175; 1:350), Benjamin's autobiographical self too can become absolutely anything else. And it is precisely because the speaking self in Benjamin can become anything else, for example a telephone, that it is the one that is addressed or meant precisely in the moment when it is mistaken for something or something else is mistaken for it. When something else is mistaken for the speaking self, it is the self which is addressed, because it has become that other object, that something else. This is to say, too, that it can be addressed and identified only because it can become anything else. If it were recognized as a self, the self could not be identified. Only in the moment when the self is mistaken for something else can it be identified. This is both the desire and the enigma of Benjamin's autobiographical self.

By the same token, to mistake the other is also an ethical obligation of the self. This is why Benjamin does not wish to "recognize anybody." If others too, like the self, are or can become something or somebody else, that is, if the ability to assume another form is not the sole privilege of the self, then to recognize and identify these others properly would mean to look for them in the guises of other objects, that is, when they are not themselves. Recognizing the other would thus not mean, as it often does today in the so-called struggles for recognition and the politics of identity, to identify and affirm others as stable selves and self-identical others. On the contrary, to affirm and recognize the other would mean for the self to acknowledge precisely those moments when the other is no longer itself but assumes a multitude of guises and forms, that is, becomes pluralized in its ability to become similar to other persons and objects.

This pluralization, even disfiguration in the act of becoming like something else is not simply a negation of experience. On the contrary, as Benjamin stresses in the fragment "On Experience," written in close proximity to the *Berlin Chronicle* and his essays on the mimetic faculty and the similar, "experience consists of lived similarities" (6:88). From this perspective, the similarities the mimetic self assumes are simultaneously disfigurations and the conditions of possibility for experience to take place. By the same token, experience is then thinkable as what disfigures it in the mimetic moment. In the mimetic act, the corporeal self forges no "causal connections" between itself and the object to which it likens itself: rather "what matters are the similarities that were lived" (6:89).

If Benjamin's self can (only) think itself in terms of its likeness to an other, such as a telephone, then the uncanny mimetic process of becoming similar that it performs is a matter of the ear and, with it, the body of the self. Indeed, we might recall in this context what Benjamin once termed *Leibähnlichkeiten* ("corporeal similarities"), which link the bodily subject to its material surroundings (6:193). The mediation that enables the mimetic process of the corporeal self to take place is linguistic, and its workings need to be read in representational terms. In this context, what Benjamin says about

Kraus's writing in 1931—only months before composing the *Berlin Chronicle*—should be understood to apply to Benjamin's writing as well. He writes: "One does not grasp his 'theory of language' if one does not recognize it as a contribution to the linguistic rules of court; one would understand the word of the other in his mouth only as a *corpus delicti* and his own only as a judging one. Kraus knows no system. Each thought has its own cell. But each cell can in an instant, and apparently prompted by a nothing, become . . . a legal chamber over which language presides" (R 254; 2:349). Benjamin stresses the corporeal nature of thoughts by linking them to cells. Like cells—basic units of living matter that sustain the body and that are structured by such features as membranes, a nucleus, and cytoplasm—thoughts have a corporeal "syntax." The corporeal nature of thoughts is in turn not tied to a system other than that of language itself. To the extent that cells and thoughts are interlaced and are both structured by language, they are both contingent upon its erratic nature, its difficulties and resistances. Indeed, language presides over them, which is to say, is situated before and in front of them, in a position of authority, guiding and controlling.

The Mnemonic Corpus

To think of the link between the mimetic capability and the corpus of the disrupted self along these lines is to make vivid Benjamin's wish, made in a 1936 fragment, that the "insight that the first material upon which the mimetic faculty attempts to operate is the human body should be put to use . . . more forcefully than it has been" (6:127). But to make visible the relays between, on the one hand, the language of the body and its cells and, on the other hand, the mimetic capabilities of the self, is also to enter the realm of memory and forgetting.

Benjamin links both memory and forgetting—the one is always traversed and threatened by the other—to the process of bodily mimesis, that is, to the moment when selves or objects assume different shapes in order to become something else. Investing the corpus with both disfiguration and forgetting, Benjamin tells us in his essay on Kafka that

> Odradek is the form which things assume in oblivion [*Vergessenheit*]. They are disfigured. The "cares of a family man," which no one can

identify, are disfigured; the vermin, of which we know all too well that it represents Gregor Samsa, is distorted; the big animal . . . is distorted. These Kafka figures are connected by a long series of figures with the primal image of disfiguration, the hunchback. Among the gestures of Kafka's tales, none is more frequent than that of the man who bows his head far down on his chest: the fatigue of the court officials, the noise affecting the doormen in the hotel. (*I* 133; 2:431)

If, as Benjamin writes in the same essay, "the most forgotten strangeness or alien land [*Fremde*] is our body—our own body" (*I* 132; 2:431), then the body is both what forgets and what is disfigured in the very moment of forgetting. The gestures that enact this disfiguring forgetting in Kafka's work are not unlike the self in the *Berlin Chronicle*. Like the ears of Kafka's doormen which are tormented by noise, the ear of Benjamin's autobiographical self is penetrated by the noise of the city. It, too, is inscribed in a chain of corporeal disfigurations that emerge as moments of forgetting precisely when the self becomes like something else. When the language of the body is forgotten or becomes illegible it enters the realm of disfiguration. It gestures toward a self that, like Kafka's literary characters Odradek or Gregor Samsa, cannot identify the origins of and reasons for its own displacement.

But the corporeal disfiguration that is forgetting is not Benjamin's only reading of the mimetic body. The rupture between remembering and forgetting is also repeated and reinscribed as the rupture that splits the realm of memory itself, that prevents memory from becoming what it is within the corpus. If, therefore, it is also in the realm of memory that the corporeal self engaged in self-portraiture attempts to articulate itself through itself or an other, we can begin to address these issues by taking seriously Benjamin's location of memory in the corpus itself. We recall that in his reading of Proust, Benjamin had tied the possibility of memory to the self's body: "Proust speaks of these 'other systems' frequently. Limbs are his favorite representation of them, and he does not tire of speaking of the memory images deposited in them, that is, how they, dependent on no prompting from consciousness, suddenly break into the latter when a thigh, an arm, or a shoulder blade suddenly takes the position in bed that they had once assumed. The *mémoire involontaire des membres* is one of Proust's favorite subjects" (*CB* 115; 1:613). If noise penetrates the ear of Benjamin's body both to act as a mnemonic trigger and to disrupt the self of the *Berlin Chronicle*, then the status of Benjamin's understanding of memory needs to be specified further.

Memory of the Limbs

Benjamin's mnemonically charged image of the apparatus is linked to his discussion of the relationship between involuntary memory and technology. In "On Some Motifs in Baudelaire," he describes this relationship as follows: "The techniques based on the use of the camera and of subsequent analogous apparati extend the range of the *mémoire involontaire*; by means of these devices they make it possible to arrest an event at any time in terms of sound and sight. Thus they become essential achievements of a society in which practice is shrinking" (*I* 186; 1:644). For Benjamin, technological apparati, such as the camera, the gramophone, or the telephone, take up the function of mnemonic devices in a culture whose capacity for memory is shrinking. But no apparatus can guarantee the stability of memory. Rather, it merely serves as a trigger for the release, within the corpus of the self, of a whole stream of paratactically arranged mnemonic images. In a technological age in which experience is always already mediated by the apparatus—what is the cinema, for instance, but a series of shocking disruptions of the experience a viewer has been strenuously trained to desire—experience becomes a parasite on the apparatus that disrupts it.[25] For the Benjaminian corpus, the apparatus is thus both the agency that occasions the disruption of experience and the medial host upon whose existence the sensuous disruption is predicated. A photograph, for instance, both disturbs the logic of experience (say, our recollection of the appearance of a certain facial feature in the other person) and also guards against the complete loss of particular memories. Upon the body of the self, it retrieves a host of mnemonic images even as it displaces the traces of other mnemonic images lodged within the same body. Similarly, the telephone's noise both disrupts the self and recalls, uncontrollably, a series of childhood memories. From the perspective of the corpus, such apparati interact with the body to make citation possible. And it is precisely within the passageways of the corpus that these citations continue to resonate.

For Benjamin, there can be no mnemonic citation that is under the conscious rule of the corpus in which it occurs. That is to say, although the corpus becomes the site on which the double coding of a mnemonic shock may take place, the paths that this mnemonic shock will take cannot be prescribed in a programmatic way or employed by this or that system. This difficulty becomes clear when Benjamin expresses his suspicion of the idea that mnemonic shocks could be steered by the free decision of an autonomous corpus. In "On Some Motifs in Baudelaire," he addresses this point with regard to Bergson's theory of experience and memory. "In Bergson," Benjamin claims, "it is as if the contemplative actualization of the stream of life were a free choice" (*I* 157f.; 1:609). In *Matter and Memory* Bergson insists on the division of memory into two modes: one mode of memory records and stores the sequential flow of everyday events and information, including dates, places, and numbers. The other mode is responsible for recording and retrieving the active or motoric abilities of a subject's biological organism, its mechanical tasks, movements, and activities, in short, a kind of memory of the body. Bergson valorizes the first mode of memory as true memory, as *mémoire pure*. But, according to Benjamin's understanding, Bergson's *mémoire pure* problematically construes conceptual or contemplative memory as an act of conscious volition. He questions Bergson's pure or true memory in terms of its essentialism. Instead, he turns to a mode of memory closer to what Bergson calls motoric memory and closer to his own concerns: Proust's *mémoire involontaire*. "Proust immediately confronts," Benjamin argues, "this involuntary memory with a voluntary memory, one that is in the service of the intellect" (*I* 158; 1:609). In Proust's *mémoire involontaire*, the self has no control over when and how mnemonic images enter its mind. (These images are conjured by a sensory impression, such as the taste of a biscuit or madeleine). But although the moment of memory is, according to Proust, arbitrary, the specific contextual constellation which gives rise to it is not. For the concept of the *mémoire involontaire*, Benjamin writes, "bears the traces of the situation out of which it was formed," and with that memory comes inscribed "the trace of the narrator like the trace of the potter's hand on the earthen vessel" (*I* 159; 1:611). The corpus of Benjamin's self, then, is invested with both a Proustian memory of the limbs and a Bergsonian motoric memory, or memory of the body, in a way that does not cease to follow the dark traces of its own constructions.

The memory of the limbs and its dangers that Benjamin here adopts can be grasped more fully within the terms of his discussion of involuntary memory in "On the Image of Proust" (1929). There, Benjamin claims that what is central to Proust's *In Search of Lost Time* is not the recording of a specific memory but rather the very process of weaving memory itself. He calls this weaving a kind of Penelopeian work of remembrance ("the weaving of his memory, the Penelope work of recollecting [*des Eingedenkens*]"; *I* 202; 2:311). Enigmatically, the weaving of memory on the subject's corpus is simultaneously the Penelope work of remembrance and the "Penelope work of forgetting."[26] Thus, remembering is also forgetting. Benjamin stages this double movement in the figure of the woven text, for "[i]f the Romans called a text a web, then hardly anybody's text is more tightly woven [*dichter*] than Marcel Proust's" (*I* 202; 2:311). The Latin designation for text, "textum" (web), which evokes the image of weaving, embodies the vicissitudes to which both text and memory are subject. Like memory, which struggles to weave its objects into existence, a text must be woven. Its semiotic strands must flow into a pattern, a dense (*dicht*) constellation of signs that may even make it literature (*Dichtung*). But like memory, a text, as a woven Penelopeian product, faces the threat of the narrative thread's unraveling. For Benjamin, the Penelopeian unweaving of a text parallels the undoing of the patterns of memory. The figure of Penelope, then, allegorizes the tension between weaving and the sudden unweaving of the text of memory. Not only does the thread of Penelope remain largely indeterminate, it also serves as a figure that comments on its own indeterminacy.

In this double gesture, memory threatens to cancel the corporeal self. As Benjamin's essay on Proust continues, what underwrites the text is not simply the author: "There is yet another sense in which memory issues strict weaving regulations. After all, only the *actus purus* of recollection itself is the unity of the text. Not the author, much less the plot. One may even say that the intermittences of author and plot are only the reverse side of the continuum of memory, the pattern on the back side of the tapestry" (*I* 202f.; 2:312). For Benjamin, the remembering self is no longer an origin or essence that reproduces itself in a textual weave. Rather, it is an effect created by the weaving of various materials into a textum and of the undoing of that weave. This view leads Benjamin to stress Proust's desire to erase the fiction of a stable self ("Proust was insatiable in emptying the simulation, the I, at one stroke") (*I* 205; 2:314). The corpus of the remembering self dissolves in order to recapture, involuntarily, the "traces" of its own memory or the memory of itself ("trace of the narrator").

How, then, may we begin to follow these mnemonic narrative traces? A key to this difficulty may well lie in Benjamin's neologistic translation of the Proustian *mémoire involontaire*, as *das ungewollte Eingedenken* (2:311). *Eingedenken*, a word borrowed from German mysticism that is not normally found in a German dictionary, is a conflation of the verb *gedenken* (to remember ceremoniously) and the predicate adjective *eingedenk* (to be mindful of, to be aware). This conflation suggests the interweaving of remembrance and an especially alert mindfulness.[27] Proust's involuntary memory is the product of a spontaneous, arbitrary eruption which, partially physiologically driven, calls forth certain images. But Benjamin's *Eingedenken* reformulates that process, adding to it the dimension of mindfulness. This mnemonic vigilance is neither conscious nor determinable by the subject's volition, yet is subtly purposeful as a narrative gesture. The mnemonic traces Benjamin wants to identify are thus themselves dialectically charged. They are, in their vigilant orientation, involuntary yet strategic, unconscious yet temporally coded, in short, they are a curious but mnemonically vital "dialectic of happiness" (*I* 204; 2:313).

The mnemonic traces Benjamin wishes to sketch on the self's corpus can also be read as traces of writing. In a related passage in *One-Way Street*, Benjamin writes that, like "ultraviolet rays, memory shows to each one in the book of life a script that invisibly, as a prophesy, glossed the text" (*W* 483; 4:142). Only for and in memory does life turn into writing, and, paradoxically, only as mnemonic activity can a thinking of what is to come take place. Reading mnemonic writing— or, simply, reading mnemonically—means reading not the future itself but rather the very promise that there will be a future. Here, Benjamin's memory inverts its intellectual "other," the perspective of the future. The promise of a future, which is linked to the activities of the present as they are mediated by the memory of the past, turns into a text. This writing is a glossing of the promise of a future which, in the mnemonic moment, can never be realized. Since this writing will have remained only faintly legible, and since writing becomes identifiable and readable only through the work of memory, its inscriptions on the reading corpus become doubly vital.

Memory and the Gap

To the extent that Benjamin thinks of the mnemonic body also in terms of an absence, a threat to its legibility, it shares its language with Freud's theory of memory. Benjamin is especially attuned to the notion of memory Freud develops in *Beyond the Pleasure Principle* (1920). In his commentary on Baudelaire, Benjamin notes the Freudian hypothesis that suggests a link between memory and consciousness. "Freud's fundamental thought," Benjamin writes, "on which these remarks are based, formulates the assumption that 'consciousness comes into being at the site of a memory trace'" (*I* 160; 1:612). The passage Benjamin quotes is from section 4 of Freud's essay. There, Freud writes that if "you consider how little is known from other sources about the genesis of consciousness, then the thought that *consciousness comes into being at the site of a memory trace* must at least be granted the significance of a somehow determined claim" (*Beyond the Pleasure Principle* 29). The movement of Freud's hypothesis is one of substitution or replacement. Consciousness comes into existence in the space in which the traces of memory engrave themselves. The simultaneous presence of consciousness and memory traces is therefore impossible. For Freud, the presence of consciousness is predicated upon an absence. Conversely, memory traces are most deeply inscribed where they are the farthest removed from consciousness.

Benjamin hopes to translate this Freudian dynamic into Proustian language: "Put into Proustian terms, this means that only what has not been 'experienced' explicitly and consciously, what has not happened to the subject as an experience, can become a component of the *mémoire involontaire*" (*I* 160f.; 1:613). Instead of being experienced and captured by consciousness, a memory trace dwells within the moment of rupture, shock, and absence. This is also the case, according to Benjamin, in Baudelaire, the theoretical teacher of Proust. Memory traces, then, can be available textually even while they remain outside conscious control. They may be inscribed in the gaps a text opens up. As Benjamin would have it, "Baudelaire's production is assigned a task. He envisioned blank spaces [*Leerstellen*] which he filled in with his poems" (*I* 162; 1:615). These gaps are the dark points of resistance through which memory becomes available to the self in a way that refuses to collapse the radical alterity between a textually mediated memory and the corporeal subject.

But, we might ask, how can these *Leerstellen*, blank spaces or gaps, which carry so much mnemonic cargo—indeed they bend under the weight of all the memory they convey—be recognized if they are, at least in the moment of writing, outside of a self's consciousness? More precisely: How can we recognize an absence when we see one? For Benjamin, a signal is needed. This signal is a trigger external to the dream that acoustically breaks with the totality of the dream or of the phantasmagoria. Phantasmagoria for Benjamin is less a strategic construct designed by those in power to blind the masses than a sort of repressed expression of mythical fear in the age of high capitalism. It is less an instance of false consciousness than a transfiguration of the products and principles of a particular symbolic order (Bolz, "Hauptstadt" 15). Ruptured by a signal, a wake-up call from the "dream-sleep" that is modernity, the phantasmagoria can be exposed as that which the corporeal self already is: a surface or façade that masks its own plurality. Such a triggering signal can be, for instance, the ringing of an alarm clock, as in the essay on surrealism, or that of the telephone, as in the *Berlin Chronicle*. Benjamin refers to such a ringing as an "alarm signal" that awakens the dreamer to an aporia.

To recognize the dream or phantasmagoria is also to allow memory traces to enter consciousness. But in the moment of ringing, of course, the memory traces flicker up only to disappear again, since they are now in the process of becoming a form of consciousness and cannot, as Freud tells us, coexist with the latter. The ringing of the telephone can thus be read as an allegorical intervention in phantasmagoria. Hearing the telephone's noise, the corporeal subject wakes up from a dream in which everything seemed natural, unconditional, and non-contingent. Waking up to the gap (*Leerstelle*) that is its corpus, the self renounces memory traces immediately after their recuperation. Noise both awakens and disrupts; it names an uncomfortable awakening. It is no accident that Benjamin privileges this uneasy awakening when he states, "Just as Proust begins his life story with the moment of awakening, so every presentation of history must begin with awakening; in fact, it must not be about anything else. This one [the *Passagen-Werk*] is about awakening from the nineteenth century" (N 52; 5:580). Indeed, in the double sense of awakening and sleep-walking that Benjamin implies, "The Now of recognizability is the moment of awakening" (N 80; 5:608).[28] It belongs to what in the *Berlin Chronicle* "determines the tone . . . of real memories" (R 26; 6:486). The most proper site of awakening for the Benjaminian corpus is thus the gap or abyss that is touched by the Now.

If the otobiography *Berlin Chronicle* turns around the ear as the site of disruption and memory, we should be careful not to rush to the conclusion that the mnemonic dimension of the ear redeems. With regard to another form of confessional writing, the journal entry, Benjamin touches upon the obscure moment in memory that interlaces the dangerous and the promising. As he writes in his essay on Goethe's *Elective Affinities*, "if it is the danger of the diary as such to lay bare prematurely the germs of memory in the soul . . . the danger must necessarily become fatal when the spiritual life expresses itself in the diary alone. Yet all the power of internalized existence stems finally from memory" (W 338; 1:178). Memory of this sort has little to do with the deliberate accessing of certain stored facts of positive knowledge on the shelves of recollection. Rather, we could say that it proceeds by shattering certain assumptions about the stability of a linear chain of recollection so that the fragments of this shattering may form a new Benjaminian constellation. This constellation may be "arrested," encountered at a standstill, and read against the grain. "It is to this immolation of our deepest self [*tiefsten Ich*] in shock," Benjamin's otobiography teaches us, "that our memory owes its most indelible images" (R 57; 6:516).[29]

Ears and Voices

What Benjamin gives us in the lyrical miniatures of his *Berlin Chronicle* is the image of an ear encased in what Adorno recalls as one of Benjamin's favorite objects: the little souvenir glass bowls in which, when shaken, snow falls onto the scene—the snow of history perhaps.[30] It is precisely in the form of such a miniature snow globe that the politics of Benjamin's ear emerges. Bloch, whom Benjamin revered as "extraordinary," indeed as "the greatest connoisseur of my writing" (C 299; B 424), gives us a hint in this regard. He once commented with admiration on Benjamin's ability to read marginal details, noting how Benjamin would all of a sudden magically illuminate a seemingly odd or insignificant detail to reveal its hidden theoretical centrality, even its status as "emblematic writing" within this or that cultural text.[31] The *Passagen-Werk* bears Bloch's intuition out. There, Benjamin himself illuminates this method of reading against the grain, in which the odd detail is thoughtfully placed into a constellation or montage of images in order to betray larger structures: "The first part of the journey will be to transpose the principle of montage into history. That is, to erect the great constructions out of the smallest, sharply fashioned building blocks. Indeed to discover the crystal of totality within the analysis of the small individual moment. . . . Debris of history" (N 48; 5:575). Without reducing the idiom of his objects to their culture or vice versa, Benjamin articulates the *relation* between the two in terms of a historical montage of debris. That an unsuspected detail can become a politically significant allegorical text—what Bloch calls the suddenly emerging *"Schrift"-Struktur,* or written structure, of the details examined by Benjamin—hints at the political resonances of the ear in Benjamin's otobiography. In this technical sense, Benjamin's ear belongs to the debris of history.

In its suspension between construction and dispersal, Benjamin's ear is a far cry from the ideologemes of the stability of meaning and selfhood that fascism propagates. If the *Berlin Chronicle* gives us an ear that is on the far side of this stability, this is not to say that a new self could be modeled on its pattern. Benjamin does not wish to hold up "his" pluralized self, the fragmented otos of his autobiography, as a program that others could simply follow, even in the resolute struggle against fascism. This would not only signal a phantasmagorical redoubling, it would also repeat National Socialism's failure to differentiate between an empirical and aesthetically simulated self. But on the far side of any facile movement of substitution, this aleatory ear does increase our awareness of how epistemological and political questions are inseparable from the tropological questions that arise in the discussion of subjectivity and corporeal selfhood.

In the same way that the self is never merely one, the ear too must be more than one. From the perspective of the *Berlin Chronicle,* being more than one or, rather, being the one who is more than one, is an eminently political concern. For Benjamin, more ears are needed, other ears for which the retreat of sound and sense remains alive. Ears must register what is not fully itself within that which penetrates them, what remains other and elusive in the hidden figures of the acoustic. To say that the ear must be more than one and that it must remain open to its own plurality and that of others, is to begin to think through the ways in which it is inhabited not only by the self (as in the passage with which we started this chapter) but also by the voices of others.

Benjamin therefore links his concerns with street and traffic noises, gramophones and telephones also to the electronically mediated acoustics of the radio. If he attempted to address, between 1929 and 1932, the years of the *Berlin Chronicle*, a plurality of ears by writing and broadcasting radio pieces for children, the voice that resounds through the radio is not the voice of singularity and straightforward meaning. In other words, it is not Hitler's voice. The voice of Hitler and the fascists penetrated the ears of the German people from radios everywhere. Indeed, cheap radios were manufactured by the Nazis to flood the market, loudspeakers were hung in the streets, and thousands of free-standing speaker-pillars were distributed across the country.[32] As Benjamin writes to Scholem on 20 July 1934 from Brecht's Danish home-in-exile, among the playwright's "great amenities is a radio, which one now needs more than ever. Thus I was able to listen to Hitler's Reichstag speech, and because it was the very first time I had ever heard him, you can imagine the effect" (C 450; B 614). Here, Benjamin's ear is penetrated by the voice of a monstrosity. The fascist voices transmitted over the radio were, as Goebbels states in his 25 March 1933 address to German radio directors, that it "would be naive to think that any person could have the power or opportunity to resist" the fascist *Geist* that has now entered the radio (*Reden* 85). After all, Goebbels explains, because the radio it meant to convince the remaining 48 percent of Germans who had not initially voted for Hitler, total fascist "mobilization . . . is one of the main tasks of radio" (89). For Goebbels, this total mobilization of the radio depends on its transmissions of a single meaning, of things that can be presented as transparent and stable significations. Stable meaning has to be manufactured, so that "the people *can* understand things," even when their fascist manipulations are far from understandable. For the voice of fascist radio, Goebbels continues, there can be nothing "that we could not make clear to the people [*wir dem Volk nicht klargemacht hätten*]" (91). "Of course," Goebbels concedes, "one must know the art of de-complicating [*entkomplizieren*] complicated matters, to simplify them, to primitivize them, to reduce them to the lowest measure. . . . This is how it is with the radio, too" (91). This is why, Goebbels states, "I consider radio to be the most modern and the most important instrument of influencing the masses" (91). Reductionism and the foreclosure of difficulty coalesce in a doctrine of transparency and sense in which competing levels of meaning are eradicated. This singularity and total coordination of meaning becomes a kind of new religion. As a Nazi radio journal states, the "art of radio wants to return from the market place to the church . . . where all listeners are surrounded by the same atmosphere. . . . Acting persons are no longer individual destinies, they are ideas, forces that move the community, that let one mouth say what moves many" (cited in Reichel 164). Whether in party speeches, public proclamations, or in the popular German live radio transmissions from the battles at the front, the electronic voice of fascism bespeaks a singular meaning that remains closed to the voices of others and to competing readings and interpretations.

But while the voice of fascism always carries the same singular message—indeed, consists of nothing but a series of repetitions and tautologies aimed at the address of a self-identical teutonic ear—Benjamin's voice reverberates as a plurality in which nothing is what it seems. Addressed to the ears of Frankfurt and Berlin, Benjamin's radio miniatures for children, the typescripts of which miraculously survived the Gestapo's confiscation of Benjamin's papers, treat such diverse topics as a visit to a brass factory, a gypsy, bootlegging, stamp fraud, witch trials, earthquakes, a crazy day, a flooding of the Mississippi river, Casper Hauser, and even "true" dog stories. Speaking on the eve of Nazi Germany, Benjamin's voice presents listeners with riddles and enigmas, a "child's garden of deconstruction."[33] Like the pages of the *Berlin Chronicle*, it refuses to let the ear be deprived of what refuses to yield itself fully.

The political "lessons" of this voice, if there are any, are ones of difference and alterity, of perplexity and deferral. The voice of the Benjaminian corpus teaches the ears of its listeners not to become like it but to share with it the sense that one voice and one set of ears are not enough. Ear and voice can never be singular; they are always already haunted by an alterity that cannot be reduced to the totalitarian terms of a single meaning. The ear that Benjamin's voice addresses is thus called upon not to foreclose a thinking of the impossible as a politically resonant act. It is in this ethical sense that Benjamin's Berlin otobiography asks us not to close our ears.

4

BENJAMIN'S EYE/I: VISION AND THE SCENE OF WRITING IN THE *BERLIN CHILDHOOD AROUND 1900*

Augenblicke, wessen Winke,
keine Helle schläft.
Unentworden, allerorten,
sammle dich,
steh.

Paul Celan, "Augenblicke"

History [*Geschichte*] breaks down into images, not into stories [*Geschichten*].

Walter Benjamin, *Das Passagen-Werk*

The *Augenblick* of Benjamin's acts of self-portraiture, that is, both their fleeting moment and their blink of the eye, can hardly be thought outside of their historical, that is, political context. This is especially true of the *Berlin Childhood around 1900*. From the beginning, the movements of this text have stood in an inverse relationship to the movements of fascism. While in 1933 Hitler and the National Socialist party work to solidify their power by increasingly uniting the *Reich*, Benjamin's autobiographical writing becomes increasingly fragmented. On 7 April 1933 a law coordinating the *Reich* with all remaining German state parliaments was instituted ("Gesetz zur Gleichschaltung der Länder mit dem Reich"), ensuring that the Nazis' politics of total coordination was enforced across Germany. By contrast, the enigmatic *Berlin Childhood*, begun only months before the Nazis' efforts at *Gleichschaltung*, remains, as Benjamin writes to Scholem in 1935, "shattered" (*zerschlagen*): "From time to time I dream of my shattered books [*träume ich meinen zerschlagenen Büchern nach*]—the *Berlin Childhood around 1900*" (C 513; B 695). *Nachträumen*: Benjamin mourns these shattered textual self-portraits by dreaming about them, longing to catch up with them in the unconscious. But he also dreams *after* them, that is, after they have taken leave of him and left behind for his thinking and dreaming only an absence and the impetus to think (after) that absence. He dreams, finally, *according to* these texts, that is, in the wake of their precepts and the drama of shattering they stage.

The *Berlin Childhood around 1900*, a book that Benjamin began in 1932—by drastically reworking parts of the *Berlin Chronicle*—and continued to revise until shortly before his death, is not only his most refined and polished surviving autobiographical document, its constellation of enigmatic miniatures also contains what Benjamin thought would be "the most precise portrait that I shall ever be able to give of myself" (C 424; B 589), "a kind of self-portrait" (C 427; B 591). The importance of this text in Benjamin's corpus cannot be overstated. It was written in close temporal and theoretical conjunction with the critical and philosophical questions that preoccupied Benjamin in the 1930s, such as memory and reproduction, politics and language, film and photography, and modernity and materialist historiography. As Adorno writes to Kracauer with uncharacteristically unrestrained enthusiasm on 21 November 1932: "Benjamin was here. He read a lot to me from his new book, the *Berlin Childhood around 1900*. I find it wonderful and utterly new. . . . I am convinced that you too will be greatly impressed with it" (*BA* 31). Even though the text was not published until 1950 under the editorship of Adorno, its place and status in Benjamin's oeuvre is next to the *Passagen-Werk*. Indeed, the *Berlin Childhood* should be read as a kind of autobiographical *Passagen-Werk*.[1] As an extensive collection of quotations and observations concerning early industrial culture and technological mediation, the *Passagen-Werk* was meant to account for the historical, cultural, and ideological specificity of modernity from a bird's-eye perspective, while the *Berlin Childhood* was to ground these reflections figuratively in the subjective experiences of a childhood. In a series of fragmentary and intricately wrought narrative images, paratactically arranged, Benjamin surveys the various quarters and neighborhoods of Berlin, its courtyards and markets, its train stations and streets, its zoo and its ice-skating rink, its monuments and amusements. The reader confronts in each textual fragment a new sign system whose mastery remains out of reach. The *Berlin Childhood*'s enigmatic texture has lead readers of Benjamin such as Burkhardt Lindner to marvel at a "secret doctrine of semiotics."[2] If the allegorical tableaux of the *Berlin Childhood* belong, as Peter Szondi remarks, "to the most beautiful prose poetry of our time" ("Hoffnung im Vergangenen" 276), their beauty is always touched by the rigorous language of an otherness that prevents the corporeal self it depicts from coming into its own.

In the *Berlin Childhood*, the language of this otherness is one of *harte Fügung* as Hermann Schweppenhäuser has observed, rhetorical figures and poetic constructions that perpetually interrupt the flow of reading and compel the reader to linger with each sentence to ponder its manifold meanings ("Physiognomie eines Physiognomikers" 149). As figures of a *harte Fügung*, the sentences of the *Berlin Childhood* are scissions or caesuras that suspend the textual self in the act of reading. Benjamin's "sentences," as Sontag once put it, "do not seem to be generated in the usual way; they do not entail. Each sentence is written as if it were the first, or the last" ("Saturn" 129). In the same way that Benjamin's sentences do not entail, they can never project the image of a coherent corporeal self.

Written during the most difficult years of Benjamin's exile and persecution, there is no page of the *Berlin Childhood* that is not touched by the images and threats of fascism. In a letter to Scholem from 3 March 1934 concerning the difficulties of finding a publisher for the book, Benjamin registers the political preoccupations that traverse his work on the text and that reveal themselves only during nightly visions—in the form of photographic negatives, as it were—to be the intensive engagements with the politics of fascism that they are: "In these times, when my imagination is preoccupied with the most unworthy problems between sunrise and sunset, I experience at night, more and more often, its emancipation in dreams, which nearly always have a political subject. I would really like to be in a position to tell you about them someday. They represent a pictorial atlas of the secret history of National Socialism" (*CBS* 100; *BW* 128). In his afterword to the posthumous publication of the *Berlin Childhood*, Adorno takes up the secret preoccupation with the political that traverses the text of Benjamin's life when he suggests that the "historical archetypes that [Benjamin] wished to develop [in the *Passagen-Werk*] out of their pragmatico-social and philosophical origin were, in the Berlin book, to flash up abruptly out of the immediacy of memory—with the force of pain felt for the irretrievable which, once it is lost, coagulates into an allegory of one's own demise." As Adorno continues, "For the images that the book conjures up to estranging proximity are neither idyllic nor contemplative. The shadow of Hitler's Reich lies cast upon them. . . . The air surrounding the sites that are about to awake in Benjamin's presentation [*Darstellung*] is deadly. Upon them falls the gaze of the condemned one, and he perceives them as condemned" (74f.). If the *Berlin Childhood*'s topography of representation is linked to something deadly, then the movements of its language stage a consistent confrontation with this deadly threat. In a constellation of figurative tableaux bearing titles such as "The Moon," "Winter Morning," "Butterfly Hunt," "The Stocking," "A Ghost," "Colors," "Society," "Two Puzzling Images," and "Victory Pillar," Benjamin's corporeal self disappears into language itself, a movement it shares with the self of Proust's *A la Recherche du Temps Perdu*, the great inspiration of, and intertext to, the *Berlin Childhood*.

Here, as in his other autobiographical texts, Benjamin stages the self's confrontation with fascism by taking recourse to the language of the body. This strategy becomes clear in a preface to the *Berlin Childhood* that Giorgio Agamben, Benjamin's Italian editor, found in 1981 in the Bibliothèque Nationale in Paris among papers that Benjamin's friend Georges Bataille had hidden there from the Nazis. Benjamin writes:

> In 1932, when I was abroad, it began to dawn on me that I would soon be forced to take a long, perhaps permanent, leave of absence from the city in which I was born.
>
> I had experienced the process of immunization as salutary to my inner life several times; I kept to it in this situation as well, intentionally conjuring up within me images—those of my childhood—which in exile incite one's homesickness the most. In the process, my feeling of longing was to conquer my spirit as little as a vaccine my healthy body. I attempted to keep the feeling at bay with my insights not into my accidental biographical irretrievability of the past but into the necessarily societal one.
>
> This procedure is responsible for the fact that the biographical traces, which show themselves more in the continuity than in the depth of experience, step back fully in these attempts. With them the

physiognomies—those of my family and my comrades. Rather, I have tried to capture the images in which the experience of a metropolis are reflected in a child of the bourgeoisie.

I think it possible that such images have their own destiny. . . . The images of my metropolitan childhood are perhaps capable of prefiguring, in their inner realm, later historical experience. (7:385)

From the beginning, Benjamin predicates his self-portrait, if it is one, on the body. If the scene of writing and the process of memory must not be touched by melancholia, Benjamin employs the rhetoric of a healthy body that must not succumb to the invading vaccine, which both attacks the body and serves to strengthen it. Yet this rhetoric of the body is tied to a twofold structure. On the one hand, to be sure, the body becomes the very site of self-portraiture. On the other hand, however, Benjamin tells us that within the language of this self-portraiture *physiognomies* fade in order for *images* to emerge. Benjamin here seems to take leave of the corpus in favor of a realm of images. But I wish to suggest that what Benjamin's language stages here is not a *retreat* from the body but rather its *displacement* into the rhetoric of the image in a way that reenacts the interpenetrating forces of *Leibraum* and *Bildraum* evoked by his essay on surrealism. This displacement also traces the shift away from the body of alterity in the *Moscow Diary* and the ear in the *Berlin Chronicle* to vision and the eye in the *Berlin Childhood*.

If Benjamin stresses a shift of emphasis toward the images of the corporeal self, we may think of them as belonging to the realm of what he calls "dialectical images." Although there are many competing definitions of it, a dialectical image for Benjamin is what breaks out of history conceived of as a teleological process.[3] "It is not," he tells us in the *Passagen-Werk*, "that the past casts its light on the present or the present casts its light on the past: rather an image is that in which the Then [*das Gewesene*] and the Now [*das Jetzt*] come into a constellation like a flash of lightning. In other words: image is dialectics at a standstill." He continues: "For while the relation of the present to the past is a purely temporal, continuous one, the relation of the Then to the Now is dialectical— not development but image[,] leaping forth [*sprunghaft*].—Only dialectical images are genuine (i.e., not archaic) images; and the place one encounters them is language" (N 49; 5:576f.). In

Benjamin's dialectical image, the historicity of an object or trope is cast in terms other than those that the temporality of historicism attaches to it. Like Benjamin's body, which, as we have seen more than once, has a language ("Language has a body and the body has a language"; 3:138), the image too belongs to language. That the body and the image share the space of language means that even when Benjamin speaks primarily of images, his language is also touched by the body. There can be no rhetoric of images that is not also a rhetoric of the body and vice versa. Therefore, if Benjamin has the "physignomies" of the *Berlin Childhood* retreat in favor of images, the body simultaneously returns in and as the rhetoric of the image. If Benjamin here stages a retreat and return of the body, he re-treats it in the reading of images. This is so because, as Benjamin tells us, "reading is the highest traditional physiognomy" (6:170).

We could say that the body of the *Berlin Childhood* belongs to the language of those images that, as Benjamin tells us in a brief speech on Proust, we recall prior to their occurrence, "images that we never saw before remembering them" (2:1064). To engage the language of these corporeal images means to be open to the reading of a radically new singularity that is simultaneously a repetition of something else (and therefore not singular). We must both recall and construct these images anew, that is, to negotiate the ways in which their rhetorical structure is both idiomatic and shared by other language.

If the body preforms historical experience, as Benjamin suggests, then the historical experience depends on this interpenetration of the image, language, and the corpus. I wish to argue in this chapter that the *Berlin Childhood* works to clarify the role of this interpenetration in the act of self-portraiture. In the *Berlin Childhood*, I would suggest, Benjamin is obsessed with the ways in which the vicissitudes of the eye simultaneously make and unmake the corporeal "I." While the problem of the subject in the *Moscow Diary* is cast in terms of the body and, in the *Berlin Chronicle*, in terms of the ear, the *Berlin Childhood* enacts it in relation to figures of the gazing eye. The *Berlin Childhood* is a text which turns on problems of vision and it can be read as a unique constellation of flashlike moments and dialectical images that stage the corpus—which is embodied by the gazing child playing on the threshold of two centuries—as hovering between affirmation and disarticulation within the rhetoric of the visual. In its refusal to reduce the visual self's body to a stable concept, the *Berlin Childhood* shares with Benjamin's other autobiographical texts the mobilization of innovative concepts that, in their vicissitudinous nature, would be useless or unemployable by the fascist machines of stable meaning.

If the foreword to the *Berlin Childhood* employs the language of a body that is to be injected with a vaccine without succumbing to it and if Benjamin's entire autobiographical project relies on the body to generate concepts that are useless for the purposes of fascism, then the rhetorical movements of these texts strive toward something that exceeds the Nazis' program of an internal renewal of the *Volk*'s body and its alleged German essence. When Benjamin evokes the body in his attempts at self-portraiture, he implicitly breaks with a certain fascist cult of the body, a fiction that generates the myth of a German corpus fully readable and present to itself as a carrier of determined political meaning. If, for Benjamin, the corpus is always also a corpse, then, for Hitler, the ultimate ideological telos of Nazism is the achievement of a "unified national body" (*Mein Kampf* 397) that arises to its political destiny. Therefore, Nazism is disdainful of those who "directed foreign blood into our national body" and thereby "contributed to that catastrophic splintering of our inner being which is expressed in German super-individualism" (390). Whereas Benjamin's corpus insists on the aporetic movement of language in the untenable constructions of a so-called identity, for Hitler, any mode of identity such as "nationality or rather race does not happen to lie in language but in the blood." For him, the infusion of the other's blood, the other's visceral alterity, into the allegedly self-identical national body can only weaken its organic wholeness. It causes "a blood mixture [that] brings about a change, which, however, means the lowering of the level of the higher race" (389). In a speech held in 1932, the year in which Benjamin began composing the *Berlin Childhood*, Hitler therefore emphasizes to the Industry Club in Düsseldorf that "the primary necessity is the restoration of a sound national German body politic aimed to strike." Hitler continues:

> In order to realize this end I founded thirteen years ago the National Socialist movement: that movement I have led during the last twelve years, and I hope that one day it will accomplish this task and that, as

the fairest result of its struggle, it will leave behind it a German body politic completely renewed internally, intolerant of anyone who sins against the nation and its interests, intolerant of anyone who will not acknowledge its vital interests or who opposes them, intolerant and pitiless against anyone who shall attempt once more to destroy or disintegrate this body politic. ("Address to the Industry Club" 141)

Hitler here takes up a trope of the fascist body he had already mobilized before, for instance in *Mein Kampf,* where he evokes it in terms of a mass phantasmagoria of an essential, organic German community:

But the community of the great demonstration not only strengthens the individual, it also unites and helps to create an *esprit de corps.* The man who is exposed to grave tribulations . . . absolutely needs that strengthening which lies in the conviction of being a member and fighter in a great comprehensive body. And he obtains an impression of this body for the first time in the mass demonstration. When from his little workshop or big factory, in which he feels very small, he steps for the first time into a mass meeting and has thousands and thousands of people of the same opinions around him, when, as a seeker, he is swept away by three or four thousand others into the mighty effect of suggestive intoxication and enthusiasm, when the visible success and agreement of thousands confirm to him the rightness of the new doctrine . . . then he himself has succumbed to the magic influence of what we designate as "mass suggestion." The will, the longing, and also the power of thousands are accumulated in every individual. The man who enters such a meeting doubting and wavering leaves it inwardly reinforced: he has become a link in the community. (*Mein Kampf* 478f.)

For Hitler, the body of the German people serves as an ideologically stabilizing concept, a single idea in which the differences and heterogeneities that traverse individual German bodies are erased in order to yield the intoxicated collective body of an essential meta-subject, the Subject-as-Body. Benjamin's autobiographical corpus, both in the *Berlin Childhood* and in other texts, can be read as a deconstruction of this ideology of the originary, authentic Subject-as-Body. In his complex stagings of the corpus, Benjamin counters Nazism's phantasmagorical constructions of the meaningful, self-identical body with a body that time and again exceeds any form of hermeneutic closure or stable meaning; he counters the idea of a single, secure, and pure meta-subject with an aleatory, dispersed subject. In contrast to Hitler's phantasm of a community of monolithic essences, Benjamin's corpus exceeds any kind of instrumentality. If Benjamin deconstructs the mythology of the fascist body, he transgresses an ideology that according to his friend Kracauer aligns "the organic connection of nature with something that the all too modest temperament takes to be soul or spirit—that is, exalting the body by assigning it meanings which emanate from it and may indeed be spiritual but which do not contain the slightest trace of reason" ("Mass Ornament" 86). The figure of Benjamin's body names this transgression.

That in the *Berlin Childhood* Benjamin develops such corporeal transgressions of fascism in the language of the gaze and the image means that he wishes to reexamine the privileges that have been accorded to vision, often called the "noblest of the senses."[4] When Benjamin's self is touched by vision, it is always already speaking of the threat of its absence: blindness and darkness. His rhetoric stages the simultaneous presence and absence of vision when the self calls upon it to provide reliable readings.[5] The brief quasi-photographic thought-images of the *Berlin Childhood* form a constellation in which the self is constantly revised. While each individual scene or node in the constellation shares a structural similarity regarding the self's visual construction and dispersal, each scene is also singular and specific to its formal context. Each time, then, the visual self assumes a different shape; each time it must be rewritten. The movement of this revision recalls the Benjaminian self that Bloch identifies in his 1928 review of *One-Way Street*: Benjamin's " 'I' is very near, but variable, indeed there are many 'I's; likewise almost every sentence starts anew, cooks differently and different things" ("Revue" 334) so that "[c]onstantly new 'I's . . . are to be seen here and extinguish one another" (335). By juxtaposing heterogeneous elements into a constellation, the *Berlin Childhood* performs Benjamin's version of a materialist historiography in which close rhetorical analyses are fruitfully linked on the body of the self to larger historical and cultural problems. The constellation of fragments reenacts the revisionary character of Benjamin's corporeal subject.

The complicated philological status of the *Berlin Childhood* also points to the central movement of the subject his self-portrait performs.[6] The many divergent *morphai* of Benjamin's text constitute a textual reenactment of the Benjaminian "subject." This subject is comprised of torn pieces and miscellaneous fragments, a specter fleeting by only to return in a different and no less transitory form. Ultimately, the problem of authorizing and validating a single textual "presence" by affixing to it a binding or intentional signature is as difficult as it is undecidable. Like its autobiography, Benjamin's corpus is constantly in flux, ceaselessly revised and rewritten. Elements of Benjamin's "self" survive from version to version, but with each new draft they undergo another transformation. Both text and self remain the same and metamorphose all at once. The "shattered" philological status of Benjamin's text thus enacts, as it were, the vicissitudes of the subject. Indeed, the shattered text is the subject's proper form.

We may begin to approach what is at stake in the *Berlin Childhood*'s visual constructions and undoings of the corporeal self by recalling Benjamin's statement in the *Passagen-Werk*, "In the fields with which we are concerned, cognition [*Erkenntnis*] comes only in lightning flashes" (N 43; 1:570). Here, in the moment of an illumination, the bolt of lightning both enables vision and blinds. In keeping with the stance of Benjamin's theses "On the Concept of History," insight here takes the form of a snapshot, a momentarily frozen image that encrypts the unique historical and subjective constellations of a particular moment in time as an event. Such a flash is a kind of caesura, a sudden break within the continuity of a narrative or an image. In this caesura, the seeing or reading self is both enabled and undone.

That Benjamin is preoccupied with the problem of vision becomes clear not only in the many metaphors of vision, images, cameras, and photography that permeate many of his well-known writings, it also emerges in the language of lesser known texts such as "A Glimpse into the World of Children's Books" (1926), where we learn that "sight is the watershed of the senses" (W 442; 4:614). He elaborates on the centrality of the visual sense in an aphorism from *One-Way Street*. There, Benjamin writes, "In the eyes we see people to the lees [*Der Blick ist die Neige des Menschen*]" (W 472; 4:125). Benjamin's use of the word *Neige* sets into motion a series of meanings that are operative throughout the *Berlin Childhood*. According to the Grimms' dictionary, *Neige*, as related to *Neigung*, denotes a person's preference, inclination, leanings, and the expression of these in a particular skill or talent. This semantic level of *Neige* refers to the positive qualities associated with the gaze, such as its capacity to organize our experience of the world in a manner consistent with the inclinations and talents of the self. But *Neige* also refers to denigration and decline; it calls the reliability and truthfulness of vision into question. A third meaning of *Neige* refers to the semantic field of sloping surfaces, of hollows and downward-leaning trajectories, and the danger of an image involuntarily sliding out of view. Yet, at the same time, once the corporeal self recognizes the vicissitudes of the gaze, once it withdraws from the scene of vision, it comes to understand that it must nevertheless keep returning to the gaze. For *Neige* can also refer to the end of something, to the marginal residue of a self thrown back upon the insufficiency that is its being. The self now lives with the knowledge of the simultaneous inevitability and inadequacy of its own hermeneutic instrument. Living in this state of instability, the gaze is the subject's worst fate—in the sense that it betrays rather than enlightens—but also its last residue, what remains when the subject has been emptied out of all other properties and qualities and submits now to a final critical inventory of its remains. After all, a further meaning of *Neige*, acquired in fifteenth-century German, names the residual content of an otherwise empty or hollow vessel, its dregs. The bodily subject is now caught between the limits of the gaze, its own contingencies and contradictions, and the promise it holds. This is how Benjamin's aphorism tells us how to read the *Berlin Childhood*. The aporia of the gaze and its *Neige* names the corporeal self between construction and dispersal.

Visual Constructions

To trace this double movement through the *Berlin Childhood*, we must understand, first, how the self appropriates vision to construct itself. Here, we may turn to a number of texts that enact the ways in which the gaze tends to aid the subject in writing itself. Like Baudelaire's Parisian flâneur, Benjamin strolls through the streets of Berlin, casting an ironically detached gaze on the spectacle the metropolis offers. He shares with Baudelaire's flâneur a look that constantly surveys and rejects, engages and re-treats.[7] The motto of the flâneur is, as we learn in the *Passagen-Werk*, "Look at everything, touch nothing" (5:968). The flâneur's gazes that Benjamin casts on Berlin are almost equally divided between those that touch exterior scenes—from "Tiergarten" to "Krumme Street" and "Beggars and Whores," from "Indoor Market" to "Accidents and Crimes" and beyond—and those that regard interior topographies such as "The Desk," "Closets," "Thick Tombs of Light Reading," or "Sewing-Box."[8] In both spheres, the gaze of the Benjaminian flâneur hopes to assure the self of its being in its reading of the many texts that public and private spaces present.

In the segment "Fever," for instance, Benjamin works to employ the language of vision to resist a certain logic of consumption that is tied to a capitalist fetishization of the commodity. This visual resistance takes the form of a finger play. Here, the ill and bedridden child secretly performs stories and scenarios under the blanket, with his fingers starring as the characters:

> I crawled in; I pulled the blanket over my head and turned my ear toward the dark abyss, occasionally feeding the silence words that returned from it as stories. From time to time, my fingers got involved and performed a scenario on their own; or they played "store" with each other, and behind the table, formed by my two middle fingers, my two pinkies nodded eagerly toward the customer who was played by myself. But my desire [*Lust*] and my power [*Macht*] to control their game grew weaker and weaker. In the end I followed almost without curiosity the activities of my fingers which operated like lazy, shady riff-raff on the outskirts of a city consumed by a fire. Impossible to trust them an inch [*Nicht möglich, ihnen über den Weg zu trauen*]. (7:405)

In their figurality, Benjamin's fingers appear to be independent of the corporeal self, as if they were details in a baroque painting (Bohrer 161). Safe from the gazes of the adults, the child displays to his own view the mechanisms that drive the logic of the adult commodity exchange one witnesses everywhere in Berlin. The child's fingers figure as customers and vendors, counters and department stores. As such, they enact the basic inventory of a capitalist logic. But, significantly, the child gradually loses interest in this spectacle of the eternal repetition of exchange. At first, he loses his desire (*Lust*) to watch the scenario—so that there is also, on the level of the implied sexual scenario, a sudden interruption of masturbation. Then he even loses control of the game altogether. Here, the logic of the commodity has entered the relentless, self-perpetuating machination that is its procedure. The imagined characters suddenly degenerate into disgusting "riff-raff" who are linked to the destruction of the city and who cannot be trusted under any circumstances. In this way, the mise-en-scène of the commodity produces in the spectator the impetus for critique, propelled by a mood of estrangement that distances him from the action of the play and its characters. In the rhetoric of the finger play, Benjamin here shares the dramatic demands of his friend Brecht.[9] The dramatic delusion of the commodity is, as Benjamin says in a speech on Brecht, "staged in its slight, torn appearance" (2:667). Epic theater under the blanket.

The reading of commodity fetishism that "Fever" implicitly stages is echoed in the segment "Indoor Market" (*Markthalle*). Here, the gazing self works to come to terms with the specific mechanisms which manufacture modes of perception that fetishize the commodity as a form of cultural consciousness. In what Benjamin experiences as the swampy, oozy prehistoric world of the market, merchants appear as secret priests of the commodity, and the *Marktfrauen* as mystic rulers over the land of fruits and birds, even as disfigured woolen giants. The primal landscape this segment conjures can be read as a literalization of the mortified primal landscape of allegory that Benjamin evokes in his study of the *Trauerspiel*. Because the landscape of this market is presented as something primeval, it would be difficult to imagine the kind of rigorous critique of the dialectic of Enlightenment for which Horkheimer and Adorno call, as the Enlightenment does not seem even to have occurred here.[10] Benjamin, mimicking the distracted but meditatively alert gaze of Baudelaire's flâneur, meanders moodily through this worldly temple of Berlin's great market, its topography of claustrophobic spaces, reeling paths, suspicious gazes, and haggling voices. Meditating on the words "markt" and "halle," Benjamin tells us: "First of all, let no one think that it was called "Markt-Halle." No, people said "Mark-Thalle"; and just as these two words were effaced in the habit of speaking to such a degree that neither one retained its original meaning, so my habit of strolling through this market effaced all the images it granted, so that none of them offered themselves to the customary concepts of buying and selling" (7:402). The customs of fossilized rhetoric ("Mark-Thalle"), which rely on the phonetic rather than the semantic qualities of the signifier, work to conceal the movements of the market and its commodities. This linguistic mortification, in which what is the commonsensical turns out to be the questionable or absurd, prevents the proper naming of the space of the commodity. Yet the child's perception of the market's multiple images and words works to interrupt and transgress the exchange of money and objects. The child reads "Mark-Thalle" critically against the grain, perhaps hearing echoes of the double encoding of the two German currencies that the word seals within its disfiguration: the contemporary *Mark* and the historical currency, the *Thaler*. The diacritical marker between the two words separates and unites them at the same time. It registers a break between them, even as it encrypts the historical continuity of currency through which the economy of the commodity operates. The self's gaze thus casts a second, critical glance at a word in order to liberate through this visual intervention the economic and historical resonances hidden with it.

This logic of the gaze that touches the commodity can be read in terms of a Marxist second glance. I wish to suggest that Benjamin's gesture here implicitly refers to a passage from *Capital* on the fetish-character of the commodity. There, in "The Fetish Character of the Commodity and Its Secret," Marx evokes the mystical properties of the commodity in a rhetoric of vision. Casting his critique of commodity fetishism in the language of the gaze, Marx employs metaphors strikingly drawn from the semantic field of vision. He tells us that a "commodity appears at first sight [*auf den ersten Blick*] a trivial, self-evident thing." He continues to structure his rejection of this superficial first glance around images of the eye ("to observe" [*betrachen*], point of view [*Gesichtspunkt*], or "very clear" [*sinnenklar*]).[11] Benjamin was well aware of Marx's passage and even includes it in "Convolute G" of the *Passagen-Werk*. If Marx analyzes the secret of the fetishized commodity in the figurative language of vision, he conceives of an elusive process of infinite substitution in which a series of displacements erases the traces of their own circulation so that the origin of the desire with which the commodity comes to be invested remains a blind spot.[12] We could say that Benjamin's segment literalizes Marx's metaphors of the eye. What Benjamin's self here shares with Marx is a sense of the necessity to reject *den ersten Blick* and to cast, instead, a *second* glance. This second glance, in the act of reading, attempts to trace the elusive movements through which a word simultaneously hides and exposes the political and cultural history inscribed in it.

If young Benjamin mobilizes the visual sense in order to empower himself and to resist the logic of certain cultural mechanisms, his gaze must be directed at the margins of his cultural text—the hidden and the peripheral. This kind of strategic looking awry is what Benjamin elsewhere admires as Kafka's secret gesture when he writes that there "is little that is so emblematic for Kafka as the suspicious gaze that he casts time and again on what is bad, disturbing, discarded as though it were something inconvenient but long familiar" (2:1199). In keeping with the movements of Kafka's gaze, Benjamin finds obscure objects and spaces endowed with a special, secret meaning. Once unearthed, these meanings may yield unanticipated insights. An example of this looking toward neglected or marginal spaces is the child's experience, in "Krumme Street," of coyly locating at the stationary store—in the background, between inconspicuous accounting books, pairs of compasses, and other office supplies—those pornographic "objectionable publications" whose special hiding place is fully invisible to the "uninitiated gaze." Only the shop decorations partake silently of the child's discoveries, "celebrat[ing] the incriminating event" (7:415). And in "The Otter," the gaze centers on the flashlike instances that shoot up erratically from the dark depths of an otter's underwater world. In the Berlin zoo, the child obstinately prefers to spend his time not with the popular animals preferred by the other children but rather at the out-of-the-way kennel of the mostly invisible—though, as it turns out, prophetic—otter. Benjamin writes:

> It was a prophetic corner. For just as there are plants of which it is said they possess the power to let one glimpse the future, so there are places that have the same gift. These are mostly abandoned sites such as tree-tops leaning against a wall, one-way streets, or front yards where no one ever spends any time. In such places it seems as though everything that is actually ahead of us were something past. It was in this part of the zoo where, whenever I lost my way and came across it, I was granted a gaze over the edge of the basin which rose up here as if it were in the center of a spa. This was the otter's kennel. (7:407)

If the *Berlin Chronicle*, which works through a rhetoric of the ear, became visible in the previous chapter as an autobiography that is an "otobiography," then the *Berlin Childhood* is here something of an "otterbiography."[13] Benjamin's gaze into the dark abyss out of which a snapshot-like image shoots up to become legible for the patient and astute reader literalizes what in "Central Park" Benjamin identifies as the core strategy of Baudelaire's poetry: "The particular beauty of the openings of so many of Baudelaire's poems: their emergence from the abyss" (*CP* 32; 1:657). Similarly, in his 1931 "Doctrine of the Similar" Benjamin speaks of "similarities" that "flash up fleetingly from the stream of things only in order to become immediately engulfed again" (*D* 68; 2:209). Enacting what Benjamin tells us is Baudelaire's rhetoric of emergence, the child's profane and specialized reading of the otter shooting up from the depths of its water basin promises to reveal a surprisingly telling image.[14] This image belongs, again, to the realm of the dialectical image which, according to the *Passagen-Werk*, "is the primal phenomenon of history" (*N* 64; 5:592).[15] Like the otter, this image is imprinted with a historical signature that points beyond itself, with the "traces of what is to come" (7:407). The child revels in the image of the otter with an insatiable visual passion. Benjamin tells us that he "could have spent days upon days with my forehead pressed to his railings without having seen enough of him," and "I watched him insatiably" (7:408). Like the children rummaging through the "Construction Site" of *One-Way Street*, where they are "irresistibly drawn by the detritus" because they can discern in it "the face that the world of things turns directly and solely to them" (*W* 449f.; 4:93), the child of the *Berlin Childhood* focuses on the marginal otter in order to understand the hidden figures of its workings. And like the children at the construction site, who become emblems of the Benjaminian material historiographer who collects the garbage of history for revolutionary purposes, he hopes to blast the existing structures and norms apart in order to confront the tropes and movements of their historicity and their political significance.[16]

That the child relies on the gaze as a potentially heuristic device also becomes clear in the initial text of the *Berlin Childhood*, "Loggias." There, Benjamin evokes the metropolitan milieu of fin-de-siècle Berlin, whose impressions and idiosyncrasies are interlaced with the early consciousness of the narrating voice. The loggias, inset balconies typical of the Wilhelminian architecture of Berlin apartment buildings, are an essential part of the child's spatial and perspectival experience of the city. As we learn in the segment "Blumeshof 12": "Of these out-of-the-way spaces, the loggia was the most important one to me, be it because the street noise pushed its way up to it in a muffled manner, be it because it offered to my gaze strange courtyards, children, and organ-grinders [*weil sie mir den Blick auf fremde Höfe mit Portiers, Kindern und Leierkastenmännern freigab*]" (7:412). The word loggias refers both to the particularity of a socially coded living space—that of the established Berlin bourgeoisie—and a demarcated viewing space from which to observe the theater of the city from a distance. ("Loggia" points back etymologically to the French "loge," a separate, privileged space for a segment of a theater's audience). From here, the child casts his glance at class demarcations. The balcony not only leads out of the maze of the upper-bourgeois apartment, it also yields a view onto the underprivileged courtyard-facing apartments, where poor children are playing on dirty pavements. Such images return with an uncanny regularity: the privileged child uneasily observes the poorer children trying to sell their beloved Christmas toys to the richer ones; a courtyard family lights its pathetic Christmas tree; or the recurring gazes that Benjamin casts into depths of the underworld of the dark cellar apartments, an image that returns to haunt the child as a surreal nightmare.[17] The child's gaze always carries with it, even if only as a fleeting phantom, the oppositional spirit and sensitivities of class consciousness.

If, from his balcony, the child breathes the very air of the city, then "it is precisely this air in which the images and allegories dwell that rule over my thinking the way the caryatids on the loggias' level rule over the courtyards of Berlin's West side [*eben diese Luft, in der die Bilder und Allegorien stehen, die über meinem Denken herrschen wie die Karyatiden auf der Loggienhöhe über die Höfe des Berliner Westens*]" (7:386).[18] These images comprise, for instance, the movements of street cars and the beating of rugs, the spastic torrents and swells of river water, the scent of fresh milk and the dim dusty roofs, the coachman's heavy boots on the pavement or the small grocer letting down the metal shutters for the night. Such images do not rule "over" the child's thinking, but rather "above" it ("*über meinem Denken herrschen*"). Benjamin's surprising preference for the dative over the accusative case makes this distinction. It implies that the signs and images of the metropolis not only determine the subject's consciousness, they also give it a perspectival domain, even as they remain strikingly elusive. From this second perspective, the images and allegories perceived by the child exist in their own configuration "above" the subject—both literally and figuratively. In order to make sense of them, the child must explode their seemingly natural and independent configuration. He must rearrange them radically by placing them in an unexpected constellation which exposes them as a text.

Benjamin illustrates this point theoretically in the seventeenth thesis "On the Concept of History." There, he writes: "Where thinking suddenly stops in a constellation saturated with tensions, it gives that constellation a shock, by which it crystallizes into a monad. The historical materialist approaches a historical subject only where it moves toward him as a monad. In this structure he recognizes the sign of a Messianic cessation of happening. . . . He seizes the opportunity to blast a specific era out of the homogenous course of history" (*I* 263; 1:703). Rejecting the concept of totality as the false veil of historical continuity, Benjamin here privileges the historical fragment that has been strategically blown out of its fossilized river bed. It is now placed in a new structure of dialectical juxtapositions and temporal discontinuities where it can be read attentively. For Benjamin, this explosion signals not an erasure of history but rather a rearticulation of an object's historicity. The grammatical shift from the accusative to the dative case that "Loggias" performs thus encodes those activities which, as Benjamin tells us, are required for an encounter with the historical that brings to light the internal differences of an object's or text's historicity.

Finally, that the child seeks to empower himself through the visual sense also becomes clear when Benjamin relies on it to stabilize a future memory in advance by relentlessly engraving certain images into his mnemonic archive. Even in light of the eventual impossibility of this project, Benjamin stresses the importance of the gaze in surveying the engaging scenes enacted in Berlin's courtyards. Here, "nothing strengthened my memory more intensely than my gaze into the courtyards with its dark loggias, one of which, shaded in the summer by an awning, was a cradle to me, one into which the city put its new citizen" (7:386). Similarly, the child's consciousness reclaims the summer light of the courtyards through the visual. "Later, from the railway, I discovered," Benjamin writes, "the courtyards anew. When, on humid summer afternoons, I looked down on them from my compartment, summer, having renounced the landscape, seemed captured in them" (7:387). The child's gaze is his instrument of constant revision and supervision, and it allows him to read the text of the city cunningly against the grain.

Reversals 1: Gazes and Sounds

So far, we have encountered rhetorical images in which the corporeal self seeks to mobilize the gaze in order to empower and construct itself. But this project is threatened by its own impossibility, its blindness. The gaze will not remain what it is, and the corporeal self cannot rely on it to provide stable insights. For instance, both the courtyard and the loggias, the child's refuges that he conquered and subsequently maintained through the eye, metamorphose upon closer inspection into less than desirable scenes. Benjamin encounters the once joyful brightness of the late morning in a surprising and consternating shift in perspectives. Now, "the late morning, when I encountered it on our loggia, had already been late morning for such a long time that it seemed to be more itself than in any other spot. I could never await it here; it was always already awaiting me" (7:387). This haunting movement from "Loggias" is mirrored throughout the texts. For example, in "Winter Morning," "the flame, as if crouched into an undersized compartment where it could hardly move because of all the coal, was looking over to me" (7:397). In both scenes, Benjamin registers the shocking moment when he realizes that he is already being looked at by the object which he had expected to subject to the surveillance of his own gaze.[19] The gaze, which was intended to perceive and dominate the other in an effort to solidify the fragile self, is cast back onto the self. To be subjected to the look of the other—and to experience the construction of the self in being perceived—means to experience oneself as contingent upon the other's activity and judgment, not as a self-identical being. To be looked at, then, engenders a loss of autonomy. The gaze of the other spatializes, temporalizes, and even corporealizes the self. That is to say, being traversed by the gaze of the other reminds the self that it is corporeal. This realization affords the self the briefest glimpse into the spatial, temporal, and bodily restrictions that situate it in a network of contingencies at any given moment. For the corporeal self that is being looked at, there can be no narrative of continuity and transcendence. The self may attempt to rupture this uneasy scene of contingency by blushing, that is, by figuratively hiding its own body from view. As Benjamin explains in the early fragment "On Shame": "Blushing with shame does not rise up from the inside, and every emerging blushing with shame, of which one sometimes

speaks, is not located in the one who feels ashamed. Rather, this
blushing pours over the ashamed one from the outside and from
the top, simultaneously erasing his shame and protecting him from
his violators. For in every dark blushing that shame pours over him,
it withdraws him from people's gazes as if under a veil. He who
feels ashamed cannot see, but he also cannot be seen" (6:69f.).
Here, the promise of the gaze transforms itself into the uncanny
absence of visibility. The very movement of this failed promise leads
to the coda of "Loggias." In a gesture of reversal that signals pending
mortification, the "child, who was once a member of the alliance,
now . . . dwells in his loggia as in a mausoleum long intended for
him" (7:388).[20] While the loggias appeared at first sight to be secure
havens for the child, they are actually crypts—empty graves whose
images work to haunt the subject's psychic apparatus.

If the self can no longer rely on the stability of the gaze, Benjamin simultaneously casts this aporia in terms of an antagonism
between the ear and the eye, between sounds and images. This
tension becomes clear in the proto-cinematic spaces of the "Imperial
Panorama." The "Imperial Panorama" (*Kaiserpanorama*) was a round
apparatus that permitted spectators seated in front of it to look at
rotating images through a set of windows. Here, the child's viewing
of the images is constantly interrupted by "a small, essentially disruptive . . . ringing which occurred during the few seconds when the
image disappeared into the background, releasing first a gap and then
the next image" (7:388).[21] Benjamin's gaze is perpetually thrown off
center by the ringing noise of the bell. In a movement that enacts
Benjamin's *Neige* as an image slipping out of view, the child cannot
focus on the visual material to be read and its meanings remain indeterminate. Here, we learn, "before I was certain, the entire structure
separating me from the wooden veneer started to shake. The image
began to waver in its small frame and, moving to the left, soon stole
out from under my glances" (7:388). Like the oversaturated image-
space of modernity, in which the self encounters, as Benjamin writes
in the *Passagen-Werk*, an undecidable "excess of information . . .
whose stimulating effects grow stronger the more information resists
any utilization" (5:560), the space of the "Imperial Panorama" is
traversed by phantom images that the self cannot arrest for good.

Benjamin takes up this rhetoric of an acoustic signal disrupting
the scene of vision in "Krumme Street." There, he writes:

Not far from the swimming-pool was the city reading hall. Even with its iron galleries it was neither too high nor too frosty for me. I sensed that I was in my proper territory. For its scent preceded it. Its scent was waiting to receive me as under a thin, mountainous layer underneath the moist, cold scent of its stairwell. I opened the iron door only shyly. Yet, I had hardly entered the hall when its silence adopted my strength.

What disgusted me most about the swimming-pool was the noisy polyphony [*Stimmenlärm*] that blended into the roaring of the pipes. It emerged already from the foyer where everyone had to purchase a leg-tag. After that, nothing could save you from the arching masses of water on the inside. It was the seat of a suspicious or cross-eyed goddess [*scheele Göttin*] who was out to take us to her breast and to nurse us from her cold chambers until there was no trace left of us in the upper world. (7:415f.)

This passage enacts the conflict between, on the one hand, the gaze as an instrument of cognition and, on the other, a polyphony of voices that threaten to unmake the self. The reading gaze is fostered by the library's silence, the absence of auditory stimulation. Here, the child, engrossed in his reading activities, can utilize his gaze in order to gain knowledge about himself and the world. Adjacent to the library is the public swimming pool whose close geographical proximity effectively intensifies the contrast to the former. If the swimming pool is the domain of the ear where a polyphony of loud voices disgusts the child, the calm reading gaze is thrown off center as the auditory overwhelms the other senses. It is hardly an accident that within the inner space of this polyphony resides the cross-eyed goddess as an emblem of the obscene and threatening denigration of vision. For Benjamin, the polyphony of voices remains irreconcilable with the insights of the gaze. To drink from the breast of the cross-eyed goddess is to drink the milk of blindness and eradication ("until there was no trace left of us in the upper world").

Reversals 2: The Photograph

That the efforts of Benjamin's corporeal subject at constructing itself are repeatedly undone is not only a matter of the competition between the visual and the acoustic senses. It also belongs to the space of photography. If Benjamin's self is both a body and an image, then what defines it is that it can never coincide with either of them. This aporia becomes visible in the segment "Mummerehlen." Here, at the photographer's studio, the self is preoccupied with the ghost of lost mimetic ability and its own inability to coincide with itself as an image.[22] Benjamin presents this inability of the corporeal self to resemble its own image as a photographic problem:

> Early on I learned to disguise [*mummen*] myself in words which were actually clouds. The gift of recognizing similarities is really nothing but a feeble vestige of the old compulsion to become and act similar. Words exercised such compulsion over me. Not those which worked to make me similar to patterns of proper behavior, but those which made me resemble apartments, furniture, clothes.
>
> But never my own image. That is why I was at such a loss when I was expected to be similar to myself. That was at the photographer's. Wherever I looked, I saw myself surrounded by screens, cushions, pedestals which lusted for my image like the shade of Hades for the blood of the sacrificial lamb. Finally I was presented in front of a coarsely painted Alpine view, and my right hand, which had to hold up a little goatee hat, cast its shadow upon the clouds and glacier-snow of the backdrop. Yet the tortured smile around the mouth of the young mountaineer is not as sad as the gaze that sinks into me from the child's face in the shadow of the household palm. . . . Like a mannequin my mother gazes at my velvet suit which seems to be over-loaded with trimmings and cut out of a fashion magazine. I, however, am disfigured by my similarity with everything that surrounds me. (4:261)

In this passage, which shares its language with Benjamin's description of a childhood photograph of Kafka, Benjamin's perpetual movement of disguising himself cancels the self's identity in the photographic image. Not only does the photographed self effectively become some-one else—the photographed Kafka whom he had described in almost the exact same language[23]—it also loses the ability to coincide with its own image. Instead of reproducing the likeness of the self's corpus, the photographic image causes the subject to become increasingly less self-identical. It resembles less and less itself and more and more its estranged surroundings. Here, the visual image prevents the child from coming into his own.[24] One could even say that the photo-graph is the child's crypt. For Benjamin, Eduardo Cadava writes, the "conjunction of death and the photographed is in fact the very principle of photographic certitude: the photograph is a cemetery. A small funerary moment, the photograph is a grave for the living dead. It tells their history—a history of ghosts and shadows—and it does so because it *is* this history" (10).

If what the corporeal self of the *Berlin Childhood* stages here can be thought of as "fairy-tale photographs," as Adorno suggests ("Nachwort" 76), then the text shares its concerns with Benjamin's 1931 essay "A Short History of Photography." To consider Benjamin's aporetic visual self from the perspective of this essay is to link it to the gaze and its auratic investments and to the trope of the "optical unconscious." If the seeing subject is not in full control of itself, this inability is related to the difference in perception between the naked eye and the camera:

> For it is another nature that speaks to the camera than to the eye: other primarily in the sense that a space interwoven with human consciousness is replaced by an unconscious one. Though it has already become customary to be able to give an account—if only coarsely—of the act of walking, nothing is known about people's posture in the moment of "stepping out." Photography, with its devices of slow motion and enlargement, reveals this posture. Only through photography do we find out about this optical unconscious, the way we find out about our drive-like unconscious through psychoanalysis. (OWS 243; 2:371)

For Benjamin, there can be no reading of the visual self that is not also a reading of the optical media. Like psychoanalysis, which attempts to explain the unconscious structure of the subject by focusing on various parapraxes that normally go unnoticed (such as slips of the tongue or the pen, or involuntary gestures), the camera's superior eye can detect those structures and movements of everyday existence that exceed the human eye's capacity for perception. Through technically mediated ways of seeing, including slow motion, enlargement, and infinite repetition, time lapse, close-up, and montage, the camera's eye may capture the brief moment of a person's stepping out into the open, or the complex microcosmos of positions and movements that are involved in a hand picking up a glass of water or a pair of scissors cutting a piece of cloth. In the Artwork essay, Benjamin gives us the corporeal image of a surgical instrument icily and precisely entering a body that has been visually fragmented into clinical images of skin, cells, and veins. The tiny point of the unintended intrusion of the present into the image that was intended to display something else can be thought in terms of this "optical unconscious." For it reveals to view what refuses to be repressed by the overall "argument" or surface meaning of the image. It touches upon—parapraxically, as it were, through "the tiny spark of contingency" (OWS 243; 2:371)— the unconscious or hidden structures of an image. The moment of futurity promised by this tiny accidental spark of the optical unconscious corresponds to the subject's ability to return the gaze of the apparatus. The promise of a future thus resides in the returnability of the gaze itself, a gaze to be found in the long past minute of futurity, "in the being-thus of the long lapsed minute," in which we are able to recognize, retrospectively, "what is to come" (OWS 243; 2:371). This historical belatedness disrupts time—the way the tiny accidental spark disrupts the temporality of the image and the way that any act of reading a text or an image always signals a belatedness, a disjunction in temporality.

Benjamin shares his interest in these photographic ruptures with Kracauer's 1927 essay "Photography." Both address the accidental intrusion of the unexpected into the carefully staged scene of early photographs.[25] As Kracauer writes, the "artistic intention is diametrically opposed to that of artistic photography" (53). Instead, he privileges the "ghostly reality" (56) of a photographic image. This thought is echoed by Benjamin in the *Passagen-Werk*, when he concludes that "old photographs appear ghostly" (5:496). Likewise, Benjamin's emphasis on fragmentation and montage as prime elements of the promise of the optical unconscious is prefigured at the end of Kracauer's essay. There, Kracauer suggests that film "realizes these possibilities whenever it combines parts and segments to create strange constructs" (62). Film, for Kracauer, can be a "play with nature cut into pieces," even a "*dream* in which the fragments of daily life become entangled" (63). Both Benjamin and Kracauer suggest that a scrupulous reading of the tiny sparks of the unusual that pierce the image may touch its ghostly nature, that is, the ways in which it eludes closure and intentionality. Juxtaposed in the constellations of a montage, these sparks are blind spots that may unravel the rhetorical structure of the image.

To be sensitive to such sparks or ruptures and to place them into an innovative montage means to be open to the experience of the auratic that they afford.[26] Through a critical immersion into these sparks and ruptures within the rhetoric of the object, the object's here and now, its idiom and singularity, its authority and authenticity, in short, its aura may be experienced. But precisely because of the instability of these instances—the ways in which they cannot be fully understood and perpetually defer meaning—the auratic threatens to turn into a specter. This is why in the same essay on photography Benjamin defines "aura" in terms of a ghostly interplay of distance and proximity: "What actually is aura? A strange weave of space and time: the singular appearance of a distance, however close it may be" (OWS 250; 2:378). In this strange weave of time and space, the singular appearance of a distance, which may be near, propels us to think the simultaneity of presence and absence that converges on the figure of the specter. During the encounter with the auratic, what is unreachably distant is also infinitely close. The apparent proximity which had sparked an identification of the auratic in the first place emerges as something absent. In the optical unconscious, the auratic hence touches the ghostly. Here, Benjamin predicates the experience of the aura upon our openness to the spectral interplay of the presence and absence of sense.

Benjamin is interested in early photography not simply as a cultural historian, but also because of the unintentional glimpse of something else that photographs allow, an excess of meaning that cannot be fully arrested. For Benjamin, it is the task of the viewer "to look, in such an image, for the tiny spark of contingency, the Here and Now, with which reality has, as it were, scorched the character of the image—for the inconspicuous place in which, in the being-thus of the long lapsed minute, what is to come nestles so eloquently still today that we, retrospectively, can recognize it" (OWS 243; 2:371). The optical unconscious that emerges in these accidental details of the image reveals the unconscious space precisely in cracks and fissures of the image as they rise from their gray background to form a new constellation. Benjamin's gaze is thus structured by a certain "bifurcation"—it attends to the historical or factual interest of the viewer at the same time that it exceeds that interest in order to reveal an unsuspected detail.

The distinction that Benjamin's bifurcation of the gaze makes within its field of vision is shared by Barthes's *Camera Lucida*. There, Barthes too differentiates between two modes of seeing: that of *studium* and that of *punctum*. By *studium* Barthes means the viewer's general interest in a particular area, such as the political testimony of a photograph or its status as a historical document. The viewer agrees to "participate in the figures, the faces, the gestures, the settings, the action" (*Camera* 26). *Punctum*, on the other hand, introduces a rupture or break in the scene of viewing; it pierces or punctuates. The *punctum* does not entail a prior choice or agreement on the part of the viewer. It disrupts the scene of the *studium*. "This second element," Barthes writes, "which will disturb the *studium* I shall therefore call *punctum*; for *punctum* is also: sting, speck, cut, little hole—and also a cast of the dice. A photograph's *punctum* is that accident which pricks me (but also bruises me, is poignant to me)" (27).

For Barthes, the *studium* is the field of unspecified desire, of general ("polite") interest, of preference for a general subject matter. It follows along the lines of the photographer's intention, and it tends to be didactic. The *punctum* is what erupts unexpectedly onto the scene of vision, what breaks the surface of the *studium* and thereby undermines the photographer's intention. Echoing Benjamin's "first reproduced human beings" (OWS 244; 2:372), such as the 1850 photograph of the philosopher Schelling, whose black coat is traversed by wrinkles that appear as an accidental extension of his solemn face, Barthes focuses on examples of the *punctum* such as a boy's big cloth hat or a young child's bad teeth in a street scene from New York's Little Italy. Likewise, in a picture titled "Idiot Children in an Institution—New Jersey, 1924" the *studium* is the obvious, tortured deformation of the children, the accidental *punctum* a boy's huge Danton-like collar and the girl's finger bandage. Barthes's differentiation of *studium* and *punctum* shares with Benjamin's bifurcation of the gaze not only an interest in the general socio-historical subject matter of the images but also a rhetorical sensitivity to the accidental spark that reveals the "here and now" of the photograph, the ways in which the hidden movements of their visual language work to disrupt their surface meaning. Here, for both Barthes and Benjamin, the corpus that is reproduced in an image cannot remain itself. It breaks down to reveal an otherness that always already traverses it. It is through liberating this otherness that the act of reading a photographed corpus is politically charged.

Reversals 3: The Ocular Gift

So far in this chapter, I have argued that Benjamin's vicissitudinous corporeal self in the *Berlin Childhood* is mediated by the sense of vision. We have seen that vision works both to construct this corporeal self and to reverse its construction. These reversals are lodged in the conflict of the visual and auditory as well as in the problem of the image of the self. Yet there is a third kind of reversal through which Benjamin stages the aporia of the seeing self. This third moment of reversal emerges in the uneasy link between the gaze and the gift.

If in the *Berlin Childhood* Benjamin forges relays between sending and receiving gazes and sending and receiving gifts, the segment "Fever" addresses these relays directly:

> I was sick a lot. This is perhaps why what others call my patience does not resemble in reality any virtue: my tendency to watch everything that I care about approach me from afar like the hours from my sickbed. I thus cannot take pleasure in a journey if I could not await the train at the station for a long time. Likewise, gift-giving has become a passion for me. I, as the one who gives, can anticipate what surprises the other well in advance. Indeed, my desire to look in this waiting period toward what is to come the way a sick man does, propped up on the pillows behind his back, later on caused women to seem all the more beautiful the more decisively and the longer I had to wait for them. (7:403)

The moments of involuntary waiting that structure and delay Benjamin's life are mediated by the gaze and the gift. Only when the self's gaze perceives the imagined traces of a coming event can its promise emerge. For Benjamin, the absence of an object of desire is both the impetus for lived experience and the triggering of a narrative. The desire mediated by this particular gaze does not result in any immediate corporeal gratification. Rather, this desire is directed at the moment in which the traces of a coming event eventually coincide with the event itself. This desire thus concerns the travel and movement of sense. As Benjamin tells us in the *Passagen-Werk*, for "parts of the past to be touched by actuality, there must be no continuity between them" (N 60; 5:587). But if the initial assessment of a lack or void generates the desire that triggers narrative in the first place, and if Benjamin locates the moment of suspense or incongruity between the traces of a coming event and its representation, then the two must never coincide. Otherwise, there could be no more narrative. Benjamin's image of ocular desire suggests that, in the temporality of its own deferral, the narrative never quite succeeds in having taken place. It is never complete. This is Benjamin's gift.[27]

If "Fever" links the gaze and the gift, it also raises questions concerning the self's temporality of looking. On the one hand, a self that discovers that it is already being looked at in the moment when it looks is mortified because it feels exposed to the contingencies that it is. On the other hand, this scene of the gaze triggers a complex economy of visual exchanges. Benjamin elaborates on this visual economy in his study of Baudelaire. There, discussing the shattering of the aura in the daguerreotype, Benjamin explains:

> What was inevitably felt to be inhuman, one might even say deadly, in daguerreotypy was the (prolonged) looking into the camera, since the camera records our image without returning our gaze. But looking at someone carries the implicit expectation that our look will be returned by the one to whom it gives itself [*dem er sich schenkt*]. Where this expectation is met (which, in the case of thinking, can attach itself equally to the intentional gaze of attentiveness and to a gaze in the straightforward sense of the word), there is an experience of the aura to the fullest extent. (CB 147; 1:646)

In this passage Benjamin equates the unrequited gaze with inhuman mortification, with a process of ocular robbery. Here, the auratic can only survive if the delicate economy of visual exchanges is maintained. Yet the gaze is only a gift insofar as any gift momentarily veils its hidden expectation of being returned—in another form—and of thus being canceled.[28] For it is only by not being returned that the gift remains what it is. But once the gift is accepted—here it is the glance by the camera—it is no longer a gift. This is so because it has entered the realm of the belongings of the receiver and is now merely property. The giver feels deceived—as Benjamin says, the glance expects a glance in return—if the gift is not returned. But if the gift *is* returned, it is no longer a gift. It is merely a participant in an economy of exchange. If it *is not* returned—and it can only not be returned if it is not even recognized *as* a gift, for if it is recognized as a gift, then that perception itself already signifies a fleeting indebtedness or recognition—then the aura is shattered and mortification lays its veil over the gazing subject. However problematic this economy of specular giving and receiving appears, the aura may be maintained, Benjamin tells us, even experienced to the fullest extent, in the reciprocal relationship of sending and then receiving the gift of a gaze.

In the moment when the self looks into the camera, it hopes for the gift of its gaze to be returned. Seizing the power that comes with instigating a look, it calls upon the apparatus to respond in kind.[29] If in this exchange of the gaze the self attempts to experience the auratic, it can access it only in the traces of a distance. In the *Passagen-Werk*, Benjamin tells us that, in the context of "trace and aura," the "trace is the appearance of a proximity, however distant what it left behind may be. Aura is the appearance of a distance, however close what it conjures up may be. In the trace, we get hold of an object; in the aura it seizes us" (5:560).[30] Here, the trace is linked to a moment of absence within the self's perception. Simultaneously, it conjures up a proximity. Therefore, the absence Benjamin's trace marks is thinkable as a distant presence. Aura, however, no matter how close the presence it cites appears to us, defers access to it. This is to say that the auratic places presence in the realm of distance in such as way as to make the possibility of a distant presence unthinkable (since the presence is already present but in its presence, *this* presence, can only be distant [*eine Ferne*]). For Benjamin, therefore, the trace can paradoxically yield presence to us, whereas the aura hides it from our view. The auratic is the moment when a thing stares at the self. The auratic emerges as something visual that prompts an object or text to "seize us." For the corporeal subject that attempts to construct itself through a visual exchange of gazes, the elusive interplay of trace and aura prevent it from coming into its own. Benjamin's self-portraits in the *Berlin Childhood* are always touched by this aporetic movement. Like the trace, the autobiographical text makes what is distant in the moment of reading—Benjamin's childhood and its Berlin milieu— appear close and graspable. But like the aura, the enigmatic rhetorical movements of the *Berlin Childhood* conjure up, in the act of reading, a melancholic sense of distance—the absent images of a Berlin that is no more and the absence of stable meanings—no matter how physically close one holds the text to one's eyes.[31]

Coda

The corporeal self that the *Berlin Childhood* enacts on the stage of vision cannot belong to the body of stable concepts craved by the fascist regime. Like the "Little Hunchback" in the text's final segment, who is always already present, hiding in manholes and cellar openings to disfigure any possible formation of the self, the gaze cannot be a reliable instrument of self-construction. Benjamin's self vanishes into the movements of its own rhetoric the way, he tells us, a Chinese painter once disappeared from the gazes of his admirers by stepping into his own picture (4:262f.). In Benjamin's self-portrait, this self takes on some of the qualities of the self in Proust and Kafka. In both writers, Benjamin observes, the self's "chambers have no local colors. . . . In these two writers the subject takes on the protective coloring of the planet which will turn gray in the catastrophes to come" (2:1221). The ghostly self of the *Berlin Childhood*, too, becomes like everything else around it. But it takes on the language of what surrounds it only to remain idiomatic and never fully legible.

To read the body of the visual self is to be thrown back upon the emptiness that is its textual form. Like the *Berlin Childhood*'s rhetorical image of the stocking that, once unrolled, presents us only with the void at its core, the visual self consists not in some essential or metaphysical realm but only in its linguistic movements. To unravel their *textum* is to unweave the self. For Benjamin's rolled-up stocking does not simply contain the gift that it brings, it also is this gift: "Now I decided to roll 'the gift' [*das Mitgebrachte*] out of its woolen bag. I pulled it towards me ever more closely until something consternating occurred: I had unpacked 'the gift' but the 'bag' in which it had been was no longer there." Benjamin continues: "I could not repeat this process often enough. It taught me that form and content, cover and the covered [*Hülle und Verhülltes*] are the same thing. It instructed me to pull truth to the fore out of literature the way that my child's hand pulled the stocking out of its 'bag'" (7:416f.).[32] What emerges from a text, what becomes legible or understandable, including perhaps the confessional self, therefore also cancels the text. This double movement literalizes the figure of unraveling: to understand but also to undo, in a comprehension that is at the same time a destruction.

Two years before his suicide under the shadow of Nazi persecution, Benjamin writes to Karl Thieme: "Let me ask you one question in conclusion: In 1932, I began writing a slender volume, *Berlin Childhood around 1900*. Perhaps you have seen the parts of it published before Hitler came to power. I have added to this book and revised it extensively in the last few weeks. It will be difficult to find a publisher for it because of its subject matter. . . . It has something to say to thousands of German refugees. . . . Do you know what this book is like? [or: "Do you have any concept of this book?"—*Haben Sie einen Begriff von dem Buch?*]" (*C* 560; *B* 755f.). Thieme cannot have a concept of Benjamin's book because it has no concepts to give. Its refusal to manufacture usable concepts is precisely what makes it speak to those who hope to resist the fascist concept-machine. If Benjamin's self cannot see eye to eye with the language of stable concepts, the haunted images of the *Berlin Childhood* belong to the Benjaminian brooder whose figurations remain constantly out of reach and who turns his own life into an allegorical text. "The brooder," Benjamin tells us in "Central Park," "whose startled gaze falls upon the fragment in his hand, becomes an allegoricist" (*CP* 46; 1:676).

EPILOGUE

TOWARD A POLITICS OF THE UNUSABLE

> Believing in progress does not mean believing that progress
> has already occurred. That would be no belief.
>
> Franz Kafka, "Oktavheft G"

> Genocide is the absolute integration. . . . Auschwitz con-
> firmed the philosopheme of pure identity as death.
>
> Theodor W. Adorno, *Negative Dialectics*

Benjamin once wrote that "all great works of literature found
a genre or dissolve one—they are, in other words, special cases" (*I* 201;
2:310). Taken together, the corpus of Benjamin's autobiographical
writings can be considered such a special case. They are a special case
not only because of their enigmatic beauty and sustained theoretical
interest but also because they mark something peculiar in Benjamin's
corpus. They stage a language in which the body of the confessional
self remains suspended between construction and dispersal. In Benjamin's autobiographies, the corporeal self acts the way he tells us
the self of Goethe's protagonists behaves in *Elective Affinities*—
it "disappears under the arch of a . . . rhetorical question, in the
perspective, so to speak, of infinite distance" (W 333; 1:171). Within
this infinite distance, the language of the vicissitudinous self's body
in turn works to exhibit a figure that, in its perpetual turnovers and
slippages, belongs to those innovative political concepts that remain

useless for the purposes of fascism and, indeed, any kind of politics of presence and transparency. If in Benjamin's innovative art of self-portraiture the body is always in re-treat—that is, both disappearing and being treated one more time—then it belongs to those concepts that elude ideologemes of self-identity and the powerful myth of stable meanings.[1] Benjamin's corpus remains unusable. The body that Benjamin's autobiographies present not only retreats but also signifies *that* it retreats, delivering a commentary on the movement of its own withdrawal. We could therefore say that his corpus dwells in the abyss that is its allegorical meaning. As Benjamin tells us in the *Passagen-Werk*, the "'abyssal' sense ['*abgründige*' *Sinn*] is to be defined as 'meaning' ['*Bedeutung*']. It is always allegorical" (5:347). The quotation marks Benjamin places around the words *abyssal* and *meaning* suggest their allegorical function. Like the body, we can access meaning, and even its abyss, only in the conditional mode, as something figurative, something that remains in quotation marks.

Our reading of the corpus in Benjamin's acts of self-portraiture has suggested that the body belongs to those concepts that can never be turned into a mere program. If the body, for Benjamin, can never be arrested once and for all, even in its undecidability, then its ethical and political importance cannot be understood in advance of a particular act of reading. "For the true critic," Benjamin writes in a 1931 fragment on "The Task of the Critic," "the actual judgment is the last thing he wrests from himself, never the basis of his undertaking" (6:171). Like that which in a fragment one year earlier Benjamin calls the "first form of criticism which refuses to judge" (6:170), the decisions that the reader must make in the act of reading are to be wrested from the act of experiencing an aporetic moment of something that cannot be decided, something that can neither be given in advance nor once and for all. Benjamin emphasizes the political importance of deferring a finite decision in a 1937 missive to Horkheimer in which he states: "To me, an important question has always been how to understand the odd figure of speech, '*to lose* a war or a court case.' The war or the trial are not the entry into a dispute, but rather the decision concerning it." He continues: "Finally I explained it to myself thus: the events involved for a person who has lost a war or a court case are truly concluded and thus for that person *any avenue of praxis has been lost*" (2:1338).[2] The possibility of political praxis is thus tied to a deferral of the absolute decision. For Benjamin, there can be no hope for transformation without the radical *keeping open* of future possibilities. As Derrida puts it in the context of the *Moscow Diary*, "one might say that Benjamin is not interested in the future or indeed that he is interested precisely in the future of the future *as in the unforseeable itself*" ("Back from Moscow" 228). This means that even a stable itinerary for fighting fascism, based on a set of transparent concepts, would only be programmatic and cooptable, foreclosing in its finitude the possibility of praxis. In his essay on Goethe's *Elective Affinities*, Benjamin reminds us that "no mode of thinking is more disastrous than that which bewilderingly bends back into the myth the very thing that has begun to grow out of it, and which, of course, through this imposed monstrosity, would at once sound an alert" (W 326; 1:163). Attempting to disrupt the fascist myth through a preconceived set of goals, any programmatic agenda such as orthodox historical materialism would only undo its own critical impulse by reinscribing into myth what it had intended to explode out of it. By contrast, Benjamin's "useless" concepts are not programmatic but aporetic. They keep the notion of a political praxis alive by refusing to be reduced to a single meaning under any circumstances—this is their ethical uselessness in a political sense.

To think the promise of the political in these terms is to illuminate a hidden connection between the earlier Benjamin of the *Trauerspiel* book and the Benjamin of the 1930s struggling overtly against the politics of fascism. In the context of the Baroque mourning play and its richly layered juxtapositions of sound and meaning, Benjamin evokes the process of becoming "afflicted by meaning [*Bedeutung*], so to speak, as if by an inescapable disease [*unentrinnbaren Krankheit*]" in terms of mournfulness and melancholia: "Here meaning is encountered, and will continue to be encountered as the reason for mournfulness [*Grund der Traurigkeit*]" (O 209; 1:383). Benjamin identifies the presence of meaning, rather than its absence, as the reason for sadness. The presence of meaning produces a melancholy stasis, a violent freezing of the possibilities that the continuing play of competing meanings and different readings may still harbor. Fascism structurally relies on this very stasis in the form of an allegedly single, determined meaning. Politically, it became a virulent German disease and, for Benjamin and millions of other victims, the ultimate "reason for mournfulness."

To think through the political in these terms also allows us to revisit Benjamin's famous final passage of the Artwork essay, which confronts the fascist aetheticization of politics with the politicization of art (*I* 242; 2:508). This passage cannot be understood in isolation from the sense of ambivalence concerning the teleological or progammatic dimensions that had led him to be suspicious of Communist politics. He was both drawn to and repelled by it. While Benjamin could never make up his mind to join the Communist Party, he was in contact with communist groups and frequented events sponsored by the Proletarian Writers' Union. In her memoirs, Asja Lacis recalls asking Benjamin why he would not help her more actively in her struggle against the social injustices inflicted by the bourgeois state and why he would not join the Communist party like his brother Georg. According to Lacis, Benjamin answered: "Well, for you it is very easy. . . . With you it is like with a horse wearing blinders. It only looks straight ahead, and the way appears straight to it. For me, it is more difficult, more complicated; I must consider many other things as well" (*Revolutionär im Beruf* 50). What interests Benjamin are the intricate interruptions of teleology—moments that give us "politics" to think again and again—rather than the instances of its mimetic execution. Just as the "work is the death mask of its conception" (W 459 4:107), mere programmatic execution is the death mask of real political progress. The trajectory of this line of thought becomes clear in a 1926 letter to Scholem, when Benjamin explains that he considers "Communist 'goals' to be nonsense and nonexistent. This does not diminish the value of Communist action one iota, because it is the corrective for its goals and because there are no meaningful *political* goals" (*C* 301; *B* 426). The value of a Communist stance can thus only be actualized on the far side of ideological programmaticity and the implementation of stable, self-identical goals. For Benjamin, the transformative power of Communist politics is tied to a moment of conceptual metamorphosis, when it ceases to remain simply itself and when its potential is lodged in an otherness on the far side of what it seems to articulate on the surface.

To be sure, the kind of political valence with which Benjamin imbricates the unexpected movements of his language cannot but cause suspicion among those who remain attached to conventional versions of Marxist intervention and the critique of ideology. Paradigmatic of this understanding of Benjamin is Habermas, whose widely read critique of Benjamin proceeds from the assumption that "there is no room in . . . ideology critique for the type of critique developed by Benjamin." "A critique that sets out to rescue semantic potential," Habermas continues, "has a highly mediated position relative to political praxis. On this, Benjamin did not manage to achieve sufficient clarity" ("Consciousness-Raising" 118). But Habermas overlooks the fact that Benjamin's political project is not to undo its mediated position in order to enter the sphere of so-called immediacy but rather to activate the radical potential that inheres in a confrontation with mediation itself. Rather than criticizing the prevailing ideology of a political situation the way that a sage enlightens the clueless and the misguided, Benjamin works to set into play a series of material and rhetorical figures that will not yield to the unmediated instrumental-izations without which no mobilization of stable political concepts and their ideologies can function. In this sense, Habermas's critique, which influenced an entire generation of Benjamin's more politically minded readers, is both correct and misleading at the same time. It is correct in its suggestion that Benjamin links questions of language to a highly mediated political stance. It is misleading in its implied conclusion that this constellation signals the eclipse of a critical engagement with the political. On the contrary, as this study has argued, Benjamin's innovative sense of the political begins to become visible precisely when the terms and concepts of the political and its presentations can no longer be taken for granted as transparent or easily comprehensible categories. The point, then, would not be to embark on a sternly triumphant quest to achieve ever greater clarity, not to mention "sufficient clarity," but rather to devise ethico-political strategies for what to do when this hoped-for clarity simply will not reveal itself. These non-programmatic strategies remain open to discussion and contestation, as they are engaged on the far side of pre-established, universally applicable norms. For Benjamin, a rigorous thinking of this challenge signals the beginning, rather than the foreclosure, of the political.

While Benjamin hoped to enlist certain Communist and Marxist strategies in his confrontation with German politics, a more radical confrontation of the movement of fascism can be located in his devel-opment of useless concepts that are constantly in re-treat. The corpus, as this study has suggested, is a prime example. Such Benjaminian concepts, which always strike at the very limits of conceptualization as such, cannot be mobilized by any kind of stable program, not even anti-fascist movements or even Marxism itself. It is no accident that Benjamin writes to Scholem in 1934, the year after Hitler's takeover, of his guardedness concerning the implementation of his concepts in the inevitably reductive form of this or that political program: "The evil—compared to those that surround us—is of so much less that it should be affirmed in every practical, productive form, except for the unpractical, unproductive form of the credo." He continues: "And this practice . . . leaves the theory (the credo, if you like) a much greater freedom than the Marxists suspect" (C 439; B 605). The credo of political theory is most useful, most itself, when it is becoming something else and when it is not used to install itself as a programmatic stance. It is most practical in the moment when it does not simply remain what it is and when it relinquishes its claims to immediate usefulness. The credo's "I believe"—which is the first phrase of the Apostle's Creed—is here also a belief in incredulity, which folds back upon itself to question the hidden assumptions of the system of beliefs in which the "I believe" could be uttered in the first place. The political significance of Benjamin's concepts is thus inscribed in the traces of their own deferrals. This is what makes Benjamin's concepts so explosive and dangerous. To read them is to experience an aporia, the "critical, dangerous moment that lies at the ground of all reading" (N 50f.; 5:578).

That Benjamin's corpus refuses to be used for this or that political agenda also means that it cannot ultimately be employed to construct a transparent, self-identical community. While the body politic of the Nazi regime functions as the site of a fully coordinated national community, the mythical *Volk*, Benjamin's body only names the impossibility or dispersal of any kind of community.[3] "The body," according to Benjamin, "is for the human being the seal of his loneliness and it will not break—even in death" (6:80). The inability of this seal—which separates the body from other bodies, which makes it singular and idiomatic—to be broken signals the irreducible difference and otherness that traverses all communities. Benjamin's sentence points to the ways in which the corpus as an aporia ruptures the imagined community of a *Volk* and the masses of a *Reich*. The seal that Benjamin evokes in terms of the body simultaneously opens up and closes off. It closes off the corporeal self from its community and constantly confronts it with its own finitude. But in this closing off it also opens up the possibility of resisting the phantasmagoria of the stable nation and the coordinated mass mobilizations upon which German fascism relied. Benjamin's seal is thus constantly in flux: it perpetually forecloses and reopens.

If Benjamin calls for innovative concepts that would be useless for the purposes of fascism, the body is a prime example because, for him, the "body passes away, is shattered as a manometer that in the moment of its highest tension explodes and, with the dispersal of its connections, becomes frail and superfluous [*hinfällig, überflüssig wird*]" (6:71). What Benjamin in the Artwork essay calls for—unusable, *unbrauchbare*—concepts has become visible in the present study in the space of a body that is *hinfällig* and *überflüssig*. The logic that connects *hinfällig, unbrauchbar,* and *überflüssig* is precisely the logic that touches upon Benjamin's corpus of concepts that retreat from the reach of fascism. While the Nazis developed the ideology of a monstrous *Lebensraum* eradicating those who would deviate from their norms, Benjamin is interested in what he calls a *Leibraum* of unusable concepts in which no corpus remains what it is.

On the far side of fascism, Benjamin's interest in the corpus belongs to his interest in things as they appear in the moment when they are about to become something else or even disappear, that is, "things in the moment of the being-no-longer [*Dinge im Augenblick des Nicht-mehr-seins*]" (5:1001). By the same token, Benjamin's body belongs to those words that, as he cites Kraus, become stranger and stranger the more you read them: "The more closely you look at a word, the more distantly it stares back at you" (2:362). This strangeness and this moment in which things become something else is the critical and dangerous moment of reading.

If this ghostly dispersal of the body names for Benjamin a certain utopian hope, this hope is not based on any kind of concrete or religious messianism, nor on a naive reversal of existing circumstances after which a new program could swiftly be implemented. On the contrary, if construction always presupposes destruction (N 60; 5:587), then the stable body's passing is also the advent of something else, something that has no name yet—"a flag," we recall, "under which sails a cargo that cannot be declared because its name is still lacking" (I 183f.; 2:301). The finitude of the body, its destruction and demise, signals Benjamin's hope that there is a "to come," a future whose contours cannot be predicted or politically evaluated in advance.

We could say that Benjamin shares his investment of utopian qualities in the body with a writer he deeply admired, the utopian novelist Paul Scheerbart, author of often grotesque fantasy and science fiction novels. Benjamin enlists him in the transformative project of a critical modernity that would also include such proper names as Brecht and Loos, Giedion and Blanqui, Bloch, Bergson, and Fourier, among others. He revisited Scheerbart's work at different stages of his career and, as we learn in a letter to Scholem, even planned to base a lengthy political treatise on it (C 168f.; B 247). Linking the self's corpus to the body politic, Benjamin remarks on "Scheerbart's utopia of the body," in which the body of the subject and the physiognomy of its culture enter a reconfigured relationship so that "the earth and mankind together form a single body" (6:148). Here, Benjamin refers to Scheerbart's 1906 novel *Münchhausen and Clarissa*, in which the characters' bodies are subjected to a phantasmatic reconfiguration at once monstrous and liberating. Throughout Scheerbart's novels, including Benjamin's favorite, *Lesabéndio: An Asteroid Novel* (1913), bodies rearrange their limbs, sport multiple heads, grow trunks in unsuspected places, interact through suction cups, turn into umbrellas, grow photographic telescope lenses out of their eye sockets, and the like. Benjamin appreciated Scheerbart's delimitation of the corpus because it was tied to potentially revolutionary impulses, a quality Benjamin also detected, more than once, in the corporeal flexibility of Disney's Mickey Mouse.[4] What Benjamin found in Scheerbart's opening up of the otherwise more rigid image of the body can perhaps best be understood in terms of what he saw as the utopian possibilities of film. Film, with its technical capabilities such as slow motion and montage, opened up areas of experience that are quotidian and pervasive but not normally accessible to cognition. If Benjamin borrows the language of Freud to designate this filmic space "the optical unconscious," we might say that in Scheerbart's comical reconfigurations of the body he saw a kind of "corporeal unconscious," a space interlaced with the hidden fabric of the bodily experiences we take for granted but hardly comprehend.

But even though Benjamin shares the utopian investment of the body with utopianists such as Scheerbart, he differs from them in that the Benjaminian body can only fulfill its political promise when it retreats from any ideological mobilization of stable, monolithic views of the world, be it reactionary or utopian. This is why he writes to Werner Kraft in 1935, "There have already been many cultures on this planet that have perished in blood and horror. It is naturally necessary for us to hope that the planet will some day experience a culture that has gone beyond both of these things—indeed, just like Scheerbart, I am inclined to assume that the planet is waiting for this. But it is terribly doubtful whether *we* will be able to present the planet this gift" (C 516; B 698). The political potential of the corpus in demise is thus to be found not in the ways in which it fulfills certain functions for *us* and on *our* behalf but rather in the ways in which it becomes something that exceeds the human subject and the politics of its particular biases. The hope that is inscribed in the unusable body is thus infinite, but not for us. As Benjamin tells us at the end of his far-reaching essay on Goethe's *Elective Affinities,* in a gesture that recalls Kafka, "The phrase 'Before you know the bodies' appears destined for a sublime irony. Those lovers never seize the body. What does it matter if they never gathered strength for battle? Only for the sake of the hopeless ones have we been given hope" (W 356; 1:201).

If the hope that is encoded in Benjamin's rejection of various transcendental signifieds or undeconstructed corporeal subjects belongs to a so-called messianic moment, what in his theses on history he terms a "*weak* messianic power" (I 254; 1:694), it behooves us to remember that, as his colleague Herbert Marcuse put it in 1964, "Benjamin's messianism has nothing to do with conventional religiosity" (24). As such, it is also much closer to the political hauntedness of the logic of what Derrida, in his rereading of Marx (and Benjamin), has termed "spectrality" than to any forms of traditional messianism.[5] While Benjamin remained influenced by his early interest in Jewish mysticism and theology, and while a quasi-theological reading of the negative dialectic always stays with him as a ghost, his notion of the theological is a figure that folds back upon itself to become something else. Thus, while Benjamin is aware of the difficulty that "gives us an experience which forbids us to regard history as completely a-theological," it is nevertheless incumbent upon us not to "attempt to write it [history] according to literally theological concepts" (N 61; 5:589). Benjamin's challenge is to think theologically without theology. His writings give us a form of religious experience that cannot be religious without always canceling its own religiosity. As Benjamin so eloquently puts it in the *Passagen-Werk,* "My thinking relates to theology the way the blotting paper does to ink. It is soaked through with it. If one were to go by the blotting paper, though, nothing of what has been written would remain" (N 61; 5:588). Theologically inflected writing is a form of language that both dictates and erases. When a text is suffused with the theological, it is always also canceled by it.

This double structure also suggests that Benjamin's valorization of unusable concepts is not a theology nor an ideology of redemption, but rather the refusal to give up hope for the futurity to come. This hope is lodged not in theology but in the gesture that both writes and erases the theological in order to keep political hope alive. Benjamin's hope is haunted by an uncanny otherness that is its condition of possibility. Just as the "true image of the past *flits* by" and just as the "past can be captured only as an image that briefly flashes up in the moment of its recognizability never to be seen again," the aporetic body that Benjamin stages in his acts of self-portraitures "threatens to disappear with every present that does not recognize that it is being addressed in the image" (*I* 255; 1:695). It is precisely in Benjamin's fleeting images and concepts, readable only in a presence that at any moment threatens to betray the self and to disappear altogether, that the political can be addressed.

While the hope with which Benjamin invests his autobiographical corpus is not theological or messianic in any traditional religious sense, it is a hope that attaches to the unpredictable ways in which the text of the body remains enigmatic. The body's demise as a stable concept—like the demise of all stable concepts—signals for Benjamin the uneasy happiness, luck, and fortune (*Glück*) that resides in destruction. "For in *Glück* all that is earthly," we read in the "Theologio-Political Fragment," "strives toward its demise, yet only in *Glück* is its demise destined to find it" (R 312f.; 2:204). Benjamin's *Glück* is measured by the extent to which demise itself remains an enigma—that is, charged with the revolutionary potential of erasure and the inability of this erasure to contain or erase its own contradictions.

Here, Benjamin shares with Nietzsche what the latter calls his "epistemological starting point," namely, the "[p]rofound aversion to reposing once and for all in any total view of the world. Fascination of the opposing point of view: refusal to be deprived of the stimulus of the enigmatic" (*Will to Power* 262). Like Nietzsche, Benjamin refuses to refuse the enigmatic. And like Nietzsche, Benjamin rejects any ideology that would rely on a single reading of the text of the world, on a program of *Gleichschaltung* of all meaning. He shares with Nietzsche, to use the language of Benjamin's essay on surrealism, "a dialectical optic that perceives the everyday as impenetrable, the impenetrable as everyday" (*R* 190; 2:307). This impenetrability, which, like Proust's work in Benjamin's commentary, "is assigned a place in the heart of the impossible" (*I* 201; 2:311), names the ethico-political commitment of Benjamin's corpus.

I hope to have begun to outline in this study the ways in which this heart of the impossible is also the place where Benjamin locates our illogical yet necessary refusal to give up all hope. One year after Hitler's seizure of power, Benjamin writes to Scholem: "I take as my starting point the small, nonsensical hope [*kleine widersinnige Hoffnung*], as well as the creatures for whom this hope is intended and yet who on the other hand are also the creatures in which this absurdity is mirrored" (*C* 453; *B* 617). The *Widersinn*, or nonsense, of Benjamin's hope is always twofold. On the one hand, hope seems hardly warranted under the prevailing political and epistemological circumstances. On the other hand, Benjamin's *Widersinn* also *is* this hope. Hope can only be located in the *Widersinn* of concepts and their refusal to be reduced to any single *Sinn* (meaning). Benjamin's hope thus emerges when it occurs as a form of opposition to fixed meanings—in the *wider* (against) of *Wider-Sinn*.

The student's political question with which I began this study— "What do we do in the meantime?"—can thus not be answered by providing any kind of stable program or recipe that putatively emerges from Benjamin's tropes, a systematic list of tasks to be carried out. Benjamin's writings do not wish us to act or think like them. Rather, as Adorno once wrote regarding the anti-fascist politics of Benjamin's *German People*, "Benjamin's book does not tempt one to imitate the texts it presents but rather provides instruction in detachment from them. Their irretrievability becomes a critique of the course the world has taken" ("On Benjamin's *Deutsche Menschen*" 333). It is like that with all of Benjamin's texts. Renouncing the temptation of false mimesis and the questionable generation of stable political itineraries, they ask us to meditate on the ways in which the disappearance they stage is itself an enactment of what must be confronted by us ethically and politically in a nondogmatic fashion—and every time anew.

Yet Benjamin's politics of unusable concepts and their figural manifestations in the negativity of rupture and deferral does not finally permit us to repose in the comfort of disowning ethical and political responsibility because we lack metaphysical foundations. On the contrary, his sentences are filled with both the never-ending unfolding of a negativity and the tone of an apocalyptic urgency that calls upon us to imagine, and even strive for, the promise of a transformation that cannot simply be implemented but is always yet to come. In Benjamin, as Cadava reminds us, the "present no longer struggles to lead knowledge, as one would lead the blind, to the firm ground of a fixed past. Instead the past infuses the present and thereby requires the dissociation of the present from itself. In other words, the past—as both the caesura and the condition of the present—strikes the present and, in so doing, exposes us to the nonpresence of the present." This is so because "the past and the present deconstitute one another in their relation" (71). For Benjamin, the ruptured present is therefore not only a site of self-differentiation but also the condition of possibility for recognizing the past as a series of ruptures that will not remain with itself but rather continues to make itself, and the present, differ from itself. To think through the promise of the past and the present is therefore to consider the ways in which they participate in an intricate economy of self-differentiations on whose survival any political hope will have rested.

What Benjamin thus leaves behind for us to learn to ask are questions about the ways in which a rupturing deconstruction of the self and its conceptual apparatus can never be thought in separation from the richnesses harbored by an occluded past and an as yet unthought future possibility. "It is the present," according to Benjamin, "which polarizes the event into fore- and after-history" (N 61; 5:588). But that the present assumes the form of a historical rupture also means that within this rupture the remnants of the past and the shadow of the future meet, binding the present inextricably to its history and to what is yet to come. If the forces of an occluded past and the signals of a future promise form, together with the ethical acceptance of political responsibility, a constellation within the rupture itself, then this constellation names precisely the rupture's transformative potential. But unlike the traditional tropes of utopian rhetoric, Benjamin's transformative rupture, if it is one, cannot be imagined in advance of this or that rhetorico-political act. It resides in its perpetual openness. For Benjamin, this openness is the political space in which one can "seize hold of a memory as it flashes up in a moment of danger" (*I* 255; 1:695) in a way that attempts to do justice to the notion that "nothing that has ever happened should be regarded as lost for history" and thus for the hope directed at what is to come (*I* 254; 1:694). It is this political love of what is to come, above and before any metaphysical foundation or programmatic certainty, that Benjamin wishes to experience. This is also why in the *Passagen-Werk* he returns to the enigmatic lines of Friedrich Hölderlin, with whose writings he had wrestled as early as 1916,[6] quoting a 1793 letter from the poet to his brother: "I love the race [*Geschlecht*] of centuries to come" (*N* 71; 5:599). For Benjamin, as for Hölderlin, the loving experience of a future resides in an experience than cannot yet be had—not simply because it cannot know what the future holds but because its condition of possibility resides in the movement of a perpetual opening-up toward what is to come in a way that would be canceled once what is to come were believed to be present.

Only because they are not decided in advance by this or that ideologeme can political *decisions* be made in the first place. This stance also differentiates Benjamin's politics from the closure and tele-theological decisionism propagated by conservative political theorists such as Carl Schmitt. Even though he expresses admiration for the methodological stance Schmitt assumes in his theory of sovereignty and the state of exception—the thesis that there is an essential link between the definition of political sovereignty and the power to decide what counts as a state of exception—Benjamin's own understanding of the *infinite* process of decision-making could not be further removed from Schmitt's.[7] While for Schmitt, later a member of the Nazi party and visible theorist for the Third Reich, political struggles move through a given epoch's apparatus of theological concepts in order to coalesce in a set of final and ultimate decisions, Benjamin's politics always defers the possibility of an absolute decision, without ever being able to extricate itself from the perpetual ethical process of wrestling with transformative decisions.[8] Only as long as no definitive decision has been made can the hope of a future improvement remain alive, because "[j]udged from the standpoint of destiny, every choice is 'blind' and leads headlong into disaster" (*W* 309; 1:140).

In order to remain alive as a hope, this future must therefore never be present. What for the Catholic Schmitt is decisionism conceived as a politics of presence and determined meaning, for Benjamin is a structure of aporetic situations that demands a politics and aesthetics of radical openness and hospitality to what cannot be decided once and for all. In contrast to the triumphant decisionism of Schmitt, for Benjamin the experience of a true decision cannot be thought in separation from the experience of a true failure. "For only this experience is able to sustain the decision," Benjamin explains, "that, beyond all other occurrences and comparisons, reveals itself to the experiencing agent as essentially singular and unique, whereas every attempt by upright human beings to found decision on lived experience sooner or later fails" (W 347; 1:190). It follows that there can be no experience of a decision that does not reveal itself as the event of a singularity which, lacking any common measure with other experiences, has always yet to be understood. Conversely, the kind of decision that is based on lived experience, that is, in comparison and analogous to some prior, other decision or experience, fails precisely because of its lack of singularity, that is, the radical uniqueness of the event and its special circumstances and issues which must be appreciated in any act of responsible decision-making. Therefore, the experience of a decision is either too radically singular to be comprehended just yet or it is a mere repetitive implementation of a policy that has been programmed in advance of the event. This dilemma signals the undecidability of the event of the decision. It is the aporia Benjamin hopes to take seriously. Here, the event of the decision will not remain itself. Benjamin puts it well in a 1931 letter to Scholem, written only four months after his missive to Schmitt: "I am determined to do my thing under any circumstances, but this thing is not always the same thing under every set of circumstances" (C 377; B 530).

To say, with Benjamin, that "there are no meaningfully *political* goals" is therefore not to disown the responsibility of the political but rather to understand it in the sense of an undecidable project that has to be perpetually engaged and strenuously revised. A new sense of the political is to be thought with every new reading of its textual manifestations. This is simultaneously the burden and the hope with which Benjamin leaves us.

On 26 September 1940, Benjamin, hoping to escape his prolonged persecution by the Nazis, finally decided to disregard the sense that in a 1931 article for the *Frankfurter Zeitung* he had ascribed to his figure of "The Destructive Character," namely, that he "lives from the feeling, not that life is worth living, but that suicide is not worth the trouble" (R 303; 4:398). Trapped in Portbou, a village on the Franco-Spanish border, he terminated his own life prematurely by taking an overdose of morphine. Benjamin's body eventually disappeared in an anonymous mass grave in a local Catholic cemetary. Although the pathos of Benjamin's tragic death has been memorialized by writers from Brecht to Arendt, from Günther Anders to Volker Braun and Heiner Müller, and has even inspired a recent American novel,[9] it was not until May 1994 that the body of one of the most significant theorists of modernity was presented with a memorial. This monument was designed for the Catalan site by the distinguished Israeli sculptor Dani Karavan. But Benjamin's corpus or corpse will not stay buried; it returns to haunt. To wrestle with the theoretical, historical, ethical, and political stakes of this haunting remains our responsibility today.

Benjamin's staging of his autobiographical corpus suggests that the closest we can come to realizing our ethical and political commitments is to learn *how to read* the elusive way in which language and the cultural texts in which it is embedded share a common fate in that they must constantly refer to each other without ever arriving at a finite decison or at full closure. Our task would be to realize what is at stake ethically and politically in thinking through this relation, even if we are unable to arrest its meanings and even if it constantly threatens to elude our grasp as though it were a phantom. The segment "A Ghost" in the *Berlin Childhood around 1900* suggests that our ability to witness this ghost is as frail as it is necessary. We see and we do not see the ghost. As Benjaminian readers and critics of culture and politics, we are bound to act the way that "in sagas, the people, witnessing a ghost's meal, realize, without actually seeing these ghosts eating and drinking, that they are holding a feast" (7:419). The rigor with which Benjamin addresses himself to the ethics and politics of language encourages us to remain faithful to the abiding difficulties that haunt the language of texts and cultures. These difficulties are our responsibility. In a Benjaminian sense, it is precisely in opening ourselves up ethically to the aporias of presentation, shared by history and aesthetics, that we may still have political hope, if there is any to be had. This commitment gestures, finally, toward what Benjamin once called something "truly revolutionary": "the *secret* signal of what is to come [*das* geheime *Signal des Kommenden*]" (P 32; 2:769).

NOTES

INTRODUCTION

1. This scenario is depicted in Benjamin's fellow Vernuche inmate Hans Sahl's recollections.

2. Thus Benjamin in a 1928 letter to Siegfried Kracauer (*BK* 59).

3. Benjamin's wish to analyze the object of his study from within (*und zwar von innen her*) links the theoretical questions of his Artwork essay to his earlier engagement with German literature. In confronting such works as Goethe's *Elective Affinities* the task Benjamin had set for himself was, as he writes in his curriculum vitae, "to illuminate the work fully from within itself" (4:218).

4. The question is Düttmann's (535). His insightful essay on Benjamin's engagement with fascism as it arises in the Artwork essay groups its discussions around concepts such as destruction, tradition, and the name.

5. These categories are suggested by Gary Smith ("Thinking through Benjamin" xxviii).

6. Kracauer employs this formulation in his essay "On the Writings of Walter Benjamin," which originally appeared in the *Frankfurter Zeitung* on 15 July 1928 and is now included in the volume of essays *The Mass Ornament* (259).

7. For a perceptive analysis of some of the rhetorical questions raised in Benjamin's theses "On the Concept of History," see Bahti. Compare also

Gagnebin, who develops a suggestive commentary on the ways in which the rhetorical or figurative nature of Benjamin's understanding of history becomes a disruptive force that hopes to avoid reducing language to a single history.

8. This suggestion is made by Geulen ("Zeit zur Darstellung" 585).

9. As Paul de Man points out in his reading of Benjamin's "The Task of the Translator," it is important to remember that pure language unfolds only in the space of a "permanent disjunction" ("Conclusions" 92). For an argument that suggests that Benjamin's enigmatic notion of "translatability"—along with its later incarnations of "critiqueability" and "reproducibility"—is one of the key terms for understanding his writing, see Weber ("Un-Übersetzbarkeit").

10. On the distinction between "parataxis," the rhetorical principle of coordinating verbal elements by placing them side by side, and "hypotaxis," the subordination of individual parts of speech to one another, see Adorno's "Parataxis: On Hölderlin's Late Poetry."

11. Benjamin here implicitly echoes a sentence from Nietzsche's anti-autobiography, *Ecce Homo*. Nietzsche too works to address the philosophical implications of the first-person singular when he explains how "with my instinctive cunning, I avoided the little word 'I' once again [*auch hier wieder das Wörtchen 'ich' umging*]" (289).

12. Thus Jean-Luc Nancy (Introduction 6).

13. For useful readings of Benjamin's general relation to French surrealism, see Cohen and Fürnkäs.

14. Compare further Tiedemann, who in his editor's introduction to the *Passagen-Werk* specifies Benjamin's general understanding of the dialectic in these terms. He speaks of Benjamin's "version of the dialectic . . . in which mediation [*Vermittlung*] retreated fully in favor of transformation [*Umschlag*] and in which the reconciliatory moment would have to yield to criticism and destruction" ("Dialectics at a Standstill" 287).

15. For extended readings that place Benjamin's question in the context of his philosophy of the name, see Schestag (589ff.) and Stiegler (71ff.).

16. See especially Kittler's *Discourse Networks 1800/1900* and *Grammophon, Film, Typewriter*.

17. Useful critical discussions and summaries of major contemporary theories of autobiography can be found in Mehlman, *A Structural Study*, and, more recently, Paul Jay, the anthology by Ashley, Gilmore, and Peters, and Robert Smith. For discussions of autobiography within the German tradition in particular, see Lehmann, Niggl, and, for Weimar Germany, Sloterdijk (*Literatur und Lebenserfahrung*). For a recent reassessment of autobiography in the context of cultural concerns, compare also the collection edited by Folkenflik.

18. For a recent discussion of the relationship between history and the subject in Benjamin, see Moses.

19. Compare Benjamin's programmatic statement in the *Passagen-Werk*: "Method of this work: literary montage. I have nothing to say. Only to show. I will purloin nothing valuable and will appropriate no witty formulations. But the rags, the garbage: I do not want to make an inventory of them but rather to do justice to them in the only way possible—to use them" (N 47; 5:574).

20. This etymological connection is pointed out by Corngold (*Necessity of Form* 282).

21. This is the term advocated throughout Lejeune's *Le pact autobiographique*, translated into English as *On Autobiography*.

22. For a recent discussion of the concept of *Darstellung*, or presentation, in Benjamin, see Frey.

23. It would be necessary to investigate the relationship between masks and the concept of the arsenal in Benjamin's language. The phrase "arsenal of masks" occurs more than once in his texts. In addition to the *Berlin Childhood*, compare, for instance, the phrase "infinite arsenal of masks," which Benjamin employs in the context of an analysis of kitsch and folk art in a fragment from around 1929 (6:185ff.)

24. In Benjamin's *Trauerspiel* book, de Man found the conceptual material for his own thinking of *prosopopeia* as the autobiographical voice from beyond the grave. There, Benjamin speaks of death masks and skulls as privileged figures of allegory. In its multiple referentiality and fractured temporality, allegory is—unlike the symbol, which suggests harmonious mediation between referential world and sign—always already an image of discontinuity and deferral. Allegory, for Benjamin, is one of the names of the temporality of death. It is a ruin touched by decay: "Allegories are, in the realm of thoughts, what ruins are in the realm of things" (O 178; 1:354).

For Benjamin, in the mortified primal landscape of the historical (what he calls "history as petrified primordial landscape"; O 166; 1:343), allegory figures as the textual mask of death. This designation is similar to what de Man would later name *prosopopeia*: For Benjamin, this "is the core of an allegorical contemplation . . . it is only significant in the stages of its decay." He continues: "So much signification, so much captivation by death because it is death that digs the jagged line of demarcation between *physis* and meaning most deeply. But if nature has always been captivated by death, it has also always been allegorical" (O 166; 1:343). In this allegorical mode, history and, by extension, the temporally inscribed voice of an absent or dead speaker "sets itself into relief in a face, no, a death's head" (O 166; 1:343). Significantly, allegory is not a name of death because of an absence or dearth of meaning, but precisely because of an excess of meaning, a dissemination of meaning that cannot easily be contained or reduced to a moment of closure

("So much signification, so much captivation by death"). This subject may well be committed to the crypt of times past, what Benjamin, in his own autobiography, calls "the icy crypt of what once was," "out of whose vault the present seems to sound back to us only as an echo" (R 59; 4:518).

25. I quote liberally from these as yet untranslated notes throughout this study.

The most extensive of these fragments is the document entitled "Outline of the Psychophysical Problem" [*Schemata zum psychophysischen Problem*]" (1922–23). It has recently been made available in English translation in the first volume of the *Selected Writings* (393–401). There, Benjamin sketches out a preliminary distinction between *Leib* (body) and *Körper* (corporeal substance). While I draw on the fragment in a general sense, I have chosen not to pursue this distinction further for several reasons. First, Benjamin himself does not sustain this distinction in his other writings, abandoning it already toward the end of the fragment itself. Second, the untenable binary opposition that the pair *Leib* and *Körper* sets up threatens to obscure the more productive and subtle insights into Benjamin's conception of the body that we can gain from the piece. As Rodney Livingston reminds us in his translator's notes, "*Körper*, the more common word, is the opposite of *Geist* (as in 'mind and body') and denotes human physicality. *Leib* is the opposite of *Seele* (as in 'body and soul') and denotes the human body as the repository of the soul; it belongs to a slightly higher register (as in *der Leib Christi*, 'the body of Christ')" (W 401). But even Livingston abandons this distinction in his translation in the latter parts of the piece, where "the contrast . . . is not crucial" (W 401). I am in agreement with Lindner who, in a note to his discussion of aura, suggests that although *Leib* is more closely related to a decaying body and *Körper* to the moment of resurrection, Benjamin generally abandons this distinction ("Benjamins Aurakonzeption" 245n. 2). For interesting and lively attempts to keep the binary alive, however, see Menke (*Sprachfiguren* 261n. 53 and 433) and Menninghaus ("Das Ausdruckslose" 58ff.). Finally, for a discussion of the general philosophical tradition of *Leib* and *Körper*, see Leder (5ff.)

26. For a brief genealogy of the body in Benjamin's early writings, compare also Weigel ("Passagen und Spuren des 'Leib-und Bildraums'" 57ff.).

27. A useful general discussion of Benjamin's messianism can be found in Rabinbach, though he ignores the question of the body. Compare also Wohlfarth ("On the Messianic Structure of Walter Benjamin's Last Reflections") and Scholem ("Toward an Understanding of the Messianic Idea in Judaism").

28. Benjamin employs this term, for instance, in "The Storyteller" (I 103; 2:458).

29. A general discussion of the relation among destruction, language, and

politics in Benjamin can be found in Düttmann. Bolz disregards this moment of violence which must problematize any revolutionary appropriation of the body for the collective and for mass movements, but simultaneously comments perspicaciously on the ethical mobilization of the masses through the collective organ ("Prostituiertes Sein" 213).

30. Nägele comments aptly on *Bildraum* and *Leibraum* with respect to the bourgeois interiority of the self, suggesting a useful reading of *Bildraum* and *Leibraum* in the context of surrealist collage and the problem of the constellation (*Theater, Theory, Speculation* 75f).

31. Henri Bergson's text is listed under the translated title *Materie und Gedächtnis* as entry number 503 in Benjamin's list of books read (7:438).

32. For instance, Bergson claims that as "my body moves in space, all the other images vary, while that image, my body, remains invariable. I must, therefore, make it a center, to which I refer all the other images. . . . I can clearly see how my body comes to occupy, within this aggregate, a privileged position" (46f.).

33. Compare further Rüffer's discussion of Riegl's and Worringer's theories of tactility. For a more general discussion of Benjamin's relation to the work of Riegl and Worringer, see Jennings ("Walter Benjamin and the Theory of Art History"). Finally, see also Kemp ("Fernbilder").

34. Although much work remains to be done to put into sharp relief the relationship between Benjamin and Klages, general discussions of it can be found in McCole (236ff.) and Fuld ("Walter Benjamins Beziehung zu Ludwig Klages").

35. For an analysis of the relation among writing, technology, and the body throughout Kafka's texts, see Neumann.

36. For a reading that links this passage to the concept of profane illumination, see Weigel (*Enstellte Ähnlichkeit* 129).

37. For one of the few sustained general treatments of the relationship between Benjamin and Nietzsche, see Pfotenhauer ("Benjamin und Nietzsche"). His essay, however, contains no discussion of the body. For examples of general discussions of the body in Nietzsche, see the comments by Nehamas (181ff.) and Mattenklott (29ff.).

38. The formulation "the body in pain" is Elaine Scarry's. In *The Body in Pain: The Making and Unmaking of the World*, she argues that the fundamental construction of culture and society is to a significant extent grounded in the body's ability to suffer. Our pain, she suggests, is simultaneously the most irreducible of subjective experiences and the most incommunicable. In the context of the politics of the unstable body, compare also Butler's perceptive general point that to "problematize the matter of bodies may entail a loss of certainty, but a loss of certainty is not the same thing as political nihilism. . . . This unsettling of 'matter' can be understood as initiating new possibilities, new ways for bodies to matter" (30).

39. In the context of the empirical fascist body, see Mosse's historical discussion of the National Socialist ideology of organicism (168), the glorified, transfigured war corps (172), as well as the stereotyped notion of a "new German" corpus, steeled and muscular (185). Compare further Hüppauf's discussion of the "birth of fascist man."

40. That this ethico-political potential of the linguistic body as something expressionless is intertwined with the act of reading becomes clear when Benjamin speaks through the voice of the Mendelssohns to emphasize the relationship of this body to interpretation. "Ever since a certain point in their development," we learn, "letters have stood on a line the way that primal images [*Urbilder*], human beings, animals, and things stood on the ground of the earth. One must not let the fact of parts of letters extending— as if beneath the earth's surface—below the lower limit of other letters keep one from looking for legs on the line when translating letters back into bodily representations. At the same level, next to them, head, eye, mouth, and hand can be in other letters, as in a young child's drawing which does not yet know the configuration and proportioning of body parts" (3:138f.).

41. Menninghaus's work has touched Benjamin's body through sensitive explications in his recent essay, "Das Ausdrucklose: Walter Benjamins Kritik des Schönen durch das Erhabene." There, he places the body, alongside other concepts such as violence, in the context of a revisitation of Kantian aesthetics and its aftermath. Menninghaus suggests that the body belongs to the moral dimension of physis because of its anti-symbolic instability. Benjamin's body, according to Menninghaus, belongs to the Benjaminian category of *das Ausdruckslose* ("the expressionless") which seals within itself both destructive and redemptive potential. According to Menninghaus, the "lack of appearance of the naked body is for Benjamin an allegory of the objection, the caesura whose non-dialectical simultaneity of destruction and salvation . . . bears the, as it were, 'blind' name of the expressionless (60). One could extend Menninghaus's argument by pointing to the ethical necessity which prevents Benjamin's corporeal self from assuming a readable and determined form. Benjamin's corporeal self remains anonymous to itself. As Benjamin tells us in a fragment from 1926, "the subject's highest moral interest is to remain anonymous to itself. . . . By virtue of the good deed it avoids making its own acquaintance" (6:59). The illegible corporeal self emerges for Benjamin as an ethical necessity.

Nägele provides innovative and lucid readings of Benjamin's theatrical stagings of the fragmented body, specifically with regard to the *Trauerspiel* study. Compare his *Theater, Theory, Speculation: Walter Benjamin and the Scenes of Modernity* and "Trauerspiel und Puppenspiel." Weigel has done much pioneering work in thematizing Benjamin's confrontation of the body, especially in relation to issues of gender. See, for example, her "Passagen und Spuren des 'Leib-und Bildraums' in Benjamins Schriften," along with the collection of essays in which this text appears (*Leib-und Bildraum: Lektüren nach Benjamin*). Compare also the chapter "Leib-und Bildraum (Benjamin)" in her *Topographien der Geschlechter: Kulturgeschichtliche Studien zur Literatur*. Bolz's work has incisively thematized questions concerning Benjamin's corporeality, especially as it relates to notions of the collective, public body of the masses and problems of technological enframement. See, for instance, his "Walter Benjamin in the Postmodern" and especially *Auszug aus der entzaubertern Welt* (125ff.).

Finally, Taussig employs Benjaminian notions of tactility in order to analyze a wide range of anthropological and political phenomena. In *The Nervous System*, he claims that what he calls Benjamin's "tactile appropriation," that is, an "everyday tactility of knowing," constitutes Benjamin's "singular contributions to social philosophy, on a par with Freud's concept of the unconscious" (144). Taussig develops this reading of Benjaminian tactility in *Mimesis and Alterity: A Particular History of the Senses*, where he intertwines it with the category of "mimesis" and employs it to analyze city spaces, buildings, cameras, and colonialisms in a variety of cultures. While I am in basic agreement with many of Taussig's insightful claims regarding Benjamin's tactile relation to the object world, I differ from his warnings against, indeed prohibitions of, close allegorical readings which for him are ultimately "manipulative" ideologies that "superimpose meaning" (*Nervous System* 147). Much could be said about this interesting interdiction, its underlying assumptions, and the ways in which much of what is interesting in Taussig's work is owed to disregarding that view.

42. Compare Kaes, Jay, and Dimendberg (*Weimar Republic* 673ff.). For a recent historical analysis of early-twentieth-century body culture, see Toepfer.

43. See the two volumes of Theweleit's *Männerphantasien*.

44. Benjamin makes a similar point a few years later when, in "On the Mimetic Faculty," he suggests that "seeing resemblances is nothing other than a rudiment of the powerful compulsion in former times to become and behave like something else" (*R* 333; 2:210).

Adorno's language of radioactivity, which registers the way that Benjamin's allegoricism sends out ever new rays of illumination and simultaneously renders its objects ever more hazardous, gestures toward the same phenomenon: "Everything which fell under the gaze of his words was transformed, as though it had become radioactive" ("Portrait" 229).

45. An example of the first tendency can be found in Wolin (183ff.), an example of the second tendency in Bolle (208).

46. For representative attempts to read Benjamin's response to fascism in literal terms see the studies by Hillach ("'Ästhetisierung des politischen Lebens': Benjamins faschismustheoretischer Ansatz—eine Rekonstruktion"

and "Der Anteil der Kultur an der Prägung faschistischer Herrschaftsmittel: Was leistet Benjamins Diagnose des Faschismus?") as well as Berman.

Symptomatic of literal readings of Benjamin's engagement with fascism is Caygill's claim that Benjamin, in his attempt to develop new concepts in the struggle against fascism, simply reproduces standard Marxist doctrines. According to this reading, Benjamin merely maintained an "analogy between his and Marx's method" so as to "rework the old concepts and where necessary introduce new concepts appropriate to the developmental tendencies of the sphere of culture" (99). But Benjamin's strategy engaged the unpredictable nature of allegory rather than "analogy" and he did not believe in any kind of "developmental tendencies" in a "sphere of culture." Rather, Benjamin pays special attention to the mortification of the cultural text, the potential of stasis, the rejection of progress, and a dialectics at a standstill, all within the movements of language and the technologies of presentation itself.

47. I am indebted here to Cadava, who usefully links these concerns to Benjamin's consideration of photography and the media spectacle, and to Nancy's "The Inoperative Community," "Our History," and the essay co-authored with Lacoue-Labarthe, "The Nazi Myth." That totalitarian regimes rely on a structure of stable meanings is also suggested by Arendt, who argues that what "convinces masses are not facts, and not even invented facts, but only the *consistency* of the system of which they are presumably part" (*Origins of Totalitarianism* 35; emphasis added).

48. Jünger's sentence (*Krieg* 5) is cited in Hillach ("Rekonstruktion" 127). I have added the emphasis.

49. If, as Lacoue-Labarthe suggests, one may conceptualize the political model of the Nazi regime as that of the *Gesamtkunstwerk*, this is because the masses respond to the image of themselves as an organic community of self-identities, as members of a transparent origin whose essence can reveal. The fascist manipulation of the masses therefore corresponds, as we will see in the next chapter with regard to the face, to the construction of an image of "a people, gathered together in their State," who are allegedly faced with "a representation of what they are and what grounds them as such" (64). This simulacrous grounding in turn corresponds to the state ideology of the spectacle in which the difference between simulations of a society and the real society is strategically erased. In such a scenario, Debord tells us in another context, the "spectacle appears at once as society itself, as a part of society and as a means of unification. As part of society, it is that sector where all attention, all consciousness, converges," so that ultimately "this sector is the locus of illusion and false consciousness; the unity it imposes is merely the official language of generalized separation" (12). Finally, for an analysis of National Socialism's *völkisch* ideology and the discourse of community, see Herf.

50. Benjamin returns to the political implications of the enigmatic phrase "to win a war" in a 1937 letter to Horkheimer (2:1338).

51. Compare Momme Brodersen's account of Benjamin's deprivation of citizenship [*Ausbürgerung*] by the National Socialists (252ff.)

52. For a critical discussion of Benjamin within Marxist debates, see Bahti and Eagleton.

53. One could argue that Benjamin's concerns with questions of representation at the expense of transparent expression places him closer to Foucault than to Habermas. For, with the Foucault of "What Is an Author," "we can say that today's writing has freed itself from the dimension of expression. Referring only to itself . . . writing is identified with its own unfolded exteriority" (142) so that what is needed is a sustained analysis of "the subject as a variable and complex function of discourse" (158).

54. These included, among others, "What Is Epic Theater?," "A Family Drama in the Epic Theater," "Brecht's *Threepenny Novel*," and "The Author as Producer." Benjamin's texts on Brecht are conveniently collected in German in a volume entitled *Versuche über Brecht*, in English under the title *Understanding Brecht*. For a general discussion of Benjamin's relation to Brecht, see Tiedemann ("Die Kunst, in anderer Leute Köpfe zu denken"). For an insightful discussion of Benjamin and Brecht in the context of the poetics of the caesura, see Nägele (*Theater* 135ff.). Witte usefully discusses the collaboration of the two in the context of their planned journal project of the 1930s, *Crisis and Criticism* (*Kritiker* 168–77). Compare further Wizisla's more recent discussion of Benjamin and Brecht in the context of the intellectual trajectory and political background of this ill-fated journal project.

55. See McCole's *Walter Benjamin and the Antinomies of Tradition* and Buck-Morss's *The Dialectics of Seeing*.

56. Compare, for instance, his discussion of Proust's noses and smells in "On the Image of Proust" (*I* 214; 2:323). See also Benjamin's quotation, in the Artwork essay, of Luc Durtain, who speaks of the technological importance of an "oto-rhino-laryngology . . . the so-called endonasal perspective procedure" (*I* 248; 1:496).

57. This is the starting point of Derrida's *Memoirs of the Blind*. For a genealogy of the eye and the ear in the context of the other senses, see the excellent study by Utz as well as Trabant's "Vom Ohr zur Stimme."

Concerning the eye's dominance, we could say with Derrida that Diderot's paradigmatic "Letter on the Blind for the Use of Those Who See" stages an obsessive meditation on the specter of blindness and the emphasis on the sense of vision that gives rise to it. Indeed, as Martin Jay has recently reminded us in *Downcast Eyes*, vision has been considered "the noblest of the senses" since the earliest texts of Western culture. This genealogy found one of its most striking formulations in the visualist language of the Enlightenment and Descartes's foundational *Discourse on Method*. This is why, as Peter Sloterdijk puts it in the *Critique of Cynical Reason*, our "eyes are the organic prototype of philosophy. Their enigma is that they not only can see but are also able to see themselves seeing. This gives them a prominence among the body's cognitive organs. A good part of philosophical thinking is actually only eye reflex, eye dialectic, seeing-oneself-see" (145; cited in Jay, *Downcast Eyes* 21).

58. Hegel's lines are cited in Muthesius (231n. 43).

59. Already in a fragment that his editors date to about 1921, Benjamin records: "Knowledge of truth. It does not exist. For truth is the death of intention" (6:48).

CHAPTER 1

1. See Hollington's concise historical discussion of Lavater and Lichtenberg in relation to Benjamin's new physiognomy.

2. Weber was the first critic to comment on the role of the face in Benjamin's engagement with fascism, and I am indebted to his discussion.

3. This point is also made by Cadava, who usefully links these concerns to the media spectacle, especially photography (53ff.). In addition to Weber's reading of the fascist face, my understanding of it is also greatly indebted to Cadava's.

4. This claim is made by Berman (48). Along these same lines, Benjamin's concern is not primarily a critique of fascism as "a politics of spectacle that precludes rational communication"—an assumption which forms the basis of Berman's criticism of Benjamin's reading of fascism. Berman argues that Benjamin loses sight of the historical specificity of fascism (51). But Benjamin's project actually works to rupture the ideology of transmission and allegedly "rational" communication itself in order to think the mimetic seductions and technologically transmitted mechanisms of power and eros through which the Nazi regime disseminated itself in the first place. At stake is a radical reading of fascist dissimulations against the grain, not the recovery or the establishment of a rationalistic, prelapsarian utopia of communicative transparency.

5. As a careful reading of Benjamin's radical disruption of the face will show, the politicized face is meant to break with the concept of mass community altogether—whether this community is simulated in the state's cultural productions or in those of the masses themselves. Benjamin's politicization of art, at least as it proceeds through the face and the corpus, provides not simply the "means by which the members of the revolutionary classes can come to see themselves as shown by themselves," as Snyder suggests. He continues: "Through this art they can test the world, accept the real, reject the illusory. They can reproduce the world in their own image—in the image that they themselves produce" (171f.). But if there is to be hope, for

Benjamin it can only become visible in the unmaking of any kind of mimetic process and the questionable image of a unified, transparent community it manufactures.

6. Kracauer's lines are cited in Karsten Witte ("Nachwort" 340). To my knowledge, Weber was the first critic to point out Benjamin's indebtedness to Kracauer's passage ("Mass Mediauras" 103n. 19).

7. See the useful historical account of Nazi film production in Reichel (180ff.).

8. This passage is cited and discussed in Lacoue-Labarthe (*Heidegger, Art and Politics* 62f.) and also in Cadava (56f.)

9. For a book-length discussion of *The Triumph of the Will*, see Loiperdinger. Compare also Elferding's analysis of the party rallies on 1 May 1933.

10. We could say that in Nazi aesthetics, the masses are given a physiognomy that strives to erase any traces of indecision or hesitation. As Sontag puts it, the "masses are made to take form, be design," in "mass athletic demonstrations, a choreographed display of bodies," the site of an aesthetics that proceeds with the rigor of "military precision" ("Fascinating Fascism" 92). It is in large part because of this military precision with which the masses are assigned a fascist countenance that Hitler praises Riefenstahl's *Triumph of the Will* as "a totally unique and incomparable glorification of the power and beauty of our Movement" (cited in Sontag 82). The seductiveness of Riefenstahl's images helped the German masses to construct the phantasm of community, a mythical essence that would become immediately visible even in the highly mediated form of its filmic face.

11. I am grateful to Jost Hermand for pointing me to this volume.

12. Weber was the first to make this point ("Mass Mediauras" 103).

13. This is also the logic through which readability is a cause for unreadability in Kafka's "Before the Law," as Derrida shows ("Before the Law" 197).

14. I thank Eduardo Cadava for pointing this line out to me.

15. The complicated and compelling relays between Levinas's and Benjamin's conceptions of the face remain to be fully investigated and can only be hinted at here. For Levinas's understanding of the face, see especially section B of *Totality and Infinity* entitled "Ethics and the Face" (194–219) and his elaborations on the phenomenology of the face in "The Paradox of Morality."

16. See Adorno's "Ernst Bloch's *Spuren*" (206).

17. Of some importance in this context is Hans Richter's aphoristic reflection on the Weimar years via the image of the head. His juxtaposition of texts and images entitled *Köpfe und Hinterköpfe* is a meditation on several key figures of the period between the two wars, including Benjamin. Richter and Benjamin both belonged to the "G-Gruppe," a group of Weimar avantgarde artists and thinkers from a variety of fields that also included Mies van

der Rohe, Man Ray, Hans Arp, John Heartfield, George Grosz, Ernst Schoen, Kurt Schwitters, Tristan Tzara, and Ludwig Hilberseimer, among others.

18. It remains to be investigated how the construction of a self's face has participated in the Western discourse of man as a sovereign subject. This problem could serve as a point of departure for a comparative reading of Benjamin and Foucault, whose final sentence of his great meditation on the questionable Western subject, *The Order of Things*, ends with a rather Benjaminian erasure of the subject's face. Foucault reaches the conclusion that in the course of a proposed rereading of the subject's privileges, "one can certainly wager that man would be erased, like the face drawn in sand at the edge of the sea" (387).

19. The historian George Mosse confirms that fascism should not be seen simply as an aberration, "a temporary response to crises, vanishing when normality is restored" (169). On the contrary, the "frequent contention that fascist culture diverged from the mainstream of European culture cannot be upheld" because "it absorbed most of what had (or proved to have) the greatest mass appeal in the past" (183). Today, as Benjamin's writings teach us, it is precisely this appeal that must continue to be thought in a deconstructive vein.

For a discussion that situates the tropes of fascism and their afterlife in the context of the ideology of "working" and "working through," see Hamacher's recent essay "Working through Working."

20. From this perspective, it would be difficult to agree with Berman's assessment of Benjamin's critique of fascism when he claims that "Benjamin's unbroken confidence in technological progress in general and the emancipatory force of the cinema in particular seem odd and no longer tenable fifty years later" (44). On the one hand, by rejecting the Benjaminian reading of fascism that emphasizes its haunted and haunting character, one would run the risk (of which Nancy and Lacoue-Labarthe, along with Benjamin himself, warn): of mistaking the current status quo as something that has somehow transcended fascism once and for all and that has made the necessity of inquiring into potentially fascist modes of representation obsolete. Likewise, Berman's claims regarding Benjamin's alleged "unbroken confidence in technological progress" need to be complicated. The status of "technological progress" in Benjamin, along with the concept of "progress" itself, is at least dialectical (in the Benjaminian sense of uncontainable *Umschlag*). For instance, careful readers of Benjamin's image of technology such as Hansen have pointed to the complex ways in which he "oscillates between a description of technical innovations and their emancipative possibilities, between historical analysis and a utopian discourse of redemption," a "dialectical movement within certain key concepts" that attempts to do justice to the dynamic simultaneity of violence and redemption encoded in technology ("Blue Flower" 210). Another group of readers would also

implicitly contradict the view that Benjamin was something of a cheerleader for technological progress. For them, Benjamin's revolutionary potential is situated precisely in his demolition of progress, his insistence on strategic *Destruktion*. As Jennings argues, "Benjamin conceived of the dialectical image as a powerful antidote to the concept of progress, for him the most salient feature in the capitalist arsenal" (*Dialectical Images* 37), so that "the salient feature of Benjamin's philosophy of history is his rejection of any notion of progress" (43). Finally, for a far-reaching meditation that takes Benjamin's unhingeing of progress as its explicit point of departure, see Adorno ("Progress").

CHAPTER 2

1. Compare in this context my discussion of the process of becoming similar in chapter 4. For a general discussion of Benjamin's notion of "disfigured similarity" and the problem of non-sensuous and non-sensical similarities [*unsinnliche Ähnlichkeiten*] see, among others, Weigel (*Enstellte Ähnlichkeit*).

2. In her memoirs, *Revolutionär im Beruf,* Lacis recalls their first encounter: "Reich had to go to Munich for a few weeks. I took [my daughter] Daga shopping on the piazza a lot. One day I wanted to buy almonds in a shop. I did not know the Italian word for almonds, and the shopkeeper did not know what I wanted. Next to me stood a man and said: 'Madam, may I help you?' 'Please,' I said. I got the almonds and walked onto the piazza carrying the boxes. The man followed me and asked: 'May I accompany you and carry the boxes?' I looked at him and he continued: 'Allow me to introduce myself—Dr. Walter Benjamin.' I said my name. My first impression: eye glasses that project light like tiny floodlights, thick dark hair, narrow nose, clumsy hands—he dropped the boxes. Overall a respectable intellectual, one of the well-to-do. He accompanied me to my house, said good-bye and asked if he could visit me. He came already the following day" (*Revolutionär im Beruf* 41f.). A few curious letters from Lacis to Benjamin have survived (see Lacis's "Briefe an Walter Benjamin"). Written with the charm of her shaky German, Lacis closes a letter from July 1936 with the hope of a reunion, "We must actually meet—[it] would be very strange [*wäre sehr sonderbar*]. Your old Asja" (573). Assuming that Lacis actually meant to write that their meeting would be special, say, *etwas Besonderes,* her parapraxis involuntarily captures something of the strangeness that was their relation. See also Lacis's memoirs in "Städte und Menschen."

Compare Scholem's recollections of the relation of Benjamin and Lacis leading up to and including Benjamin's Moscow visit (*Friendship* 122ff.). On the philological tension between the *Moscow Diary* and the travel essay "Moscow," from which Benjamin's personal reflections on Lacis are carefully excised, see Smith, "Zu Benjamins 'Moskauer Tagebuch': Fragen an den Herausgeber."

3. It would be necessary to pursue the many relays between the *Moscow Diary* and the *Berlin Childhood around 1900* along the lines of an erotics of reading. An excellent starting point in the *Berlin Childhood* is the segment "Awakening of the Sexus" (7:431ff.). Compare also the segment "Spirit and Sexuality/Nature and Body" (W 395f.; 6:81f.) in the fragment "Outline of the Psychophysical Problem" (W 393ff.; 6:78ff.). For a general discussion of Benjamin's eros of language, see Weigel (*Enstellte Ähnlichkeit* 147ff.).

4. If, as we recall, Benjamin suggests that the "insight that the material upon which the mimetic faculty attempts to operate is the human body should be put to use more forcefully than it has" (6:127), then the 1925 travel essay "Naples," co-authored with Lacis, gestures in a similar direction. One senses the admiration with which it is reported that locals have the ability to turn their bodies into central cultural functions or quotidian objects, for instance, "they have the ability to turn their body into a table" (R 171; 4:314). In this strange text written together by two friends who will never come together, Benjamin and Lacis remark upon the importance of the semiotic dimension of the body in a way that emphasizes the function of the body as a tactile text in which "ears, nose, eyes, breast, and armpits are signal stations taken up by the fingers. This line-up reoccurs in their fastidiously specialized eroticism" (R 173; 4:316).

5. For a useful general discussion of the creaturely in Benjamin's rearticulation of the historical, see the recent study by Hanssen (150ff.).

6. This aspect of Benjamin's interest in the new factuality is pointed out by Boym (119, 122).

7. Similarly, he elaborates in a later passage apropos of the methodology of historical materialism on how the "first part of the journey will be to transpose the principle of montage into history. That is, to erect the great constructions out of the smallest, sharply fashioned building blocks. Indeed to discover the crystal of totality within the analysis of the small individual moment. That is, to break with historical vulgar naturalism. To grasp the construction of history as such. In the structure of commentary. Debris of history" (N 48; 5:575).

8. Compare Benjamin's treatise on the female hat and its genital significations in "Convolute B" (5:131).

9. Witte points to this letter and the identification between reading and the body that it makes (*Intellectual Biography* 198), albeit in the context of the redemption brought by death.

10. Compare Benjamin's metaphor of aging and his discussion of wrinkles in his Proust essay (I 211f.; 2:320ff.). For an excellent general meditation on the concept of relation, including its significance for Benjamin's notions of translation, allegory, and history, see Fynsk.

11. I am indebted in my discussion to Nancy's reading of the touch in "Corpus." For a different meditation on the touch that takes its point of departure from Nancy's work, see Derrida's "*Le Toucher*: Touch/to touch him."

12. The alterity inscribed within the touch of the body is also linked to Benjamin's general attitude toward the constellation of nature, creatureliness, and touching—namely, one of horror and disgust. Already in a letter from 30 July 1913, he writes to Herbert Belmore: "I was of the opinion that a horror of nature is the test for a true experience of nature. He who does not feel horrified by nature has no idea of how to begin to treat nature" (C 48; B 83). And later, speaking of Weimar Germany in *One-Way Street*, he emphasizes the political dimension of this constellation by criticizing the body politic's "dark drives of the animal" which reign "with animal insensibility but without the insensate intuition that animals possess" (W 451; 4:95).

For a discussion of Benjamin's reading of nature as demonic and phantasmagoric as well as its relation to the religious philosophy of Hermann Cohen, see Jennings (*Dialectical Images* 67ff.). Cf. in this context, Witte (*Kritiker* 48ff.). For a discussion of the early Benjamin's understanding of nature in the context of Wyneken and the German youth movement, see McCole (46f.).

13. This reading is sustained by a little-known unpublished fragment entitled "On the Theory of Disgust," like *One-Way Street*, from 1928, which reads like an extension of Benjamin's aphorism: "There is no human being that is free of disgust. It is only thinkable that someone, throughout his whole life, never encounters the sight, the smell, the taste, or other sensory impression which calls forth his disgust. Every human being could explore the animal which conjures up his most intense disgust, if one only knew it well enough. Perhaps a tiny life form, a bacillus that one notices under the microscope" (6:88). From the perspective of the human, there can be no other to the experience of disgust in the moment of an encounter.

14. For a discussion of some of the further implications of this thought-image, see Weigel (*Enstellte Ähnlichkeit* 147–50).

15. The connection between Benjamin's passage from "Socrates" and the Derridean critique of phallogocentrism is forged by Hörisch (52).

16. This perpetual confrontation also expresses itself in other forms. For instance, because the narrator of the *Moscow Diary* can never coincide with, or "consume," the other, he shifts his desire to other objects of potential gratification, most notably food. In numerous passages, the rejected or depressed Benjamin devours food in a kind of sudden eating frenzy. "In the afternoon I see Asja only briefly," Benjamin laments; "[s]he had had an argument with Reich about living arrangements and sends me away. I read Proust in my room while scarfing down marzipan" (MD 16; 6:298). Or:

"Back in my room I lay down on the bed and read Proust while eating the candied nuts we had bought because Asja likes them" (*MD* 43; 6:326). He describes himself eating "once again" "a sweet roll" in the pastry shop (*MD* 120; 6:407), and candy after dinner (*MD* 390; 6:390). Indeed, "when tea was finally served, I shamelessly stuffed myself with biscuits" (*MD* 96; 6:383). And another time, there "was a fairly rich assortment of food and tea on the tea table and without having to be encouraged I ate a great deal" (*MD* 101; 6:386).

Though he cannot control these urges, the narrator is not blind to their existence either. As Benjamin comments on these fits of devouring: "I notice how the great need for rest that has come over me now that I have been delivered from my agonizing dependence on Asja discovers ever new sources through which it satisfies itself. Above all, of course, food and drink" (*MD* 59; 6:344). The narrator shifts the trajectory of his unfulfilled desire away from Lacis and onto the devouring of food—a process of substitutive gratification, the Freudian *Ersatzbefriedigung*. In the *Moscow Diary*, this substitutive gratification shifts toward a form of painful addiction ("agonizing dependence"—he is first addicted to Lacis, then to food), that is, from lust to devouring. Thus, while the concrete manifestation of the relation to the desired other metamorphoses, the very *structure* of that relation—addiction itself—does not. The narrator's addiction reveals itself not as an aberration but as a radicalization of the problematic desire that flows through the entire text and that, in the unconscious, becomes a symptom of the decentered subject itself. The text charts the traces of desire as addiction, even as it presents addiction as what may potentially guard against the total annihilation of the subject's existence. After all, for Benjamin, addiction is a form of ontological vigilance. As he explains in his drug protocols of 1932, "in a great many cases, a main motive for addiction is to increase the addict's suitability for life's struggle" (6:605).

Benjamin engaged in this kind of life's struggle also in the sphere of literature, and especially on the terrain of writers to whom he was addicted, such as Proust and Aragon. In his essay "On Proust," Adorno recalls that "Benjamin once told me that he did not want to read one word more of Proust than he had to translate, because otherwise he would fall into an addictive dependency that would impede him in his own production" (313). Benjamin also conveys the cautious excitement of the literary addict in a letter to Adorno from 1935 regarding Aragon's *Paysan de Paris*, of which "[e]venings, lying in bed, I could never read more than two or three pages . . . because my heart started to pound so hard that I had to put the book down" (*C* 488; *B* 663).

From a different perspective, it would be necessary to investigate this struggle for existence along the lines of Lacan's distinction between the

NOTES TO CHAPTER 2

body's real and symbolic death as outlined by Žižek in his essay on Benjamin's theses on the concept of history, "Walter Benjamin: Dialektik im Stillstand."

In a 1915 essay from his student years, "The Life of Students," Benjamin conceives of another kind of substitutive gratification, namely that offered by the prostitute. In a peculiar turn of argument, he suggests the essential complementarity of the academic mind and the (non-bourgeois) eros as a natural commodity. It is the task of the university, Benjamin claims, "to form—out of intellectual life—into a unity what is sadly looking at us, in the distorted and disfigured form of the torso of an intellectual eros, as the intellectual independence of the creative producer (in the fraternities) and as the unmastered force of nature (in prostitution)" (W 44; 2:84). Some twenty years later, in the *Passagen-Werk*, the prostitute figures as an emblem of the masses and of commodity fetishism. There, Benjamin writes: "Love of the prostitute is the apotheosis of our empathy for the commodity" (5:475). Compare, in the orbit of "The Life of the Students," Benjamin's short statement on erotic education (2:71).

17. Compare Shapiro, who remarks on this contradiction as developed by Nancy.

18. Julia Kristeva suggests that a subject's very existence is dependent upon its identification with an ideal other. By naming the self as an image to be read, this process of identification aids the subject in constructing a preferred self-image. Through such an idealized relationship, the self becomes part of the other, and the two are woven into a symbolic interdependence. It is precisely this relationship that drives the subject to establish imaginary objects of desire in the first place (253). According to Kristeva, the other is a (potentially hostile) means of constructing the ideal self. The other promises the possibility that the self might discern itself at the same time that it threatens to obscure the conditions of such enlightenment. Although the narrating voice of the *Moscow Diary* is eventually denied access to the other—and in particular the other's body—that voice is to a certain degree empowered by the other's potential presence, enabling the subject, at least momentarily, to think of itself as a form of self-consciousness. The other, then, is understood "not as a 'pure signifier' but as the very space of metaphorical shifting" (254). From this perspective, Benjamin depends on Lacis—who, as his other, is nothing but the reflection of his subject-positions—though he is ultimately denied the full identification with (or consummation of) the other that is necessary for the construction of a coordinated self-image.

19. In my discussion of presence of mind, I am indebted to Menke's fine account (*Sprachfiguren* 352ff.). For a different discussion of presence of mind, see Weidmann (*Flanerie, Sammlung, Spiel* 119ff. and "Geistesgegenwart: Das Spiel in Walter Benjamins Passagenarbeit").

20. Weidmann discusses this passage in the context of the problem of the game in Benjamin ("Das Spiel" 532).

21. For an extended reading of this thought-image, see Weidmann ("Das Spiel" 531ff.).

22. Compare further Menke's suggestive extension of *Geistesgegenwart* into the material scene of reading (*Sprachfiguren* 360).

23. Chow links questions of death, decay, and necrophilia in Benjamin to a consideration of the category "gender."

24. These lines are from "Nationalsozialistische Erziehung. Kampf-und Mitteilungsblätter des Nationalsozialistischen Lehrerbundes für den Gau Groß-Berlin (1932–34)," as cited in Briegleb (104).

25. In this connection, compare also Benjamin's meditation in an early fragment on "Psychology": "When I speak with a human being and a doubt about him rises within me, his image becomes cloudy. I still see him but I can no longer perceive him" (6:66).

26. Here, I follow Derrida's elaboration of the tear in *Memoirs of the Blind* (126).

CHAPTER 3

1. Compare Carol Jacobs, who in her fine reading of the *Berlin Chronicle*, "Walter Benjamin: Topographically Speaking," develops Benjamin's labyrinthine entanglement in the textual structure of his Berlin topography.

2. In focusing on the ways in which the self of the *Berlin Chronicle* interacts with noise, I follow the lead of Manfred Schneider, who was the first critic to comment on the function of noise in the Berlin autobiographies within the context of criminalistic storage and retrieval systems, police archives, and psycho-electronic patterns of public identification. While Schneider's pioneering reading remains indispensable and should be regarded as complementary to the one I am proposing here, I differ with his approach in several vital respects. While I agree with Schneider's assessment that noise disturbs Benjamin's self, I do not share his focus on the psychological and criminalistic concerns that link the subject to the police archive. While Schneider's readings of the acoustic realm refer to the *Berlin Childhood*, mine refer to the *Berlin Chronicle*. Schneider takes the *Berlin Chronicle* simply as an early version of the *Berlin Childhood*, while I try to remain faithful to the different projects they embody. To be sure, there are many relays and overlaps between the two texts, but a majority of the textual material in each one is not shared by the other. Unlike Schneider, I disagree with the notion that Benjamin's Berlin autobiographies become increasingly preoccupied with the acoustic at the expense of the image. On the contrary, as I hope to show in the following chapter, vision and the image dominate the *Berlin Childhood*, while the ear and the acoustic are more central to

the *Berlin Chronicle*. Likewise, I do not agree with Schneider's overall thesis that the twentieth century is marked by a transition from the visual to the acoustic. In more ways than one, ours is the culture of the image. If anything, the *Berlin Chronicle* stages a transitional moment in a culture moving from the acoustic to the visual. Finally, and most importantly, I wish to argue here that the acoustic self is suspended rather than simply negated, a theoretically and politically significant difference I discuss below.

3. As Sieburth rightfully reminds us, "Benjamin's passion for the diminutive is well-documented; Scholem reports his admiration for two grains of wheat in the Jewish section of the Musée Cluny on which the complete *Shema Israel* had been inscribed. The smaller the object, Hannah Arendt observes, the more likely it seemed to Benjamin that it could contain in the most concentrated form everything else—reduction in size having as its corollary a recovery of primal pattern (as in the Goethean *Urphänomen*) or a distillation of synecdochical cosmic design (as in the Leibnizian monad)" (13). In this context, compare also Lacis's reflections on the poems Benjamin wrote for her in his miniature handwriting that she could only decipher with the help of a magnifying glass (*Revolutionär im Beruf* 71).

4. Fuld's biography records the bleak contents of the various good-bye notes (*Zwischen den Stühlen* 226f.). For a vivid account of Benjamin in Ibiza in 1932, see the recollections of Jean Selz, to whom Benjamin read part of his memoirs and with whom he initiated the project of translating his autobiographical pages into French.

5. Jacobs's essay on the *Berlin Chronicle*, "Topographically Speaking," is a joyous exception.

6. See also Gary Smith's discussion of this passage ("Thinking through Benjamin" xviif.).

7. The English translation seems to omit this passage.

8. The pervasive sound of the military bands and the rumbling of the coach wheels in early twentieth-century Berlin is registered, in remarkably similar language and tone, in another autobiography, Nabokov's *Speak, Memory*: "A military band (Germany, at the time, was the land of music), manned by an uncommonly jerky conductor, came to life every ten minutes or so but could hardly drown the ceaseless, sweeping rumble of wheels" (205). Compare also the astute descriptions of Berlin traffic and street noise in Döblin's 1929 epic novel, *Berlin Alexanderplatz*, to which Benjamin dedicated an important review essay, "Crisis of the Novel" (3:230ff.).

9. He writes: "So on these erring paths I became especially familiar with the stations, each with its outskirts [*Weichteile*] like a city: the Selesian, Stettin, Görlitz stations, and Friedrichstraße" (R 12; 6:472).

10. It would be useful to understand this noise also in terms of Kracauer's reading of the modern "mass ornament," precisely to the extent that cultural noise aspires to the status of a seeming extra or elusive excess that

secretly structures one's cultural existence. See his 1927 essay "The Mass Ornament," of which Benjamin was well aware.

11. In the wealth of acoustic figurations of the *Berlin Chronicle*'s compendium of noise it is also worth noting the all-pervasive ringing of the school bell emitting the signal that comes to structure, even overdetermine, the lives of young Benjamin and his fellow pupils (*R* 51; 6:510f.). The alarm signal functions both as an ordering device of the pupil's otherwise unstructured, even chaotic, academic existence (*Getrappel, Lärmen, Geschwätz*) and as a disruptive, authoritarian signal, the sheer shrillness of which evokes unease. At the same time, however, the youth enjoys in these situations his most intimate contacts with the desirable maid—perhaps a first figuration of what in the *Berlin Childhood* will later be called "Awakening Sexus." Moreover, the intrusion of cultural noise produces in the youth an utter disgust with the masses at the same time that it is linked to his (desired or fantasized) relationship to his mother. In this way the noise of the masses—much like rhetorical irony itself, which has the power simultaneously to construct and destroy intimacy and the effect of love—both distances and endears.

12. Apparently missing in the English translation.

13. Cited in Walter ("Reimen und Stehlen" 97). For an extended meditation on the politics of noise, compare Attali.

14. Jacobs remarks on the link made here between the ability to decipher a map and a sense of physical direction ("Topographically Speaking" 505).

15. This is the term Schneider suggests to designate the self's *negation* (119).

16. Menninghaus has cast this transitory "in-betweenness" interestingly in terms of a Benjaminian *Schwellenkunde* or doctrine of thresholds, where, in "a world so structured by thresholds, threshold activities, and threshold creatures, the break-down or leveling of thresholds signals not an act of liberation but of catastrophe, of the intrusion of chaos into a mythologically formed world" (*Schwellenkunde* 40).

17. These scholars are among those who have, in tracing such medial formations of subjectivity, devoted specific attention to the problem of hearing and the telephone. See Kittler's *Discourse Networks 1800/1900; Grammophon, Film, Typewriter*; and *Draculas Vermächtnis: Technische Schriften*. Compare also Schneider; Rickels's "Kafka and Freud on the Telephone" as well as his *Aberrations of Mourning* (279–93); and especially Ronell's *The Telephone Book: Technology, Schizophrenia, Electric Speech*. Investigating "the transcendental predicament of accepting a call" (5), Ronell shows how the telephone operates as a "synecdoche for technology" (7). She demonstrates how the "ear, eye, even skin, have been divested of authority as they acquire technical extension and amplification in media" (109), investigating the extent to which the human subject has become a product of technology. Finally, for a brief account that traces the relation between the ear and

language from Derrida back to Herder, see Trabant ("Language and the Ear"). I thank Hans Adler for pointing me to this last text.

18. See Friedrich Podszus's letter to Gräfin Johanna Rogendorf von Mollenburg, in which he reports meeting Benjamin regularly at "Wolff's telegraph office" (cited in Puttnies and Smith, *Benjaminia* 30).

19. In the year before the *Berlin Chronicle* was written, Kracauer already had thematized, in the text "The Haunted Entertainment Bar" written for the *Frankfurter Zeitung*, the ghostly character of the telephone (*Straßen in Berlin* 89ff.).

20. To my knowledge, Schneider was the first reader to have commented on the image of the telephone in Benjamin's *Berlin Childhood around 1900*.

21. On this point, compare also Schneider (107).

22. These protocols are chronologically, formally, conceptually, and rhetorically related to the *Berlin Chronicle*. Compare Scholem's afterword to Benjamin's *Berlin Chronicle*, in which he traces the *Chronicle*'s lines "O brown-baked column of victory / With children's sugar in winter days"— which later, in slightly altered form, became the motto of the *Berlin Childhood*—to a surrealistic poem Benjamin wrote in conjunction with his drug experiments ("Nachwort zu Benjamins *Berliner Chronik*" 176f.).

23. It would be necessary to trace the many relays between the noise that penetrates Benjamin's ear and Adorno's elaborations of problems of what he calls fetishistic, atomistic, and dissociative modes of hearing ("Über den Fetischcharakter in der Musik und die Regression des Hörens").

24. Hamacher elaborates on the moment in which Benjamin can become like anything else, specifically clouds, throughout "The Word 'Wolke'— If It Is One." My understanding of becoming similar is indebted to this essay. I have also profited from Cadava's similar reading of this mimetic act in the relation between Benjamin and Kafka (106ff.). For an extended complementary reading of Benjamin's becoming similar to the telephone, compare Schneider (130ff.).

25. For a discussion of the temporal dimension of the shock mediated by the modern machine, see Tiedemann (*Studien* 81f.). Also compare Pfotenhauer's discussion of the "reception of shock" as a shift in the dimension of time (*Ästhetische Erfahrung* 76ff.).

Benjamin's understanding of memory is indebted to Bergson's theory, elaborated in *Matter and Memory*, that memory proceeds by shocks. Bergson states that a "sharp shock, a violent emotion, forms the decisive event to which they [memories] cling; if this event, by reason of its sudden character, is cut off from the rest of history, they follow it into oblivion. We can understand, then, that the oblivion which follows a physical or moral shock includes the events which immediately preceded it" (171). Memory organizes itself around trauma, shock, and the rupture of experience. The constant influx of moments of shock gives rise to the fragments of consciousness to which memories attach themselves. Every such moment, by extension, is what Baudelaire, in "The Painter of Modern Life," calls a "memory which has acquired the habit of registering in a flash the general tone and shape, the outline pattern" of the recollection enabled by shock (407).

Moreover, Benjamin's "tone of true memory" places the telephone within the orbit of Freudian *Nachträglichkeit* (belatedness or retroactivity). The child stores and codes certain scenes as memories without being able to interpret them. Only later, during certain developmental phases, such as the Oedipal phase, or under the psychological stress of certain traumatic situations, do these inscriptions return to the self. Benjamin's telephonic noise could be read as producing such a stressful instance.

26. See also Nägele's perceptive commentary on this passage (*Theater, Theory, Speculation* 56). The image of remembrance and forgetting in this context may be profitably read in conjunction with Benjamin's theory of melancholia (Pensky 193).

27. Compare McCole's explanation of *Eingedenken* (260).

28. Compare further Adorno's letter on the dream as a model of dialectical subjectivity and Benjamin's response (N 54f.; 5:582).

29. This immolation of the material self in the shock of memory is also related to Benjamin's rearticulation of the subject in the creative act. Here, the self is never the critical agency of its own acts of writing and producing, not even when such an act is linked to the category of memory.

In this context, see Jennings for a reading of Benjamin's theory of (art) history in the orbit of Worringer and Riegl: "Benjamin's late work contains two distinct but often complementary theories of the relationship between history and the literary text. The first is unambiguously psychological, a theory of memory and its relation to the creative process; the second, a theory of the collective determination of the individual work, is so oriented to the text (or cultural object) itself that the producer of the text or artifact all but disappears" ("Walter Benjamin and the Theory of Art History" 79). Compare further Habermas ("Excursus on Benjamin's Theses") and, for a related discussion of the relays between Benjamin's textualist and materialist concerns, the essay by Corngold and Jennings, "Walter Benjamin in Recent Critical Perspective."

30. Adorno's report on Benjamin's affection for these objects is handed down to us through Szondi's 1962 "Walter Benjamin's City Portraits" (29).

31. Bloch writes, "Precisely and at least most visibly this: that, under the light shed on them by Benjamin, the centrality of things that are peripheral, out of the way, and even eccentric could emerge with so much skin-tight precision, and that they then, illuminated as a real written image, become 'emblematic'" ("Recollections" 343).

To illustrate this point, Bloch recalls strolling along Berlin's *Kurfürstendamm* with his bride Karola one day, when the couple happened to spot

Benjamin, the physiognomist of the object world, walking slowly, his head lowered and oddly tilted to the side, apparently rapt in thought. Having heard so much about her husband's friend but never having met him in person, Karola Bloch politely but quickly inquired after what Benjamin had been pondering. Benjamin slowly looked up and responded: "Madam, have you ever noticed the sickly appearance of the marzipan figures?" (341).

That Bloch shared the philosophical stance of Benjamin's penetrating gaze at the unexpected detail becomes clear in a letter to Benjamin dated 30 April 1934 in which Bloch evokes their common "looking entirely elsewhere [*ganz anderswohin blicken*]" ("Briefe an Benjamin" 653).

32. The fascists' dissemination of the radio is mentioned in Mosse (*Nazi Culture* xxx) and discussed in detail by Reichel (160).

33. I borrow this term from Mehlman's extended essay on Benjamin's radio scripts for children, *Walter Benjamin for Children*.

CHAPTER 4

1. Adorno was the first reader to comment on the *Berlin Childhood* as a "subjective" counterpart to the *Passagen-Werk* ("Nachwort" 74). That Benjamin himself thought of the *Berlin Childhood* as an autobiographical pendant to the *Passagen-Werk* is suggested by Weigel (*Enstellte Ähnlichkeit* 31).

2. Lindner proposes this term with regard to the segment "Loggias" ("Archäologie" 30).

3. The fullest discussion of the "dialectical image" along the trajectory of Benjamin's development can be found in Jennings (*Dialectical Images.*)

4. Compare in this context Heidegger's claim, in "The Time of the World Picture," that modernity, starting with Descartes, turned itself fully into images. According to Heidegger, in modernity there is no image *of* the world. Rather the world as such *is* image. The transformation of the world into image corresponds to the advent of the modern subject, whose representational demands are ultimately based on historical violence: the subject forces that which is given (*das Seiende*) to turn itself into images to be read exclusively on the site embodied by the subject itself. Through a process of quasi-consumption, the gazing subject now claims to speak in the name of the world which it had first turned into an image—a form of double violence. Heidegger suggests that visuality and the site of the image are the ground upon which modern culture and its subject problematically operate.

For a detailed survey of the ways in which the Western tradition privileges vision in philosophical speculation and for modern critiques of vision, see Martin Jay's *Downcast Eyes*. Compare also the collection *Modernity and the Hegemony of Vision*, edited by David Levin and Crary's archaeology of vision, *Techniques of the Observer.*

Because Benjamin shares his language and concerns with the philo-sophical tradition that thematizes vision, and because he breaks with this tradition to reformulate its terms, he both belongs to the tradition and does not belong to it. He alters the tradition even as he echoes it. The tradition survives in him but becomes something else. We could therefore say that the Western tradition of writing about vision inhabits Benjamin as a ghost—and he inhabits it as a ghost.

5. In the visual world of the *Berlin Childhood* there is no "behind" or "depth of meaning," but only surfaces to be read. Hart Nibbrig suggests that in "the texts of the *Berlin Childhood*, the deepest layer becomes the most superficial one. It is not made transparent with regard to a deeper meaning hidden behind the world. But the illumination of the surface does not persist; time and again it coagulates into materiality. The victory column remains a stone, and the otter, an otter; what the child encounters in them in not attached to them" (725).

6. Benjamin's editors, Tiedemann and Schweppenhäuser, as well as Bernd Witte ("Bilder der Endzeit") explain the complicated textual status of the *Berlin Childhood*. When in December 1926 Benjamin published the first three pieces of what was to become his childhood autobiography, he could not have foreseen the consternation that the multiple versions of his text would cause his readers. These three pieces, originally published under the title "Children" in the Berlin journal *Literarische Welt*, were expanded to six texts which appeared two years later as "Enlargements" in *One-Way Street* in 1928. The "Enlargements" can be regarded as the prototype of the *Berlin Childhood*. They contain the central preoccupations of the later autobiography: the reading child fully engrossed in texts, inhabiting a special reading space in which he fortifies his resistance to the restrictive and mystifying rules and norms of adult society and in which he experiences a subversive literary jouissance; the child who arrives late at school and must now endure cruel punishment and subjugation; the secret sensuous joys of candy as the prefiguration and guilt of sexual intercourse; young Benjamin, riding on a carousel, unveiling his joyous coincidence with the external world as the ancient "ecstasy of power"; the child, in a mode befit-ting Benjamin's materialist historiographer, strategically collecting garbage and other superfluous objects; or, finally, the various rooms of a haunted *Gründerzeit*-apartment that becomes a negative second nature and prevents the child from coming into his own.

In October 1931, Benjamin signed a contract with *Literarische Welt* that obliged him to contribute short texts in quarterly installments chronicling life in Berlin. Benjamin never completed the assignment. A fragmentary chronicle of childhood memories was published in book format in 1970 by Scholem as *Berlin Chronicle*. The *Berlin Chronicle* and the *Berlin Childhood* are, despite their partial overlap, quite distinct. Most of the material in each one has no equivalent passage in the other. In the autumn of 1932, Benjamin, now living with a friend in Italy, lends his autobiography the quality of fragmentation and allegoricism that characterizes the published versions of the *Berlin Childhood*. In the hermeticization of his short texts, Benjamin enacts the necessity of the fragmentary form for the allegorical project of his self-portrait that challenges even subtle readers. On 24 July 1933, Benjamin thus announces in a letter to Jula Rath that his *"Berlin Childhood around 1900,* of which you unfortunately understood so little and in which there is so much to understand, is growing by a some few but important pieces" (*C* 423; *B* 587). At the same time, Benjamin is quite aware of the significance, both theoretical and biographical, that this peculiar textual constellation possesses. In keeping with the principle that underlies a good part of his production, namely, to intertwine highly personal material with theoretical and philosophical reflections of aesthetic, historical, and socio-political significance, Benjamin now poetizes and fragments his text even more. Benjamin wished to undermine his textual self through the new (vis-à-vis the *Berlin Chronicle*) or redoubled (vis-à-vis "Children") emphasis on narrative rupture.

In 1934, after the Nazi seizure of power, Benjamin offers the book manuscript of *Berlin Childhood* to several publishers, including Kiepenheuer and Erich Reiss, to no avail. A significant revision of the text in the spring of 1938 did not lead to a book publication. But at least several pieces of the text appeared in the exile journal *Maß und Wert,* published and edited with the assistance of Thomas Mann. Only in 1950, ten years after Benjamin's suicide and under the editorship of Adorno, did the *Berlin Childhood* finally appear as a book. Until recently, this "Adorno version" was considered the most reliable text. But various editorial developments since then have made the philological status of the text a delicate matter.

In their annotations to the *Gesammelte Schriften*, Benjamin's editors, Tiedemann and Schweppenhäuser, differentiate among five main versions of the text (7:691ff.). There is (a) a handwritten convolute begun in autumn 1932, the "Felicitas-Exemplar," which had already been consulted in volume four of the first edition of the *Gesammelte Schriften*; (b) the version from late 1932, dedicated to Benjamin's son and thus called the "Stefan-Exemplar," which has only recently been made accessible; (c) the version Rexroth used for the first publication of the *Gesammelte Schriften* in 1972 and which relies mainly on Adorno's editions of 1950 and 1955, called the "Adorno-Rexroth version"; (d) the (presumably) 1938 version of the text, found in 1981 by Benjamin's Italian editor Giorgio Agamben in the *Bibliothèque Nationale* in Paris, the *Handexemplar komplett* as Benjamin himself wrote diagonally across the title page; this is the latest surviving version organized by Benjamin himself and only one of two—the other being version "e"—that contain the author's own table of contents as well as a significant and heretofore unknown "Preface"; and (e) a 1932–33 version found recently in the archives of the University of Gießen; a full autopsy of this manuscript still remains to be made available.

Though there is no definitive proof that the *Handexemplar komplett* is indeed Benjamin's 1938 version, indirect evidence, marshaled from his letters and from recorded conversations, makes a convincing case. Readers of the 1938 version who are familiar with the Adorno-Rexroth version may be surprised to find that many pieces have been drastically shortened and a good number eliminated altogether. Such texts seemed, for at least three decades, an integral part of the *Berlin Childhood*. In the absence of a definitive historical-critical edition, the 1938 Paris manuscript follows most closely Benjamin's own textual *constellation* of the individual segments. In my reading, I generally follow the 1938 version and consult previous versions when appropriate.

Such philological questions about the status of Benjamin's text are not as extraneous as they may at first appear. Indeed, they perform the constantly revised status of Benjamin's autobiographical self which, with each new draft, undergoes another transformation. The "shattered" philological status of Benjamin's text thus enacts, as it were, the vicissitudes of the subject.

7. An excellent extended analysis of the cultural image of the flâneur can be found in Herbert. For a recent discussion of the *Berlin Childhood* that stresses Benjamin's reading of Baudelaire, see Günter (154ff.).

8. This division into exteriority and interiority is pointed out by Bohrer (567).

9. Compare Benjamin's commentaries on Brecht, especially "What Is Epic Theater?" (*I* 147ff.; 2:532ff.) as well as the compilation of his writings on Brecht in *Understanding Brecht*. For a useful commentary on this essay, see Stern.

In a diary entry from 29 June 1938, Benjamin relates his exiles' conversations with Brecht, in which the playwright links epic theater to the theatrical sphere of the child: "Brecht talks about epic theater; he mentions the children's theater in which errors in presentation, functioning as estrangement effect, endow a performance with epic traits" (*Versuche über Brecht* 115; 6:534). Finally, for a reading of the constellation of Benjamin and Brecht, see Arendt's *Benjamin und Brecht: Zwei Essays*.

10. This point is suggested by Witte (*Intellectual Biography* 147).

11. The full passage from *Capital* reads: "A commodity appears, at first sight [*auf den ersten Blick*], a trivial, self-evident thing. Its analysis shows that it is a very problematic thing, abounding in metaphysical subtleties and theological peculiarities. So far as it is a use value, there is nothing mysterious about it, whether we observe [*betrachten*] it from the point of view [*Gesichtspunkt*] that by its properties it is capable of satisfying human needs, or from the point that those properties are the product of human

labor. It is as very clear [*sinnenklar*] that man, by his industry, changes the forms of the materials furnished by Nature, in such a way as to make them useful to him. The form of wood, for instance, is altered by making a table out of it. Yet, for all that, the table continues to be that common, sensory thing, wood. But as soon as it steps forth as a commodity, it is changed into something transcendent. It not only stands with its feet on the ground, but, in relation to all other commodities, it stands on its head and evolves out of its wooden brain grotesque ideas, far more wonderful than if it voluntarily started to dance" (71).

12. Compare also Eagleton, who relates the moment of commodity fetishism in Benjamin to Lacan's field of vision of the imaginary (25ff.). For a general critique of Eagleton's Marxist readings of Benjamin, see Norris. On commodity fetishism in Benjamin more generally, see further Jennings (*Dialectical Images* 73f.) and Buck-Morss (*Dialectics of Seeing* 187ff.). Finally, for a useful analysis of Benjamin's more general reading of capitalism in the context of Weber and Nietzsche, see Steiner's recent commentary on the fragment "Capitalism as Religion."

13. I thank Thomas Y. Levin for presenting me with the gift of "otterbi-ography."

14. Schneider also notes the relay between the otter's emergence and the moment of flashing up in the "Doctrine of the Similar" (130).

15. If the gaze into the otter's unsung kingdom, which is situated among the dead-end streets and dim corners where no other visitor of the zoo normally treads, affords Benjamin an ocular epiphany in which something peculiar happens to temporality, then past and future enter a new relationship. We may recall the definition given by Friedrich Schlegel, the Romantic theorist whom Benjamin studied meticulously, of the historian as a prophet turned backwards (33). Here, Benjamin implicitly cites and inverts Schlegel's language, showing the *prophet to be a historian turned forward* ("as though everything that is actually ahead of us were something past").

16. That the conceptual role model for the materialist historiographer, whether in the *Berlin Childhood* or in *One-Way Street*, should be the child and his playful, irreverent gaze is consistent with Benjamin's general privileging of the child. He was an avid collector of children's books and toys, and his expertise on children's culture led him to write several influential essays and book reviews on the topic. The anthology *Walter Benjamin und die Kinderliteratur*, edited by Klaus Doderer, presents a number of sustained discussions on this aspect of Benjamin's corpus.

In the *Berlin Childhood*, there can be no doubt that the child's perceptual mode is privileged and radically different from that of the adult world. As the reader learns in "Two Enigmatic Images": "Back then the bank of adulthood appeared separated from me by the river ribbon of many years, much like that bank of the canal from which a bed of flowers looked toward me and which

I had never trod upon during my strolls at the governess's side" (7:401). The difference between the cognitive world of the child and that of the adult world is enacted in the sphere of vision, in which only the child can perceive (and enjoy) the moody jouissance of the flower bed looking at the human passers-by. Scholem comments on Benjamin's fascination when he suggests that it is "one of Benjamin's most important characteristics that throughout his life he was attracted with almost magical force by the child's world and ways. This world belongs to the most persistent and abiding themes of his reflections, and indeed, everything he wrote on this subject counts among his most perfect pieces" ("Walter Benjamin" 175). The figure of the child enables Benjamin to link the disparate strands of theology, philosophy, belletrism, and the revolutionary impetus. As Buck-Morss claims, what "Benjamin found in the child's consciousness, badgered out of existence by bourgeois education and so crucial to redeem (albeit in new form), was precisely the unsevered connection between perception and action that distinguished revolutionary consciousness in adults" (*Dialectics* 263).

In "A Glimpse into the World of Children's Books" (1926), the only text Benjamin ever devoted entirely to his extensive and beloved collection of children's books, he concretizes something of the force with which the child's gaze in the *Berliner Kindheit* penetrates the world of images. Here, it is not the objects that "come forth to meet the picturing child from the pages of the book; instead, through looking the child enters into those pages, becoming suffused, like a cloud, with the riotous colors of the world of pictures" (W 435; 4:609). The child is thus an "imaging" (*bilderndes*) subject and, through the activity of "imaging," he accesses the world of already given images. The young Benjamin translates this visual cross-illumination into a critical vocabulary that helps him to evaluate the given world of the image and to affix to this image a vital inscription: "With the same compelling demand for a description [*Beschreibung*] that is found in such images, they awake the word in the child. Just as the child describes [*beschreibt*] these images in words, so he literally inscribes [*beschreibt*] them: he scribbles on them" (W 436; 4:610). In the literalization that transforms the German verb *beschreiben* or "to depict" into "to inscribe," the child arrests the flickering image and marks it forever as his own by engraving it with the traces of his pen. Benjamin elaborates on this method in his 1929 *Denkbild* entitled "San Gimignano": "To find words for what is before one's eyes—how difficult that can be. But when they do come, they bang away at the real with little hammers until they drive forth the image as if from a copper plate" (4:364). The child can now engage in a reading of his cultural and political constellation. The double textual movement of *beschreiben* as de-scription and in-scription renders the child a potentially subversive subject.

17. Compare on this point Lindner ("Archäologie" 30). For different

readings of "Loggias," see also Schweppenhäuser (159) as well as the extended readings of this segment—in the only two book-length treatments of the *Berlin Childhood* thus far—by Stüssi (130ff.) and Muthesius (33ff.).

18. Benjamin here also implicitly invokes another meaning of loggias, that of the architectural porch held up by columns carved into human shape (as one might find them in Athens). In Florence, the loggia is an outdoor sculpturing display, a copy of which can be found in Munich. Benjamin's term *Loggienhöhe*, or height of the loggia, thus superimposes Berlin (and Paris) on Munich, Florence, and Athens to create a network of topographical relays. I thank Victor Udwin for pointing out these architectural relays to me. Springer takes Benjamin's text as a point of departure for a detailed art-historical discussion of Berlin's "Victory Column" monument and the problem of *Historienmalerei*.

19. The evocative segment "The Little Hunchback" also belongs to this structure. Here, Benjamin tells of his strolls through Berlin during which he encounters cellar openings and holes in the concrete: "The trap-doors opened less to the outdoors than to the subterranean realm. Hence the curiosity with which I looked down through the bars of the grating on which I was standing; I wanted to take in from the basement the sight of canary bird, a lamp, or an inhabitant. If I was unsuccessful in this pursuit during the day, the following night would occasionally turn tables on me, and in my dreams gazes that apprehended me [*die mich dingfest machten*] were aimed at me from such underground holes" (7:429f.). Benjamin's gaze is directed into the abyss, the margins of the cityscape, but the other's gaze is always already there, looking at him: "The little man always got there first . . . he blocked my way" (7:430), and the "little man often stood like this. Yet I never saw him. He always only saw me" (7:430). Benjamin again evokes the hunchbacked dwarf—*ein buckliger Zwerg*—at the beginning of his "Theses on the Concept of History" (*I* 253; 1:693). For a useful discussion of Benjamin's hunchbacked dwarf, see Wohlfarth ("Märchen für Dialektiker").

20. See also Schweppenhäuser's comments on the political relationship among the mausoleum, the citizen, and death (171).

21. Compare also Benjamin's thought-image "Imperial Panorama" in *One-Way Street* (W 450ff; 4:94ff.).

The specific significance of the visual space of the "Imperial Panorama" for Benjamin's concept of the subject is further illustrated in a little known typescript probably written between 1930 and 1933, entitled "The Second Self: A New Year's Eve Story to Think About." As an intertext to the segment in the *Berlin Childhood*, this literary fragment works to set into motion some of the uncanny qualities of a self that is visually constructed. Krambacher, a poor and lonely bachelor, embarks on a drinking orgy on New Year's Eve in the false hope that someone will join him on this occasion. When no one does, he decides to wander through the deserted streets. Through the windows of a pathetic-looking, run-down pub, he discerns the faint outlines of a sign that reads "KAISERPANORAMA." The advertisement on the front door promises a grand gala performance for the night—a visual journey through the past year. Upon entry, Krambacher sees that the establishment is deserted, except for the old owner who abruptly rises from his sleep, proclaiming that he has been waiting for just the "right one." The owner promises to show Krambacher a man who shares his worries, thoughts, denied impulses, and inferiority complexes without resembling him in other ways: "Now, what are these impulses?" muses the old man, "They are the pressure that the second self exerts on the handle of the door that leads to their life. Now you will see why you kept this door locked" (7:297). The visual journey in twelve images begins, complete with explanations by the old man who for each picture scoots over to another chair. On some of the images, the second self can actually be seen, on others only the "situations in which it wanted to involve the first." The switching of the pictures is accompanied by a ringing noise, and the last ringing is drowned out by the roaring of the New Year's bells; Krambacher awakes in his chair, holding an empty punch glass.

"The Second Self" playfully conjures up the notion of the visual construction of selfhood as an attempt, on the part of the subject, to become coextensive with an impersonal "already given" rather than with an original or an "essentially different." The "already given" could have been assumed as the second self by anyone willing to be convinced of the appropriateness of that second image for its redoubling—regardless of the actual or empirical properties of the "already given." That is why the coy owner so eagerly assures Krambacher that he is indeed "the right one," whose second self embarks upon an odd journey within the *Kaiserpanorama.* Despite the owner's insistence to the contrary, the reader is led to conclude that the experiences presented to Krambacher as those of his (proper) unconscious psychological upheaval would have fit any passerby randomly entering the pub. These images are not original at all; they are infinitely reproducible and ready to be appropriated by this or that "self." Benjamin's tale suggests that the moment of identification must be one of deception. It is the phantasmagorical assumption of a tailor-made unfolding of the subjective unconscious.

22. Compare further Hamacher's reading of words and clouds in the context of Benjamin's essay "Doctrine of the Similar" ("The Word 'Wolke' "). On sensuous correspondences as mimetic potential in Benjamin, see Menninghaus (*Sprachmagie*) and, more recently, the studies by Bub and Sdun. In this context, see also Jacobs's general comments on the status of figurative correspondences in Benjamin, particularly metaphor ("Image of Proust").

23. Compare also my discussion of *mummen* in relation to Benjamin's theory of mimesis in the previous chapter. For a seminal reading of photography and the problem of history in Benjamin, see Cadava. See also the

recent study by Rugg, who thoughtfully reads the *Berlin Childhood* as a "photographic autobiography in disguise" (133).

For readings that elaborate on the striking similarities in the language Benjamin uses here and in his description of Kafka's photograph both in his essay on Kafka and in "Short History of Photography," see, among others, Stüssi (189ff.), Witte (*Intellectual Biography* 11ff.), Cadava (115ff.), and Rugg (168ff.). Finally, for a recent reading of the constellation of Kafka and Benjamin in the language of gesturing and naming, see Hamacher's "Die Geste im Namen. Benjamin und Kafka." The historical development of Benjamin's concept of photography is traced in Krauss's recent overview.

24. This passage stages a multiple displacement. First, the text depicts the inability of the child to constitute himself, to become what he is. The text then depicts Benjamin, in the visual moment of the photograph, as violently assimilated to his negative second nature, the oppressive *Gründerzeit* furniture and the sentimental studio props. Second, the title "Mummerehlen" comes to Benjamin from an ancient book of children's verse in which a character is called *die Muhme Rehlen*. Because this word has no meaning for the child who is not familiar with *Muhme*—an older German word for aunt—for him "the creature turned into a ghost: the Mummerehlen" (4:260). Hence the signifier "Mummerehlen" enacts a rhetorical disfiguration that yields a ghost. Third, the text "Mummerehlen" was originally intended as the initial text of *Berlin Childhood*. It was to stand as the most complete "self-portrait" Benjamin is capable of writing, one thoroughly interlaced with the presence of a ghost. Eventually, however, the text was relegated farther back into the book when Benjamin moved the "Loggia" into first position. Fourth, in the 1938 version of the *Berlin Childhood*, Benjamin deletes from the passage the entire photographic scene. The text "Mummerehlen" is itself a trace of inscriptions and cancellations, a text about a ghost that strangely becomes a kind of ghost itself.

25. Benjamin's discussion of the optical unconscious through the camera belongs to a whole discursive field of the time. As Hansen points out, the "attribution of psychic, physiognomic, even psychoanalytic faculties to the camera is a topos of early 1920's film theory, notably in Jean Epstein and Béla Balázs," though Benjamin's specific thinking of the optical unconscious is most intimately indebted to Kracauer's 1927 essay "Photography" (Hansen, "Blue Flower" 208). "Prefiguring the superimposition of modernity and prehistory that Benjamin was to advance in his essay on Surrealism and the *Passagen-Werk*," Hansen suggests, "Kracauer's reflections on photography locate the radical function of the medium (intercut with an analysis of its ideological, mythological function) in the arbitrary moment of exposure, the moment of chance that might capture an aspect of nature at once alienated and released from the tyranny of human intention—the 'dregs of history'" (208).

26. For an extended discussion of Benjamin's concept of the auratic, compare Stoessel and, more recently, Recki and Lindner ("Benjamins Aurakonzeption"). Compare also Ferris, who suggestively analyzes the relays between Benjamin's concepts of aura and history.

27. Benjamin's preoccupation with the act of waiting is operative throughout the *Berlin Childhood*. He shares this interest in waiting with Kracauer's 1922 essay "Those Who Wait," a meditation on the dispersed modern subject as the one who waits. For the many scenes of waiting, see especially the putti scenes in "Tiergarten" (7:395) or Benjamin's late arrival at school in "Too Late" (7:395) and the break in temporality he associates with it.

For a recent argument that suggests that Benjamin's figures of waiting are interwoven with his delineations of ambivalence and the erotic, see Geulen ("Genealogy of Gender" 166).

28. My discussion of the gift is indebted to Derrida's *Given Time*.

29. In this connection, compare the passage in *One-Way Street* in which Benjamin states that with regard to his love, Asja Lacis, "of the two of us, I had to be, at any price, the first to see the other. For had she touched me with the match of her eyes, I would have gone up like a powder keg" (W 461; 4:110).

30. Compare the discussions by Menke (*Sprachfiguren* 360f.) and Haverkamp (78), who each comment on this passage in the general context of the dialectical image. For a different discussion of trace and aura in the context of the *Passagen-Werk*, see Jauss.

31. On this point, I am indebted to Haverkamp's discussion (78). Compare also the correspondence between the gaze and the auratic in a preparatory note to Benjamin's 1935 essay "On the Mimetic Faculty." There, he suggests that the relation between the gaze and the auratic is predicated upon the object world always already looking at the subject, particularly the stars (2:958).

32. Compare also Menke's useful reading of this passage in the general context of the textuality of Benjamin's images ("Bild—Textualität" 48ff.).

EPILOGUE

1. For a general political meditation that focuses on the problem of retreating, see *Retreating the Political* by Lacoue-Labarthe and Nancy.

2. Benjamin's lines are cited in Tiedemann's "Historical Materialism," and I use the translation found there (182).

3. For recent meditations on the philosophical and political implications of post-communal thinking, see Nancy's "The Inoperative Community" and Agamben.

4. On Benjamin's reading of Mickey Mouse, compare, among others, Hansen ("Of Mice and Ducks").

5. See Derrida, *The Specters of Marx: The State of the Debt, the Work of Mourning, and the New International,* especially the passages devoted to Benjamin's "weak messianic force" (55 and 180–81n. 2). For a discussion of Benjamin's rearticulation of messianism, compare Jennings (*Dialectical Images* 58ff.) and Wohlfarth, "On Some Jewish Motifs in Benjamin." A more recent discussion of Benjamin's relation to messianism and Jewish theology is offered by Ullmann.

6. Compare especially Benjamin's early essay "Two Poems by Friedrich Hölderlin" (W 18ff; 2:105ff.). For a probing reading of this text, see Corngold's "Benjamin's 'Affective Understanding' of Hölderlin's Odes 'The Poet's Courage' and 'Timidity.'"

7. That parts of Benjamin's book on the *Trauerspiel* are methodologically indebted to Schmitt's pre-Hitler work on political theology and state sovereignty is well known. It becomes evident, for example, in the text's explicit references to Schmitt as well as in a letter that Benjamin wrote to Schmitt when he sent him a copy of the text on 9 December 1930 (1:887). Benjamin also mentions the influence of Schmitt's methodology on the *Trauerspiel* study in a 1928 curriculum vitae (6:219).

8. Weber makes this point in "Taking Exception to Decision: Walter Benjamin and Carl Schmitt" (18). For further discussion of the relationship between Benjamin and Schmitt, see also the respective studies by Figal, Rumpf, and Bolz (*Auszug aus der entzauberten Welt* 85ff.).

9. I am referring to Jay Parini's *Benjamin's Crossing.*

WORKS CITED

Adorno, Theodor W. "Benjamin the Letter Writer." In *The Correspondence of Walter Benjamin, 1910–1940*. By Walter Benjamin. Ed. Gershom Scholem and Theodor Adorno. Trans. Manfred Jacobson and Evelyn Jacobson. Chicago: University of Chicago Press, 1994. xvii–xxii.

———. "Erinnerungen." In *Über Walter Benjamin*. Ed. Rolf Tiedemann. 2d rev. ed. Frankfurt am Main: Suhrkamp, 1990. 78–84.

———. "Ernst Bloch's *Spuren*. On the Revised Edition of 1959." In *Notes to Literature*. Vol. 1. Trans. Shierry Weber Nicholson. New York: Columbia University Press, 1991. 200–15.

———. "Introduction to Benjamin's *Schriften*." In *On Walter Benjamin: Critical Essays and Recollections*. Ed. Gary Smith. Cambridge: MIT Press, 1988. 2–17.

———. "Nachwort zur *Berliner Kindheit um neunzehnhundert*." In *Über Walter Benjamin*. Ed. Rolf Tiedemann. 2d rev. ed. Frankfurt am Main: Suhrkamp, 1990. 74–77.

———. "On Benjamin's *Deutsche Menschen*, a Book of Letters." In *Notes to Literature*. Vol. 2. Trans. Shierry Weber Nicholson. New York: Columbia University Press, 1992. 328–33.

———. "On Proust." In *Notes to Literature*. Vol. 2. Trans. Shierry Weber Nicholson. New York: Columbia University Press, 1992. 312–17.

————. "Parataxis: On Hölderlin's Late Poetry." In *Notes to Literature*. Vol. 2. Trans. Shierry Weber Nicholson. New York: Columbia University Press, 1992. 109–49.

————. "A Portrait of Walter Benjamin." In *Prisms*. Trans. Samuel Weber and Shierry Weber. Cambridge: MIT Press, 1981. 227–41.

————. "Progress." Trans. Eric Krakauer. In *Benjamin: Philosophy, Aesthetics, History*. Ed. Gary Smith. Chicago: University of Chicago Press, 1989. 84–101.

————. "Über den Fetischcharakter in der Musik und die Regression des Hörens." In *Gesammelte Schriften*. Vol. 14. Ed. Rolf Tiedemann. Frankfurt am Main: Suhrkamp, 1984. 14–50.

Adorno, Theodor W., and Walter Benjamin. *Briefwechsel 1928–1940*. Frankfurt am Main: Suhrkamp, 1994.

Agamben, Georgio. *The Coming Community*. Trans. Michael Hardt. Minneapolis: University of Minnesota Press, 1993.

Arendt, Hannah. "Introduction. Walter Benjamin: 1892–1940." In *Illuminations*. By Walter Benjamin. Trans. Harry Zohn. New York: Schocken, 1968. 1–55.

————. *The Origins of Totalitarianism*. New York: Harcourt Brace Jovanovitch, 1973.

————. *Walter Benjamin, Bertolt Brecht: Zwei Essays*. Munich: Piper, 1971.

Ashley, Kathleen, Leigh Gilmore, and Gerald Peters, eds. *Autobiography and Postmodernism*. Amherst: University of Massachusetts Press, 1994.

Attali, Jacques. *Noise: The Political Economy of Music*. Minneapolis: University of Minnesota Press, 1985.

Bahti, Timothy. "History as Rhetorical Enactment: Walter Benjamin's Theses 'On the Concept of History.'" *Diacritics* 9.3 (1979): 2–17.

Barthes, Roland. *Camera Lucida: Reflections on Photography*. Trans. Richard Howard. New York: Noonday, 1993.

————. "The Face of Garbo." In *Mythologies*. Trans. Annette Lavers. New York: Noonday, 1988. 56–57.

————. *The Pleasure of the Text*. Trans. Richard Miller. New York: Hill and Wang, 1975.

Bataille, Georges. *Erotism: Death and Sensuality*. Trans. Mary Dalwood. San Francisco: City Lights, 1986.

Baudelaire, Charles. "The Painter of Modern Life." In *Selected Writings on Art and Literature*. Trans. P. E. Charvet. London: Penguin, 1972. 390–435.

Benjamin, Walter. *Briefe*. Ed. Gershom Scholem and Theodor Adorno. Frankfurt am Main: Suhrkamp, 1966.

————. *Briefe an Siegfried Kracauer: Mit vier Briefen von Siegfried Kracauer an Walter Benjamin*. Marbach: Theodor W. Adorno Archiv, 1987.

———. "Central Park." Trans. Lloyd Spencer. *New German Critique* 34 (1985): 32–58.

———. *Charles Baudelaire: A Lyric Poet in the Era of High Capitalism.* Trans. Harry Zohn. London: New Left Books, 1973.

———. *The Correspondence of Walter Benjamin, 1910–1940.* Ed. Gershom Scholem and Theodor Adorno. Trans. Manfred Jacobson and Evelyn Jacobson. Chicago: University of Chicago Press, 1994.

———. "Doctrine of the Similar." Trans. Knut Tarnowski. *New German Critique* 17 (1979): 65–69.

———. *Gesammelte Schriften.* 14 books in 7 vols. Ed. Rolf Tiedemann and Hermann Schweppenhäuser. Frankfurt am Main: Suhrkamp, 1972–89.

———. *Illuminations.* Ed. Hannah Arendt. Trans. Harry Zohn. New York: Schocken, 1968.

———. *Moscow Diary.* Ed. Gary Smith. Trans. Richard Sieburth. Cambridge: Harvard University Press, 1986.

———. "N [Theoretics of Knowledge; Theory of Progress]." Trans. Leigh Hafrey and Richard Sieburth. In *Benjamin: Philosophy, Aesthetics, History.* Ed. Gary Smith. Chicago: University of Chicago Press, 1989. 43–83.

———. *One-Way Street and Other Writings.* Trans. Edmund Jephcott and Kingsley Shorter. London: New Left Books, 1979.

———. *Origin of German Tragic Drama.* Trans. John Osborne. London: New Left Books, 1977.

———. "Program for a Proletarian Children's Theater." Trans. Susan Buck-Morss. *Performance* 1.5 (1973): 28–32.

———. *Reflections.* Ed. Peter Demetz. Trans. Edmund Jephcott. New York: Schocken, 1978.

———. *Selected Writings.* Volume 1: *1913–1926.* Ed. Marcus Bullock and Michael Jennings. Cambridge: Harvard University Press, 1996.

———. "Theories of German Fascism." Trans. Jerolf Wikoff. *New German Critique* 17 (1979): 120–28.

———. *Understanding Brecht.* Trans. Anna Bostock. London: New Left Books, 1973.

———. *Versuche über Brecht.* Ed. Rolf Tiedemann. Frankfurt am Main: Suhrkamp, 1971.

———, trans. "Die Photographie von der Kehrseite." By Tristan Tzara. *G* 1 (1923): 39–40.

Benjamin, Walter, and Gershom Scholem. *The Correspondence of Walter Benjamin and Gershom Scholem: 1932–1940.* Ed. Gershom Scholem. Trans. Gary Smith and Andre Lefevere. New York: Schocken, 1989.

———. *Walter Benjamin/Gershom Scholem: Briefwechsel, 1933–1940.* Ed. Gershom Scholem. Frankfurt am Main: Suhrkamp, 1980.

Bergson, Henri. *Matter and Memory.* Trans. N. M. Paul and W. S. Palmer. New York: Zone, 1991.

Berman, Russel. "The Aestheticization of Politics: Walter Benjamin on Fascism and the Avant-Garde." *Stanford Italian Review* 8.1–2 (1990): 35–52.

Bloch, Ernst. "Briefe an Walter Benjamin 1934–1937." In *Briefe 1903–1975.* Vol. 2. Ed. Karola Bloch et. al. Frankfurt am Main: Suhrkamp, 1985. 649–68.

———. *Geist der Utopie.* Frankfurt am Main: Suhrkamp, 1985.

———. *The Principle of Hope.* Trans. Neville Plaice et. al. Cambridge: MIT Press, 1986.

———. "Recollections of Walter Benjamin." Trans. Michael Jennings. In *On Walter Benjamin: Critical Essays and Reflections.* Ed. Gary Smith. Cambridge: MIT Press, 1988. 338–45.

———. "Revue Form in Philosophy." In *Heritage of Our Times.* Trans. Neville and Stephen Plaice. Berkeley: University of California Press, 1991. 334–37.

———. *Spuren.* Frankfurt am Main: Suhrkamp, 1985.

———. "Über den sittlichen und geistigen Führer oder die doppelte Weise des Menschengesichts." In *Philosophische Aufsätze zur objektiven Phantasie.* Frankfurt am Main: Suhrkamp, 1969. 204–10.

Bohrer, Karl Heinz. *Der Abschied. Theorie der Trauer: Baudelaire, Goethe, Nietzsche, Benjamin.* Frankfurt am Main: Suhrkamp, 1996.

Bolle, Willi. *Physiognomik der Moderne: Geschichtsdarstellung bei Walter Benjamin.* Cologne: Böhlau, 1994.

Bolz, Norbert. *Auszug aus der entzauberten Welt: Philosophischer Extremismus zwischen den Weltkriegen.* Munich: Fink, 1989.

———. "Der bucklichte Zwerg." In *'Magnetisches Hingezogensein oder Schaudernde Abwehr': Walter Benjamin 1892–1940.* Ed. René Buchholz and Joseph A. Kruse. Stuttgart: Metzler, 1994. 42–58.

———. "Prostituiertes Sein." In *Antike und Moderne: Zu Walter Benjamins 'Passagen.'* Ed. Norbert Bolz and Richard Faber. Würzburg: Königshausen und Neumann, 1986. 191–213.

———. "Statt eines Vorworts: Hauptstadt Paris." In *Passagen: Walter Benjamins Urgeschichte des neunzehnten Jahrhunderts.* Ed. Norbert Bolz and Bernd Witte. Munich: Fink, 1984. 12–16.

———. "Walter Benjamin in the Postmodern." *New Comparison* 18 (1994): 9–23.

Boym, Svetlana. "The Obscenity of Theory: Roland Barthes' 'Soirées de Paris' and Walter Benjamin's *Moscow Diary.*" *Yale Journal of Criticism* 4.2 (1991): 105–28.

Brecht, Bertolt. "Notizen zu Heinrich Manns 'Mut.'" In *Gesammelte Werke.* Vol. 19: *Schriften zur Literatur und Kunst 2.* Frankfurt am Main: Suhrkamp, 1968.

Briegleb, Klaus. *Unmittelbar zur Epoche des NS-Faschismus: Arbeiten zur politischen Philologie 1978–1988.* Frankfurt am Main: Suhrkamp, 1989.

Brodersen, Momme. *Spinne im eigenen Netz—Walter Benjamin: Leben und Werk.* Bühl-Moos: Elster, 1990.

Bub, Stefan. *Sinnenlust des Beschreibens: Mimetische und allegorische Gestaltung in der Prosa Walter Benjamins.* Würzburg: Königshausen und Neumann, 1993.

Buck-Morss, Susan. *The Dialectics of Seeing: Walter Benjamin and the Arcades Project.* Cambridge: MIT Press, 1989.

Butler, Judith. *Bodies That Matter.* New York, Routledge, 1993.

Cadava, Eduardo. *Words of Light: Theses on the Photography of History.* Princeton: Princeton University Press, 1997.

Caygill, Howard. *Walter Benjamin: The Colour of Experience.* London: Routledge, 1998.

Celan, Paul. "Augenblicke." In *Gedichte*, vol. 2. By Paul Celan. Frankfurt am Main: Suhrkamp, 1987. 113.

Chow, Rey. "Walter Benjamin's Love Affair with Death." *New German Critique* 48 (fall 1989): 63–86.

Cohen, Margaret. *Profane Illumination: Walter Benjamin and the Paris of Surrealist Revolution.* Berkeley: University of California Press, 1993.

Corngold, Stanley. "Benjamin's 'Affective Understanding' of Hölderlin's Odes 'The Poet's Courage' and 'Timidity.' " In *Complex Pleasure: Forms of Feeling in German Literature.* Stanford: Stanford University Press, 1998. 150–70.

———. *Franz Kafka: The Necessity of Form.* Ithaca: Cornell University Press, 1988.

Corngold, Stanley, and Michael Jennings. "Walter Benjamin/Gershom Scholem." *Interpretation* 12 (1984): 357–66.

———. "Walter Benjamin in Recent Critical Perspective." *Modern Language Studies* 16.3 (1986): 367–73.

Crary, Jonathan. *Techniques of the Observer: On Vision and Modernity in the Nineteenth Century.* Cambridge: MIT Press, 1990.

Debord, Guy. *The Society of the Spectacle.* Trans. Donald Nicholson-Smith. New York: Zone Books, 1994.

de Man, Paul. *Aesthetic Ideology.* Ed. Andrzej Warminski. Minneapolis: University of Minnesota Press, 1996.

———. "Autobiography as De-Facement." In *The Rhetoric of Romanticism.* New York: Columbia University Press, 1984. 67–81.

———. *Blindness and Insight: Essays in the Rhetoric of Contemporary Criticism.* Minneapolis: University of Minnesota Press, 1988.

———. " 'Conclusions': On Walter Benjamin's 'The Task of the Translator.' " In *The Resistance to Theory.* Minneapolis: University of Minnesota Press, 1986. 73–105.

Derrida, Jacques. "Back from Moscow, in the USSR." In *Politics, Theory, and Contemporary Culture*. Ed. Mark Poster. New York: Columbia University Press, 1993. 197–235.

———. "Before the Law." Trans. Avital Ronell and Christine Roulston. In *Acts of Literature*. Ed. Derek Attridge. New York: Routledge, 1992. 181–220.

———. *Given Time: 1. Counterfeit Money*. Trans. Peggy Kamuf. Chicago: University of Chicago Press, 1992.

———. *Memoirs of the Blind*. Trans. Pascale-Anne Brault and Michael Naas. Chicago: University of Chicago Press, 1993.

———. *The Ear of the Other: Otobiography, Transference, Translation*. Trans. Peggy Kamuf. Ed. Christie McDonald. Lincoln: University of Nebraska Press, 1988.

———. *Positions*. Trans. Alan Bass. Chicago: University of Chicago Press, 1981.

———. *Specters of Marx: The State of the Debt, the Work of Mourning, and the New International*. Trans. Peggy Kamuf. London: Routledge, 1994.

———. " 'This Strange Institution Called Literature': An Interview with Jacques Derrida." In *Acts of Literature*. Ed. Derek Attridge. New York: Routledge, 1992. 33–75.

———. "*Le Toucher*: Touch/to touch him." *Paragraph* 16.2 (1994): 122–57.

Döblin, Alfred. *Berlin Alexanderplatz*. Munich: Deutscher Taschenbuch Verlag, 1987.

———. "Von Gesichtern, Bildern und ihrer Wahrheit." Introduction to *Antlitz der Zeit: Sechzig Aufnahmen deutscher Menschen des 20. Jahrhunderts*. By August Sander. Munich: Transmare, 1929. 7–15.

Doderer, Klaus, ed. *Walter Benjamin und die Kinderliteratur: Aspekte der Kinderkultur in den zwanziger Jahren*. Weinheim: Juventa, 1988.

Düttmann, Alexander Garcia. "Tradition and Destruction: Benjamin's Politics of Language." Trans. Debbie Keates. *MLN* 106.3 (1991): 528–54.

Eagleton, Terry. *Walter Benjamin, Or Towards a Revolutionary Criticism*. London: Verso, 1981.

Elferding, Wieland. "Von der proletarischen Masse zum Kriegsvolk: Massenaufmarsch und Öffentlichkeit am Beispiel des 1. Mai 1933." In *Inszenierung der Macht: Ästhetische Faszination im Faschismus*. Ed. Klaus Behnken and Frank Wagner. Berlin: Neue Gesellschaft für bildende Kunst, 1987. 17–50.

Ferris, David. "Aura, Resistance, and the Event of History." Introduction to *Walter Benjamin: Theoretical Questions*. Ed. David Ferris. Stanford: Stanford University Press, 1996. 1–26.

Figal, Günter. "Vom Sinn der Geschichte: Zur Erörterung der politischen Theologie bei Carl Schmitt und Walter Benjamin." In *Dialektischer*

Materialismus. Ed. Emil Angehrn et. al. Frankfurt am Main: Suhrkamp, 1992. 252–69.

Folkenflik, Robert, ed. *The Culture of Autobiography: Constructions of Self-Representation*. Stanford: Stanford University Press, 1993.

Foucault, Michel. *The History of Sexuality*. Trans. Robert Hurley. New York: Vintage, 1990.

———. "Nietzsche, Genealogy, History." In *Language, Counter-Memory, Practice*. Ed. Donald Bouchard. Trans. Donald Bouchard and Sherry Simon. Ithaca: Cornell University Press, 1977. 139–64.

———. *The Order of Things: An Archeology of the Human Sciences*. New York: Vintage, 1973.

———. "What Is an Author?" In *Textual Strategies*. Ed. Josué Harari. Ithaca: Cornell University Press, 1979. 141–60.

Freud, Sigmund. *Beyond the Pleasure Principle*. Trans. James Strachey. New York: Liveright, 1950.

Frey, Hans-Jost. "On Presentation in Benjamin." Trans. Michael Shae. In *Walter Benjamin: Theoretical Questions*. Ed. David Ferris. Stanford: Stanford University Press, 1996. 139–64.

Fuld, Werner. *Walter Benjamin: Zwischen den Stühlen. Eine Biographie*. Munich: Hanser, 1979.

———. "Walter Benjamins Beziehung zu Ludwig Klages." *Akzente* 28 (1971): 274–86.

Fürnkäs, Josef. *Surrealismus als Erkenntnis: Walter Benjamin—Weimarer Einbahnstraße und Pariser Passagen*. Stuttgart: Metzler, 1988.

Fynsk, Christopher. *Language and Relation*. Stanford: Stanford University Press, 1996.

Gagnebin, Jeanne-Marie. *Zur Geschichtsphilosophie Walter Benjamins*. Erlangen: Palm und Enke, 1978.

Gasché, Rodolphe. "Saturnine Vision and the Question of Difference: Reflections on Walter Benjamin's Theory of Language." In *Benjamin's Ground: New Readings of Walter Benjamin*. Ed. Rainer Nägele. Detroit: Wayne State University Press, 1988. 83–104.

Geulen, Eva. "Toward a Genealogy of Gender in Walter Benjamin's Writings." *The German Quarterly* 69.2 (1996). 161–80.

———. "Zeit zur Darstellung: Walter Benjamins 'Das Kunstwerk im Zeitalter seiner technischen Reproduzierbarkeit.'" *MLN* 107.3 (1992): 580–605.

Goebbels, Joseph. *Goebbels-Reden*. Vol. 1. Ed. Helmut Heiber. Düsseldorf: Droste, 1971.

———. "Why Are We Enemies of the Jews?" Trans. Louis Snyder. In *The Weimar Republic Sourcebook*. Ed. Anton Kaes, Martin Jay, and Edward Dimendberg. Berkeley: University of California Press, 1994. 137–38.

Goethe, Johann Wolfgang. *From My Life: Poetry and Truth*. Trans. Robert

Heitner. Ed. Thomas Saine and Jeffrey Sammons. New York: Suhrkamp, 1987.

Günter, Manuela. *Anatomie des Anti-Subjekts: Zur Subversion autobiographischen Schreibens bei Siegfried Kracauer, Walter Benjamin und Carl Einstein.* Würzburg: Könighausen und Neumann, 1996.

Habermas, Jürgen. "Excursus on Benjamin's Theses on the Philosophy of History." In *The Philosophical Discourse of Modernity: Twelve Lectures.* Trans. Frederick G. Lawrence. Cambridge: MIT Press, 1990. 11–16.

———. "Walter Benjamin: Consciousness-Raising or Rescuing Critique?" In *On Walter Benjamin: Critical Essays and Recollections.* Ed. Gary Smith. Cambridge: MIT Press, 1988. 90–128.

Hamacher, Werner. "Die Geste im Namen: Benjamin und Kafka." In *Entferntes Verstehen.* Frankfurt am Main: Suhrkamp, 1998. 280–323.

———. The Word 'Wolke'—If It Is One." Trans. Peter Fenves. In *Benjamin's Ground: New Readings of Walter Benjamin.* Ed. Rainer Nägele. Detroit: Wayne State University Press, 1988. 147–76.

———. "Working through Working." Trans. Matthew Hartman. *Modernism/Modernity* 3.1 (1996): 23–55.

Hansen, Miriam. "Benjamin, Cinema, and Experience: 'The Blue Flower in the Land of Technology.' " *New German Critique* 40 (1987): 179–224.

———. "Of Mice and Ducks: Benjamin and Adorno on Disney." *South Atlantic Quarterly* 92.1 (1993): 27–61.

Hanssen, Beatrice. *Walter Benjamin's Other History: Of Stones, Animals, Human Beings, and Angels.* Berkeley: University of California Press, 1998.

Hart Nibbrig, Christiaan. "Das déjà vu des ersten Blicks: Zu Walter Benjamins 'Berliner Kindheit um Neunzehnhundert.' " *Deutsche Vierteljahrsschrift* 47.4 (1973): 711–29.

Haverkamp, Anselm. "Notes on the Dialectical Image (How Deconstructive Is It?)." *Diacritics* 22.3–4 (1992): 70–80.

Heartfield, John and Kurt Tucholsky. *Deutschland, Deutschland über alles: Ein Bilderbuch von Kurt Tucholsky und vielen Fotografen. Montiert von John Heartfield.* Berlin: Neuer Deutscher Verlag, 1929.

Heidegger, Martin. *Being and Time.* Trans. John Macquarrie and Edward Robinson. New York: Harper and Row, 1962.

———. "The Principle of Identity." *Identity and Difference.* Trans. Joan Stambaugh. New York: Harper and Row, 1969. 23–41.

———. "The Time of the World Picture." In *The Question Concerning Technology and Other Essays.* Trans. William Lovitt. New York: Garland, 1977. 115–54.

Herbert, Robert. *Impressionism: Art, Leisure, and Parisian Society.* New Haven: Yale University Press, 1991.

Herf, Jeffrey. *Reactionary Modernism: Technology, Culture, and Politics in*

Weimar and the Third Reich. Cambridge: Cambridge University Press, 1984.

Hillach, Ansgar. "Der Anteil der Kultur an der Prägung faschistischer Herrschaftsmittel: Was leistet Benjamins Diagnose des Faschismus?" In *Walter Benjamin: Profane Erleuchtung und rettende Kritik,* ed. Norbert Bolz and Richard Faber. Würzburg: Königshausen und Neumann, 1985. 231–65.

―――. " 'Ästhetisierung des politischen Lebens': Benjamins faschismustheoretischer Ansatz—eine Rekonstruktion." In *Walter Benjamin im Kontext.* Ed. Burkhardt Lindner. Königstein/Ts.: Athenäum, 1985. 127–67.

Hitler, Adolf. "Address to the Industry Club." In *The Weimar Republic Sourcebook.* Ed. Anton Kaes, Martin Jay, and Edward Dimendberg. Berkeley: University of California Press, 1994. 138–41.

―――. *Mein Kampf.* Trans. Ralph Manheim. Boston: Houghton Mifflin, 1943.

Hollington, Michael. "Benjamin and Physiognomy." *Southern Review* 25 (1992): 49–60.

Hörisch, Jochen. "Objektive Interpretation des schönen Scheins." In *Walter Benjamin: Profane Erleuchtung und rettende Kritik.* Ed. Nobert Bolz and Richard Faber. Würzburg: Könighausen und Neumann, 1985. 50–66.

Horkheimer, Max, and Theodor W. Adorno. *Dialectic of Enlightenment.* Trans. John Cumming. New York: Herder and Herder, 1972.

Hüppauf, Bernd. "The Birth of Fascist Man from the Spirit of the Front: From Langemarck to Verdun." In *The Attractions of Fascism: Social Psychology and Aesthetics of the "Triumph of the Right."* Ed. John Milfull. New York: Berg, 1990. 45–76.

Jacobs, Carol. "Walter Benjamin: Image of Proust." In *The Dissimulating Harmony: The Image of Interpretation in Nietzsche, Rilke, Artaud, and Benjamin.* Baltimore: Johns Hopkins University Press, 1978. 87–110.

―――. "Walter Benjamin: Topographically Speaking." *Studies in Romanticism* 31.4 (1992): 501–24.

Jameson, Fredric. "Benjamin's Readings." *Diacritics* 22.3–4 (1992): 19–34.

Jauss, Hans Robert. "Spur und Aura: Bemerkungen zu Walter Benjamins Passagen-Werk." In *Studien zum Epochenwandel der ästhetischen Moderne.* Frankfurt am Main: Suhrkamp, 1989. 189–215.

Jay, Martin. *Downcast Eyes: The Denigration of Vision in Twentieth-Century French Thought.* Berkeley: University of California Press, 1993.

Jay, Paul. *Being in the Text: Self-Representation from Wordsworth to Roland Barthes.* Ithaca: Cornell University Press, 1984.

Jeffrey, Ian. *Photography.* London: Thames and Hudson, 1981.

Jennings, Michael. *Dialectical Images: Walter Benjamin's Theory of Literary Criticism.* Ithaca: Cornell University Press, 1987.

————. "Walter Benjamin and the Theory of Art History." In *Walter Benjamin, 1892–1940. Zum 100. Geburtstag.* Ed. Uwe Steiner. Bern: Lang, 1992. 77–102.

Jünger, Ernst, ed. *Krieg und Krieger.* Berlin: Junker und Dünnhaupt, 1930.

Kaes, Anton, Martin Jay, and Edward Dimendberg, eds. *The Weimar Republic Sourcebook.* Berkeley: University of California Press, 1994.

Kafka, Franz. *Diaries 1910 to 1913.* Trans. James Stern and Elisabeth Duckworth. New York: Schocken, 1973.

Kemp, Wolfgang. "Fernbilder. Benjamin und die Kunstwissenschaft." In *Walter Benjamin im Kontext.* Ed. Burkhardt Lindner. Königstein/Ts.: Athenäum, 1985. 224–57.

Kittler, Friedrich. *Discourse Networks 1800/1900.* Trans. Michael Metteer and Chris Cullers. Stanford: Stanford University Press, 1990.

————. *Draculas Vermächtnis: Technische Schriften.* Leipzig: Reclam, 1993.

————. *Grammophon, Film, Typewriter.* Berlin: Brinkmann und Bose, 1986.

Klages, Ludwig. *Ausdrucksbewegung und Gestaltungskraft.* In *Sämtliche Werke.* Vol. 6: *Ausdruckskunde.* Ed. Ernst Frauchinger et. al. Bonn: Bouvier, 1964. 139–313.

————. *Prinzipien der Charakterologie.* In *Sämtliche Werke.* Vol. 4: *Charakterkunde I.* Ed. Ernst Frauchinger et. al. Bonn: Bouvier, 1976. 95–182.

————. "Vom Traumbewußtsein." In *Sämtliche Werke.* Vol. 3: *Philosophie III.* Ed. Ernst Frauchinger et. al. Bonn: Bouvier, 1974. 155–238

Kracauer, Siegfried. "Anmerkungen über Portrait-Photographie." In *Schriften.* Vol. 5, book 3. Frankfurt am Main: Suhrkamp, 1990. 196–98.

————. "The Mass Ornament." In *The Mass Ornament.* Ed. and trans. Thomas Y. Levin. Cambridge: Harvard University Press, 1995. 75–86.

————. "On the Writings of Walter Benjamin." In *The Mass Ornament.* Ed. and trans. Thomas Y. Levin. Cambridge: Harvard University Press, 1995. 259–64.

————. "Photography." In *The Mass Ornament.* Ed. and trans. Thomas Y. Levin. Cambridge: Harvard University Press, 1995. 47–63.

————. *Straßen in Berlin und anderswo.* Frankfurt am Main: Suhrkamp, 1964.

————. "Those Who Wait." In *The Mass Ornament.* Ed. and trans. Thomas Y. Levin. Cambridge: Harvard University Press, 1995. 129–40.

Krauss, Rolf. *Walter Benjamin und der neue Blick auf die Photographie.* Ostfildern: Cantz, 1998.

Kristeva, Julia. "Freud and Love: Treatment and Its Discontents." In *The Kristeva Reader.* Ed. Toril Moi. New York: Columbia University Press, 1986. 238–71.

Lacis, Asja. "Briefe an Walter Benjamin." In *Russen in Berlin: Literatur, Malerei, Theater, Film. 1918–1933.* Ed. Fritz Mierau. Leipzig: Reclam, 1987. 573–76.

————. *Revolutionär im Beruf: Berichte über proletarisches Theater, über Meyerhold, Brecht, Benjamin und Piscator.* Ed. Hildegard Brenner. Munich: Rogner und Bernhard, 1971.

————. "Städte und Menschen: Erinnerungen." *Sinn und Form* 21.6 (1969): 1326–57.

Lacoue-Labarthe, Phillippe. "The Aestheticization of Politics." In *Heidegger, Art, and Politics.* Trans. Chris Turner. Oxford: Basil Blackwell, 1990.

Lacoue-Labarthe, Philipppe, and Jean-Luc Nancy. "The Nazi Myth." Trans. Brian Holmes. *Critical Inquiry* 16 (1990): 291–312.

————. *Retreating the Political.* Ed. Simon Sparks. London: Routledge, 1997.

Leder, Drew. *The Absent Body.* Chicago: University of Chicago Press, 1990.

Lehmann, Jürgen. *Bekennen-Erzählen-Berichten: Studien zur Theorie und Geschichte der Autobiographie.* Tübingen: Niemeyer, 1988.

Lejeune, Philippe. *On Autobiography.* Trans. Paul Eakin. Minnesota: University of Minnesota Press, 1989.

Lendvai-Dircksen, Erna. *Das deutsche Volksgesicht.* Berlin: Drei Masken, 1934.

Levin, David, ed. *Modernity and the Hegemony of Vision.* Berkeley: University of California Press, 1993.

Levinas, Emmanuel. "The Paradox of Morality: An Interview with Emmanuel Levinas." In *The Provocation of Levinas: Rethinking the Other.* Ed. Robert Bernasconi and David Wood. London: Routledge, 1988. 168–80.

————. *Totality and Infinity: An Essay on Exteriority.* Pittsburgh: Duquesne University Press, 1969.

Lindner, Burkhardt. "Benjamins Aurakonzeption: Anthropologie und Technik, Bild und Text." In *Walter Benjamin 1892–1940. Zum 100. Geburtstag.* Ed. Uwe Steiner. Bern: Lang, 1992. 217–48.

————. "Das *Passagen-Werk,* die *Berliner Kindheit* und die Archäologie des 'Jüngstvergangenen.'" In *Passagen: Walter Benjamins Urgeschichte des neunzehnten Jahrhunderts.* Ed. Norbert Bolz and Bernd Witte. Munich: Fink, 1984. 27–48.

Loiperdinger, Martin. *Der Parteitagsfilm "Triumph des Willens" von Leni Riefenstahl: Rituale der Mobilmachung.* Opladen: Leske and Budrich, 1987.

Marcuse, Herbert. "Revolution und Kritik der Gewalt: Zur Geschichtsphilosophie Walter Benjamins." In *Materialien zu Benjamins Thesen "Über den Begriff der Geschichte": Beiträge und Interpretationen.* Ed. Peter Bulthaup. Frankfurt am Main: Suhrkamp, 1975. 23–27.

Marx, Karl. *Capital.* Trans. Samuel Moore and Edward Aveling. New York: International, 1967.

Mattenklott, Gert. *Der übersinnliche Leib: Beiträge zur Metaphysik des Körpers.* Reinbek bei Hamburg: Rowohlt, 1982.

McCole, John. *Walter Benjamin and the Antinomies of Tradition.* Ithaca: Cornell University Press, 1993.

Mehlman, Jeffrey. *A Structural Study of Autobiography: Proust, Leiris, Sartre, Lévi-Strauss.* Ithaca: Cornell University Press, 1974.

———. *Walter Benjamin for Children: An Essay on His Radio Years.* Chicago: University of Chicago Press, 1993.

Menke, Bettine. "Bild—Textualität: Benjamins schriftliche Bilder." In *Der Entzug der Bilder: Visuelle Realitäten.* Ed. Michael Wetzel and Herta Wolf. Munich: Fink, 1994. 47–65.

———. *Sprachfiguren: Name—Allegorie—Bild nach Walter Benjamin.* Munich: Fink, 1991.

Menninghaus, Winfried. "Das Ausdruckslose: Walter Benjamins Kritik des Schönen durch das Erhabene." In *Walter Benjamin 1892–1940. Zum 100. Geburtstag.* Ed. Uwe Steiner. Bern: Lang, 1992. 33–76.

———. *Schwellenkunde: Walter Benjamins Passage des Mythos.* Frankfurt am Main: Suhrkamp, 1986.

———. *Walter Benjamins Theorie der Sprachmagie.* Frankfurt am Main: Suhrkamp, 1980.

Moses, Stéphane. "Geschichte und Subjektivität: Zur Konstitution der historischen Zeit bei Walter Benjamin." In *Das Subjekt der Dichtung: Festschrift für Gerhard Kaiser.* Ed. Gerhard Buhr, Friedrich Kittler, and Horst Turk. Würzburg: Königshasuen und Neumann, 1990. 153–78.

Mosse, George. "Toward a General Theory of Fascism." In *Masses and Man: Nationalist and Fascist Perceptions of Reality.* Detroit: Wayne State University Press, 1987. 159–96.

———, ed. *Nazi Culture: Intellectual, Cultural, and Social Life in the Third Reich.* New York: Grosset and Dunlap, 1966.

Müller, Heiner. "Glückloser Engel 2." In *Glückloser Engel: Dichtungen zu Walter Benjamin.* Ed. Erdmut Wizisla and Michael Opitz. Frankfurt am Main: Fischer, 1992. 29.

Muthesius, Marianne. *Mythos, Sprache, Erinnerung: Untersuchungen zu Walter Benjamins "Berliner Kindheit um neunzehnhundert."* Basel: Stromfeld, 1996.

Nabokov, Vladimir. *Speak, Memory: An Autobiography Revisited.* London: Weidenfeld and Nicholson, 1967.

Nägele, Rainer. *Echoes of Translation: Reading between Texts.* Baltimore: Johns Hopkins University Press, 1997.

———. *Theater, Theory, Speculation: Walter Benjamin and the Scenes of Modernity.* Baltimore: Johns Hopkins University Press, 1991.

———. "Trauerspiel und Puppenspiel." *Leib-und Bildraum: Lektüren nach Benjamin.* Ed. Sigrid Weigel. Cologne: Böhlau, 1992. 9–34.

Nancy, Jean-Luc. "Corpus." Trans. Claudette Sartiliot. In *The Birth to Presence*. Stanford: Stanford University Press, 1993. 189–207.

———. "The Inoperative Community." In *The Inoperative Community*. Trans. Peter Connor. Minneapolis: University of Minnesota Press, 1991. 1–42.

———. Introduction. In *Who Comes after the Subject?* Ed. Eduardo Cadava, Peter Connor, and Jean-Luc Nancy. New York: Routledge, 1991. 1–8.

———. "Our History." Trans. Cythia Chase et.al. *Diacritics* 20.3 (1990): 97–115.

Nehamas, Alexander. *Friedrich Nietzsche: Life as Literature*. Cambridge: Harvard University Press, 1985.

Neumann, Gerhard. "Nachrichten vom 'Pontus': Das Problem der Kunst im Werk Franz Kafkas." In *Franz Kafka: Schriftverkehr*. Eds. Wolf Kittler and Gerhard Neumann. Freiburg: Rombach, 1990. 164–98.

Nietzsche, Friedrich. *Beyond Good and Evil*. Trans. R. J. Hollingdale. Harmondsworth: Penguin, 1973.

———. *Ecce Homo: How One Becomes What One Is*. In *On the Genealogy of Morals and Ecce Homo*. Ed. and trans. Walter Kaufmann. New York: Vintage, 1989. 215–82.

———. *Thus Spoke Zarathustra*. In *The Portable Nietzsche*. Ed. and trans. Walter Kaufmann. New York: Penguin, 1982. 103–439.

———. *The Will to Power*. Trans. Walter Kaufmann and R. J. Hollingdale. New York: Random, 1967.

Niggl, Günter, ed. *Die Autobiographie: Zu Form und Geschichte einer literarischen Gattung*. Darmstadt: Wissenschaftliche Buchgesellschaft, 1989.

Norris, Christopher. "Image and Paradox: Readings of Walter Benjamin." In *The Deconstructive Turn: Essays in the Rhetoric of Philosophy*. London: Methuen, 1984. 107–27.

Olney, James. "Autobiography and the Cultural Moment: A Thematic, Historical, and Bibliographical Introduction." In *Autobiography: Essays Theoretical and Critical*. Ed. James Olney. Princeton: Princeton University Press, 1980. 3–27.

Parini, Jay. *Benjamin's Crossing*. New York: Henry Holt, 1997.

Pensky, Max. *Melancholy Dialectics: Walter Benjamin and the Play of Mourning*. Amherst: University of Massachusetts Press, 1993.

Pfotenhauer, Helmut. *Ästhetische Erfahrung und gesellschaftliches System: Untersuchungen zum Spätwerk Walter Benjamins*. Stuttgart: Metzler, 1975.

———. "Benjamin und Nietzsche." In *'Links hatte sich noch alles zu enträtseln': Walter Benjamin im Kontext*. Ed. Burkhradt Lindner. Frankfurt am Main: Syndikat, 1978. 100–126.

Proust, Marcel. *Remembrance of Things Past* [*A la recherche du temps perdu*]. Trans. C. K. Scott Moncrieff. New York: Random House, 1961.

Puttnies, Hans, and Gary Smith. *Benjaminiana: Eine biographische Recherche.* Giessen: Anabis, 1991.

Rabinbach, Anson. "Between Apocalypse and Enlightenment: Benjamin, Bloch, and Modern German-Jewish Messianism." In *In the Shadow of Catastrophe: German Intellectuals between Apocalypse and Enlightenment.* Berkeley: University of California Press, 1997. 27–65.

Recki, Birgit. *Aura und Autonomie: Zur Subjektivität der Kunst bei Walter Benjamin und Theodor W. Adorno.* Würzburg: Königshausen und Neumann, 1988.

Reichel, Peter. *Der schöne Schein des Dritten Reiches: Faszination und Gewalt des Faschismus.* Munich: Hanser, 1991.

Richter, Hans. *Köpfe und Hinterköpfe.* Zürich: Arche, 1967.

Rickels, Laurence. *Abberations of Mourning: Writing on German Crypts.* Detroit: Wayne State University Press, 1988.

———. "Kafka and Freud on the Telephone." *Modern Austrian Literature* 22.3–4 (1989): 211–26.

Riefenstahl, Leni. *Hinter den Kulissen des Reichsparteitag-Films.* Munich: Zentralverlag der NSDAP Franz Eher, 1935.

Riegl, Alois. *Die spätromantische Kunsttheorie.* Wien: Staatsdruckerei, 1901.

Rilke, Rainer Maria. *The Notebooks of Malte Laurids Rigge.* Trans. John Linton. Travistock Square: Hogarth Press, 1930.

———. *Die Sonette an Orpheus.* In *Sämtliche Werke.* Vol 1: *Gedichte. Erster Teil.* Frankfurt am Main: Insel, 1955. 727–73.

Ronell, Avital. *The Telephone Book: Technology, Schizophrenia, Electric Speech.* Lincoln: University of Nebraska Press, 1989.

Rüffer, Ulrich. "Taktilität und Nähe." In *Antike und Moderne: Zu Walter Benjamins Passagen.* Ed. Norbert Bolz and Richard Faber. Würzburg: Königshausen und Neumann, 1986.

Rugg, Linda. *Picturing Ourselves: Photography and Autobiography.* Chicago: University of Chicago Press, 1997.

Rumpf, Michael. "Radikale Theologie: Walter Benjamins Beziehung zu Carl Schmitt." In *Walter Benjamin: Zeitgenosse der Moderne.* Eds. Peter Gebhardt et.al. Kronberg/Ts.: Scriptor, 1976. 37–51.

Sahl, Hans. "Walter Benjamin in the Internment Camp." Trans. Deborah Johnson. In *On Walter Benjamin: Critical Essays and Recollections.* Ed. Gary Smith. Cambridge: MIT Press, 1988. 346–52.

Sander, August. *Antlitz der Zeit: Sechzig Aufnahmen deutscher Menschen des 20. Jahrhunderts.* Munich: Transmare, 1929.

Scarry, Elaine. *The Body in Pain: The Making and Unmaking of the Modern World.* Oxford: Oxford University Press, 1985.

Scheerbart, Paul. *Lesabéndio: Ein Asteroiden-Roman.* In *Dichterische Hauptwerke.* By Paul Scheerbart. Stuttgart: Goverts, 1962. 521–719.

————. *Münchhausen und Clarrisa: Ein Berliner Roman.* Berlin: Oesterheld, 1906.

Schestag, Thomas. "Asphalt." *MLN* 106.3 (1991): 589–621.

Schlegel, Friedrich. *Schriften zur Literatur.* Munich: Deutscher Taschenbuch Verlag, 1985.

Scholem, Gershom. "Nachwort zu Benjamin's *Berliner Chronik.*" In *Walter Benjamin und sein Engel: Vierzehn Aufsätze und kleine Beiträge.* Ed. Rolf Tiedemann. Frankfurt am Main: Suhrkamp, 1983. 174–79.

————. Preface. In *Moscow Diary.* By Walter Benjamin. Ed. Gary Smith. Trans. Richard Sieburth. Cambridge: Harvard University Press, 1986. 5–8.

————. "Toward an Understanding of the Messianic Idea in Judaism." In *The Messianic Idea in Judaism and Other Essays on Jewish Spirituality.* Trans. Michael Meyer. New York: Schocken, 1971. 1–36.

————. "Walter Benjamin." Trans. Lux Furtmüller. In *On Jews and Judaism in Crisis: Selected Essays.* Ed. Werner Dannhauser. New York: Schocken, 1976. 172–97.

————. *Walter Benjamin: The Story of a Friendship.* Trans. Harry Zohn. Philadelphia: Jewish Publication Society of America, 1981.

Schneider, Manfred. *Die erkaltete Herzensschrift: Der autobiographische Text im 20. Jahrhundert.* Munich: Hanser, 1986.

Schweppenhäuser, Hermann. "Physiognomie eines Physiognomikers." In *Zur Aktualität Walter Benjamins.* Ed. Siegfried Unseld. Frankfurt am Main, Suhrkamp, 1972. 139–71.

Sdun, Dieter. *Benjamin's Käfer: Untersuchungen zur bildlichen Sprache Walter Benjamins im Umkreis der Einbahnstraße.* Frankfurt am Main: Lang, 1994.

Selz, Jean. "Erinnerung." In *Über Walter Benjamin.* Frankfurt am Main: Suhrkamp, 1968. 37–51.

Shapiro, Gary. "Jean-Luc Nancy and the Corpus of Philosophy." In *Thinking Bodies.* Ed. Juliet MacCannell and Laura Zakarin. Stanford: Stanford University Press, 1994. 52–62.

Sieburth, Richard. "Benjamin the Scrivener." In *Benjamin: Philosophy, Aesthetics, History.* Ed. Gary Smith. Chicago: University of Chicago Press, 1989. 13–37.

Simmel, Georg. "Die ästhetische Bedeutung des Gesichts." In *Das Individuum und die Freiheit.* Frankfurt am Main: Fischer, 1993. 140–45.

Sloterdijk, Peter. *Critique of Cynical Reason.* Trans. Michael Eldred. Minneapolis: University of Minnesota Press, 1987.

————. *Literatur und Lebenserfahrung: Autobiographien der Zwanziger Jahre.* Munich: Hanser, 1978.

Smith, Gary. Afterword. In *Walter Benjamin: Moscow Diary.* Trans. Richard

Sieburth. Ed. Gary Smith. Cambridge: Harvard University Press, 1986. 137–46.

———. "Thinking through Benjamin: An Introductory Essay." In *Benjamin: Philosophy, Aesthetics, History*. Ed. Gary Smith. Chicago: University of Chicago Press, 1989. vii–xlii.

———. "Zu Benjamins 'Moskauer Tagebuch': Fragen an den Herausgeber." *Alternative* 32–33 (1980): 140–42.

Smith, Robert. *Derrida and Autobiography*. Cambridge: Cambridge University Press, 1995.

Snyder, Joel. "Benjamin on Reproducibility and Aura: A Reading of 'The Work of Art in the Age of Its Technical Reproducibility.'" In *Benjamin: Philosophy, Aesthetics, History*. Ed. Gary Smith. Chicago: University of Chicago Press, 1989. 158–74.

Sontag, Susan. "Fascinating Fascism." In *Under the Sign of Saturn*. New York: Farrar, Straus, Giroux, 1980. 73–105.

———. "Under the Sign of Saturn." In *Under the Sign of Saturn*. New York: Farrar, Straus, Giroux, 1980. 109–34.

Springer, Peter. "Panorama der Dauer—Inferno des Wandels: Historienmalerei in Walter Benjamins *Berliner Kindheit um Neunzehnhundert*." In *Historienmalerei in Europa: Paradigmen in Form, Funktion und Ideologie*. Eds. Ekkehart Mai and Anke Repp-Eckert. Mainz: Zabern, 1990. 347–67.

Steiner, Uwe. "Kapitalismus als Religion: Anmerkungen zu einem Fragment Walter Benjamins." *Deutsche Vierteljahrsschrift* 72.1 (1998): 147–71.

Stern, Howard. *Gegenbild, Reihenfolge, Sprung: An Essay on Related Figures of Argument in Walter Benjamin*. Berne: Lang, 1982.

Stiegler, Bernd. *Die Aufgabe des Namens: Zur Funktion des Eigennamens in der Literatur des 20. Jahrhunderts*. Munich: Fink, 1994.

Stoessel, Marleen. *Aura: Das Vergessene Menschliche. Zur Sprache und Erfahrung bei Walter Benjamin*. Munich: Hanser, 1983.

Stüssi, Anna. *Erinnerung an die Zukunft: Walter Benjamins Berliner Kindheit um Neunzehnhundert*. Göttingen: Vandenhoeck and Ruprecht, 1977.

Syberberg, Hans-Jürgen. *Die freudlose Gesellschaft: Notizen aus dem letzten Jahr*. Munich: Hanser, 1981.

Szondi, Peter. "Hoffnung im Vergangenen: Über Walter Benjamin." In *Schriften*. Vol. 2. Frankfurt am Main: Surkamp, 1978. 278–94.

———. "Walter Benjamin's City Portraits." In *On Walter Benjamin: Critical Essays and Reflections*. Ed. Gary Smith. Cambridge: MIT Press, 1988. 18–32.

Taussig, Michael. *Mimesis and Alterity: A Particular History of the Senses*. New York: Routledge, 1993.

———. *The Nervous System*. New York: Routledge, 1992.

Theweleit, Klaus. *Männerphantasien*. 2 vols. Frankfurt am Main: Roter Stern, 1977–78.

Tiedemann, Rolf. "Dialectics at a Standstill: Approaches to the *Passagen-Werk*." Trans. Gary Smith and André Lefevere. In *On Walter Benjamin: Critical Essays and Reflections*. Ed. Gary Smith. Cambridge: MIT Press, 1988. 260–91.

———. "Historical Materialism or Political Messianism? An Interpretation of the Theses 'On the Concept of History.'" In *Benjamin: Philosophy, Aesthetics, History*. Ed. Gary Smith. Chicago: University of Chicago Press, 1989. 175–209.

———. "Die Kunst, in anderer Leute Köpfe zu denken: Brecht—kommentiert von Walter Benjamin." In *Versuche über Brecht*. By Walter Benjamin. Ed. Rolf Tiedemann. Frankfurt am Main: Suhrkamp, 1971. 175–208.

———. *Studien zur Philosophie Walter Benjamins*. Frankfurt am Main: Suhrkamp, 1965.

Toepfer, Karl. *Empire of Ecstasy: Nudity and Movement in German Body Culture, 1910–1935*. Berkeley: University of California Press, 1997.

Trabant, Jürgen. "Language and the Ear: From Derrida to Heidegger." *Herder Yearbook*. Ed. Karl Menges et. al. Columbia, S.C.: Camden House, 1992. 1–22.

———. "Vom Ohr zur Stimme: Bemerkungen zum Phonozentrismus zwischen 1770 und 1830." In *Materialität der Kommunikation*. Ed. Hans Ulrich Gumbrecht and K. Ludwig Pfeiffer. Frankfurt am Main: Suhrkamp, 1988. 63–79.

Tucholsky, Kurt. *Deutschland, Deutschland über alles: Ein Bilderbuch von Kurt Tucholsky und vielen Fotografen. Montiert von John Heartfield*. Berlin: Neuer Deutscher Verlag, 1929.

Ullmann, Wolfgang. "Walter Benjamin und die jüdische Theologie." In *Aber ein Sturm weht vom Paradiese her: Texte zu Walter Benjamin*. Ed. Michael Opitz and Erdmut Wizisla. Leipzig: Reclam, 1992. 96–122.

Utz, Peter. *Das Auge und das Ohr im Text: Literarische Sinneswahrnehmung in der Goethezeit*. Munich: Fink, 1990.

Walter, Klaus. "Reimen und Stehlen: Brecht und HipHop." In *drive b: Brecht 100*. Ed. Marc Silberman. Berlin: Theater der Zeit and International Brecht Society, 1997. 97–101.

Weber, Samuel. "Mass Mediauras, or: Art, Aura and Media in the Work of Walter Benjamin." In *Mass Mediauras: Form, Technics, Media*. Ed. Alan Cholodenko. Stanford: Stanford University Press, 1996. 76–107.

———. "Taking Exception to Decision: Walter Benjamin and Carl Schmitt." *Diacritics* 22.3–4 (1992): 5–18.

———. "Un-Übersetzbarkeit: Zu Walter Benjamins 'Aufgabe des Übersetzers.'" In *Die Sprache der Anderen*. Ed. Anselm Haverkamp. Frankfurt am Main: Fischer, 1997. 121–45.

Weidmann, Heiner. *Flanerie, Sammlung, Spiel: Die Erinnerung des 19. Jahr-hunderts bei Walter Benjamin*. Munich: Fink, 1992.

———. "Geistesgegenwart: Das Spiel in Walter Benjamins Passagenarbeit." *MLN* 107.2 (1992): 521–47.

Weigel, Sigrid. *Entstellte Ähnlichkeit: Walter Benjamins theoretische Schreib-weise*. Frankfurt am Main: Fischer, 1997.

———. "Leib-und Bildraum (Benjamin)." In *Topographien der Geschlechter: Kulturgeschichtliche Studien zur Literatur*. Hamburg: Rowohlt, 1990. 18–39.

———. "Passagen und Spuren des 'Leib-und Bildraums' in Benjamins Schriften." In *Leib-und Bildraum: Lektüren nach Benjamin*. Ed. Sigrid Weigel. Cologne: Böhlau, 1992. 49–64.

Witte, Bernd. "Bilder der Endzeit. Zu einem authentischen Text der *Berliner Kindheit* von Walter Benjamin." *Deutsche Vierteljahrsschrift* 58.4 (1984): 570–92.

———. *Walter Benjamin: An Intellectual Biography*. Trans. James Rolleston. Detroit: Wayne State University Press, 1991.

———. *Walter Benjamin: Der Intellektuelle als Kritiker*. Stuttgart: Metzler, 1976.

Witte, Karsten. "Nachwort." In *Das Ornament der Masse*. By Siegfried Kracauer. Ed. Karsten Witte. Frankfurt am Main: Suhrkamp, 1977. 335–47.

Wizisla, Erdmut. "'Krise und Kritik' (1930/31): Walter Benjamin und das Zeitschriftenprojekt." In *Aber ein Sturm weht vom Paradiese her: Texte zu Walter Benjamin*. Ed. Michael Opitz and Erdmut Wizisla. Leipzig: Reclam, 1992. 270–302.

Wohlfarth, Irving. "'Immer radikal, niemals konsequent. . . .' Zur theo-logisch-politischen Standortsbestimmung Walter Benjamins." In *Antike und Moderne: Zu Walter Benjamins 'Passagen.'* Ed. Norbert Bolz and Richard Faber. Würzburg: Königshausen und Neumann, 1986. 116–37.

———. "Märchen für Dialektiker: Walter Benjamin und sein 'bucklicht Männlein.'" In *Walter Benjamin und die Kinderliteratur: Aspekte der Kinderkultur in den zwanziger Jahren*. Ed. Klaus Doderer. Weinheim: Juventa, 1988. 121–76.

———. "On Some Jewish Motifs in Benjamin." In *The Problems of Moder-nity*. Ed. Andrew Benjamin. London: Routledge, 1989. 157–215.

———. "On the Messianic Structure of Walter Benjamin's Last Reflec-tions." *Glyph* 3 (1978): 148–212.

Wolin, Richard. *Walter Benjamin: An Aesthetic of Redemption*. 2d rev. ed. Berkeley: University of California Press, 1994.

Worringer, Wilhelm. *Abstraktion und Einfühlung*. Munich: Piper, 1976.

Žižek, Slavoj. "Walter Benjamin: Dialektik im Stillstand." *Fragmente* 29–30 (1989): 149–60.

INDEX

addiction as ontological vigilance, 262n. 16
Adler, Hans, 267n. 17
Adorno, Gretel, 140, 166
Adorno, Theodor W., 15, 23, 35, 36, 49, 51, 58, 60, 65, 73, 79, 81, 88, 95, 129, 158, 193, 200–202, 211, 221, 241, 248n. 10, 253n. 44, 259n. 20, 262n. 16, 267n. 23, 268n. 28, 268n. 30, 269n. 1
Agamben, Giorgio, 202, 271n. 1, 278n. 3
allegory: in Benjamin and de Man, 249n. 24; and body, 62–63; as life, 229; meaning and, 232; and reading practice, 76; relation to face, 106; as ruin, 249n. 24; versus symbol, 21, 77, 106
Anders, Günther, 245
anthropological materialism, 58

Arendt, Hannah, 23, 82, 254n. 47, 272n. 9
Aragon, Louis, 60, 262n. 16
Arp, Hans, 258n. 17
Atget, Eugène, 114
Attali, Jacques, 266n. 13
aura, 223–24, 226–27
autobiography: and chronicle, 46–47, 49, 166–67; as crypt, 250n. 24; as displacement of self, 34; as montage, 47; as otobiography, 171–73, 176, 193–94; as pact, 48; and the problem of genre, 48–51; as prosopopeia, 50; in relation to memory, 175; significance for Benjamin's work, 32–34; and textual archaeology, 41–48, 179–80; as thanatography, 176. *See also* self-portraiture and cultural analysis

avoidance of theory, 136–37

Bahti, Timothy, 247n. 7, 255n. 52
Barthes, Roland, 110, 137, 224–25
Bataille, Georges, 202
Baudelaire, Charles, 60, 88, 94, 105,
    191, 209, 211, 214, 226, 268n.
    25, 272n. 7
Belmore, Herbert, 261n. 12
Bely, Andrei, 130
Benjamin, Walter: and body in
    Kafka, 65–67; and Brecht, 83–84,
    255n. 54, 272n. 9; development
    of ideas on body, 52–69; and
    ethics, 32; on facial wrinkles,
    105–6, 260n. 10; and figurative
    nature of the political, 12, 15,
    21, 27–28, 30–31; history in, 13,
    33, 39–41; hope in, 12, 132, 160,
    244–46, 256n. 5; imbrication
    of private and public sphere,
    155; importance of child in, 76,
    273n. 16; in internment camp,
    19–20; and Levinas, 109–10;
    and Nietzsche on body, 67–69;
    and Nietzsche on epistemology,
    240–41, 251n. 37; and politics of
    the unusable 12–14, 20–21, 23,
    93, 205, 229, 231–46; on progress,
    258n. 20; readability as cause
    for unreadability, 107–8; reading
    of fascism, 13, 19, 20, 24–25;
    69–70, 75–85, 93–123, 200–207,
    228–29, 231–46 (see also national
    socialism); relation to body in
    Klages, 64–65; and relation of
    text and context, 23–32, 194;
    and Scheerbart, 238–39; and
    Schmitt, 243, 279n. 7
Benjamin, Walter, works of:
    "Announcement of the Journal
    Angelus Novus," 99; "Arten des
    Wissens" (Kinds of knowledge),
    256n. 59; "Aufzeichnungen

zu Drogenversuchen" (Drug
protocols), 130, 181, 262n.
16; "Ausgraben und Erinnern"
(Excavating and remembering),
179–80; *Berlin Chronicle*, 14,
32–33, 34, 42, 46, 48–49, 51,
85–86, 129, 163–98, 200, 203–4,
213, 264nn. 1, 2, 266n. 11, 267n.
19, 267n. 22, 270n. 1; *Berliner
Kindheit um neunzehnhundert*
(*Berlin Childhood around 1900*)
12, 14, 32–33, 38, 50, 60, 81,
85–87, 113, 129, 158, 166–67,
170, 176–77, 183, 199–229, 245,
249n. 23, 260n. 3, 264n. 2, 266n.
11, 269n. 1, 270nn. 5, 6, 272n.
7, 273n. 16; "Bert Brecht," 211;
"Brezel, Feder, Pause, Klage,
Firlefanz" (Pretzel, quill, break,
sorrow, nonsense), 76; "Central
Park," 150, 214, 229; *Charles
Baudelaire*, 60, 94, 105, 107, 186,
226; "Das Skelett des Wortes"
(The skeleton of the word), 131;
"Das zweite Ich" (The second
self), 275n. 21; "Der Weg zum
Erfolg in dreizehn Thesen"
(The way to success in thirteen
theses), 156; "Destructive
Character," 148, 245; *Deutsche
Menschen* (German people), 79,
241; "Die Aufgabe des Kritikers"
(The task of the critic), 232;
"Die Erkenntnis" (Cognition),
59, 260n. 4; "Die glückliche
Hand" (The lucky hand), 157;
"Die politische Gruppierung der
russischen Schriftsteller" (The
political formation of Russian
writers), 129; "Die Theorie"
(Theory), 69; "Doctrine of the
Similar," 44, 214, 273n. 14, 276n.
22; "Erfahrung und Armut"

(Experience and poverty), 67, 75; "Erotische Erziehung" (Erotic education), 263n. 16; "Erste Form der Kritik" (First form of criticism), 119, 204; "Franz Kafka," 39, 65–66, 136, 185–86; "Franz Kafka: Beim Bau der Chinesischen Mauer" (Franz Kafka: While Building the Great Wall of China), 65; "Gedacht ist alles" (Everything is thought), 90; "Glimpse into the World of Children's Books," 208, 274n. 16; "Goethe's Elective Affinities," 12, 14, 31, 89, 145, 161, 168, 193, 231, 233, 239, 243, 244; "Grundlage der Moral" (Foundation of morals), 131–32, 252n. 41; "Hashish in Marseilles," 94, 122; "Image of Proust," 105, 122, 126, 148, 189, 231, 241, 255n. 56, 260n. 10; "Karl Kraus," 52, 163, 185, 237; "Krisis des Romans" (Crisis of the novel), 265n. 8; "La Traduction—Le Pour et le Contre," 84, 108, 121; "Lebenslauf" (Curriculum vitae), 27, 247n. 3, 279n. 7; "Life of Students," 263n.16; "Literaturgeschichte und Literaturwissenschaft" (Literary history and literary scholarship) 26; "Materialien zu einem Selbstportrait" (Materials for a self-portrait), 183; "Moscow," 70, 130, 132–34, 137; *Moscow Diary*, 14, 32–33, 55, 85–86, 125–62, 165–66, 170, 203, 204, 260n. 3, 261n. 16, 263n. 18; "Napels," 260n. 4; "Neue Dichtung in Russland" (New Russian literature), 133, 158;

"Notizen 4" (Notes 4), 156–57; "On Language as Such and the Language of Man," 28–29, 30, 91; "On the Mimetic Faculty," 183, 253n. 44, 278n. 31; "On the Program of the Coming Philosophy," 15, 170; "On Some Motifs in Baudelaire," 59, 187, 188, 191–92; *One-Way Street*, 33, 45, 55, 57, 61, 69, 74, 76–77, 83, 89, 128, 138, 142–43, 148, 151, 155–57, 159, 160, 166, 181, 190, 207, 208, 214, 234, 261n. 13, 273n. 16, 275n. 21, 278n. 29; *Origin of the German Mourning Play*, 27, 55, 62–63, 67, 78, 84, 89, 105, 142, 183, 211, 233, 249n. 24, 279n. 7; "Outline of the Psychophysical Problem," 69, 236, 250n. 25, 260n. 3; "Pariser Brief I" (Parisian letter I), 99; *Passagen-Werk* (Arcades Project), 13, 22, 25, 31, 36, 45, 47, 73, 75, 88, 94–95, 104–5, 108–9, 114, 131, 134, 136, 138, 163–64, 193–94, 200, 203–4, 208–9, 212, 214, 218, 222, 225–27, 232, 236, 237, 239–40, 242–43, 249n. 19, 260nn. 7, 8, 263n. 16, 269n. 1; "Probleme der Sprachsoziologie" (Problems of the sociology of language), 29, 59; "Program for a Proletarian Children's Theater," 246; "Programm der literarischen Kritik" (Program of literary criticism), 95; "Proximity and Distance," 150, 154; "Psychologie" (Psychology), 54, 264n. 25; "Review of Anja and Georg Mendelssohn, *Der Mensch in der Handschrift*" (The human being in its handwriting), 14, 52, 71, 252n. 40; "Review of Fjodor Gladkov, *Zement"* (Concrete), 107, 158; "Review of Paul Léautaud, *Le théatre de Maurice Boissard, 1907–1923,"* 34; "Russian Toys," 137; "San Gimignano," 16; "Short History of Photography," 107, 115, 118, 221–25; "Socrates," 152, 261n. 15; "Strenge Kunstwissenschaft (Rigorous study of art)," 59; "Storyteller," 31, 74, 148, 167, 237, 250n. 28; "Surrealism," 22, 35, 55, 57–58, 94, 97, 203, 241; "Task of the Translator," 30, 41, 77, 121; "Theologico-Political Fragment," 240; "Theories of German Fascism," 79, 81; "Theses on the Concept of History," 13, 38, 40, 61, 67, 69, 95, 120–21, 158, 208, 216, 240, 243, 275n. 19; "Tod" (Death), 35, 157, 237; *"Trauerspiel* and Tragedy," 25; "Two Poems by Friedrich Hölderlin," 279n. 6; "Über das Grauen" (On horror), 159; "Über die Ehe" (On marriage), 149–50; "Über die Scham" (On shame), 217–18; "Übung" (Exercise), 157; "Wahrnehmung und Leib" (Perception and body), 61; "Work of Art in the Age of Its Technical Reproducibility," 21, 79, 81, 88–89, 94–96, 122, 221–22, 234, 237; "Zu Scheerbart" (On Scheerbart), 238; "Zur Astrologie" (On astrology), 126; "Zur Erfahrung" (On experience), 184; "Zur Lage der russischen Filmkunst" (On the situation of Russian film), 129; "Zur Theorie des Ekels" (On the theory of disgust), 261n. 13

Bergson, Henri, 58–60, 175–76, 188, 238, 251nn. 31, 32, 267n. 25
Berman, Russell, 79, 254n. 46
body: and apocatastasis, 56; and corpse, 62–63; and death, 63; development of in Benjamin, 52–69; as hermeneutic machine, 134; and history, 55–58, 68–69; inscription of, 67; as *Körper* and as *Leib*, 250n. 25; and limits of intelligibility, 62–63, 72, 135, 164–65; and memory, 59–60, 172–74, 268n. 25; as political site, 14, 68, 72, 91–92; in relation to language 14, 52, 54, 60, 62, 71–72, 252n. 40; as resisting closure, 60, 61, 173; and stylization, 130–31; and technology, 56, 266n. 17; as unusable concept, 22, 72, 159, 166, 172–73, 205; and violence, 57; and writing, 59, 66, 131
body-space (*Leibraum*), 55, 57, 155, 203, 237, 251n. 29. *See also* image-space
Blanqui, Louis Auguste, 238
Bloch, Ernst, 36, 60, 61, 73, 86, 95, 110, 111, 112, 113, 161, 193, 207, 238, 268n. 31
blushing, 217–18
Bohrer, Karl-Heinz, 272n. 8
Bolle, Willi, 22, 253n. 45
Bolz, Norbert, 38, 73, 251n. 29, 253n. 41, 279n. 8
Braun, Volker, 245
Brecht, Bertolt, 38, 83, 86, 88, 95, 98, 171, 195, 238, 255n. 54, 272n. 9
Breton, André, 60
Brodersen, Momme, 255n. 51
Buber, Martin, 27, 135–37

Buck-Morss, Susan, 84, 127, 255n. 55, 273n. 12, 274n. 16
Butler, Judith, 251n. 38

Cadava, Eduardo, 220–21, 242, 254n. 47, 256n. 3, 257n. 8, 257n. 14, 267n. 24, 276n. 23
Cassirer, Ernst, 110
Caygill, Howard, 79, 254n. 46
Celan, Paul, 20
Chow, Rey, 264n. 23
Cohen, Hermann, 135
Cohen, Margaret, 248n. 13
Cohn [-Rath], Jula, 128, 167, 271n. 6
community, 96–97, 99, 102, 120, 236–37, 254n. 49, 256n. 5
constellation, 87–88, 94, 193, 207, 126
Corngold, Stanley, 81, 249n. 20, 268n. 29, 279n. 6
corpus. *See* body
creaturely, the, 135, 137, 145, 261n. 12

Debord, Guy, 254n. 49
Deleuze, Gilles, 90
De Man, Paul, 27, 50–51, 103–4, 169, 248n. 9
departure, 160–62
Derrida, Jacques, 27, 53, 74, 136, 152, 171–72, 233, 239, 255n. 57, 257n.13, 261n. 11, 264n. 26, 267n. 17, 278n. 28, 279n. 5
dialectical image, 203–4
Diderot, Denis, 255n. 57
Dimendberg, Edward, 253n. 42
disgust (*Ekel*), 148–49, 261n. 12, 261n. 13
Disney, Walt, 238
Döblin, Alfred, 114, 265n. 8
Dürer, Albrecht, 65
Durtain, Luc, 255n. 56
Düttmann, Alexander García, 83, 247n. 4, 250n. 29

Eagleton, Terry, 255n. 52, 273n. 12
ethics, 72–73, 81, 93, 122, 137, 197, 232, 241–46, 252n. 41

Ferris, David, 278n. 26
Foucault, Michel, 69, 255n. 53, 258n. 18
Fourier, François, 238
Frankfurt School, 82, 98
Freud, Sigmund, 60, 191–92, 238
Freund, Gisèle, 114
Frey, Hans-Jost, 249n. 22
friendship, 128–29, 160–62
Fuld, Werner, 251n. 34, 265n. 3
Fürnkäs, Josef, 248n. 13
Fynsk, Christopher, 260n. 10

Gagnebin, Jeanne-Marie, 248n. 7
Gasché, Rodolphe, 23
George, Stefan, 31, 64
Geulen, Eva, 248n. 8, 278n. 27
ghosts, 51, 63, 69, 70, 80, 94, 131, 147, 150, 161–62, 174–75, 176, 220, 222, 223, 237, 239, 245, 267n. 19, 269n. 4, 277n. 24
G-Gruppe (G-Group), 114, 257n. 17
Giedion, Sigfried, 164, 238
gift, 225–28
Gleichschaltung (total coordination), 80, 241
Goebbels, Joseph, 80, 97, 100, 195–96
Goethe, Johann Wolfgang von, 32, 41, 48, 135, 145, 161, 169, 231, 233, 239
Gogol, Nikolaj, 105
Goldstein, Kurt, 29
Grosz, George, 258n. 17
Guattari, Félix, 90
Gundolf, Friedrich, 64, 169
Günter, Manuela, 272n. 7

Habermas, Jürgen, 82, 234–35, 255n. 53, 268n. 29
Hamacher, Werner, 32, 258n. 19, 267n. 24, 276nn. 22, 23
Hamann, Johann Georg, 170
Hansen, Miriam, 258n. 20, 277n. 25, 278n. 4
Hanssen, Beatrice, 260n. 5
Harlan, Veit, 100
Hart Nibbrig, Christiaan, 270n. 6
Haverkamp, Anselm, 278nn. 30, 31
Heartfield, John, 122, 258n. 17
Hegel, Georg Wilhelm Friedrich, 35, 89, 256n. 58
Heidegger, Martin, 37, 44, 82, 88, 269n. 4
Heinle, Fritz, 38, 166
Herder, Johann Gottfried von, 267n. 17
Herf, Jeffrey, 254n. 49
Hermand, Jost, 257n. 11
Hessel, Franz, 167
Hilberseimer, Ludwig, 258n. 17
Hill, David Octavius, 114
Hillach, Ansgar, 79, 253n. 46
historical materialism, 20, 40, 82, 153
Hitler, Adolf, 79, 96, 98, 100, 105, 195, 199, 205–7, 236, 241
Hoffmann, E. T. A., 105
Hofmannsthal, Hugo von, 41, 135
Hölderlin, Friedrich, 31, 89, 243
Hollington, Michael, 256n. 2
Hörisch, Jochen, 261n. 15
Horkheimer, Max, 21, 60, 95, 158, 211, 232, 255n. 50
Hüppauf, Bernd, 252n. 39
hypotaxis, 49, 166, 248n. 10. *See also* parataxis

image-space (*Bildraum*), 55, 57, 203, 251n. 29. *See also* body-space
impossible possibility, 15, 197

impotence, 144, 150–52, 158
intention, 89–90

Jacobs, Carol, 264n. 1, 265n. 5, 266n. 14, 276n. 22
Jameson, Fredric, 37
Jauss, Hans Robert, 278n. 30
Jay, Martin, 253n. 42, 255n. 57, 269n. 4
Jay, Paul, 248n. 17
Jennings, Michael, 81, 87, 251n. 33, 259n. 20, 261n. 12, 268n. 29, 269n. 3, 273n. 12, 279n. 5
Joël, Ernst, 181
Jünger, Ernst, 74, 80, 254n. 48

Kaes, Anton, 253n. 42
Kafka, Franz, 12, 31, 39, 47, 58, 65–67, 115, 185, 213, 220, 228, 239, 257n. 13, 267n. 24
Kant, Immanuel, 71, 170
Karavan, Dani, 245
Käutner, Helmut, 100
Keller, Dora, 128
Kemp, Wolfgang, 251n. 33
Kittler, Friedrich, 38–39, 176, 248n. 16, 266n. 17
Klages, Ludwig, 64–65, 67, 71, 251n. 34
Klee, Paul, 122
Kommerell, Max, 64
Kracauer, Siegfried, 23, 24, 55, 60, 73, 86, 95, 97–98, 110, 113, 118–19, 127, 200, 207, 222, 247nn. 2, 10, 257n. 6, 265n. 10, 267n. 19, 277n. 25, 278n. 27
Kraft, Werner, 239
Kraus, Karl, 52, 163, 185, 237
Kristeva, Julia, 263n. 18
Krull, Germaine, 114

Lacan, Jacques, 262n. 16, 273n. 12
Lacis, Asja, 86, 125–26, 128–29, 132, 135, 137–55, 159–62, 165–66,

234, 259n. 2, 260n. 4, 261n. 16, 264n. 3, 278n. 29
Lacoue-Labarthe, Philippe, 71, 119–20, 254n. 47, 254n. 49, 257n. 8, 258n. 20, 278n. 1
Lavater, Johann Kaspar, 95, 256n. 1
Leder, Drew, 250n. 25
Lehmann, Jürgen, 248n. 17
Lehmann, Walter, 112
Leibähnlichkeiten (corporeal similarities), 126, 184
Lejeune, Philippe, 249n. 21
Lelevich, Grigory, 130, 135
Lendvai-Dircksen, Erna, 102, 118
Levin, Thomas Y., 273n. 13
Levinas, Emmanuel, 109–10, 257n. 15
Lichtenberg, Georg Christoph, 95, 256n. 1
Liebeneiner, Wolfgang, 100
Lindner, Burkhardt, 201, 250n. 25, 269n. 2, 274n. 17
Livingston, Rodney, 250n. 25
Loos, Adolf, 238
Lukács, Georg, 83, 110, 153
Luther, Martin, 31

Mann, Heinrich, 98, 105
Mann, Thomas, 271n. 1
Marcuse, Herbert, 239
Marcuse, Ludwig, 110
Marx, Karl, 212, 239
Mattenklott, Gert, 251n. 37
Mayakovsky, Vladimir, 130
McCole, John, 84, 167, 169, 251n. 34, 255n. 55, 261n. 12
meaning as illness, 233
Mehlman, Jeffrey, 248n. 17, 269n. 32
memory: and archaeology of the self, 41–48; and the corpus, 185–93; and technology, 177–80
Mendelssohn, Anja, 71
Mendelssohn, Georg, 71

Menke, Bettine, 157, 250n. 25, 263n. 19, 264n. 22, 278n. 30, 278n. 32
Menninghaus, Winfried, 73, 137, 250n. 25, 252n. 41, 266n. 16, 276n. 22
messianism, 82, 84, 239–40, 279n. 5
mortification, 63, 77, 153, 226, 249n. 24
Moses, Stéphane, 249n. 18
Mosse, George, 71, 252n. 39, 258n. 19, 269n. 32
Mühsam, Erich, 115
Müller, Heiner, 123, 245
Muthesius, Marianne, 275n. 17
myth, 71, 233

Nabokov, Vladimir, 265n. 8
Nachträglichkeit (belatedness or retroactivity), 268n. 25
Nägele, Rainer, 54, 73, 251n. 29, 252n. 41, 255n. 54, 268n. 26
Nancy, Jean-Luc, 62, 71, 119–20, 248n. 12, 254n. 47, 258n. 20, 261n. 11, 263n. 17, 278n. 1, 278n. 3
national socialism, 71, 74, 79–84, 95, 99, 194; as aestheticization of politics, 121–22; and the body, 200–207; filmic production of the face in, 99–101; as master narrative, 119–21; mythical structure of, 119–21; and radio, 195–97, 269nn. 32, 33; and stable meaning, 79–81, 104, 196; and total coordination, 159, 194–97, 199, 254n. 47. *See also* Benjamin, Walter: reading of fascism
Nehamas, Alexander, 251n. 37
Neumann, Gerhard, 251n. 35
Nietzsche, Friedrich, 50, 53, 58, 67, 108, 154, 171, 240–41, 248n. 11, 251n. 37, 273n. 12

noise, 86, 163–98, 218–19, 265n. 8, 265n. 10, 266n. 11, 266n. 13, 267n. 23

Olney, James, 50
other, the: and the corpus, 137–43; and touching 146–50; transformations of, 153–54
Ovid, 109

parataxis, 130, 187, 200, 248n. 10. *See also* hypotaxis
Pfotenhauer, Helmut, 251n. 37, 267n. 25
phantasmagoria, 192–93, 206, 237
photography, 87, 102–3, 114, 187, 200, 208, 276n. 23, 277n. 25; as autobiographical problem, 219–24; and Neue Sachlichkeit (New Matter-of-Factness), 136
physiognomy: 67, 94–95; of the city, 133–34; and fascism, 93–123; and language, 59, 72; in photography, 118–19; and recollection, 202–3; as unarticulated, 135
Podszus, Friedrich, 267n. 18
politics: and aporia, 104, 231–46; and figurative language, 76–84; and prosopopeia, 103, 104, 108–9
prostitution, 263n. 16
Proust, Marcel, 31, 58–60, 88, 94, 105, 126, 134, 142, 148, 186, 188–91, 202, 204, 228, 241, 262n. 16

Rabinbach, Anson, 82, 250n. 27
Ray, Man, 258n. 17
Reich, Bernhard, 152–53
Reichel, Peter, 257n. 7, 269n. 32
Richter, Hans, 257n. 17
Rickels, Laurence, 176, 266n. 17
Riefenstahl, Leni, 100, 118
Riegl, Alois, 59, 251n. 33, 268n. 29

Rilke, Rainer Maria, 77, 86, 95, 112–13, 148
Ronell, Avital, 176, 180, 266n. 17
Rosenzweig, Franz, 69
Roth, Joseph, 133
Rousseau, Jean-Jacques, 32
Rüffer, Ulrich, 251n. 33
Rugg, Linda, 277n. 23
Rychner, Max, 31

Sahl, Hans, 247n. 1
Sander, August, 114–18
Scarry, Elaine, 251n. 38
Scheerbart, Paul, 238–39
Schestag, Thomas, 248n. 15
Schlegel, Friedrich, 273n. 15
Schleiermacher, Friedrich, 31
Schmitt, Carl, 243–44, 279n. 7
Schneider, Manfred, 176, 264n. 2, 266n. 15, 266n. 17, 267nn. 20, 21, 267n. 24, 273n. 14
Schoen, Ernst, 35, 60, 167, 258n. 17
Scholem, Gershom, 11, 34, 60, 65, 67, 127–28, 166–67, 195, 201, 234, 236, 241, 244, 250n. 27, 259n. 2, 267n. 22, 274n. 16
Schweikart, Hans, 100
Schweppenhäuser, Hermann, 94, 201, 275n. 17, 275n. 20
Schwitters, Kurt, 258n. 17
self: and bodily stylization, 130; and disappearance, 231, 240; and displacement of other, 183–84; historical moment of Benjamin's, 37–41; as performance in Nietzsche, 58; and presence of mind, 155–56; relation to language, 35–36, 41; relation to technology, 38–39, 176–83; and textual revision, 207–8; touching the other, 146–50; undoing of, 15, 35–37; 41, 85, 190, 268n. 29. *See also* subject

self-portraiture and cultural analysis, 13–14, 48, 85, 103, 199, 232

Selz, Jean, 265n. 4

sex and interpretation, reading, and writing, 86, 126, 138–42, 151–52, 160

Sieburth, Richard, 265n. 3

Simmel, Georg, 86, 95, 110–11, 113, 174

Sloterdijk, Peter, 248n. 17, 256n. 57

Smith, Gary, 127, 247n. 5, 260n. 2

Smith, Robert, 248n. 17

Sontag, Susan, 201, 257n. 10

sphinx's face as political enigma, 107

Springer, Peter, 275n. 18

Staudte, Wolfgang, 100

Steiner, Uwe, 273n. 12

Steinhoff, Hans, 100

Stiegler, Bernd, 248n. 15

Stoessel, Marleen, 278n. 26

Stone, Sasha, 114, 166

Stüssi, Anna, 275n. 17, 277n. 23

subject: as absence, 57; Benjaminian analysis of, 35; Hegelian definition of, 35; and the idealized imaginary other, 263n. 18; in modernity, 35–39; as multiplicity, 67; and the requirement of anonymity, 131–32. *See also* self

substitutive gratification (*Ersatzbefriedigung*), 262n. 16, 263n. 16

Syberberg, Hans-Jürgen, 100

Szondi, Peter, 201, 268n. 30

Taussig, Michael, 73, 253n. 41

Theweleit, Klaus, 74, 253n. 43

Thieme, Karl, 229

Tiedemann, Rolf, 95, 248n. 14, 255n. 54, 267n. 25

Toepfer, Karl, 253n. 42

touch, the, 138, 141–42, 146–50, 158, 261nn. 11, 12

Trabant, Jürgen, 255n. 57

truth: as death of intention, 89, 256n. 59; and deferral of sense, 232–33; in modernity, 78; relation to face, 109; relation to language, 41, 77; relation to photograph, 77

Tucholsky, Kurt, 122

Tzara, Tristan, 258n. 17

Udwin, Victor, 275n. 18

Utz, Peter, 255n. 57

Van der Rohe, Mies, 257–58n. 17

Verhoeven, Paul, 100

Vertov, Dziga, 127

vision: and class demarcations, 215; and the commodity, 210–12; and the gift, 225–27; versus hearing, 217–19; and Heidegger's world picture, 269n. 4; and photography, 219–25

vitalism (*Lebensphilosophie*), 64, 68, 74

Voß, Johann Heinrich, 31

Wagner, Richard, 95

Weber, Max, 273n. 12

Weber, Samuel, 95, 248n. 9, 256nn. 2, 3, 257n. 6, 257n. 12, 279n. 8

Weidmann, Heiner, 263nn. 19, 20, 21

Weigel, Sigrid, 73, 250n. 26, 251n. 36, 252n. 41, 259n. 1, 260n. 3, 261n. 14, 269n. 1

Windelband, Wilhelm, 59

Wissig, Eugen, 167

Witte, Bernd, 23, 37, 127, 260n. 9, 261n. 12

Witte, Karsten, 257n. 6

Wizisla, Erdmut, 255n. 54

Wohlfarth, Irving, 84, 250n. 27, 275n. 19, 279n. 5

Wolin, Richard, 21, 253n. 45

Worringer, Wilhelm, 59, 251n. 33, 268n. 29

Wyneken, Gustav, 67, 261n. 12

Youth Movement, 37, 38, 67, 74, 261n. 12

Zeitschrift für Sozialforschung (Journal of social research), 29

Žižek, Slavoj, 263n. 16

BOOKS IN THE KRITIK: GERMAN LITERARY THEORY
AND CULTURAL STUDIES SERIES

Walter Benjamin: An Intellectual Biography, by Bernd Witte, translated by James Rolleston, 1991

The Violent Eye: Ernst Jünger's Visions and Revisions on the European Right, by Marcus Paul Bullock, 1991

Fatherland: Novalis, Freud, and the Discipline of Romance, by Kenneth S. Calhoon, 1992

Metaphors of Knowledge: Language and Thought in Mauthner's Critique, by Elizabeth Bredeck, 1992

Laocoon's Body and the Aesthetics of Pain: Winckelmann, Lessing, Herder, Moritz, Goethe, by Simon Richter, 1992

The Critical Turn: Studies in Kant, Herder, Wittgenstein, and Contemporary Theory, by Michael Morton, 1993

Reading After Foucault: Institutions, Disciplines, and Technologies of Self in Germany, 1750–1830, edited by Robert S. Leventhal, 1994

Bettina Brentano-von Arnim: Gender and Politics, edited by Elke P. Frederiksen and Katherine R. Goodman, 1995

Absent Mothers and Orphaned Fathers: Narcissism and Abjection in Lessing's Aesthetic and Dramatic Production, by Susan E. Gustafson, 1995

Identity or History? Marcus Herz and the End of the Enlightenment, by Martin L. Davies, 1995

Languages of Visuality: Crossings between Science, Art, Politics, and Literature, edited by Beate Allert, 1996

Resisting Bodies: The Negotiation of Female Agency in Twentieth-Century Women's Fiction, by Helga Druxes, 1996

Locating the Romantic Subject: Novalis with Winnicott, by Gail M. Newman, 1997

Embodying Ambiguity: Androgyny and Aesthetics from Winckelmann to Keller, by Catriona MacLeod, 1997

The Freudian Calling: Early Viennese Psychoanalysis and the Pursuit of Cultural Science, by Louis Rose, 1998

By the Rivers of Babylon: Heinrich Heine's Late Songs and Reflections, by Roger F. Cook, 1998

Reconstituting the Body Politic: Enlightenment, Public Culture, and the Invention of Aesthetic Autonomy, by Jonathan M. Hess, 1999

The School of Days: Heinrich von Kleist and the Traumas of Education, by Nancy Nobile, 1999

Walter Benjamin and the Corpus of Autobiography, by Gerhard Richter, 2000

Heads or Tails: The Poetics of Money, by Jochen Hörisch, translated by Amy Horning Marschall, 2000

Dialectics of the Will: Freedom, Power, and Understanding in Modern French and German Thought, by John H. Smith, 2000